Thematic Guide
to
British Poetry

Thematic Guide
to
British Poetry

Ruth Glancy

Greenwood Press
Westport, Connecticut • London

Library of Congress Cataloging-in-Publication Data

Glancy, Ruth F., 1948–
    Thematic guide to British poetry / Ruth Glancy.
        p.   cm.
    Includes bibliographical references and indexes.
    ISBN 0–313–31379–2 (alk.   paper)
    1. English poetry—Themes, motives.   2. English poetry—Handbooks, manuals,
etc.   I. Title.
    PR502.G55   2002
    821.009—dc21   2002023252

British Library Cataloguing in Publication Data is available.

Library of Congress Catalog Card Number: 2002023252
ISBN: 0–313–31379–2

First published in 2002

Greenwood Press, 88 Post Road West, Westport, CT 06881
An imprint of Greenwood Publishing Group, Inc.
www.greenwood.com

Printed in the United States of America

The paper used in this book complies with the
Permanent Paper Standard issued by the National
Information Standards Organization (Z39.48–1984).

10 9 8 7 6 5 4 3 2 1

Contents

ᏇᎠᎲᎤ

Contents

Introduction

Over the centuries, the British Isles has contributed a remarkable catalog
of inventions and discoveries to human progress, but perhaps its most
highly valued and enduring gift has been seven centuries of poetry. As
the years roll on and the legacy of poems grows, how can we hope to
find our way through such a vast wealth of verse, much of it as fresh,
relevant, and compelling as it was when it was first composed? The
purpose of this book is to offer a guide to students, teachers, librarians,
and general readers who are interested in reading and studying poetry
from the point of view of its subject matter, the essential question of
what it is "about."

Collections of poetry are often referred to as "treasuries," "garlands,"
or "gardens," attesting to the intrinsic value of a literary form that illu-
minates human activity in surprising and often unforgettable ways.
When we speak of a poem having a "theme," we are referring to a poem
that brings a particular human perspective to the subject matter. A poet
can write an objective description of an event such as a wedding, or a
natural creature such as a nightingale, but unless the poem expresses—
overtly or subtly—the poet's attitude to the subject, the poem does not
have a theme. Compare, for example, John Clare's poem "Mouse's Nest"
(1835) with Robert Burns's poem "To a Mouse" (1785). Although both
poems are included in this survey in the Nature section, only Burns's
poem has a "theme" that can be readily identified. Both poets describe
the overturning of a mouse's nest and the small creature's discomfort.
But while Clare's poem is simply descriptive of the nest and its owner
(he finds the mother mouse "grotesque" and alien from him, thus hinting
at the theme of man's relationship to nature), Burns goes further in pondering this relationship. His exposing of the nest with his plow is an
example of "man's dominion," trampling thoughtlessly over the neat,

well-ordered lives of our fellow creatures. The central theme of the poem is thus a modern one: man's responsibility to the created world. But Burns provides another theme as well, one that could place the poem among those that deal with fate, or ambition, or even regret. The sudden loss of the mouse's home reminds him that people, too, often find their "best laid plans" swept away by chance. (John Steinbeck found the title for his novel *Of Mice and Men* [1937] in Burns's poem, attesting to the universality of the theme.) Finally, Burns introduces the theme of regret and loss when he envies the little mouse its inability to grieve over its lost home or fear for future losses, as we do. Clare's poem is "about" a mouse's nest, but Burns's poem is "about" the joys and sorrows that a consciousness of time and chance brings to human creatures. Of course, most poems express their theme less explicitly than does Burns's "To a Mouse." Poetic devices such as irony, tone, diction, rhythm, and rhyme are all employed by good poets to convey their particular view of human experience. Discovering a poem's theme thus requires the reader to listen carefully to the poet's unique voice.

Many poems have several themes. Are Shakespeare's sonnets about love, or death, or time? Often they comment profoundly on all three, and readers will often disagree about which theme the poet intended to be uppermost. Gerard Manley Hopkins's fine lyric "Pied Beauty" (1877) is a devotional poem reminding us to praise God for the beauties of the created world. The careful depiction of that world makes it also a "nature" poem, but in this survey the poem is discussed under "Beauty," because while many poems are hymns of praise to the natural world, few poems draw our attention so memorably to the startling beauty of odd, irregular, even commonplace details: the colors on a trout's side, the patchwork-quilt effect of fields, the irregular markings on a cow's back. We think of poems about beauty as usually being hymns of praise to beautiful women (and therefore they are also often love poems), but the relationship between the beautiful object and the one who finds it beautiful can be explored in a variety of ways through poetry. This survey is thus not intended to be prescriptive; rather, it is intended to place the major poems in English literature into groups so that they may be usefully compared with others on that topic. Poems that lend themselves to other interpretations are cross-referenced to other themes in the survey.

Twenty-nine themes, arranged alphabetically, have been selected as being representative of the major concerns of British poets over seven centuries. Some themes, such as love, death, and nature, have remained universally popular with poets (these themes have been subdivided in an attempt to bring some order to the vast number of poems available). Others, such as the active and contemplative lives, seem to be less relevant today. Within each section, the poems are usually discussed chronologically so that readers can trace the development and decline of interest in themes over the centuries. Often this development is linked to historical events—wars, religious upheaval, the Industrial Revolution—or to more gradual changes in human outlook and experience. Attitudes to marriage, for example, as dramatized in the poetry, have altered radically from Chaucer's time to our own, but marriage is still of keen interest to poets.

Because of the huge number of excellent British poems, many of the discussions are very brief. The intention is not to provide a detailed analysis but rather to draw the reader's attention to the poems that have added fresh insights and striking expression to that theme. Teachers are encouraged to use the survey as a source for essay or study topics that require students to compare poems on the same theme. Or themes may be usefully compared; poems about the active and contemplative lives are often similar to those about innocence and experience, which in turn relate to poems about old age. An index at the end of the *Guide* makes it easy to find all discussions of a poet, so the book may also be used for the study of individual poets or periods. Not included are the many poems written as tributes to other poets, the enormous number of such tributes making such a topic unmanageable.

Following each theme, the reader will find a list of the poems discussed in that section, arranged in order of the discussion, with a listing of some of the anthologies in which each poem can be found. Abbreviations for the anthologies correspond to those used in the *Columbia Granger's Index to Poetry in Anthologies* (11th ed., Columbia University Press). Many of the poems discussed in this survey are readily available in any standard collection of poetry (and there are literally hundreds of poetry anthologies; readers are advised to consult *Granger's Index* for complete listings of books in which the poems can be found). Other poems are harder to find, but they have been included either because they contribute usefully to that particular theme, or because they have been overlooked by many anthologists and deserve to be better known. These poems can be found in editions of the collected works of a particular poet, rather than in large anthologies.

In an appendix at the end of the *Guide*, readers will find biographical sketches of the poets, briefly outlining their lives and literary interests. While short, these summaries will help students to place the poets in their time and milieu. Following that section, a bibliography carefully selected for students lists helpful critical studies of poetry to broaden the necessarily limited discussion of individual poems included here. In general, this survey concentrates on the poems' expression of a theme rather than on technical matters of versification and poetic language, always recognizing, however, that the two are interdependent in a good poem. As the eighteenth-century poet Alexander Pope wisely said, "The sound must seem an echo to the sense." In this brief survey, matters of "sound" must give way to the discussion of "sense." Although the poet Edward Thomas is quite correct in saying that the best poetry cannot be paraphrased, many of the poems surveyed receive just such a cursory description. The intention of this book is to provide a path for readers into the abundant world of British poetry in all its variety and richness. On discovering these poems for themselves, readers will both enrich their own lives immeasurably and help to keep alive a literary tradition that has for seven centuries colored and altered our conception of the universe and our place in it as poets and readers.

Anthologies of British Poetry and Abbreviations Used

ତ୍ର≀∿⌒୧

The following anthologies contain some of the more obscure poems discussed in this *Guide*. These anthologies also contain many of the more popular poems, but the listings at the end of each theme do not include them if the poem is more readily available in the anthologies listed above.

AIW   *Ain't I a Woman! A Book of Women's Poetry from around the World.* Illona Linthwaite, ed. New York: Peter Bedrick Books, 1988.

CaPo   *Cavalier Poets; Selected Poems.* Thomas Clayton, ed. Oxford: Oxford University Press, 1978.

EnRePo   *English Renaissance Poetry: A Collection of Shorter Poems from Skelton to Jonson.* John Williams, ed. 2nd ed. Fayetteville: University of Arkansas Press, 1990.

EnRP   *English Romantic Poetry and Prose.* Russell Noyes, ed. Oxford: Oxford University Press, 1956.

InPS   *An Introduction to Poetry.* Louis Simpson, ed. 3rd ed. New York: St. Martin's Press, 1986.

MoBrPo   *Modern British Poetry.* Louis Untermeyer, ed. 7th rev. ed. New York: Harcourt, Brace, and World, 1962.

NBLV   *The Norton Book of Light Verse.* Russell Baker, ed. New York: W. W. Norton, 1986.

NIP   *The Norton Introduction to Poetry.* J. Paul Hunter, ed. 3rd ed. New York: W. W. Norton, 1986.

NOBE   *The New Oxford Book of English Verse, 1250–1950.* Helen Gardner, ed. Oxford: Oxford University Press, 1972.

NoP   *The Norton Anthology of Poetry.* Alexander W. Allison et al., eds. 3rd ed. New York: W. W. Norton, 1983.

OxAEP-2   *The Oxford Anthology of English Poetry.* Vol. 2. John Wain, ed. Oxford: Oxford University Press, 1990.

OxBSP   *The Oxford Book of Short Poems.* P. J. Kavanagh and James Michie, eds. Oxford: Oxford University Press, 1985.

OxBTC   *The Oxford Book of Twentieth-Century English Verse.* Philip Larkin, comp. Oxford: Oxford University Press, 1973.

WiR   *The Wind and the Rain. An Anthology of Poems for Young People.* John Hollander and Harold Bloom, eds. Garden City, New York: Doubleday, 1961.

Dates provided for poems are either the date of composition or the date of publication, if the composition date is unknown.

Active and Contemplative Lives

∽⌒⌒⌒∾

What is the best kind of life—a busy, social one in the urban world of politics, commerce, and conversation, or a retired, thoughtful one in the country, the only company one's own thoughts? This question was frequently debated in the Middle Ages and the Renaissance, when contemplation meant a profound state of prayer, deeper than meditation, that brought the soul into union with God. The contemplative life often meant retirement to the cloisters of a convent or monastery, and the dichotomy was thus sometimes seen as the contrast between a worldly, materialistic life and a spiritual, ascetic one. In *The Canterbury Tales* (c. 1387), Chaucer's less-than-perfect clergy often reject the contemplative in favor of the active, and seek secular pleasures outside the cloisters. More commonly, poems on this theme approach it from the point of view of the person caught up in the active, competitive world who yearns for a more simple, solitary life. The contemplative life is also associated with melancholy, however, and in his influential study, *The Anatomy of Melancholy* (1621), Richard Burton considered it almost a disease that could be avoided by pursuing an active life among good company. Despite Burton's warning, the yearning for a contemplative life remains strong among poets, perhaps because they are particularly drawn to the solitude of their own imaginations.

One of the earliest poems to glorify the state of the quiet, contemplative mind is the late sixteenth-century poem "My mind to me a kingdom is," often credited to Sir Edward Dyer but more recently thought to be written by Edward de Vere. Published in 1588, it has always been one of the most popular Elizabethan lyrics. The poet rejects the allures of a life in high society—the "princely pomp" and "wealthy store" of the aristocrat, the wit of the courtier, and the beauty of the court ladies. He is captured by none of these attractions because his mind "doth serve for all." He pities those caught up in the quest for wealth and fame because they fall as easily as they rise, and the precarious nature of their position leads to worry and unhappiness. Like most poems whose aim is to contrast two opposing points of view, the lyric relies on antithesis and irony to emphasize the poet's choice of life: "They poor, I rich; they beg, I give;/They lack, I leave; they pine, I live." Living free from ambition and competition, the poet enjoys the benefits of a "quiet mind." Rather than relying for his happiness on material possessions or the downfall of other people, he finds peace of mind in health, a clear conscience, and his own solitude.

Another Elizabethan lyric on this theme is found in Robert Greene's play *Farewell to Folly* (1591). "Sweet are the Thoughts that Savor of Content" contrasts the quiet mind of the poor man with the worries and vicissitudes of the wealthy. Beggars, the poet says, sleep easily in their beds, and contentment is found more readily in the cottage than in the palace. "A mind content both crown and kingdom is." Many poems on this theme value the contemplative life because its "riches" are open to all; the poets are seeking to reassure the humble that their station in life contains spiritual treasure of much greater worth than the material treasures of the wealthy.

The contrast between the active and contemplative lives is most fully and delightfully developed in the seventeenth century by John Milton, who devoted a whole poem to each idea. He wrote "L'Allegro," or "the cheerful man," and "Il Penseroso," or "the contemplative man" (c. 1631), as companion poems, contrasting the two states of mind in parallel form. While mood—cheerfulness and melancholy—is the central idea of the poems, the moods are connected to active and contemplative lives, and unlike most other poets, Milton does not favor one kind of life over the other. Rather, he recognizes that most people vacillate between the two moods, seeking company when cheerful and solitude when thoughtful or sad. The contrast is often expressed in music, as in Schumann's "Florestan and Eusebius," or in the movement from allegro (quick) to adagio (slow), as Milton's title suggests.

"L'Allegro" and "Il Penseroso" are early works, probably written after Milton had attended Cambridge University and returned to his family home in rural Buckinghamshire. The poems depict his life at that time, when as Il Penseroso he pursued a solitary life of study and reflection at Horton, breaking out from time to time as L'Allegro, spending a carefree day with his friends in London. Unlike the two Elizabethan lyrics, Milton's poems do not attach the theme to class; rather, they attempt to dramatize the mood of the cheerful man and the mood of the pensive man through the use of language and image.

The contrast between the moods is heightened by the parallel form of the two poems. "L'Allegro" portrays the speaker's day from morning to night, and "Il Penseroso" portrays his night, from evening to morning. Both poems begin with the banishing of the unwanted emotion—Melancholy from L'Allegro's world and Mirth from Il Penseroso's—and the welcoming of the chosen one: the nymph Mirth for L'Allegro and the pensive nun Melancholy for Il Penseroso. Next, the poet calls on the companions of Mirth—including Jest, Jollity, Quips, and "Laughter holding both his sides"—and the companions of Melancholy—including Peace, Quiet, Leisure, Contemplation, and Silence. The main sections of the poem "L'Allegro" describe the pleasures of the morning, afternoon, evening, and night, which include lively farmyard scenes ("While the cock with lively din/Scatters the rear of darkness thin"), busy daytime activities of plowmen, milkmaids, and shepherds, and a youthful village dance and dinner. The day culminates in the city among the "busy hum of men," where the speaker attends a comedy by Ben Jonson or Shakespeare. L'Allegro's life is surrounded by noise and activity. Even at night there is no darkness in the description, but rather the brilliancy of elegant parties and lively theaters. The details reinforce the active interrelationship of the human and natural worlds. The poet asks to be admitted to Mirth's "crew," and the whole world is awakened by the lark, the cock, and the hounds, who "cheerly rouse the slumbering morn." Just as the country people are by the nature of their work involved in the landscape and the animals, the townspeople are also involved with each other as storyteller and listener, actor and audience. Even the ladies need admirers on whom their eyes can "rain influence." Like the characters he describes, the poet derives pleasure from a feeling of active and purposeful union with his surroundings, a union typified by the reference to Orpheus in the last lines. Orpheus's fame lay in his ability to communicate with the inanimate objects of nature. Thus the active life is typified by a joyful sense of harmonious unity between all of creation.

Il Penseroso's account begins at night, and the setting conveys his inner melancholy and solitary detachment from the world. While in "L'Allegro" the natural elements have an active purpose (the sun is a "great potentate," and the mountains provide rest for "labouring clouds"), in "Il Penseroso" the moon wanders aimlessly, with no purpose, stooping occasionally to avoid a cloud as a pensive walker might bend over to avoid the branch of a tree. The poet's self-sufficiency in his contemplation is emphasized through detail. The nun looks at the ground with a "sad leaden downward cast," unlike the plowman, the mower, and the shepherd, who look at the fields as the source of their work. Unlike L'Allegro, Il Penseroso is not actively stirred by the sounds of the birds; in fact, he does not even hear the nightingale, which should herald his night as the lark awoke the dawn of L'Allegro's day. The curfew sounds far off and does not call him as the bell had called the farm workers. The solitary speaker walks unseen in the darkness, or retreats to a "high lonely tower" where his lamp may be seen from a distance. Like the lamp, the poet is remote from his surroundings, a tower complete unto himself. Here his thoughts lead him to the tragic tales of old, in contrast to L'Allegro's attendance at a comedy. When morning comes, rather than the active life of farm and village, Il Penseroso seeks a secluded spot where he may be hidden "from day's garish eye," and where sleep may bring him "some mysterious dream." While L'Allegro ends his poem with a plea for music that takes away cares, Il Penseroso seeks a church service in a "studious cloister," where the stained-glass windows cast "a dim religious light" and the organ and choir "bring all Heaven before my eyes." Finally, Il Penseroso will end his days in "peaceful hermitage," his only companions the stars above and the herbs at his feet. Each poem describes the landscape, activities, people, and thoughts to which we are attracted when feeling either cheerful or melancholic, active or contemplative.

Both poems are written in iambic tetrameter, the rhythm of the nursery rhyme. But Milton's careful use of sound brings to life the contrast between the active, mirthful life and the contemplative, melancholy one. "L'Allegro" is filled with short, lively phrases such as the famous lines, "Come, and trip it as you go/On the light fantastic toe." "Il Penseroso," in contrast, creates the pensive mood of the speaker through long, subdued, and soft sounds. His lonely room contains only a cricket on the hearth and him, and the only sound is "the bellman's drowsy charm/ To bless the doors from nightly harm."

Milton does not prefer one life over the other. Both poems can be seen as expressing a desire for spiritual enlightenment, and both paths are valid. At the end of "L'Allegro" the speaker finds that music releases a harmony within himself that has been typified by the harmonious details of the poem. The poet's communion with the external world has brought about a sense of peace. For Il Penseroso, happiness comes from within, the result of reading, dreaming, and contemplation. In his sonnet "On His Blindness" (1652?), Milton relates these contrasting personalities to the hierarchy of angels and also to human worshipers. God values both the busy, active messengers who do good works, and the contemplative thinkers who also serve when they patiently and faithfully "stand and wait."

Another poet interested in active and contemplative lives was Abraham Cowley (1618–1667). As a supporter of the royal family of the Stuarts, who had been exiled after the execution of Charles I in 1649, he was also exiled and worked as a spy for the Royalist cause. After being imprisoned for this work, he pondered escaping the intrigues and politics of the court by fleeing to a contemplative life in America. In a preface to his poems in 1656, he writes of this escape, which was not to seek gold but to "forsake this world forever, with all the *vanities* and *Vexations* of it, and to bury myself in some obscure retreat there. . . . " Cowley never did go to America, but he ended his days in a seclusion that he envisaged in "The Wish" (1647). Like the Elizabethan poets, the speaker of "The Wish" seeks retirement from "the busy world" where pride, ambition, flattery, and malice make life miserable. Cowley uses the metaphor of a bee hive to contrast the busy beelike world of the city with his country retreat. The "honey" of the active world soon cloys, and the buzzing and stinging of city life become unendurable. In his retreat he will have few friends but many books and a loving mistress. Like Greene, Cowley plays on the notion of "wealth" and "riches" to contrast the treasures of the natural world of his garden with the material wealth of the city. His only fear, he concludes, is that other people will see how delightful his secluded life is and will flock there too, creating yet another city. Many modern seekers after "wilderness" at the end of the twentieth century have discovered that Cowley's fear was well founded.

Cowley's small house and large garden are typical of a recurring motif in literature that deals with active and contemplative lives. The garden has played a central role in Western literature because of the biblical importance of the Garden of Eden, the site of man's innocence before the Fall. When Adam and Eve ate the fruit of the tree of knowledge, they were expelled from the garden into the real, mortal world. In English poetry the garden sometimes takes the place of the pastoral world of classical literature, the Golden Age where innocent nature is represented by shepherds tending their flocks on idyllic, sunny hillsides, untroubled by the storms of human or natural strife. Like Pastoral poetry, garden poetry sometimes became love poetry, most memorably in the thirteenth-century French allegory *The Romance of the Rose*. Here, as in most garden imagery, the garden was the site of courtly or idealized love, a platonic love that upheld the ideal of innocence in the Garden of Eden. The garden was a retreat from the busy world for the lovers, who had no interest in the affairs of others. It represented the best of the natural world of trees, flowers, and streams; but unlike the real world that also contains raging rivers, treacherous mountains, and deep forests concealing wild beasts, the garden was safe because it was enclosed and cultivated. In its ordered seclusion it was the perfect setting for the contemplative life.

The most famous English poem to set the contemplative life in a garden is Andrew Marvell's "The Garden," written in the 1650s and composed of nine octaves of iambic tetrameter rhyming in couplets. The tone of the poem is ironic and good humored as Marvell parodies the conventional garden love poem by arguing that the joys of the garden are best appreciated alone. Like earlier poets writing on this theme, he begins by valuing repose over the "uncessant labors" of men who seek glory and fame, using images of growth to make the contrast. While the ambitious man is crowned by only one or two plants, such as the palm, oak, or bay, all symbolic of victory, the contemplative man has all nature at his disposal. He has looked for quiet and innocence "in busy companies of men," but finds them only in the garden. The third stanza rejects the garden as a site for romantic love; no white or red, the emblems of female beauty, are as amorous as "this lovely green." He chastises lovers for carving their mistresses' names in the trunks of the trees, whose beauty, he argues, far exceeds the beauty of the women named. He continues the joke in stanza four by reminding the reader of the Greek myths in which a woman is pursued by a god, only to be turned into a tree. Because Marvell's garden has no women in it, it is the Garden of Eden without Eve. Love is there, but it is sensual rather than sexual love. The images are suggestive and erotic, but deliberately unattached to a woman: ripe apples drop about the speaker's head, "luscious clusters" of grapes explode in his mouth, peaches reach into his hands, and melons trip up his feet. He "falls" on the grass, but it is an innocent fall because women have been banished from the garden.

The second half of the poem moves from bodily pleasure to the pleasures of the mind in quiet contemplation. Marvell draws on Plato for an image of the mind creating ideal forms, just as God does. In a passage that prefigures the Romantic poets of the nineteenth century, the speaker is found "transcending" the real world of the garden to create an ideal natural world: "Annihilating all that's made/To a green thought in a green shade." Having made this imaginative leap, the speaker finds his soul freeing itself from the body, transformed into a bird that rests, preening and singing, in the tree overhead. This image of the soul as bird is a favorite one in English poetry, explored also in John Keats's "Ode to a Nightingale" (1819). From this ecstasy of pure contemplation the speaker again rails at women, but the tone remains ironic, the criticism undercut by the lightness of image. He jokes about how happy Eden must have been before Eve arrived, but the lines "After a place so pure and sweet/What other help could yet be meet!" remind us through the play on "helpmate" that the poet is enjoying his parody of the courtly love tradition that glorified the woman in the garden. Adam, he concludes, had to have his troublesome Eve because "to live in paradise alone" would have been to have had two paradises, and no man could bear such happiness.

The poem concludes with a description of a sun dial skillfully created in the garden with flowers and herbs. Always temperate, the garden of contemplation is blessed with a "milder sun" that marks time through a fragrant clock of flowers that tells the passage of time to the bees as well as to the speaker. Rather than the mechanical clock time of the busy world, time in the garden is a part of its natural beauty. The prelapsarian ideal is complete with the banishing of not just Eve and sexual love, but also human time and therefore mortality.

A more traditional expression of the theme is found in Alexander Pope's short "Ode on Solitude," written, Pope claimed, in 1699, when he was eleven years old, and based on a poem by Horace, a Roman writer whose influence on Pope and his contemporaries was profound. The speaker yearns for a simple country life, tending a few acres, self-sufficient, enjoying peace of mind, sound sleep, innocence, and meditation. Let me "steal [hide] from the world," the speaker concludes; he asks only to live and die unknown and unlamented, reiterating the theme's general condemnation of the pursuit of fame and ambition in the active life.

Pope gives the theme a comic twist in his "Epistle to Miss Blount" (c. 1710), a gently satiric poem written to Teresa Blount, the sister of his good friend Martha Blount. Teresa had been complaining loudly about her parents' having exiled her to the country when she had been enjoying the delights of London society, and Pope pokes fun at her enforced contemplative life. Surrounded by "dull aunts, and croaking rooks," poor Teresa has to endure "prayers three hours a day," a solitary tea, and an early bedtime. The only beau is a jolly squire, rough mannered and coarse, who "loves you best of all things—but his horse." Forced into lonely contemplation, Teresa stares into the fire and conjures up images of the sophisticated life she is missing in town, but when the images fade she is left "in lone woods, or empty walls." At the end of the poem Pope mildly chastises Teresa for her ill humor when he imagines himself in a contrasting state in London. Pretending to be in love with her, he concludes that while she dreams of the active life, he yearns for the contemplative one, and, standing on a busy street, he conjures up pictures of her in her rural retreat. When the picture vanishes, he falls into the same bad humor that has befallen her: "Vexed to be still in town, I knit my brow,/Look sour, and hum a tune—as you may now." Pope delighted in teasing young women about their bad moods and ill humor, and here he makes use of the convention of the active and contemplative lives to make fun of the young woman's love for society and dislike of her own company.

A very different female attitude to country life is offered by Alexander Pope's friend Anne Finch, countess of Winchilsea, in her long poem "The Petition for an Absolute Retreat," published in 1713. Finch was considerably older than the frivolous Teresa when she wrote the poem, so it is not surprising that her view of the quiet, contemplative life is more mature. Finch sees "those Windings and that Shade" (a phrase that recurs regularly throughout the almost 300 lines of rhyming couplets) as offering her freedom from the sort of pressures that Teresa's social life offers a woman. She wants to be free from social climbing, vanity, and the competition for admirers that Pope satirizes in his portrait of Teresa and in "The Rape of the Lock" (1714). Finch offers a portrait of her retreat that, like Marvell's garden, is Edenlike. She will not have to work because her food—plain and wholesome—will be provided naturally. Cherries and peaches will, as in Marvell's garden, be within easy reach. In her retreat, Anne Finch will enjoy a more natural dress, with perfumes and colors provided by flowers rather than chemists. Here the poem recalls the lyrics about natural versus contrived beauty by Robert Herrick and Ben Jonson ("Delight in Disorder" [1648] and "Still to be Neat" [1609]), written in the previous century. Finch's easy garments will respond to the wind, "Gently waving, to express/Unaffected carelessness."

Surprisingly, Finch does not eschew company in her "absolute retreat," as does Marvell in his garden. At the beginning of the poem she bans vain, frivolous, and worldly people, but she does want the company of "A *Partner* suited to [her] mind," someone who also slights "Fame and Splendour, Wealth and Pride." The retreat is truly prelapsarian, free from "Rage, and Jealousy, and Hate," the attributes of fallen man. Ardelia (Finch's poetic name for herself) and her friend Arminda will learn more from the contemplation of nature than they would among "Crowds, and Noise." This enjoyment of the natural world tends more to the Romantic movement of the early nineteenth century than to the more rational one of the eighteenth century, but Finch does find in nature's lessons both pleasure and "use"; let us not idly lounge in our retreat she tells her companion, but rather "Let each moment be improved." After describing various historical figures who made the mistake of giving up their contemplative lives for fame and possessions, only to meet with disastrous ends, Finch concludes that the "contemplations of the Mind" that she pursues in her retreat will lead her to spiritual peace and contentment. Let others seek fame, applause, and the pleasures of good food and merry times; in her contemplative life "all Heaven shall be surveyed/From those Windings and that Shade."

A contemporary of Pope and Anne Finch, the Welsh lawyer-turned-painter and clergyman John Dyer is remembered now mainly for his contribution to the theme of the active and contemplative lives, "Grongar Hill" (1726). Describing the river Towy and the surrounding hills, Dyer finds in the quiet country life a respite from greed and acquisitiveness. Like other poets writing on this theme, he contrasts material wealth with the spiritual wealth to be found in nature. Peace of mind cannot be found in the palaces of the mighty. While Dyer's descriptions of the Welsh mountains are at times banal (a banality only exaggerated by his excessive use of exclamation marks), they also evoke a wild and uncivilized beauty, very different from the orderly and cultivated gardens beloved by the eighteenth-century rationalists. He looks ahead to the Romantic poets of the next century, and has added a phrase to the language:

But transient is the smile of fate!
A little rule, a little sway,
A sunbeam in a winter's day,
Is all the proud and mighty have
Between the cradle and the grave.

William Cowper's long poem "The Task" (1785), too long to be fully considered in this discussion, is also central to the theme of the active and contemplative lives. A biography of Cowper by Lord David Cecil is titled *The Stricken Deer* (1929) after one section of the poem in which Cowper describes his retreat from the world as akin to that of a deer, wounded by a hunter's arrow, that hides itself away in the forest. There, he says, he was found by Christ, similarly wounded by the world of men. Burdened throughout his life by depression that led eventually to madness, Cowper was naturally attracted to the contemplative, solitary life of the English countryside that he eulogizes in the poem. Writing just before the French Revolution, he shared with Jean-Jacques Rousseau a belief in liberty and the superiority of the natural world over the civilized world. A gentle man who hated hunting and kept a tame hare, Cowper in "The Task" gave us the well-known aphorism "Variety's the very spice of life."

The Romantic poets who followed Cowper—William Wordsworth, Samuel Taylor Coleridge, John Keats, and Percy Bysshe Shelley—continued to champion the rustic, rural, contemplative life rather than the active, sophisticated, social life of the city coffeehouse and salon where many of the eighteenth-century writers had congregated. The Romantic movement (approximately 1800–1830) was a democratic one that extolled the life of the common man, especially country people such as shepherds and plowmen. In this volume the poetry of the Romantics is discussed under the themes of "Art, Imagination, and Inspiration" and "Nature" because their interest was with the power of the natural world rather than just its place in the contemplative life. For the Romantics, the natural world of field and birdsong was the inspiration for their imaginations and the source of their creative power as poets.

A late Romantic, Emily Brontë rejects the active life and embraces a private, imaginative world in "O! Thy bright eyes must answer now" (1844). Emily's life, like that of her novelist sisters Charlotte and Anne, was essentially contemplative, bounded by the remote village of Haworth and the surrounding Yorkshire moors where they passed most of their lives. But in the publishing of their poetry and novels, Emily apparently envisioned a kind of fame and worldliness that she chooses to reject in the poem. Her creative impulse, personified as a "God of visions," has to explain to her Reason why she chose to pursue her personal visions and "cast the world away." It has usually been assumed that Emily was too shy and insecure to seek the wider world, but in the poem she claims to have "persevered to shun/The common paths that others run." She has chosen a "strange road," disdaining the wealth, power, glory, and pleasure that she claims to have at one time sought. She admits, though, that her literary "offerings" were merely "careless gifts" that deserved to be "despised." Now, rather than pursuing the pleasures of worldly fame, she has chosen to commune only with her own imagination, her "God of visions" who is at the same time her "slave," her "Comrade," and her "King." In the last three stanzas Bronte explains what she means by these three conflicting relationships with her Muse. Brontë thus dramatizes her contemplative life by personifying her imagination as somehow separate from herself, a force that both governs her ("my king,") and does her bidding ("my slave"). Her sister Charlotte described her imagination similarly, as a dominant male figure of whom she was both frightened and beloved. Emily concludes by acknowledging the power of a God who is beyond doubt or despair because he is essentially her "own soul." Her account of the contemplative life is thus much more personal and introspective than that of the male poets who describe it in terms of their surroundings: their gardens and rural life.

Alfred, Lord Tennyson, the most prolific and popular poet of the nineteenth century (he was poet laureate for forty-two years), wrote on a large range of topics, but many of his poems were written in the shadow of an early tragedy, the death of his close friend Arthur Hallam at the age of just twenty-two. Hallam died suddenly in Vienna while on a European tour, and when the news reached Tennyson in England, he at once turned to poetry for the release of his intense grief. Wisely, he chose to write a monologue, a poem spoken by a character quite separate from himself, in this case Ulysses, the hero of Homer's epic *The Odyssey* (Ulysses is the Roman name for Odysseus). In "Ulysses" (1833) Tennyson tried to encourage himself to go on living after the death of Arthur, and the poem became an attempt to value the active life. Its poignancy and beauty, however, derive from the intense sense of loss that underlies the old adventurer's words. Tennyson would go on to spend seventeen years creating his long tribute to Arthur Hallam, *In Memoriam* (1850), but he later noted that the intensity of his grief was most evident in the poem written immediately after Hallam's death: "There is more about myself in 'Ulysses,' which was written under the sense of loss and that all had gone by, but that still life must be fought out to the end. It was more written with the feeling of his loss upon me than many poems in 'In Memoriam.' "

The poem takes up Ulysses' story where Homer left off in *The Odyssey*. Ulysses, king of Ithaca, has returned home after a long absence, fighting in the Trojan War (the subject of Homer's *The Iliad*) and then taking ten years to bring his crew safely home (the subject of *The Odyssey*). As the poem opens, Ulysses is standing on a rocky crag in Ithaca, gazing out to sea and lamenting the dull, routine life that now oppresses him after the adventures of the past. He is "idle," the hearth "still," the crags "barren." His wife is old, and his people are a "savage race,/That hoard, and sleep, and feed, and know not me." Ulysses is not ready to settle down into a contemplative life, ruling his island: "I cannot rest from travel; I will drink/Life to the lees." As Ulysses reviews his adventurous life, he speaks with longing of his past greatness, when, "for always roaming with a hungry heart," he visited other places and people and became "a name." He remembers his fellow warriors and mariners with whom he battled "on the ringing plains of windy Troy." Now he has become a "gray spirit yearning in desire." He speaks dismissively of his son Telemachus, who is dull enough to take over his kingship. The language he uses to describe his son and their people implies Ulysses' sense of superiority. Telemachus will use "slow prudence," or caution, to "make mild/A rugged people, and through soft degrees/Subdue them to the useful and the good." Damning with faint praise, Ulysses finds Telemachus "blameless" and "decent" in the carrying out of "common duties" far beneath the interest of the great adventurer: "He works his work, I mine."

"Ulysses" seems on the surface to make a convincing case for the active life. The aging king is not going to sink into retirement: "How dull it is to pause, to make an end,/To rust unburnished, not to shine in use!/ As though to breathe were life!" The poem concludes with a moving long address to his fellow mariners, urging them to sail away over the "dark, broad seas" one more time. Tennyson desperately wanted to be convinced by his old speaker. He is only twenty-four but he feels the chill of death through the loss of his friend. In his black despair he tries to urge himself to go on living, to set sail again, but his acute sense of loss haunts the language and sounds of the poem, undercutting Ulysses' battle cry for action. The contemplative life of Milton's Il Penseroso dominates the poem despite Ulysses' attempts to deny it. In a powerful metaphor describing experience as an arch through which "gleams that untraveled world," Ulysses finds that the arch's "margin fades" as he approaches it; in other words, the untraveled world of the future is a mirage, unattainable. That he is traveling toward death, not life, is suggested by many of the sounds and images in the poem. Ulysses reminds his mariners that they are old, that "Death closes all; but something ere the end,/some work of noble note, may yet be done." That line, with its hesitant conditional verb "may" rather than the future tense "shall," is followed by a reminder that they may be sailing only to their deaths:

The lights begin to twinkle from the rocks;
The long day wanes; the slow moon climbs; the deep
Moans round with many voices.

The long, sad sounds of these lines, emphasizing the dying of the day, prepare us for Ulysses' reminder that "It may be that the gulfs will wash us down." The poem concludes with a final cry to action, that Ulysses and his warriors are "strong in will/To strive, to seek, to find, and not to yield." But Tennyson's intense grief has permeated every line of the poem, undercutting the active with the melancholic, the sun-dappled sea giving way to "dark, broad seas" that "gloom" with the coming of night. Perhaps unwittingly, Tennyson has merged L'Allegro and Il Penseroso into an unforgettable poem that speaks of the failure of the human will wholly to banish melancholy.

A well-known but minor twentieth-century poem on this theme is W. H. Davies's short lyric "Leisure" (1928). In seven couplets of iambic tetrameter Davies pleads to be given time to "stand and stare," time to appreciate the natural world of squirrels and starry skies amid the cares of a busy life. A more successful and compelling poem is William Butler Yeats's "The Lake Isle of Innisfree." Probably Yeats's most anthologized poem, it epitomizes the "escape" from the modern industrial world that is now always associated with romanticism, or with Henry David Thoreau's retreat to a cabin on Walden Pond. Yeats wrote the poem in 1888 when he was living in, and hating, London. He begins with his decision to return to Innisfree, a small, uninhabited island on a lake in western Ireland. There he will build a small cabin and live alone and simply, enjoy the natural world that he idealizes in a few sharp images: the buzz of bees, the "purple glow" of the sky, the evening beating of birds' wings. He will be self-sufficient, his humble wants supplied by the garden and bee hive. The images harken back to an earlier time, when buildings were not brick but clay. Like the earlier poets writing in praise of the contemplative life, the speaker seeks peace in his solitary retreat. Only at the end of the poem do we realize the poignancy of his opening line, which declares he "will arise and go now." The statement, with its demonstrative future tense (I *will*), is repeated, but we learn that the little cabin and its idealized surroundings exist, and will continue to exist, only in the city dweller's imagination. He continually hears the sounds of the lake water lapping, but he hears it while standing fixedly on the gray streets of the town. The sounds of the poem recreate the gentle, soothing sounds of wave and wind in contrast to the harsh noises of the city. The last line, which tells us that he hears the water lapping in the world's heart, reminds the reader of all that the modern industrial city dweller has lost by being separated from the natural pulse of the earth. The lake isle can never be more than a dream, a recollection of a lost

Elysium, the garden before the Fall. But perhaps Yeats's vision is not wholly bleak. His speaker can still hear and respond to the deep forces of nature, immutable under the concrete of the active, busy life. It is the imagination that allows the contemplative mind to reach into the still heart of things and be nourished by it.

Poems that contrast the active and contemplative lives offer us insight into the unresolved tensions that have always pulled at the human heart. The modern psychologist would refer to these lives as those of the extrovert and the introvert, and most of us have a tendency toward one or the other. Poets, perhaps, will always lean toward the life of contemplation, just as twenty-first-century city-dwellers will often yearn to escape from the "fast lane" of modern, technology-driven life into the quieter paths of stream and field so finely described in contemplative poetry.

❦

"My mind to me a kingdom is," anonymous; attributed to Edward de Vere or Sir Edward Dyer
> ImPo; TrGrPo-1

"The Poor Estate" ("Sweet are the Thoughts that Savor of Content"), Robert Greene
> TrGrPo-1

"L'Allegro" and "Il Penseroso," John Milton
> ImPo; NAEL-1; OAEL-1; TFi; TrGrPo-1

"The Wish," Abraham Cowley
> TrGrPo-1

"The Garden," Andrew Marvell
> BL; ImPo; NAEL-1; OAEL-1; OBEV; SB; TFi; TrGrPo-1

"Ode on Solitude" ("Happy the man, whose wish and care"), Alexander Pope
> ImPo; TrGrPo-1

"Epistle to Miss Blount," Alexander Pope
> NAEL-1

"The Petition for an Absolute Retreat" (excerpt), Anne Finch
> BL

"Grongar Hill," John Dyer
> ECP; SB; TrGrPo-1

"The Task" (excerpts), William Cowper

ECP; NAEL-1; OAEL-1

"O! Thy bright eyes must answer now," Emily Brontë
TrGrPo-2

"Ulysses," Alfred, Lord Tennyson
BAVP; ImPo; NAEL-2; OAEL-2; OBEV; TFi; TrGrPo-2

"Leisure," W. H. Davies
TFi; TrGrPo-2

"The Lake Isle of Innisfree," William Butler Yeats
NAEL-2; TFi; TrGrPo-2

Art, Imagination, and Inspiration

Ↄↄ⌒ↄↄ

All poets are vitally concerned with the springs of their creativity. Where do their words come from? The Greeks personified their artistic inspiration in the figures of the Muses, nine goddesses who made possible the writing of poetry, drama, and music. British poets throughout the ages have also looked beyond their own souls for inspiration, seeking it often in beautiful women, nature, or God. Others find inspiration within themselves, in a nonrational realm often identified as the imagination.

Sir Philip Sidney, one of the finest of the Renaissance poets, wrote a sonnet cycle of 108 sonnets and eleven songs in the courtly love tradition titled *Astrophil and Stella* (1582). Astrophil, the young courtier, tells the story of his devoted but disappointed love for a beautiful married lady. The convention that an unattainable, virtuous woman could be the poet's Muse began with the Italian poets Dante and Petrarch in the thirteenth and fourteenth centuries. Beatrice was the inspiration for Dante's *Divine Comedy* (c. 1310–1321), and Petrarch wrote his love sonnets for Laura; both women, like Sidney's Stella, were based on real women from the poets' own lives, but in the poetry they became abstractions that transcended any one woman. Stella is Astrophil's "star," an unattainable, perfect, and lovely woman who leads him on his distracted path of adoration. In Sonnet 1 he sets out his reason for writing the poems: Stella will read them, realize his suffering, and pity him. Astrophil explains that he read other love poets to try and find the right words to "paint the blackest face of woe," but "Invention" could not be inspired by such study. The poet writes with some irony and humor about his writer's block. Comparing himself to a pregnant woman in the throes of labor, he concludes with an image of the poet biting his pen in frustration before hearing his Muse remind him to "look in thy heart and write."

In Sonnet 41, Astrophil credits Stella with inspiring him in a tournament. A courtier in the court of Queen Elizabeth I (with whom he quarreled because he opposed her marriage to a Catholic), Sidney often took part in jousting competitions. In the poem he ponders his victory: why was he the winner? The members of the audience find different reasons for his success: for the horsemen it was his horsemanship; for the townsfolk it was his strength; for other jousters it was his experience; for "lucky wits" it was merely chance; for his family it was inherited talent. But the poet rejects all of these suggestions (with some humor, as clearly all of the reasons are valid). No, he replies, he won because Stella was watching, and her "heavenly face/Sent forth the beams" that gave him the power to win the prize.

In Sonnet 74, Sidney returns to the subject of Stella as the inspiration for his poetry rather than for his prowess on a horse. In the first quatrain he rejects the Greek Muses as his source, humorously undervaluing his talent that would be scorned by them. As a "poor layman" with a "vulgar brain," he could not summon the Muses to his aid. In the second quatrain he claims not to know what poets mean when they speak of inspiration, but he asserts that he is never inspired by the words of other poets. Why, then, does he find it easy to write good poetry that is admired by the "best wits"? As in Sonnet 41, the wits guess several unspecified reasons, all rejected by the poet. The answer is simple: his words are sweet because his lips are inspired by Stella's kiss.

Birds and their varied and powerful songs, which seem to speak directly to the heart of listening mankind, have for centuries symbolized the freeing of the soul from the body and the poet's gift of transforming everyday words into transcendent lyrics. One of the most loved bird poems is Percy Bysshe Shelley's "To a Skylark" (1820). Shelley saw the poet as a prophet whose creative gifts gave him the power to be a voice for political change. A radical, Shelley saw the French Revolution as the beginning of a worldwide movement toward democracy. But the new century had seen the collapse of many of the reforms begun in 1789, and Shelley despaired that the times were becoming increasingly restrictive and reactionary. In his *Defence of Poetry* he wrote that "poets are the unacknowledged legislators of the world."

The famous opening lines of "To a Skylark" find in the pure sounds of the bird's song not just nature, but art:

> Hail to thee, blithe Spirit!
>   Bird though never wert—
> That from Heaven, or near it,
>   Pourest thy full heart
> In profuse strains of unpremeditated art.

Just as the long last line of this opening stanza gives us a sense of the bird's song, so the repetition in each stanza of a long closing line continues to imitate the sound of the bird as well as spiraling outward in a movement that imitates the bird's soaring into the sky. The bird unites the two refined elements of creation and imagination, air and fire, as it springs from the earth "like a cloud of fire," recalling Shelley's admiration for the rebel Prometheus, who brought fire to mankind. The bird disappears into the sky, becoming a part of it, but its song seems to fill the heavens from a source now unseen. The poem then attempts to describe the bird—a rapturous sound high in the sky—through simile. What is most like it? The brightness of its fluid notes surpasses raindrops from a rainbow cloud. Is it like a poet "hidden/In the light of thought" whose words, once published, stir a sympathetic chord in the reader? Is it like a maiden shut away in a tower (as in "The Lady of Shalott" [1833]) whose love-sick music "overflows her bower"? Is it like a glow-worm whose light emerges from its hidden spot among the flowers, or is it like a rose "embowered" in green leaves, whose scent pours out on the wind? Each of the images is of a hidden source of something magical—music or light or fragrance—that pours in profusion into the world to surprise and transform us, just as the notes of the hidden bird's song pour over the poet. Each of the images is "joyous, and clear and fresh." But the sky-lark's music "doth surpass" them all.

The poet then asks the bird to teach him what "sweet thoughts" have inspired his song. Human song, however glorious, has "some hidden want." Why is the bird's song so perfect? Clearly the skylark is free from human cares—languor, or annoyance, or "love's sad satiety." His joy is unalloyed, whereas ours is always tempered by regret or longing: "Our sweetest songs are those that tell of saddest thought." And yet Shelley recognizes that even if we were as free from worry as the bird, we could not approach the beauty and joy of its song. He ends the poem by appealing to the bird to teach him something of his inner gladness, because "the world should listen then—as I am listening now." Shelley prays for a voice like the skylark's to arrest and transform his human audience.

Some birds have been called upon more than others in this quest for the expression of the poet's art, and the nightingale in particular has been the subject of many British poems. According to Greek mythology, the nightingale was originally Procne, whose husband King Tereus raped her sister, Philomel, and cut out her tongue. Philomel communicated her plight to Procne by weaving a message into a cloth. In revenge, Procne killed her young son (who resembled his father) and fed him to Tereus. The gods in pity turned the voiceless sister, Philomel, into a swallow, who cannot sing, and Procne into the nightingale, whose poignant, sad song forever regrets the murder of her child. Because later Roman writers reversed some details of the story, they turned the voiceless Philomel into the nightingale, and her name has been associated with nightingales in British poetry ever since. A Middle English lyric, "The Cuckoo and the Nightingale," established another tradition that sees the nightingale as the friend of love, unlike the cuckoo, its enemy. If lovers hear the nightingale in spring, their love will blossom, but if they hear the cuckoo (the usual harbinger of spring), they will be disappointed. John Milton refers to this convention in his first sonnet, "O Nightingale" (1630), where he calls on the bird to sing to him before the cuckoo can call and doom his love affair to failure. Milton links love and poetry in the last line of the sonnet, when he tells the nightingale that as a poet he serves both the Muse of poetry and Love, and that the bird is wedded to both through legend and its "liquid notes," so much more musical than the sound of the "shallow Cuckoo," the "rude Bird of Hate."

Anne Finch, countess of Winchilsea, an Augustan poet writing at the end of the seventeenth century, also praises the nightingale for its beautiful song, which her poem "To the Nightingale" (1713) tries to emulate through its irregular rhythm. Just as the bird's song is unfettered, its phrases both "short, or long," so the lines of the poem vary between iambic pentameter at the beginning and trochaic trimeter, with an additional stress at the end of the line ("Poets wild as thee, were born"). Both bird and poet sing best when "unconfin'd" and when not attempting to please, but both are beset by cares, a comparison emphasized by the use of an alexandrine at the end of the first stanza (an iambic hexameter, whose extra syllable draws attention to it and brings the stanza to a close). This line also highlights an unusual aspect of the rhyme scheme. The poem is written in rhyming couplets with the exception of a triplet and the final long line, which rhymes surprisingly with the seventh line of the thirteen-line stanza. Finch is drawing attention to the presence of "cares" in the lives of both bird and poet, and perhaps such sorrow is necessary to inspire their songs: "... th'unhappy Poet's Breast,/Like thine, when best he sings, is plac'd against a Thorn." In the myth, Philomel was said to press her breast against a thorn when she sang to remind herself of the pain of the rape. The unexpected suddenness of "Thorn," with its Christian associations of suffering, startles the reader and prepares for the second, longer (twenty-two lines) stanza. While in the first stanza the poet has been waiting for the nightingale to sing, the second begins with the anticipated song, the poet's "Muse," which will fulfill its promise of inspiration. But at once the poet realizes that she cannot find words to emulate the bird's song. " 'Twill not be!" shifts the long second stanza into a new address to the bird, as the poet now urges the bird to give up its sweet harmonies and "Let Division shake thy Throat." But here, too, the poet is left behind in frustration, and she chastises the nightingale, asking if it plans to sing until June, ignoring its nest-making duties. At the end of the poem, the poet realizes that she has been criticizing the bird out of jealousy. Unable to fit words to the nightingale's beautiful song, poets can only "censure what we cannot reach."

One of the three odes John Keats wrote on the subject of poetic imagination and art was inspired by the nightingale's song. In the spring of 1819, at an age (twenty-three) when most people feel that the world is before them, full of promise and interest, Keats was facing the prospect of death. When he was only fourteen, his mother had died of tuberculosis, a disease that claimed his younger brother Tom in December 1818. Knowing that he, too, was almost certainly doomed to an early death, Keats threw himself into the writing of poetry, and the topic of immortality through art was understandably uppermost in his mind. "Ode to a Nightingale" (1819) opens with the poet's sense of deep melancholy as he sits in a garden, listening to the nightingale's song in the trees overhead: "My heart aches, and a drowsy numbness pains/My sense, as though of hemlock I had drunk. . . ." The bird's song contains the sounds of summer and warmth, of unalloyed happiness and peace. In the second stanza the poet yearns for a drink that will transport him to such a world, a glass of wine "tasting of Flora and the country green," or "a beaker full of the warm South. . . ." Under the influence of such an evocative taste bursting in his mouth, he might "fade away into the forest dim" with the bird. The third stanza catalogs the pain and sorrow of human life: "the weariness, the fever, and the fret"; the losses of old age, and worse, the cruelty of a world where "youth grows pale, and spectre-thin, and dies"; and the speed with which beauty fades (Keats had recently fallen in love with Fanny Brawne). But in stanza four he rejects the aid of wine, recognizing that he can enter the bird's immortal world "on the viewless wings of Poesy." At once he is with the nightingale, in another world lit only by the light of heaven. "Tender is the night" where he finds himself. Stanza five describes this new world, but the sounds and images recreate a world muffled and darkened, where the senses are dulled as hearing and sight lose their keenness. Despite this fading of images, however, the stanza is still highly evocative of scent and color, almost through their absence. He "cannot see" the flowers at his feet, and can only guess at the spring scents in the "embalmed darkness." But for the reader, "the fruit-tree wild;/White hawthorn, and the pastoral eglantine;/Fast fading violets . . . and . . . the coming musk-rose, full of dewy wine" are rich with perfume and soft hues. The last line of the stanza contains a powerful onomatopoeia that captures the muted sensations of the bird's world: "The murmurous haunt of flies on summer eves."

In stanza six the poet, recalling how often in the past he has thought death a welcome respite from the cares of the real world, is tempted to submit now, when his soul seems to be already separated from his body through the immortal song of the nightingale:

> Now more than ever seems it rich to die,
> To cease upon the midnight with no pain,
>   While thou art pouring forth thy soul abroad
>   In such an ecstasy!

But the stanza concludes with the reminder that if he gives himself up to death, even though the bird will continue to sing his "high requiem" the poet will no longer be able to hear it. Stanza seven separates the bird from the poet, recalling how its song has given it immortality. Keats recalls the long history of the nightingale, a bird connected in ancient legend with emperors and clowns. His imagination sees the bird's song piercing the "sad heart" of the biblical Ruth, when, exiled to the land of her dead husband and "sick for home,/She stood in tears amid the alien corn." The stanza ends with one of the most evocative and haunting images in British poetry when Keats tells the bird that its voice has

> Charm'd magic casements, opening on the foam
>   Of perilous seas, in faery lands forlorn.

The richly allusive word "forlorn" (it means "long ago" but also "forsaken") jolts the poet back into the real world in the concluding stanza, reminding him that "the fancy" (his imagination) cannot really take him into the bird's immortal world. When in his fancy he attempted to follow the bird, he lost consciousness, and his senses, so essential to the poet, became dulled. Recalled from his imaginative union with the bird, he bids it farewell as the bird flies away and its "plaintive anthem fades/ Past the near meadows, over the still stream,/Up the hill-side; and now 'tis buried deep/In the next valley-glades." The lines echo the retreat of the bird's haunting song as it fades into silence. Keats is left in the garden, questioning his reverie: did he dream the "embalmed darkness" where his imagination took him on the wings of the bird's song?

The melancholy of many of Keats's poems derives from his sense that he cannot live in a perpetual present like the nightingale. The bird is immortal because the song that charmed the emperors is somehow the same song that comforted Ruth and inspired the poet. But the poet's world is temporal and therefore he and his brother are subject to death. His consolation is his ability to hear and be deeply moved by the nightingale's song; for a few moments, he can become one with the bird. But ironically, living in the pure world of the imagination proved to be death to the poet's sensations and therefore his ability to create.

Melancholy is at the center of Robert Bridges's poem "Nightingales" (1893). Written as a dialogue between the poet and the birds, it recalls Keats's ode in the poet's desire to find the ideal, natural world of eternal spring where the nightingales learned their song. But the nightingales reply that their inspiration is not an ideal world at all; rather, their song comes from a deep sense of regret and loss (perhaps a reference to the Roman version of the Philomel story, in which the wronged sister, left mute by her sister's husband, is given a haunting, poignant voice by the gods). The birds dream by day, and by night they "pour [their] dark nocturnal secret" into the hearts of suffering humanity.

Keats wrote six odes in 1819, and they are generally regarded as his finest works and among the most important of the poetry written by the Romantic poets. Several of them take up the subject of art and the imagination, a topic of vital interest to Keats, who had rejected a medical career in favor of the much less lucrative one of poet. In "Ode to Psyche" Keats addresses Psyche, the Greek goddess identified with the human soul. In Greek mythology, Psyche, a beautiful young woman, unwittingly becomes the lover of Eros (Cupid), the god of love. She is forbidden to see her lover, who comes to her only in the dark, but she disobeys the order and lights a lamp, discovering Eros's identity. He leaves her, but after many trials inflicted by Eros's mother, Aphrodite (or Venus), Psyche is reunited with him and eventually becomes a goddess. In his ode, Keats tells the goddess that he wants to give her the honor due to her that she has never received, coming late to the pantheon of gods and goddesses. The poet is seeking inspiration for his "tuneless numbers" as he tells of either dreaming or having a waking vision of Psyche in the arms of Eros, enclosed in a sylvan glade of shady trees and "deepest grass." The poet worships the pagan goddess, who has come "too late" for the honors offered to the earlier pre-Christian deities. Inspired by his vision, Keats offers to be her choir, her voice, her lute, her pipe, her incense, her shrine, her grove, her oracle, and her prophet, who will speak back to her the inspiration he derives from her. In the last stanza the poet offers to be her priest, and his temple will be "in some untrodden region of [his] mind." This idea leads him to visions of the transforming power of the imagination, inspired by the soul's (Psyche's) union with love (Eros). The earlier vision of Psyche and Eros in the forest glade is transformed into a glade of the mind, "new grown with pleasant pain." Instead of trees, "branched thoughts" shall flourish; his "working brain" will create through the "gardener Fancy" a rich and varied landscape for Psyche to inhabit. The poem ends with Keats's favorite image of a casement opening, now to let "warm Love in." Keats's imagination will make possible the union of soul and love through the medium of "pleasant pain." In a letter to his brother accompanying the poem, Keats had explained this reference to the connection between suffering and creation: "Do you see not how necessary a World of Pains and troubles is to school an Intelligence and make it a soul?"

The best-known of Keats's odes on the subject of art and creativity is his "Ode on a Grecian Urn," which was written in the same year, 1819.

Like "Ode to Psyche" it was influenced by Keats's interest in the Greek world, partly inspired by his frequent visits to the Greek antiquities rooms in the British Museum. As in "To a Nightingale," its subject is the poet's recognition of an immortal world, the world of the bird and the urn. In the first stanza the poet is looking at the design on the urn, marveling at the still wholeness and separateness of the work of art. The urn, an "unravish'd bride of quietness," represents the pure world of art, immortal and flawless. In relating the story that is told in images on the urn, Keats captures in his ode this other world where the music from the pipes, heard only in the mind, is sweeter than music that comes to us through the ears. The story on the urn is of young love. A piper pursues a beautiful girl, and Keats envies them their immortality because their love is always before them; it can never grow old or descend into the disappointment of human passion.

In the fourth stanza, Keats describes another scene on the urn, a procession of people following a priest and a heifer, solemnly on their way to a sacrifice. These figures are shown on the urn, but more vital is a scene that is *not* on the urn: Keats creates in the reader's mind a vision of the town from which the people have come. "Emptied of its folk, this pious morn," the "little town" is silent in the story told in the urn, and will forever be silent. Its citizens are frozen on the urn on their way to the sacrifice, and will never return to tell the town's story. The stanza recalls Keats's opening address to the urn as the "unravish'd bride of quietness,/Thou foster-child of silence and slow time." The urn and its picture are outside of human time; they tell a human story of time and change, but in themselves are eternal.

Keats returns to this idea in the last stanza, when he tells the urn that its stillness takes him out of the realm of consciousness into an understanding of immortality. He appears to envy the urn its detachment from human affairs when he refers to it as "Cold Pastoral!" While generations of people shall suffer, live, and die, the urn will live on unchanged. At the end of the poem, the urn speaks to the poet in a famous address that has created endless critical debate: " 'Beauty is truth, truth beauty,—that is all/Ye know on earth, and all ye need to know.' " Controversies rage over whether the urn says just the first five words, or the whole passage. Depending on the answer, what does the urn mean, and do the lines belong artistically to the poem as a whole? In "truth" and "beauty" Keats is referring to the ideal world of art, as represented by the urn and its story. In telling a very human story of pursuit, passion, suffering, and sacrifice (and in being created by a sculptor), the urn both contains human experience and transcends human mortality. Art gives permanence by reaching beyond the emotions; at the same time it provides consolation and comfort because it "shalt remain, in midst of other woe. . . ." Keats's ideal world of art ("truth") can be apprehended through the senses. Its unheard music is sweeter than the heard, and the silence of the urn speaks directly to the human heart.

Keats's first poem about artistic inspiration was his 1816 sonnet "On First Looking into Chapman's Homer." He wrote this much-loved poem in the heat of the moment the morning after he and his friend Charles Cowden Clarke spent the night reading a translation of Homer by George Chapman, an Elizabethan poet. The sonnet abounds in rich imagery drawn from Elizabethan exploration and discovery. The octave (the first eight lines of the sonnet) elaborates a metaphor in which Keats is the explorer in the "realms of gold," or the world of literature. "Much have I travell'd," he says, but the "wide expanse" ruled by Homer was unknown to him until Chapman's translation took him into that "pure serene" air. The sestet develops two similes of exploration to explain Keats's sense of wonderment on entering Homer's world. He is "like some watcher of the skies/When a new planet swims into his ken," an image taken from a contemporary account of Herschel's discovery of Uranus. The second simile compares Keats to "stout Cortez" when, with his men, he first saw the Pacific Ocean, "Silent, upon a peak in Darien." The poet's sense of inspiration encompasses earth and heaven as Keats decides to follow his literary calling.

Wind is an archetypal symbol of inspiration, being the "breath" of nature (and "inspire" means to 'breathe into'). The most powerful of wind poems is "Ode to the West Wind" (1819) by Percy Bysshe Shelley. Like his "To a Skylark," the poem is a plea for inspiration to become a voice for democracy, but it is much more than just a political polemic. Shelley tells us that he wrote the poem "in a wood that skirts the Arno, near Florence, on a day when the tempestuous wind, whose temperature is at once mild and animating, was collecting the vapors which pour down the autumnal rains." Written in *terza rima* form (three-line stanzas linked by rhyme: lines one and three of each stanza rhyme with line two of the preceding stanza), the poem moves with the force and energy of the wind it addresses. Shelley's subject is the cycle of death and rebirth in nature and in human affairs. The autumn wind that, like an invisible enchanter, furiously whirls the dead leaves, also drives the seeds to their "dark wintry bed" where they lie, "each like a corpse within its grave." But the west wind of spring, the "azure sister," blows a more gentle breeze over the "dreaming earth," to awaken the seeds into life again. The autumn wind is thus both "destroyer and preserver," seemingly forcing the seeds into their death while actually ensuring their safety beneath the ground.

While the first section depicts the effect of the wind on the leaves and the land, in the second stanza we see its effect on the clouds, and in the third, on the sea. The poem surges with the wind across land and sky, driven by the prophetic voice of the poet that culminates at the end of each section with the exhortation, "oh, hear!" A lull in Section 3 contains an evocative description of the blue Mediterranean in midsummer, as the poet calls to mind the "old palaces and towers/Quivering within the wave's intenser day" before the autumn wind rends the surface of the sea and disturbs even the "oozy woods" of the ocean floor. The last two sections move to the poet's personal response to the wind, culminating in his request to be inspired by it so that as a poet he can revitalize the democratic movement. The fourth section regrets that, as he is not a leaf, a cloud, or a wave, he seems to be beyond the influence of the wind. Like many of the Romantic poets, he recalls that as a boy he was closer to natural forces and would have been instinctively inspired by the wind. Now he is bowed down by the cares of the world and is no longer like the wind, "tameless, and swift, and proud." In a rapture of emotion often associated with romanticism, the poet declares, "I fall upon the thorns of life! I bleed!" But in the last section he finds that he is still responsive to the wind's power, and he begs it to inspire his poetic voice that, now he is older, is tinged with sadness. The poem concludes with a metaphor from the opening when the poet asks the wind to "drive [his] dead thoughts over the universe/Like withered leaves to quicken a new birth!" Perhaps recalling Shakespeare's metaphors in his sonnet "That time of year thou mayst in me behold," (1609), Shelley then compares his words to "ashes and sparks" from an "unextinguished hearth" that the wind can spread, rekindling political change. In the last line Shelley unites the natural cycle of death and rebirth with the cyclical nature of human history: "If Winter comes, can Spring be far behind?" The poet, inspired by the wind, nature's "destroyer and preserver," can be a prophet for a new age through his poetry.

Another Romantic poem about inspiration is Samuel Taylor Coleridge's unfinished fragment "Kubla Khan." Coleridge wrote about its composition in his preface to the poem, written some years later and not necessarily entirely accurate. According to the preface, in the summer of 1797 Coleridge had retired to a lonely farm in the west of England to recover from an illness. After taking opium (a usual painkiller at the time), he had fallen asleep while reading *Purchas's Pilgrimage* (1613) which contains the lines "Here the Kubla Khan commanded a palace to be built, and a stately garden thereunto. And thus ten miles of fertile ground were enclosed within a wall." According to Coleridge, he slept on for three hours, and in a dream composed from 200 to 300 lines of poetry; the composition was rather a state in which "all the images rose up before him as *things* with a parallel production of the correspondent expressions, without any sensation of consciousness of effort." When he awakened he had a "distinct recollection of the whole" and immediately wrote down the poem as we have it. At that point he was interrupted by a visitor and was unable to return to the vision until later. Because of this account of its creation, the poem has often been viewed as the purest expression of the creative process or dream vision. The poem seems to be conveying in images the world of the imagination, and it establishes the poet as the creator, able to reconcile opposites and encompass all of creation, in the manner of the Mogul's building of his "sunny pleasure dome."

The exotic landscape of Xanadu is the setting for the descent into the unconscious mind. Alph, the "sacred river," runs "through caverns measureless to man/Down to a sunless sea." Other images in the opening lines create a sense of enclosure: ten miles of "fertile ground" are "girdled round" with "walls and towers"; gardens blossom with perfumed trees, "enfold[ed]" by ancient forests. This sense of security and peace is shattered in the second part of the poem, however, as the vision moves farther down into a "savage place!" where a "mighty fountain" bursts out "with ceaseless turmoil seething" from a chasm. The vision is exotic and wild, but not dangerous, because as well as being "savage" it is also "holy and enchanted." As the fountain throws up "huge fragments" of rock in its turmoil, it also flings up the sacred river Alph. The vision continues to deepen as we follow the meandering Alph through "wood and dale" into "caverns measureless to man," until at last it "sank in tumult to a lifeless ocean." At this central point, Kubla "heard from far/Ancestral voices prophesying war!" The world of the imagination seems to be continually threatened by the "real" world.

The poem then returns to the opening image of the pleasure dome, which seems to hang midway between the real and imaginary worlds; from it can be heard the music of fountain and caves. The dome itself is a "miracle" that seems paradoxically to share both worlds, a "sunny pleasure-dome with caves of ice!" In the final eighteen lines of the poem Coleridge abruptly switches his vision to "a damsel with a dulcimer" whom he had seen in an earlier flight of imagination. Just as the words of *Purchas's Pilgrimage* inspired the first vision, remembering the damsel's music has the power to conjure up other exotic worlds in the poet's mind. Through music he will "build that dome in air," recalling the building of castles in the air, a usual metaphor for the creation of visions in the mind. The ambiguity of the poem is stressed in the last few lines, however, when the poet describes his rapture as both transcendently beautiful and alarming. The "caves of ice" in the mind of the poet manifest themselves in "his flashing eyes, his floating hair!" a vision of madness that inspires the cry of "Beware! Beware!" The poet, enclosed in his imaginary world, becomes a dangerous force from whom his companions in the real world must seek the magical protection of a circle woven three times around him. The danger is ambiguous, though, because his companions feel a "holy dread" in the presence of one who "on honeydew hath fed,/And drunk the milk of Paradise."

A major poet for much of the Victorian age, and poet laureate for over forty years, Alfred, Lord Tennyson explored the role of the artist in "The Lady of Shalott" (1833), an early poem whose striking images and symbols can be interpreted in many ways. A narrative poem, it tells the story of a beautiful lady who is imprisoned in a tower on an island in a river near the town of Camelot. Held captive by the knowledge that a curse hangs over her if she even looks out of the window, the lady patiently sits day after day weaving "a magic web with colours gay." Because she cannot look out of the window, she looks instead into a mirror, which reflects the active life of the people of Camelot going about their business. These "shadows of the world" are brightly colored, unlike the muted blues and grays of the tower and the barren room. At first the lady seems content with her lonely artistic life, but when she sees a bride and groom go by she begins to realize what she is missing and to resent her isolation: "I am half sick of shadows," she declares. In Part 3, her new restlessness is challenged by the sight of bold Sir Lancelot, who rides, plumed and dazzling, into her vision in the mirror. Unable to resist the pull of love, the lady strides to the window and looks out, bringing the curse into effect: "Out flew the web and floated wide;/The mirror cracked from side to side." The lady leaves her tower, only to die. She goes down, finds a boat moored among the rushes, writes her name on the prow, lies down in the boat, and drifts down to Camelot. The townspeople, who have known her only by her song, hear her singing again, but they find her dead as the boat slides into the town.

The poem lends itself to diverse interpretations. What are we to make of the enigmatic symbols—the web, the mirror, the island, and the tower? Many of the symbols in the poem are recurrent ones in literature. The color blue, connected with the room, and the lilies that grow around the tower are both symbols of the Virgin Mary, for example. The imprisoned maiden is a well-known motif, found in fairy tales like *Sleeping Beauty*, and often interpreted in terms of a young woman's awakening into sexual love and marriage. The story itself is a re-telling of the Arthurian legend of the fair maid of Astolat, as told by Malory (although Tennyson denied this source, claiming to have found the story in an Italian *novella*, to which he added the web, the tapestry, and the mirror). These symbols suggest that the poem can also be seen to concern the life of the artist. The lady's picture is a representation of the real world, not the real world itself. But in the poem her picture is one step further removed from the real because she works from the image in a mirror, a reflection of the real world outside the window. The world of art is removed from the real world, and therefore from time and change. Like the figures in Keats's urn, the lady and her tapestry are immortal, provided she remains isolated from the real world. But when she realizes that this isolation also means a life devoid of love, she chooses to embrace the real, mortal world rather than the ideal world of art. In making that choice she brings on the "curse" of mortality: her death. Tennyson wrote of the lady's predicament, "The new-born love for something, for some one in the wide world from which she has been so long secluded, takes her out of the region of shadows, into that of realities."

Robert Browning, a contemporary of Tennyson, is now best known for his brilliant dramatic monologues. In these poems the speaker is talking to an implied listener, whose side of the conversation is unrecorded but implied by the monologue. The poem is "dramatic" because the conversation is set in a location that is described through the poem, and some sort of action takes place during the course of the conversation. Most importantly, through the monologue the speaker unconsciously reveals his real character, which is always at odds with his own view of himself. Browning wished to give his reader "the gift of seeing," a glimpse into the "separate spiritual drama" that plays out in each of us. Two of Browning's dramatic monologues (c. 1853) are spoken by historical figures, both Italian Renaissance painters, and they offer contrasting attitudes to art and its relationship to life. We meet Fra Lippo Lippi on a street in Florence, trying to explain to the night watchmen why he, a friar, is prowling about the streets as dawn is breaking. Andrea del Sarto is talking to his wife, Lucrezia, in their room one autumn at twilight. While he talks she gazes out of the window, awaiting the arrival of her cousin (and lover). The poems illustrate the decay of Renaissance art as Browning sees it, with Fra Lippo Lippi's exuberant love of live and art representing the beginning of the period (the poem takes place in spring), and Andrea del Sarto's resigned, self-pitying sense of failure representing the decline of the movement. Fra Lippo Lippi is forced to defend himself and his art. What is he, a holy man, doing in such a part of town? The poem explores the relationship between the sensual and the spiritual, arguing for the integration of the flesh and the spirit in life and in art. Fra Lippo Lippi has run afoul of his church masters, who represent the medieval view of art against which the Renaissance was rebelling. He argues that the world of the flesh is not a snare but a part of God's glory, and his exuberant, colorful language exudes energy and spirituality. Andrea del Sarto, in contrast, is immobile and impotent, married to a woman whose infidelity and materialism were well known. Andrea's sense of failure as an artist and a husband pervades the poem as he whiningly complains about his lack of success, sometimes blaming it on her moral bankruptcy (she wanted him to paint for money), and then apologizing and blaming the times. Andrea del Sarto is known as the "faultless painter" because technically he was more skillful than Raphael and Michelangelo. But unlike them he is soulless, timid, and emotionally sterile. Whereas Fra Lippo Lippi's art is vibrant and robust, intended to glorify God through conveying the richness of creation, Andrea del

Sarto's is mean and narrow, the product of a man who stole from the king of France and saw his own parents die in poverty. He rightly describes himself as "the weak-eyed bat no sun should tempt/Out of the grange whose four walls make his world." Fra Lippo Lippi, in contrast, has fled the four walls of the monastery to find life as it is lived. His love for life is ironically summed up by Andrea del Sarto, who vacillates between a recognition of all he has lost and a self-pitying attempt to excuse and justify himself: "Ah, but a man's reach should exceed his grasp,/Or what's a heaven for?" In the next line, Andrea tells the truth about his own failure to attempt works requiring more than his dull, limited technical skill: "All is silver-gray/Placid and perfect with my art: the worse!" Browning's criticism of the valuing of "perfection" over creativity and daring was shared by his contemporary, the famous art critic John Ruskin.

Browning's artists, like many poets, are concerned with the springs of their creativity. Andrea's wife was his Muse, but a flawed one. The contemporary poet Seamus Heaney found his muse in his rural Irish roots. His 1966 poem "Digging" is often printed first in selections from his work because it is Heaney's declaration that he is striking out from the farming background of his father and grandfather to become a poet. The poem opens with the poet writing, the pen resting in his hand, "snug as a gun." Under his window, his father is digging potatoes, as he has been doing for twenty years. His talent with a spade was learned from his father, and the poem moves from the father's skill to the grandfather's, as the poet remembers taking milk to the old man as he dug peat in the bogs of Ireland. Heaney finely brings to life the skill—artistry—of the farmers, bred to the soil and able to wield a spade with grace and dignity. But the poet is a new generation, and he will keep alive the connection between man and nature in his own way. Just as the memories of his grandfather rise in his imagination, he will recreate those memories for others. He has no spade, so he will dig with his pen. The metaphor serves as a cogent reminder of the vital role of the artist—painter or poet—in the ever-changing world of human affairs.

❦

Sonnet 1, *Astrophil and Stella* ("Loving in truth, and fain in verse my love to show"), Sir Philip Sidney

ImPo; NAEL-1; OAEL-1; OBEV; TFi; TrGrPo-1

Sonnet 41, *Astrophil and Stella* ("Having this day my horse, my hand, my lance"), Sir Philip Sidney

NAEL-1

Sonnet 74, *Astrophil and Stella* ("I never drank of Aganippe well"), Sir Philip Sidney

    NAEL-1

"To a Skylark," Percy Bysshe Shelley

    ImPo; NAEL-2; OAEL-2; TFi; TrGrPo-2

"O Nightingale," John Milton

    OAEL-1

"To the Nightingale," Anne Finch

    BL; ECP

"Ode to a Nightingale," John Keats

    ImPo; NAEL-2; OAEL-2; OBEV; TFi; TrGrPo-2

"Nightingales," Robert Bridges

    ImPo; OAEL-2; TFi; TrGrPo-2

"Ode to Psyche," John Keats

    NAEL-2; OAEL-2; TFi

"Ode on a Grecian Urn," John Keats

    ImPo; NAEL-2; OAEL-2; OBEV; TFi; TrGrPo-2

"On First Looking into Chapman's Homer," John Keats

    ImPo; NAEL-2; OAEL-2; OBEV; TFi; TrGrPo-2

"Ode to the West Wind," Percy Bysshe Shelley

    ImPo; NAEL-2; OAEL-2; OBEV; TFi; TrGrPo-2

"Kubla Khan," Samuel Taylor Coleridge

    ImPo; NAEL-2; OAEL-2; OBEV; TFi; TrGrPo-2

"The Lady of Shalott," Alfred, Lord Tennyson

    BAVP; NAEL-2; OAEL-2; TFi; TrGrPo-2

"Fra Lippo Lippi," Robert Browning

    BAVP; NAEL-2; OAEL-2

"Andrea del Sarto," Robert Browning

    BAVP; NAEL-2; OAEL-2

"Digging," Seamus Heaney

    NAEL-2

Beauty

Beauty has always been a favorite topic for poets, who are perhaps akin to artists in being particularly sensitive to what pleases the mind and the senses, whether it be a beautiful landscape or a beautiful woman. Many poets would consider that in writing poetry they are seeking beauty in language and form. But what is beauty? An interesting discussion of this question can be found in James Joyce's novel *A Portrait of the Artist as a Young Man* (1916), in which the hero, Stephen Dedalus, explains that Saint Thomas Aquinas's definition of beauty requires three qualities: wholeness (the recognition of the separateness of the object), harmony (the recognition of the relationship of its parts), and radiance (the recognition of its "whatness"). According to Joyce, through Dedalus, art is beautiful when it arrests the mind, and he refers to Percy Bysshe Shelley's likening of the poet's mind to a fading coal in the moment of the apprehension of beauty. Dedalus also considers the appreciation of female beauty, another favorite topic for poets.

The Ancient Greek philosopher Plato was the first writer to attempt a definition of beauty. Plato theorized that the objects in the world around us were merely shadows of a real essence, or form, that existed in an ideal, unchanging world. The most important of these forms was beauty, which for Plato was also goodness. Beautiful things in our world are merely the shadows of that ideal beauty. Many English poets were intrigued by Plato's theory of forms and based their poems about beauty upon it. In his sonnets, for example, Shakespeare upsets Plato's theory in order to flatter his beautiful male subject, arguing in Sonnet 53 ("What is your substance, whereof are you made" [1609]) that the young man is the substance, or form, of beauty, of which all other beautiful people (such as Adonis and Helen of Troy) are merely the shadows.

The Romantic poets writing at the beginning of the nineteenth century were particularly interested in beauty as it related to art and nature. When John Keats's Grecian urn (1819) made its famous pronouncement, "Beauty is truth, truth beauty," it was referring to beauty as an ideal, a perfect state similar to Plato's idea of the form, that could be apprehended by the mind. Percy Bysshe Shelley personified "intellectual" or ideal beauty as a spirit in his "Hymn to Intellectual Beauty," conceived while he was boating on Lake Geneva with Lord Byron in the summer of 1816. Although writing about beauty in the Platonic sense—that there is a perfect beauty in an ideal world, of which our own world is merely the shadow—Shelley also conveys his sense of the beauty of the real world, however shadowy, as evidenced by Lake Geneva. He wrote to a friend that the poem was "composed under the influence of feelings which agitated me even to tears."

The hymn addresses the "Spirit of BEAUTY," which in the opening lines Shelley compares to an "awful shadow of some unseen Power" that "Floats though unseen amongst us." In working out the human relationship to this immortal force, Shelley uses similes to draw attention to Beauty's evanescence as it is apprehended by man. It is like summer winds, moonbeams, dusk, night clouds, or "memory of music fled." But its subtlety just makes it "yet dearer for its mystery." Beauty's fleeting presence enriches human thought and experience, but in its transience it also leaves us often in a "dim vast vale of tears, vacant and desolate." The fleeting nature of Beauty as Shelley comprehends it continues to dominate the poem. In the third stanza he speaks of other poets' attempts to capture it through "frail spells" that only serve to remind us that the human world is fragile and mortal. Only the spirit of Beauty "gives grace and truth to life's unquiet dream." The poem continues to focus on the spirit's power in the human rather than the natural world, seeing Beauty as the source of human compassion. Like the other Romantic poets, Shelley speaks of his childhood as the time when he first apprehended this ideal Beauty. Having sought immortality in the graveyard, looking for ghosts, the young boy suddenly sensed the spirit's shadow touching him. The poet says he retained that perception and devoted his life to recalling it. Reiterating his belief that poets have the power to bring about social reform, Shelley tells the spirit that through the poet it will "free/This world from its dark slavery." The final stanza recollects Wordsworth's "Ode: Intimations of Immortality" (1807), in which the poet finds a gentler solace in nature than the vivid apprehension of nature that he experienced in his youth. Shelley's young self had first passively sensed the spirit of Beauty in the spring, symbolic of his own youth. Now, in autumn and at the end of the day, Shelley finds a greater harmony and actively calls on the spirit of Beauty to bring calm and love to his mature years. He in turn will continue to worship this life-giving power.

Another fine poem on the subject of beauty in nature is Gerard Manley

Hopkins's "Pied Beauty" (1877). This short lyric thanks God for "pied," or "dappled," things: skies, the dots on the side of a trout, glossy chestnuts, finches' wings, the random coloring of plowed and fallow fields, and the diversity of human work and the tools that accompany it. With characteristic energy and abruptness, Hopkins praises the beauty of the world's variety and oddness—"Whatever is fickle, freckled." In a series of short contrasts—"swift, slow; sweet, sour; adazzle, dim"—he recognizes that all of God's creation is beautiful, however apparently flawed or imperfect it may seem. Unlike Shelley, an atheist, Hopkins has no trouble identifying the source of the world's extraordinary beauty.

Many poems, and particularly Renaissance poetry, are concerned with the beauty of women. The subject is as old as recorded history, going back to women like Delilah and Salome in the Bible, and Helen of Troy, whose face "launched a thousand ships" when a Trojan, Paris, stole her from her Greek husband, Menelaus, and brought about the Trojan War. The beautiful woman is often seen as the temptress, the siren who lures men into danger and brings about their downfall. Many times poems about female beauty focus on the discrepancy between the fair face and the cruel heart; the poet is often lamenting his unrequited passion. In "No Second Troy" (1908), William Butler Yeats used the story of Helen of Troy as the basis for his complaint against Maud Gonne, whom he had passionately loved in vain for many years. The poem compares Helen's power to bring about war to Maud Gonne's patriotic and often violent defense of Ireland against England. The poet begins by asking why he should "blame her" for making his life miserable (she rejected his marriage proposals several times), and for inciting Irishmen to violent action against the English (although they lacked the courage to follow through). By comparing Maud to Helen, Yeats gives her a nobility of purpose that could not be happy in passively accepting Irish subservience to England; he also ascribes Helen's beauty to her, a refined beauty "like a tightened bow" that is "not natural" in these post-heroic days because it is "high and solitary and most stern." The meaning of the title is revealed at the end of this short lyric when Yeats suggests that Maud Gonne—beautiful, talented, and fiercely dedicated to her cause—belongs to the age of heroes. She tried to teach "ignorant men" and would have "hurled the little streets [of Ireland] upon the great [of London]. . . ." The poet's ambivalence is evident in the final line: Maud was too heroic for her time, but when he asks, "Was there another Troy for her to burn?" he reminds us that such large souls are also dangerous, especially to those who seek to come close to them.

Unrequited love of a beautiful woman was a favorite theme of the Renaissance poets, whose inspiration was the courtly love tradition brought to England from Italy. The Italian poet Petrarch was the most pervasive influence on the early English poets' attitude to female beauty.

Petrarch idolized his Laura in his poetry, depicting her as a woman whose beauty turned her into a goddess. The Petrarchan tradition relied on similes and metaphors (or "conceits," if the metaphor was an unusual one) that became standard in courtly love poetry. The poet would paint a portrait of an unattainable and unrealistic beauty: eyes shone like stars or suns; skin was as white as milk or snow; lips were as red as cherries or coral; cheeks were as red as roses; teeth were like pearls; hair was like gold. The rose itself became the favorite metaphor for beauty, exemplifying the delicacy, fragility, freshness, color, and naturalness of the lovely woman.

Many poets took as their theme the transience of beauty, often glorying in the poem's ability to immortalize the woman's fleeting good looks. In his sonnet "Brittle Beauty" (1557), Henry Howard, earl of Surrey, elaborates on this theme. In the first twelve lines he finds a series of different ways to describe the pain of finding that beauty does not last: its frailty is "dangerous," "costly," "slippery," "hard to attain," "false and untrue," the "enemy to youth," and "bitter sweet." In the closing couplet, beauty is compared to fruit affected by frost that in its ripeness is already doomed to decay. In 1592 Samuel Daniel wrote a sonnet sequence to Delia that observes the traditional Petrarchan conventions of the lovesick poet lamenting the cruelty of his beautiful and unattainable lady. In "When men shall find thy flower, thy glory, pass," he baits Delia with the transience of her beauty. When she looks in her mirror and finds her beauty gone, she need not despair because the effects of her beauty live on in him. Her cruelty exists still in his wounds, and though her flame is gone, the heat remains in him, as does his faith in her. The source of his fire (her beauty) is spent, now that her hair is turning white ("when winter snows upon thy sable hairs"), and he has the last laugh because she can only see his passion and repent her cruelty in scorning his love. The next sonnet begins with this line, offering Delia the Renaissance poet's traditional gift of immortal beauty through his poem: when "frost of age hath nipt thy beauties near," the poet's pencil will bring them to life again.

Edmund Spenser, like Surrey, a Renaissance writer famous for his sonnets, describes his mistress's beauty and cruelty in his sonnet "So oft as I her beauty do behold" from *Amoretti* (1595). In the octave he wonders from what substance she was formed that made her so distressingly beautiful but cruel. Rejecting the four elements of earth, water, air, and fire, he argues in the sestet that she is formed from the sky, the source of her "haughty looks" but also of the heavenly purity of her love. This compliment tempers his earlier charges of cruel capriciousness ("she doth freeze with faint desire") and leads to the closing couplet in which he pleads with her to find in her heavenly medium a little mercy for his lovelorn plight. The beauty did take pity on him; Elizabeth Boyle married Spenser in 1594.

Many Elizabethan lyrics elaborated upon Petrarch's conceits in amusing and surprising ways. Thomas Campion's famous lyric "There is a garden in her face" (1617) begins with the conventional comparison of a woman's complexion to roses and lilies. In this "heav'nly paradise" the poet finds cherries growing on her lips, but none may buy them until " 'Cherry-ripe!' themselves do cry." The two succeeding stanzas conclude with this line, emphasizing the poet's regret that the woman is unapproachable until she seeks a kiss herself. The metaphor is expanded in the second stanza and again uses conventional comparisons in finding that the cherries (her lips) enclose a row of "orient pearl" (her teeth); when the lady laughs, her mouth looks "like rosebuds filled with snow." In the final stanza the poet brings the lady's features to life as an army guarding her lips, the "sacred cherries" that he hopes will eventually give access to his desires. Her eyes watch "like angels," and her eyebrows, shaped like bows, become real bows that can shoot deadly arrows ("piercing frowns") at anyone who attempts to approach her lips. The poem ends with the refrain that only when the lips themselves cry "cherry-ripe" may they be kissed.

In his song "Rose-Cheeked Laura" (1602), Campion departs from his title's conventional metaphor by comparing Laura's beauty to "silent music." The beauty of the unsung music complements the loveliness of her face, and their harmony is heavenly. His own "dull notes" cannot reach the perfection of her silent music, formed from "beauty purely loving." The song is an example of quantitative meter, the alternation of long and short syllables (as practiced by Greek and Roman poets) rather than the more common English style of stressed and unstressed syllables.

Thomas Carew expands on the Petrarchan conventions in his song "Ask me no more where Jove bestows" (1640). Each of the five four-line stanzas begins with the words "Ask me no more" as the poet, addressing the woman, answers her five questions concerning where frail but beautiful things go when they die: the "fading rose" of June can be found in her "beauty's orient deep"; the "golden atoms of the day" retire to her hair; the nightingale "winters" in her throat; falling stars become fixed in her eyes; and the immortal phoenix (which dies and is reborn from its ashes) "in your fragrant bosom dies." The metaphors of rose, sun, nightingale, star, and phoenix are conventional ones, but Carew's song, relying on soft and soothing sounds, brings them to life with grace and ease in a lyric that was frequently set to music.

One of the most famous poems on the subject of female beauty is Shakespeare's anti-Petrarchan Sonnet 130, "My mistress' eyes are nothing like the sun" (1609). Following on from the first negation, the poem catalogs the standard Petrarchan metaphors and denies the mistress any of those fine qualities: coral is far redder than her lips; snow is white, but her breasts are "dun"; black rather than golden wires adorn her head. The next quatrain refuses to transfer the attributes of inhuman objects to her. Real roses are "damasked red and white," but her cheeks are not. Her breath is not as delightful as perfume. Music is more pleasing than the sound of her voice. These refusals to give her idealized beauties culminate in the rejection of her as a goddess (which the poet admits never to have seen)—for his mistress walks on the ground. Here the poet prepares for the closing couplet, where the apparent insults of the poem are turned into praise instead. Goddesses do not exist, he says, but real women do, and his mistress is "as rare" as any of the conventional sonnets' idealized women. In fact, her fineness gives the lie to these imaginary beauties. This famous sonnet is a tribute to the ordinary woman's attractiveness. As Mirabell says of his beloved Millamant in Congreve's witty play *The Way of the World* (1700), "I like her with all her faults, nay, like her for her faults."

Many of Shakespeare's sonnets discuss beauty in relation to love or the passing of time, and they will be discussed under those themes in this survey. Sonnet 106, "When in the chronicle of wasted time" (1609), departs from Petrarchan conventions, basing its praise of the beautiful person (man or woman? the poem does not say) on a comparison between the poet's effort to do justice to that beauty and the attempts of earlier poets to praise the beauties of their time. The sonnet relies on the notion of biblical typology, which recognized people and events in the Old Testament as prefiguring people and events in the New Testament. Shakespeare makes the connection clear when he says that the praises of the old writers were "but prophecies/Of this our time, all you prefiguring. . . ." Lines eleven and twelve are ambiguous but appear to suggest that because the old poets had "divining eyes" they were able to describe the perfect beauty of the poet's friend (just as the old prophets knew that Christ was coming). The closing couplet regrets that modern-day poets lack the old writers' skill: they have "eyes to wonder, but lack tongues to praise." The old poets had greater skill because they apprehended the present beauty's perfection in the earlier type. New poets, dazzled with the brilliance of the beauty, are speechless with wonder.

Other Renaissance poets wrote about beauty in women rather than in an individual woman, but they were not always complimentary. In "Beauty" (1647), Abraham Cowley writes about the diversity of definitions of female beauty, corresponding to the variety of human skin colors and features. From beauty's (and women's) inconstancy he moves to beauty's (and women's) shallowness: beauty is finest in dim light, being but a "false coin" that conceals the dross within. In the last stanza he compares female beauty not to a rose but to a tulip, which is merely a painted flower with no medicinal value, smell, or taste. The tulip is short-lived and so is the man's appreciation for the woman's beauty, "whose flames but meteors are,/Short-liv'd and low, though thou wouldst seem a star. . . ." His final attack on female beauty is that it does not exist at all; while it pretends to "dwell richly in the eye," it actually exists only in the fancy. In "The Scrutiny" (1649), Richard Lovelace's satirical speaker recognizes his lover's beauty but argues for inconstancy because other women are beautiful too, and deserve his attention. He may find that his lover's brown hair is the finest, but he "must search the black and fair,/Like skillful mineralists that sound/For treasure in un-plowed-up ground." If she proves to be the most beautiful, he will return to her "even sated with variety."

A more generous account of the variety of female beauty is found in Thomas Campion's "Give beauty all her right!" (c. 1613), where the poet acknowledges the equal power to please of different types of beauty from different times and places. He challenges the poems that idealize one woman's beauty as casting into the shade all others, finding that "Helen, I grant, might pleasing be,/And Rosamond was as sweet as she." Rosamond Clifford, mistress of Henry II, was a well-known Elizabethan beauty.

A counter-tradition grew up beside the poems that idealized female beauty. These poems often criticized women's attempts to make themselves more beautiful through makeup, elaborate hair styling, and dress, arguing that natural beauty is much more attractive. In Ben Jonson's "Clerimont's Song" (or "Still to be Neat") from the play *Epicoene* (1609), the speaker tells the woman that although she artfully hides her props (the powders and perfumes), "All is not sweet, all is not sound." In the second stanza he asks her to be simple, with "robes loosely flowing, hair as free." The "adulteries of art" may fool his eyes, but they do not touch his heart. Jonson is also talking about art in general in the poem, preferring the art that enhances nature (in the second stanza) to the art that conceals or tries to improve on nature. Robert Herrick's famous "Delight in Disorder" (1648) makes the same point, but more sensuously. The poem does not refer to the woman directly; rather, she is depicted through her unruly dress, whose "sweet disorder" implies through metonymy (the clothes standing for the woman) the woman's openness to sexual advances. The disorder "kindles in clothes a wantonness"; a loosely thrown shawl becomes a "fine distraction." Carelessly placed lace, cuffs, and "ribbands" lead to a "tempetuous petticoat" that seems to be calling to the poet. An untied shoe completes a picture that "bewitches" the poet far more than "too precise" art could ever achieve. Another of Herrick's short lyrics, "Upon Julia's Clothes" (1648), makes the same point in six mellifluous lines that echo the subject of the poem:

Whenas in silks my Julia goes
Then, then (methinks) how sweetly flows
That liquefaction of her clothes.

The poet is captivated by the sight of silk, fluid and apparently unfettered, suggesting (he hopes) the woman's own lack of constraint.

Another Cavalier poet, Richard Lovelace, concentrates on the beautiful woman's hair in "To Amarantha" (1649) when he urges her to leave her hair unbraided. Here, too, the language suggests sexual banter; his "curious hand or eye" is itching to free her hair from its confines. Once freed, it will be played with by "its calm ravisher the wind," which wishes to "wanton" over it. The poem ends with a delightful return to the Petrarchan conceit of golden hair. In ribbons the hair is benighted, so the woman is asked to free it: "Like the Sun in's early ray;/But shake your head, and scatter day!"

Edmund Spenser, in Sonnet 37 from *Amoretti*, amusingly plays on the same conceit of the woman's golden hair as imprisoned. But now it is the admirer who is in danger of being captivated by the golden net that covers the beautiful hair. When a man's "frail eyes" are caught in the net, his weak heart becomes an easy prey for her. In the sestet, Spenser warns his eyes against becoming entangled in the alluring golden mass of hair and net. Only a fool would exchange his freedom for fetters, "though they golden be."

The most famous attack on conventional female beauty, especially the artificial beauty that is produced by bottles and lotions, is Jonathan Swift's "The Lady's Dressing Room" (1732). Celia issues from her chamber after five hours of primping and preening, a "goddess . . . arrayed in lace, brocade, and tissues." Her innocent lover, Strephon, sneaks in to her room, and the rest of the poem catalogs his horrified discovery that beneath Celia's apparently flawless exterior lies all the dirt and grime of human bodily functions. In all his writings Swift's main satirical attack is on human pride, and in this poem he viciously undermines the idealization of female beauty and the eighteenth-century glorification of the human form. Strephon, like the hero of Swift's *Gulliver's Travels* (1726), sees the imperfections of the body as through a magnifying glass (Gulliver's eye-opening occurs in the land of the Brobdingnagian giants); both men become misanthropic, seeing human beings as coarse, repulsive, foul-smelling creatures. In the poem, Swift claims to "pity wretched Strephon, blind/To all the charms of womankind" and wishes Strephon would learn to think like the poet, and "bless his ravished eyes to see/Such order from confusion sprung,/Such gaudy tulips raised from dung." While humiliating the pride of the beautiful Celia and her ardent admirer (for whose praise she spends so much time preparing), Swift also reveals his equally passionate distaste for the less noble aspects of the human condition.

Swift's attack on female beauty did not go unanswered: Lady Mary Wortley Montagu replied in a poem titled "The Reasons That Induced Dr. Swift to Write a Poem Called the Lady's Dressing Room" (1734). Montagu's response is an attack on Swift personally, however, as she describes Swift himself visiting the room of "Betty," a prostitute. When he fails to perform, he blames his inability on her lack of hygiene, which he threatens to reveal in print to warn away other customers. "Betty" has the last word when she retorts that she will use his poem for toilet paper. Petrarchan admiration of a silent goddess on a pedestal was dealt a death blow by this coarse debate.

Perhaps to avoid both the Renaissance idealization of female beauty and the eighteenth-century critique of it, later ages steered away from it altogether. Two Romantic poets, however, wrote lyrics for specific women in terms rather different from the Petrarchan conventions that depicted the face in particular. Lord Byron, a notorious womanizer, wrote "She Walks in Beauty" (1814) in appreciation of his cousin by marriage, Mrs. Robert John Wilmot, a widow who appeared at a ball in a black gown decorated with spangles. Her dress gave rise to Byron's simile that she resembled "the night/Of cloudless climes and starry skies." The perfection of her dress he sees reflected in the "nameless grace" of her dark hair, but the poem becomes a tribute to the expression on the widow's face. Like the starry night, her face reflects a serene, peaceful mind and an innocent, loving heart. The poem was set to the music of Isaac Nathan as one of the *Hebrew Melodies* (1815).

William Wordsworth wrote "She Was a Phantom of Delight" in 1804 on first seeing Mary Hutchinson, who became his wife. The poem encapsulates the notion of love at first sight: in the first stanza, the lovely woman must be an apparition, who will disappear as suddenly as she appeared. Playing on the Petrarchan conventions, the poet describes her eyes as twilight stars, sparkling and dark, as is her hair. In every other way, however, she is springtime and dawn, a sprite "to haunt, to startle, and way-lay." The second stanza gives human form to this apparition while retaining the spirit that first captivated him. In the "household motions" of her womanly form he recognizes freedom and youth, and in her face he sees a nature that will respond to the many emotions of human life. Stanza three speaks of the "pulse" that animates the whole, the essence of the woman that makes her what she is: a "perfect Woman, nobly planned," embodying "Endurance, foresight, strength, and skill." The final couplet returns the poem to its opening as the poet recognizes that the "phantom" that first arrested him is still there in the human form, "bright/With something of angelic light."

Whether writing about the beauty of the natural world or the beauty of a lovely woman, (or young man, in some of Shakespeare's sonnets), poets have found in beauty a captivating power that engages their imaginations and inspires them to write. The poem itself then often becomes the greater beauty, the art that arrests the mind by bringing wholeness, harmony, and radiance to its subject. Just as Jonson's speaker is charmed more by "sweet neglect" than by powder and perfume, the subtly artful poem strikes not just the eyes but the heart.

econo

Sonnet 53, "What is your substance, whereof are you made," William Shakespeare

ImPo; OAEL-1; OBEV

"Hymn to Intellectual Beauty," Percy Bysshe Shelley

ImPo; NAEL-2; OAEL-2

"Pied Beauty," Gerard Manley Hopkins

BAVP; ImPo; NAEL-2; OAEL-2; OBEV; TFi; TrGrPo-2

"No Second Troy," William Butler Yeats

NAEL-2; OAEL-2; TFi

"Brittle Beauty," Henry Howard, earl of Surrey

TrGrPo-1

"When men shall find thy flower, thy glory pass," from *Delia*, Samuel Daniel

NAEL-1

"So oft as I her beauty do behold," Edmund Spenser

TrGrPo-1

"There is a garden in her face," Thomas Campion

ImPo; NAEL-1; OAEL-1; TFi

"Rose-Cheeked Laura," Thomas Campion

NAEL-1; OAEL-1; TFi

"A Song" ("Ask me no more where Jove bestows"), Thomas Carew

ImPo; NAEL-1; TFi

Sonnet 130, "My mistress' eyes are nothing like the sun," William Shakespeare

ImPo; NAEL-1; OAEL-1; TFi

Sonnet 106, "When in the chronicle of wasted time," William Shakespeare

ImPo; NAEL-1; OAEL-1

"Beauty," Abraham Cowley
    ImPo; TrGrPo-1

"The Scrutiny," Richard Lovelace
    TrGrPo-1

"Give beauty all her right!" Thomas Campion
    TrGrPo-1

"Clerimont's Song" ("Still to be Neat"), Ben Jonson
    NAEL-1; OAEL-1; TFi; TrGrPo-1

"Delight in Disorder" ("A sweet disorder in the dress"), Robert Herrick
    BL; ImPo; NAEL-1; OAEL-1; OBEV; SB; TFi; TrGrPo-1

"Upon Julia's Clothes," Robert Herrick
    BL; ImPo; NAEL-1; OAEL-1; OBEV; TFi; TrGrPo-1

"To Amarantha," Richard Lovelace
    BL; TrGrPo-1

Sonnet 37, *Amoretti* ("What guyle is this, that those her golden tresses"),
Edmund Spenser
    NAEL-1; TrGrPo-1

"The Lady's Dressing Room," Jonathan Swift
    NAEL-1

"The Reasons That Induced Dr. Swift to Write a Poem Called the Lady's
Dressing Room," Lady Mary Wortley Montagu
    BL; NAEL-1

"She Walks in Beauty," George Gordon, Lord Byron
    ImPo; OBEV; NAEL-2; TFi; TrGrPo-2

"She Was a Phantom of Delight," William Wordsworth
    ImPo; OAEL-2; TFi; TrGrPo-2

Carpe Diem

∽⌒⌒⌒∽

Like so many themes in British poetry, *carpe diem* came to the British poets from the classical writers of ancient Greece and Rome. The phrase comes from the first century B.C. Latin poet Horace, who in Ode, I. xi, tells his mistress that their future is in the hands of the gods. Life is short, so they must "enjoy the day," for they do not know if there will be a tomorrow. The theme was particularly popular in seduction poems of the seventeenth century, whose young male poets followed Horace in reminding a would-be mistress that time flies, and they should enjoy their love before they grow too old. The theme became well known through translations and adaptations of the first century B.C. Roman poet Catullus's lyric "Vivamus mea Lesbia, atque amemus." In Thomas Campion's version, "My sweetest Lesbia, let us live and love" (1601), for example, the poet argues that while the sun and stars may set, they rise again, whereas when our "little light" sets "we sleep one ever-during night." Ben Jonson's adaptation, "Come, my Celia, let us prove,/While we can, the sports of love" (a song from his play *Volpone* [1606]), is delightfully brief and light hearted, as most poems on this theme are. Jonson tells Celia that the sin is not in enjoying their love but in letting the world know about it. "Why should we defer our joys?" he tells her, summing up the heart of the *carpe diem* theme.

Robert Herrick, a Cavalier poet who was known as the first of the "sons of Ben" (or followers of Ben Jonson), wrote many lyrics for a number of probably fictional women, many of them on the subject of life's brevity. In "Corinna's Going A-Maying" (1648), he urges a young beauty to rise early on May Day morning to enjoy the coming of spring in the traditional village May Day rituals of rebirth and the flowering of young love. "Our life is short," he reminds her, "And, as a vapor or a drop of rain,/Once lost, can ne'er be found again." Herrick's "To the Virgins, to Make Much of Time" (1648) opens with the famous stanza,

> Gather ye rosebuds while ye may,
>   Old time is still a-flying;
> And this same flower that smiles today,
>   Tomorrow will be dying.

Herrick urges the young women to marry while they are young, "when youth and blood are warmer," because in no time they will be old and unwanted.

The short-lived beauty of the rose was a favorite metaphor for poets writing on the *carpe diem* theme. Edmund Waller, a contemporary of Herrick, in "Go, Lovely Rose!" (1645) sends a rose to his mistress to remind her of the ways in which she resembles the flower. Addressing the flower, he notes that they are both "sweet and fair," and they both deserve to be admired; the woman should not hide her beauty, just as the rose does not languish unappreciated in a desert but blooms for all to see. There is a hint of complaint in the opening stanza when the poet asks the rose to "tell her that wastes her time and me," that she is like the rose. But the woman receives a violent shock when the last stanza opens with the command to the rose, "Then die!" The woman, seeing the rose's early demise, will, he hopes, appreciate that beautiful women, like beautiful roses, are short-lived and should take advantage of the poet's desire to admire and win them. In "To Phyllis" (1645), Waller is even more direct, urging his mistress to sleep with him now because their youth and beauty will soon disappear, taking love with them. He argues that their "present love" is the truth and must be consummated because their past may not have been as noble and their future is left to the gods, who are notoriously fickle in their attachments.

Abraham Cowley also argued the *carpe diem* theme in "The Epicure" (1656), a short paraphrase from the Greek poet Anacreon, who praised love and wine. This slight lyric contains many of the images now associated with the carefree life. Beginning "Fill the bowl with rosy wine,/ Around our temple roses twine," the poem goes on to assure us that "Today is ours. What do we fear? . . . Banish business, banish sorrow./ To the gods belongs tomorrow."

The best of the seventeenth-century *carpe diem* poems is Andrew Marvell's "To His Coy Mistress" (1681). Marvell's tone is bantering as he tries to coax his lady out of what he imagines to be mere coquettishness. "Had we but world enough, and time," he tells her, they could happily continue their flirtation. He then wildly exaggerates that enviable position, imagining her by the Ganges searching for rubies while he remains in dull Humberside, England. Their courtship could extend from before

Noah's days to the Last Judgment, giving him time to spend hundreds of years praising her many attributes. The poem gently satirizes both the woman's desire to be flattered and the lover's extravagant flattery; she deserves such eons of wooing and he would love to indulge her in it. But alas, he reminds her in the second half of the poem, "at my back I always hear/Time's winged chariot hurrying near." Now the speaker's importuning becomes more pointed, and rather than the picturesque fading rose of earlier *carpe diem* poems, Marvell's images of life's brevity are stark and disturbing. He brings before his mistress's gaze the vision of her body in the tomb, with only worms now to "try/That long-preserved virginity." Here, too, his tone is bantering as he remarks offhandedly, "The grave's a fine and private place,/But none, I think, do there embrace."

The third section of the poem also departs from the conventional love lyric of the Cavalier poets as he begs his mistress to give in to the fire in her bosom. While turtle doves are the traditional birds of love, Marvell compares himself and his coy mistress to "amorous birds of prey" who need to devour time before time devours them. The closing petition is violent as he urges his suit, his impatience driving the poem in sound and image:

> Let us roll all our strength and all
> Our sweetness up into one ball,
> And tear our pleasures with rough strife
> Thorough the iron gates of life.

The correlation between sex and death, hinted at in earlier *carpe diem* poems, is conveyed with energy and wit in Marvell's treatment of the theme. Few later writers attempted to better him.

❧

"My sweetest Lesbia, let us live and love," Thomas Campion
    NAEL-1; OAEL-1; TFi
"Song: To Celia" ("Come, my Celia, let us prove"), Ben Jonson
    OAEL-1; TFi; TrGrPo-1
"Corinna's Going A-Maying," Robert Herrick
    NAEL-1; OAEL-1; TFi
"To the Virgins, to Make Much of Time," Robert Herrick
    BL; ImPo; NAEL-1; OAEL-1; TFi
"Go, Lovely Rose," Edmund Waller

NAEL-1; OBEV; TFi

"To Phyllis," Edmund Waller

TrGrPo-1

"Fill the bowl with rosy wine," Abraham Cowley

TrGrPo-1

"To His Coy Mistress" ("Had we but world enough, and time"), Andrew Marvell

BL; ImPo; NAEL-1; OAEL-1; OBEV; TFi; TrGrPo-1

Christmas Poems

John Milton's poem "On the Morning of Christ's Nativity" was written for Christmas 1629, when Milton was only twenty-one and just deciding that he would serve God and his countrymen as a poet. Most of the poem is a hymn offered to the "infant God" through the poet's Muse, who will hasten to present it to the Christ child before the Wise Men arrive with their gifts. The hymn—twenty-seven eight-line stanzas—tells the story of Christ's birth, beginning with a description of winter that recalls the Puritan belief that the expulsion of man from the Garden of Eden (the Fall) resulted in the fall of Nature also. Nature is hiding her "foul deformities" behind white snow that makes a pretense of innocence, reminding us that all of creation was waiting for the birth of Christ the redeemer. Even the sun hid before the greater glory and light of God made manifest on earth. The first few stanzas also praise God for sending peace to the earth on this special morning, a peace that was known to have reigned in the Roman Empire at that time. Drawing on the Pastoral convention of classical poetry, in which shepherds lived and sang in an ideal, prelapsarian world, the hymn suggests that the coming of Christ meant the promise of a return to a perfect state through his redemptive grace. The shepherds hear heavenly music, normally out of the reach of mortal ears, and Nature too hears the harmony of the music and interprets it as ushering in a new age in which heaven and earth will once again be united. Truth, Justice, and Mercy will replace Sin and Vanity, even Hell itself, through the redeeming power of Christ.

In stanza sixteen Milton moves away from this vision of the Garden of Eden restored. No, he says, the crucifixion and the Day of Judgment are still to come, and Christ's birthday is celebrated as the beginning of a new era in which the old pagan beliefs are swept away by "the dreaded Infant's hand."

Less well known now than Milton's poem is Robert Southwell's "The Burning Babe," published in 1602 and much admired by Ben Jonson. The poem, which contains sixteen iambic heptameter lines rhyming in couplets (a line known as a "fourteener" because it contains fourteen syllables), tells of the poet's vision of a "burning babe all burning bright" that suddenly appears in the air above him. The child, who is weeping bitterly, radiates a scorching heat that he explains to the poet comes from his deep love for humanity. He laments that "none appear to warm their hearts," and the poem becomes a powerful allegory of Christ's sacrifice: "The metal in this furnace wrought are men's defiled souls." As the Christ child disappears into the winter night, the poet realizes that the vision has ushered in Christmas day.

Christmas was not widely celebrated outside of church until the mid-nineteenth century, when the traditions that we know today—Christmas trees, cards, games, and festivities—became popular with city families as well as country folk. The landed gentry had always honored the season on a small scale before the Puritan Interregnum (1649–1660) had banned any celebration of Christmas. But with the help of Prince Albert, who popularized the German tradition of Christmas trees, and Charles Dickens, who brought Christmas to the working poor of England through *A Christmas Carol* (1843), the Victorians embraced Christmas as, in Scrooge's nephew's words, "a kind, forgiving, charitable, pleasant time . . . when men and women seem by one consent to open their shut-up hearts freely." Alfred, Lord Tennyson structured his long poem "In Memoriam A.H.H." (1850) around three Christmases, the changing celebration of which illustrates the passage of his grief for his dead friend, Arthur Hallam. The first Christmas section is number 28, written in 1833, not long after Hallam's death. Tennyson's remarkable ability to fulfill Alexander Pope's dictum that "the sound must seem an echo to the sense" (*An Essay on Criticism*, 1709) is evident in the five four-line stanzas that make up Section 28. Feeling isolated and shut out from human life and religious faith, Tennyson describes the church bells echoing back and forth between the four parishes surrounding Tennyson's family home in Lincolnshire. The lines perfectly echo the back and forth movement of the bells as they swing to and fro, bringing "Peace and goodwill, goodwill and peace,/Peace and goodwill, to all mankind." But the sounds of the bells also "swell out and fail, as if a door/Were shut between me and the sound." In his grief, Tennyson cannot accept the message of the bells, and he vacillates between grim isolation and a yearning for reassurance in a motion that is perfectly caught in the swaying of the bells. In the fourth stanza he almost seeks the oblivion of death, hoping that another Christmas will not find him still on earth. But in the fifth stanza he cannot resist the power of the bells and their message of Christian hope. He heard them as a boy, and now "they bring me sorrow touched with joy,/The merry, merry bells of Yule."

The eight stanzas comprising Section 30 describe the Tennyson family's attempts to carry on without Arthur (he had been engaged to Alfred's sister Emily) on that first Christmas after his death. With "trembling fingers" they decorate the house with holly and take up their old games, "making vain pretense/Of gladness." Silently, they form a circle of hands (an image that recurs throughout the poem) and seek the comfort of Christian belief in an afterlife for Hallam, promised by Christ's birth. The tone of the poem is still somber, however, and the closing appeal to the coming of dawn and hope is muted.

Section 78 describes the second Christmas after Hallam's death. Again the family is weaving holly around the hearth, but now "silent snow" falls "calmly," unlike the more painful rain of the first Christmas. The poem suggests a sense of emptiness and waiting, the snow muffling sound and creating a sense of the world suspended, as in James Joyce's story "The Dead" (1914). Again they play the games of their childhood, but "over all things brooding slept/The quiet sense of something lost." The second Christmas poignantly exemplifies the stage of grief in which the tears of the previous year have dried, and in that apparent recovery from grief there lies an even greater pain: "O last regret, regret can die!" In the poem's movement from empty loss to a vital sense of Hallam's continued presence in another state of being, this section employs the recurrence of Christmas and all its associations to describe the progress of grieving. Only when Tennyson can give up the human, mortal Hallam, whose actual presence he misses so intensely, can he begin to realize Hallam's immortal existence. At the end of this section he accepts the passing of the first, acute grief, and his recognition that the sorrow can remain even when his tears have dried recalls Wordsworth's description of "thoughts that do often lie too deep for tears" in his "Ode: Intimations of Immortality" (1807).

The third Christmas is prepared for in Sections 104 and 105. The Tennysons have moved—only one church is tolling its bell in the misty night—and the poet senses that this break with the past is necessary to his recovery. In this new land, free from memories, "all is new unhallowed ground." He asks that they not try to take up their old customs but just let the coming of dawn and the cycle of natural life signal the season. Section 106 contains the well-known Christmas refrain,

> Ring out the old, ring in the new,
>   Ring happy bells, across the snow:
>   The year is going, let him go;
> Ring out the false, ring in the true.

Again Tennyson's matching of sound and sense brings the ringing of the bells to life in the back and forth motion of the lines. That motion also dramatizes the lesson of the section, which takes up Thomas Carlyle's battle cry for a new religious faith that throws out the old, empty rituals and brings in a rejuvenated, spiritual Christianity. Ring out social injustice, he says, and ring in "sweeter manners, purer laws." Ring out greed, false pride, slander, and wars—the evils of a world that has been divorced from true spirituality; ring in love, peace, and compassion. Finally, he asks to "ring in the Christ that is to be," marked by a Christmas that is nearing the end of the millennium. Only a reborn faith, experienced by the world at large, can bring an end to the evils of injustice and war. The rebirth of faith that Tennyson hopes for in the third Christmas embraces his new sense that Hallam has received eternal life through Christ.

A more disturbing view of the end of a Christian era and the dawning of a new one is offered in William Butler Yeats's "The Second Coming." Written in 1919, in response to the cataclysmic changes brought about by World War I, the Russian Revolution, and the Irish troubles, the poem dramatizes Yeats's theory that human history goes through 2,000-year cycles, each new cycle being the antithesis of its predecessor. The birth of Christ marked the beginning of one 2,000-year cycle that is now nearing its end, and Yeats sees the "second coming" of Christ as ushering in a very different era. At the end of the second millennium, Yeats sees a world that has spun away from Christ's teachings into a terrifying abyss of anarchy and bloodshed.

The second stanza inverts the biblical references to Christ's return on the Day of Judgment as described in Revelation. This "Second Coming" at the end of the twentieth century will be very different from the birth of Christ. In a horrifying vision, Yeats wonders, what kind of monster can it be, rising, blind and ruthless, out of the desert. Through the darkness, and surrounded by birds of prey, this beast makes its way to Bethlehem. The beast has been slumbering in "stony sleep" since before Christ's birth (and the image of the beast as half-lion, half-man suggests the ancient Egyptian Sphinx), but the Christian era, ushered in by the "rocking cradle" in Bethlehem, has "vexed" the beast to "nightmare." The poem moves forward with a frighteningly relentless force as it traces the rising of the beast in the desert and its chillingly gradual but inevitable crawling toward birth at the beginning of a new cycle of human history.

The speaker of T. S. Eliot's "The Journey of the Magi" (1927) is one of the three wise men who brought gifts to the infant Jesus at his birth. The poem recalls Milton's hymn because Eliot, too, sees the birth in terms of the inevitable Easter death. The reason for Christ's birth was the redemption of the world through his death on the cross, and in "The Journey of the Magi" the old man, looking back, sees the birth and the death as the same event, wondering for which one they had been led on their difficult journey at the very worst time of year. After making their way through the snow and cold, they seem to arrive at the crucifixion site of three trees before finding the stable. The poem ends, as does Milton's, with the effects of the birth of Christ on the old ways. The wise men return to their own country but they cannot now accept pagan beliefs. The magus feels out of place "with an alien people clutching their gods." Like all the Christmas poems, then, "The Journey of the Magi" sees Christ's birth as a transformation, the bringing of light to the darkness. Although Eliot shares Yeats's sense that at the end of the twentieth century Christendom will have lost touch with the spirit born in the stable, only Yeats fears the inevitable overthrow of that light.

❧

"On the Morning of Christ's Nativity," John Milton
    ImPo; NAEL-1; OBEV
"The Burning Babe," Robert Southwell
    NAEL-1; OAEL-1; OBEV; SB; TFi; TrGrPo-1
Selections from "In Memoriam A.H.H.," Alfred, Lord Tennyson
    BAVP; NAEL-2; OAEL-2
"The Second Coming," William Butler Yeats
    ImPo; NAEL-2; OAEL-2; OBEV; TFi
"The Journey of the Magi," T. S. Eliot
    ImPo; NAEL-2; TFi; TrGrPo-2

Death

No age in poetry, spoken or written, has failed to take up the most human of themes: the end of life. It was central to the old ballads, narrative poems handed down orally for centuries and only recorded as recently as the eighteenth century. One of the best known of the ballads, "The Wife of Usher's Well" tells the chilling story of three sons who are drowned at sea. Their grieving mother's plea that they be returned to her "in earthly flesh and blood" is answered one night in November, and their joyous mother orders a celebratory feast, not recognizing that they are ghosts. The boys' hats are "o' the birk," or strewn with birch, a sign that they have come from the world of the dead; as the cock crows to herald the day, they remind each other that they can stay no longer. Like all ballads, "The Wife of Usher's Well" achieves its power through repetition, understatement, and a powerful rhythm.

Many of Shakespeare's sonnets are concerned with death while focusing more specifically on love, time, or immortality. In this survey those sonnets will be found under their more dominant themes. In Sonnet 71, "No longer mourn for me when I am dead" (1609), death is the central topic as the speaker warns his friend against grieving over his loss. Do not remember me, he pleads, if doing so will make you sad. If you read this poem after I am gone, do not even speak my name, but "let your love even with my life decay." The couplet tells the friend that the world mocks those who grieve too long. There is an irony in Shakespeare's tone, however, that reminds the reader that the poet is giving this instruction in a poem that is intended to remind the friend of its author.

Many poems on death see it as the great leveler that brings equality to king and peasant. Shakespeare's "Fear No More the Heat of the Sun," from *Cymbeline* (1623), cheerfully reminds us of this impartiality. In four stanzas of six lines each, this delightful song tells us not to worry about life's problems—the weather, the ups and downs of fortune, the bigger threats of witchcraft and ghosts—when death comes, life's vicissitudes are over for all of us, regardless of station: "Golden lads and girls all must,/As chimney-sweepers, come to dust."

A very different Renaissance poem on the theme of man's equality in the face of death is Thomas Nashe's "A Litany in Time of Plague," (or "Adieu! farewell earth's bliss!" from his play *A Pleasant Comedy Called Summer's Last Will and Testament* [1592]). Each of the six stanzas contains three couplets of leaden six-syllable lines, dominated by one-syllable words that toll like a death-knell, culminating in each stanza with the line "I am sick, I must die." A final refrain concludes each stanza: "Lord, have mercy on us!" In the face of death the rich man cannot buy his safety any more than the hero of old could defy death with his sword. Still well known are the lines from stanza three: "Beauty is but a flower/Which wrinkles will devour;/Brightness falls from the air,/Queens have died young and fair,/Dust has closed Helen's eye./I am sick, I must die."

Many Christian poets have written about the defeat of death through Christ's resurrection. The most famous of these poems is probably John Donne's Holy Sonnet "Death, Be Not Proud" (1633), in which the poet addresses Death to remind it that it is powerless. Rather than the "mighty and dreadful" tyrant that rules over mankind, Death is just a more pleasurable form of the rest and sleep it resembles. Donne reminds Death that it, too, is in the hands of "fate, chance, kings, and desperate men," all of which can unexpectedly bring it about. But the final over-throw of Death's dominion occurs in the final couplet, when "One short sleep past, we wake eternally,/And Death shall be no more: Death, thou shalt die." Donne's contemporary George Herbert similarly addresses Death in his poem "Death" (1633), where he makes a striking comparison between death's power before and after the coming of Christ. The open-ing lines describe the body several years after death, an "uncouth, hid-eous thing, Nothing but bones," a wordless mouth gaping open. The second half of the poem introduces Christ's sacrifice and resurrects the dry bones of the first two stanzas. Christ's death "did put some blood into thy face." Now death is desirable, "fair and full of grace." At the final resurrection, "all thy bones with beauty shall be clad."

Thomas Gray, an eighteenth-century poet, is best known now for two poems about death, both inspired by the loss of his old school friend Richard West at the age of twenty-five. "A Sonnet on the Death of Mr. Richard West" (1742) contrasts the poet's misery with the cheerfulness of a spring morning, and laments that the one person who would have understood his grief is the one now gone. Not long after, Gray began "Elegy Written in a Country Churchyard" (1751) which is still one of the most popular of all English poems, overflowing as it is with memorable lines that evoke the English countryside and the rural way of life. Its nighttime setting of a graveyard establishes many of the conventions of the Gothic novel that would be made popular by Gray's friend Horace Walpole in his *The Castle of Otranto* (1765): an "ivy-mantled tower," a "moping owl," and a graveyard and its sleeping inhabitants, shaded by the gnarled yew tree. Written in quatrains rhyming abab, the poem moves from an evocative sense of place (a "lowing herd," a "glimmering landscape," a beetle that "wheels his droning flight," and the "drowsy tinklings" of the sheep bells) to an evocation of the lives of the people who sleep beneath the grass at the speaker's feet. The poem becomes a tribute to the contemplative lives of country people as it develops the themes often connected with death: the vanity of the earthly pursuit of power and glory ("the paths of glory lead but to the grave"); the greater value of homely pursuits ("the short and simple annals of the poor"); the talents in country people that are never allowed to blossom ("Full many a flower is born to blush unseen,/And waste its sweetness on the desert air"). Such quiet heroism exists "far from the madding crowd's ignoble strife." From this general portrait of the village people, the narrator focuses his attention on one particular gravestone where an epitaph, rudely cut in the stone, tells a brief history of a life once lived. Now he allows a "kindred spirit," reading the stone, to remember the man's life in the village, from his youth to his being laid to rest in the churchyard. The poem concludes with the epitaph itself, inspired by Gray's grief at the loss of his friend Richard West, "a youth to Fortune and to Fame unknown." The poem brings quiet resignation to Gray's tribute to his friend, established in the evocative opening description, developed in the portrait of the villagers, and finally brought to completion in the epitaph, which requests the reader to leave the dead in his final repose in "the bosom of his Father and his God."

One of Robert Burns's finest songs is "Afton Water" (1789), like many poems both a love song and a lament for the dead. Burns wrote most of his poems in the Scots vernacular, the language of the country people in southwestern Scotland where he farmed, but "Afton Water" is one of his best poems in standard English. The poem is a gentle address to the river, urging it not to waken Mary, his beloved who lies "sleeping" beside it. The poem evokes the milder aspects of the countryside—the scene he depicts is of tree, bird, stream, and valley, echoing the poet's acceptance of Mary's death. He speaks of her as though she were still alive, which suggests that to the poet she was indeed still a part of the natural world in which she rests: "My Mary's asleep by thy murmuring stream,/Flow gently, sweet Afton, disturb not her dream." The Mary of the poem was Mary Campbell, a maid-servant to whom he proposed (on the banks of a stream—all his lyrics to Mary use a river as metaphor), but she died before they could marry. Burns wrote several fine lyrics on the loss of his "Highland Mary" (1799), including one of that title, in which he characteristically compares her to a flower: "But oh! fell death's untimely frost, That nipt my flower sae early!/Now green's the sod, and cauld's the clay,/That wraps my Highland Mary." On an anniversary of her death, after he had married Jean Armour, he wrote "To Mary in Heaven" (1799) remembering their brief love affair on the banks of the river Ayr. Time, he says, has just made the memory of that time more acute: "Time but th' impression stronger makes,/As streams their channels deeper wear."

The Victorian age (1837–1901) was preoccupied by death in all its aspects, partly because Queen Victoria herself went into extended mourning after the death of her beloved husband, Albert, in 1861. Victorian funerals were ornate occasions, and death figured prominently in the popular art of the day. The death of children particularly appealed to Victorian sentimentality. The Victorian poet Christina Rossetti wrote many poems about death from a Christian perspective, but they are surprisingly varied in their approach. Often, Rossetti is concerned with the state of death itself, and she does not always depict it as a union with God; whereas some Christian imagery sees Christ's defeat of death as the defeat of night altogether (the soul thus moves from day into day), Rossetti often writes about a state of limbo, or sleep, that precedes the Day of Judgment. In frail health for most of her life, and the daughter of an invalid father, she found life a struggle, with the cares and worries almost too great to bear, so she often describes death as a reward and a release from suffering. In "Up-Hill" (1858), the journey through life is an uphill road, closing in night at an inn where the weary traveler will find rest among those who have toiled up the path before her. "Sleeping at Last" (1896), written shortly before her own death, depicts in Rossetti's characteristically gentle and rhythmic cadences death as a welcome relief from "the struggle and horror" of life; the woman is "sleeping at last in a dreamless sleep locked fast." But even here an element of horror at the body in death creeps in with the reminder that the body is "Cold and white, out of sight of friend and lover/Sleeping at last." "Rest" depicts the sleep of death as a timeless, soundless stasis—"Her rest shall not begin and end, but be"—until the awakening on the "morning of Eternity." "After Death" (1849) depicts a dead child as not sleeping at all but conscious of its grieving father weeping over its body. The death-bed scene takes an unexpected turn when the child recalls, "He did not love me living; but once dead/He pitied me." The child finds it "sweet" to know that the father "is warm tho' I am cold." In her lyrical "When I Am Dead, My Dearest" (1848), Rossetti recalls Shakespeare's Sonnet 71, discussed above, as she warns in the first stanza against mourning her loss or sentimentalizing her burial: "And if thou wilt, remember,/And if thou wilt, forget." The second stanza moves to the dead poet herself, who, "dreaming through the twilight/That doth not rise nor set," will be oblivious of all earthly senses: "Haply I may remember,/And haply may forget." In "Remember" (1862) she urges the mourner, "Better by far you should forget and smile/Than that you should remember and be sad."

Emily Brontë's "Remembrance" (1845) was a part of Emily's and her sister Anne's stories about an imaginary island called Gondal. Fifteen years after the death of her lover, the heroine speaks to him of her continuing love for him but acceptance of his loss. Remembering that he is "Cold in the earth, and the deep snow piled above thee!" the speaker tells him that she has been faithful to his memory while continuing to be swept along by the tide of the living. She did not give in to her initial despair but chose to carry on "without the aid of joy." Even now, she cannot "indulge in Memory's rapturous pain": "Once drinking deep of that divinest anguish,/How could I seek the empty world again?"

Alfred, Lord Tennyson, the poet laureate and favorite poet of Queen Victoria, wrote frequently about death because of the loss of his friend Arthur Hallam, not just in the major work "In Memoriam A.H.H." (1850), discussed in the "Death of the Young," section, but also in his small lyrics. "Break, Break, Break" (1834) demonstrates Tennyson's remarkable ability to convey meaning through sound. The poem contrasts the harsh monosyllables of the opening lines ("Break, break, break,/On thy cold gray stones, O Sea!") with the smoothly flowing lines that follow: "And I would that my tongue could utter/The thoughts that arise in me." Standing on the seashore, Tennyson finds in the waves breaking on the cold stone a perfect metaphor for his inability to give voice to the grief he is suffering. The poem widens out from the stones on the shore to the sounds of the greater seascape: a fisherman's boy playing with his sister; a sailor lad singing on his boat. "The stately ships go on/To their haven under the hill," reminding the poet again of his loss. As in so many of his poems, Tennyson here echoes the ebb and flow movement of the sea in the alternation of a long flowing line (the wave coming in) with a shorter one (the wave receding): "But the tender grace of a day that is dead/Will never come back to me."

The sound of the sea ebbing and flowing is even stronger in Tennyson's most famous poem about death, "Crossing the Bar." He wrote it on the inside of a used envelope during the short ferry crossing from the Isle of Wight (where he then lived) to the mainland in October 1889 after a serious illness. Tennyson requested that this poem always appear at the end of any collection of his poetry (a request not always honored). "Crossing the Bar" (leaving the safety of the harbor) uses as its central metaphor the familiar notion that many people die during the night, as the tide turns and starts to go out. Speaking of his own death, Tennyson asks that his loved ones not grieve at his departure because the ship that will take him to his final rest is piloted by God. Tennyson echoes 1

Corinthians 13, "For now we see through a glass darkly; but then face to face," when he says, "I hope to see my Pilot face to face/When I have crossed the bar." Asked why the pilot remained on board after the ship had left the harbor, Tennyson replied that the Pilot has always been on board, "but in the dark I have not seen him." The Pilot is "that Divine and Unseen who is always guiding us." The poem achieves its greatest effect through the powerful rush of emotion in the long lines that imitate the waves pouring onto the land before they recede in the short line that follows: "And may there be no moaning of the bar/When I put out to sea." "When that which drew from out the boundless deep/Turns again home." "And may there be no sadness of farewell,/When I embark."

Robert Browning's "Prospice" (1861), which means "look into the distance," is about the poet's own death. It similarly alternates long and short lines, but the effect is very different, as is the central metaphor: climbing a difficult mountain. "Fear death?—to feel the fog in my throat,/The mist in my face,/When the snows begin, and the blasts denote/I am nearing the place." Now, the rhythm depicts not a gentle tide but a vigorous battle. The rhythm is predominantly anapestic ("Yet the strong man must go"; "And the barriers fall"): three-syllable feet composed of two unstressed syllables followed by a stressed syllable. Anapests give the sense of rapid movement; the meter is that of a horse galloping. Now death is not welcomed but feared: it is "the Arch Fear in a visible form." And yet the poem moves from fear to acceptance. Just as Tennyson crosses the bar, Browning attains the summit of the mountain and receives his reward. This last, best fight must be met with courage, not shrunk from: "I would hate that death bandaged my eyes, and forbore,/And bade me creep past." At the final moment, the raging battle will give way to peace, "then a light, then thy breast," as Browning is once again united with his beloved wife, Elizabeth Barrett, whose death shortly before inspired the writing of the poem.

"Prospice" invites comparison with a famous twentieth-century poem, Dylan Thomas's "Do Not Go Gentle into That Good Night" (1951), inspired by the last illness of Thomas's father. Like Browning, Thomas depicts dying as a fight that must be fought to the end; but whereas Christian poets have depicted this battle as one that death loses because of Christ's victory over death, for Thomas there is only defeat that must be resisted at all costs. The poem is written predominantly in monosyllables, which slow the rhythm and add to the sense of impotent rage, very different from Browning's energetic anapests. The old, dying men of Thomas's poem "rage against the dying of the light." Because they have left things undone or unsaid, they have not fully lived. The bitterness of the tone derives from Thomas's address to his father in the last stanza, where he invokes him to "curse," and "bless," him with his "fierce tears." The conflict in the son's emotions at his father's impending death is finely felt and strongly expressed in this poem that has found many sympathetic readers.

One of Thomas's early poems, written in 1933, just before his nineteenth birthday, powerfully imagines Thomas's own death, but while the language of the poem is as violent as that of "Do Not Go Gentle," the theme of the poem is much less bitter. "The Force That Through the Green Fuse Drives the Flower" examines the force that will bring about Thomas's death just as surely as the death of the "crooked rose." The poem moves through several similar similes; thus, his blood is driven by the same force that allows water to carve deep ravines in rock. Paradoxically, the force that creates is also the force that destroys, but this unity is a consolation to Thomas, despite the harshness of his images of destruction.

D. H. Lawrence wrote a series of poems about the illness (through cancer) and death of his mother. His close relationship with her was at the center of his first novel, *Sons and Lovers* (1913). In "Suspense" (1910) he waits in a London suburb, where he is teaching, for news of her death. In the first stanza, the news coming from the north is identified with a wind that blows the birds and a train that "rushes stampeding down" to the south "from the darkening north." There is fear in the images, and a sense of helplessness; he can only wait for news. While the first stanza moves from north to south, the second focuses on the poet, waiting helplessly in the south and fixedly looking north, his whole being riveted, like a compass needle, on the "lode of her agony." He is waiting for news that she, and by implication, he, are "free" from the pain of her illness. The poem captures the tension between wishing for release from suffering and dreading the coming of the darkness, a curious state of suspension in which time both flies (in the wind and the train) and stands still (in the steadfast needle).

Lawrence uses Tennyson's alternation of long and short lines in "The Bride" (1911) to contrast the old body of his mother, lying in state after her death, with the young body of the girl she once was. At first the long lines celebrate her youthfulness, while the short, abrupt ones remind us that it is illusory. But the poem moves to an acceptance that the youthful look is in fact a reflection of her soul's freedom. In death she has regained her youthful innocence and promise, a promise perhaps not borne out by her life: he imagines that she is dreaming the "perfect" thoughts of a bride. The lines are a poetic rendering of Mrs. Morel's death in *Sons and Lovers* (1913). "Silence," "Sorrow," and "Brooding Grief" all evoke the poet's emotions at different times following his mother's death: the ability of tiny details to call up intense feelings of loss; the deep silence of the lost voice undercutting the noises of everyday life. Lawrence closed the series with "Troth with the Dead" (1911), a powerful evocation of his sense of oneness with his lost mother through the image of the sinking moon, which he sees as uniting the land of the living and the land of the dead. The half that is hidden in darkness he imagines as still shining in his mother's hair; the half he sees is a sign of our commitment to the dead. Just as the moon still shines in the land of darkness, even though we cannot see it, so love means that the dead are "lost and yet still connected" to us. Eerie lights shine from one side of the moon to the other, and in his own heart he senses that his mother's love still brings light, "weird and blue," to his life. The image recalls Tennyson's movement from grief and dark despair to a sense of being connected to Arthur Hallam in an endless circle. Lawrence refers to the moon as a "broken coin," and the word "broken" recurs twice more; but the brokenness turns out to be only an illusion because the other half of the moon or coin exists below the horizon, or in the earth where his mother lies.

The late-Victorian writer Thomas Hardy wrote "After the Last Breath" in response to his mother's death in 1904. Hardy alternates long and short lines to fine effect in the poem, achieving a sense of the balance between grief and relief at the loss of an invalid. In each of the five stanzas, the long third line runs over into an abrupt fourth and final line that echoes the finality of death. The poem speaks of the sense of dislocation after the invalid has died: the medicine bottles, now no longer required; the pillow, now no longer needing to be smoothed; the watchers, their lives now no longer on hold. The form of the poem deftly conveys the monumental shift that death brings to those left behind, once the beloved is no longer the "prisoner . . . of Time."

Hardy wrote a series of poems after the sudden death in 1912 of his first wife, Emma Gifford, from whom he had become increasingly estranged. In "The Walk" (1912) he compares his solitary walk to the top of a nearby hill now, after her death, with a previous walk, when she was alive but did not accompany him. Now he will return to an empty room. "The Voice" (1912) describes the poet's sense that he hears the voice of his dead wife, but it is her voice as it was when they were young, not the tones of their later, troubled marriage. The poem speaks in a lilting cadence of Hardy's regret that he lost the woman he loved twice, when she changed and when she died. The long, evocative lines of the first three stanzas abruptly alter into a sharp and perhaps self-indulgent sense of the poet's solitude: "Thus I; faltering forward. . . ." Having dismissed the idea of a ghostly voice in favor of its being just the wind, Hardy returns in the final stanza to the notion that it is his dead wife who calls. This sense that his wife is haunting him inspired "The Shadow on the Stone" and "The Haunter" (1916). The speaker in the latter is his wife's ghost, who wants to communicate with the poet, now that it is too late. The poet's own sense of regret is strong in the poem, and through the ghost's desire to be with him he is able to express his recognition of his guilt in the breakdown of the marriage. The reader senses that Hardy wrote this poem for his wife as an acknowledgment of his love for her and his appreciation of her love for him, which during their later years together he was unable to recognize. Now the ghost wants the poet to know that she recognizes his continued faith. In seeking him out, she wishes to bring him peace.

A similar but much earlier poem in which a dead wife haunts the poet is John Milton's sonnet "Methought I saw my late espoused saint" (1658). Two of Milton's wives died soon after giving birth—his first wife, Mary Powell, and his second wife, Katherine Woodcock—but the subject of this poem is likely to be Katherine, whose face he never saw because he became blind before meeting her. She appears to him in a dream vision, "vested all in white, pure as her mind," her face veiled (as it was to him in life) but with "love, sweetness, goodness" radiating from her pure form. Just as she leans to embrace him, the vision vanishes, leaving him in the darkness of his blind grief: "I waked, she fled, and day brought back my night."

Stevie Smith's "Not Waving but Drowning" (1957) is probably the best known of twentieth-century poems about death. Just twelve lines tell a simple story of a man who is rescued too late from a fatal swim in the sea; the implication is that the people on shore misunderstood his cries for help, mistaking them for a cheery wave, which they probably returned. Their casual reaction is recorded also, as they accuse him of being a practical joker whose jokes finally got the better of him. But the little poem chillingly concludes with the dead man's attempt to tell them that his death in the sea was emblematic: constantly misunderstood, he had lived all his life in the cold, calling for help and being ignored. The poem strikes a chord with early-twenty-first-century readers who see in it modern man's sense of alienation in a world where human communication often breaks down into misunderstanding.

Alienation is central to Edward Thomas's moving poem "Rain" (1916), written during World War I (after he enlisted but before he went to France), when Thomas's own death and the death of his friends was uppermost in his mind. Perhaps no other British poem more eloquently links death to the world of nature than does this evocation of the sound of rain falling. Alone in his "bleak hut," Thomas is led by the sound of the falling rain to thoughts of his death, when he will lie below the earth, unable to hear the rain falling or appreciate its cleansing. This thought leads him to remember his friends, hoping that none of them is dying now, or lying, helpless, listening to the rain. By the end of the poem Thomas has "dissolved" into the rain, unable to love anything except death itself: "If love it be towards what is perfect and/Cannot, the tempest tells me, disappoint."

From the early poets' grappling with death as an abstraction, to the modern poets' attempts to come to terms with the loss of children, parents, and lovers, this theme has lent itself to poetic forms as surely as love has found its expression in poetry. Many a tombstone is engraved with a verse, but few epitaphs are as simply memorable as Robert Louis Stevenson's "Requiem," written by him for this purpose and found on his grave in Samoa, where he died in 1894:

> Under the wide and starry sky,
> Dig a grave and let me lie.
> Glad did I live and gladly die,
>   And I laid me down with a will.
> This be the verse you grave for me:
> *Here he lies where he longed to be;*
> *Home is the sailor, home from the sea,*
>   *And the hunter home from the hill.*

❦

"The Wife of Usher's Well," anonymous

   ImPo; NAEL-1; OAEL-1; TFi; TrGrPo-1

Sonnet 71, "No longer mourn for me when I am dead," William Shakespeare

   ImPo; NAEL-1; TFi

"Fear No More the Heat of the Sun" (from *Cymbeline*), William Shakespeare

   ImPo; OBEV; TFi; TrGrPo-1

"A Litany in Time of Plague" ("Adieu! Farewell earth's bliss!"), Thomas Nashe

   NAEL-1; OAEL-1; OBEV; TFi; TrGrPo-1

Holy Sonnet ("Death, Be Not Proud"), John Donne

   ImPo; NAEL-1; OAEL-1; OBEV; Tfi; TrGrPo-1

"Death," George Herbert

   NAEL-1

"A Sonnet on the Death of Mr. Richard West," Thomas Gray

   BL; TrGrPo-1

"Elegy Written in a Country Churchyard," Thomas Gray

   BL; ECP; ImPo; NAEL-1; OAEL-1; OBEV; TFi; TrGrPo-1

"Afton Water" ("Flow gently, sweet Afton"), Robert Burns

   ImPo; NAEL-2

"Up-Hill," Christina Rossetti

   BAVP; NAEL-2; OAEL-2; TFi; TrGrPo-2

"Sleeping at Last," Christina Rossetti
    NAEL-2; TrGrPo-2

"Rest," Christina Rossetti
    OAEL-2; TrGrPo-2

"After Death," Christina Rossetti
    BAVP; NAEL-2

"When I Am Dead, My Dearest," Christina Rossetti
    NAEL-2; OAEL-2; TFi; TrGrPo-2

"Remember," Christina Rossetti
    OAEL-2; TFi; TrGrPo-2

"Remembrance," Emily Brontë
    BAVP; ImPo; OBEV; NAEL-2; TFi; TrGrPo-2

"Break, Break, Break," Alfred, Lord Tennyson
    BAVP; ImPo; NAEL-2; TFi; TrGrPo-2

"Crossing the Bar," Alfred, Lord Tennyson
    BAVP; ImPo; NAEL-2; OAEL-2; TFi; TrGrPo-2

"Prospice," Robert Browning
    ImPo; NAEL-2; TrGrPo-2

"Do Not Go Gentle into That Good Night," Dylan Thomas
    TFi; NAEL-2; OAEL-2

"The Force That Through the Green Fuse Drives the Flower," Dylan Thomas
    NAEL-2; OBEV; TFi

"Suspense," D. H. Lawrence
    MoBrPo

"The Bride," D. H. Lawrence
    OxBTC

"Troth with the Dead," D. H. Lawrence
    not anthologized; available in editions of Lawrence's poetry

"After the Last Breath," Thomas Hardy
    not anthologized; available in editions of Hardy's poetry

"The Walk," Thomas Hardy
    NAEL-2; OBEV

"The Voice," Thomas Hardy
    NAEL-2; OAEL-2; OBEV; TFi

"The Haunter," Thomas Hardy
    NOBE
"Methought I saw my late espoused saint," John Milton
    ImPo; NAEL-1; OAEL-1; TFi
"Not Waving but Drowning," Stevie Smith
    OAEL-2; OBEV; NAEL-2; TFi
"Rain," Edward Thomas
    NAEL-2; OBEV
"Requiem," Robert Louis Stevenson
    BAVP; OBEV; TFi; TrGrPo-2

Death of the Young

⚜

This most poignant of themes is also one of the most difficult for serious poets. Mawkish verse on the loss of a child fills the obituary pages of daily newspapers, and maudlin sentiment is always near at hand when writers attempt highly charged emotional themes. The great poets can avoid it, however, by seeking fresh and surprising images and diction rather than the familiar and heavily emotive language of the conventional eulogy. This section includes poems not just about children but also about premature death: the loss of young people in their prime, those whose potential is abruptly and unexpectedly extinguished. Poems about young people who have died in war are discussed in the War section.

Ben Jonson is famous for three fine poems about the death of children, two of the children his own. "On My First Daughter" is a tribute to Mary, who died at the age of just six months; "On My First Son" (1603) concerns the death of Benjamin at the age of seven. Both poems are twelve lines of rhyming couplets, the first written in iambic tetrameter and the second in iambic pentameter. They are, however, very different in tone and content. The tribute to the infant Mary appears to be an attempt to comfort his wife, the grieving mother, with conventional Christian consolation. The baby was a gift to them, the young parents, from heaven, and therefore she is "heaven's due" and the father should not regret returning her to God. As an infant she is still innocent, and her namesake Mary will "in comfort of her mother's tears" make her a part of Mary's "virgin train," a special, honored place. The baby's soul is safe, but the poem closes with a moving reminder of their little daughter's fragile, tiny body: "This grave partakes the fleshly birth./Which cover lightly, gentle earth." These lines are a paraphrase from the first-century A.D. Roman poet Martial, who in Epigram V. xxxiv requests "may no hard earth cover her gentle bones: do not lie heavily on her, Earth; she was not a heavy weight on you."

Two other poems employ Martial's disturbing contrast between hard, cold earth and small, fragile body. One of Ben Jonson's "sons" (the poets who admired and followed him), Robert Herrick, startles the reader in his four-line poem "Upon a Child" (1648):

Here a pretty baby lies
Sung asleep with lullabies;
Pray be silent, and not stir
Th' easy earth that covers her.

The shock in the last line—when the reader realizes that the baby is not just napping, but sleeping her long sleep—draws attention to the unnaturalness of the death of a child. Herrick finds the earth "easy," unlike Jonson, who followed Martial in pleading with the earth to lie gently, like a soft blanket, on the sleeping baby. The twentieth-century playwright Oscar Wilde, writing about the death of his sister in childhood in "Requiescat" (1881) (a prayer for the repose of the dead), also focuses on the stark contrast between the little girl's beautiful, innocent body and the heavy weight of coffin and stone that lies upon her breast. The reader is asked to "tread lightly" and "speak gently," for the child can hear and feel beneath the snow, even though her bright hair is now tarnished, her youth "fallen to dust." At the end of the poem the poet's grief takes over, however, in the thought that she hears nothing and rests in peace. The poet, in contrast, is buried with her but also alive and suffering the grief of her loss: "All my life's buried here./Heap earth upon it."

Ben Jonson wrote two other famous poems about the death of children. In the poem to his daughter discussed above, his classical references and traditionally Christian consolations suggest a certain detachment from his daughter's death in comparison to the greater grief of his wife, the mother, for whom he is offering comfort. "On My First Son," written in 1603, probably eight years after the death of Mary, is much more personal because the boy was seven, and the father had formed a close attachment to him. The poem begins with a farewell to Ben, "thou child of my right hand, and joy," the "right hand" referring to the name Benjamin, which in the original Hebrew means "son of the right hand," or fortunate. The poem then elaborates on the idea, central to Christian thought, that one must not put too much reliance on other human beings. Jonson calls it his sin that he hoped too much for the boy; like Mary, Ben was only lent to him, and he has had to give him back on the seventh anniversary of his birthday, the "just day." In the second quatrain Jonson wishes he could give up all his fatherly connections to the boy and, instead of holding on to him, recognize that, in dying, his son has been saved from the miseries of human life: "world's, and flesh's rage," and the pain of growing old. Bidding the boy rest in peace now, his father calls him his "best piece of poetry"—created by the poet as surely as his poetry. The poem concludes by reiterating that it is a sin to become too attached to people because if we "like too much" we are unwilling to accept the will of God, which has taken Ben from him.

One of Ben Jonson's best-known poems is his "Epitaph on S.P., a Child of Queen Elizabeth's Chapel" (1616). S.P. was Salomon Pavy, a child actor in Queen Elizabeth's acting company who died in 1602 at the age of thirteen. Writing as a poet rather than a father, Jonson still evokes pity for the young boy, beginning with his gentle urging to "Weep with me all you that read/This little story." Jonson plays upon the boy's talent as an actor to explain the untimely death of this child, beautiful "in grace, and feature." So good was he at playing old men that the Fates mistook him for one and took him to heaven. Seeing their mistake, they tried to give him a second life, "But, being so much too good for earth,/Heaven vows to keep him." Part of the attractiveness of the poem is its rhythm. Written in six quatrains of alternating rhyme (abab, cdcd, and so on), the poem is composed of lines that are not consistently iambic or trochaic, but every second line contains five syllables, while the remaining lines alternate between seven syllables and eight. The result is a lyrical movement, almost swinglike, in each quatrain, that suggests the boy's youth and contributes to the poem's attempt to make his death seem less unnatural and more fitting. The tone is playful rather than elegiac, but the simple emotion of the opening lines remains at the heart of the poem.

Some of the finest lyrics about the death of children are understandably written by women poets. The late-Victorian poet Alice Meynell captures the inconsolable grief of the mother in two simple quatrains titled "Maternity" (1913). The first four lines remember the death of a newborn baby (an only child) ten years earlier, when friends offered the mother the consolation that the baby was in heaven. The mother's answer, which begins in line four, continues into the second stanza with the mother's acknowledgment that the baby, "born in pain," is "not now forlorn." But in the last two lines of the poem the woman's abiding grief is poignantly contrasted with the baby's freedom from life's misery: "But oh, ten years ago, in vain,/A mother, a mother was born."

Elizabeth Jennings, writing in the twentieth century, considers consolation and loss in "For a Child Born Dead" (1979). Addressing her lost baby, the mother finds that because the baby never lived, she does not know how to think about him; there was no "warm and noisy room" of the child's life against which to know now its opposite. The consolation is an ironic one: the baby's character cannot be distorted or altered in his mother's memory because the child has never had the chance to create memories. His "clear refusal of the world" is uncomplicated by having lived. But in the final two lines Jennings finds in this clarity a bitter consolation that grief could be so "pure."

Katherine Philips's "On the Death of My First and Dearest Child, Hector Philips" (1655) is more emotional but still compelling as the mother's description of her loss (she was married for over six years before her boy was born, but he lived for only forty days) gives way to a personal address to her lost baby. All she can offer him in her lonely grief (the "unconcerned world" cannot comfort her) is her talent as a poet, but "tears are [her] muse, and sorrow all [her] art." "Piercing groans" will be his elegy, and "these gasping numbers" her last attempt at poetry. She did, in fact, write more, and bore another baby the following year, who outlived her. Less tortured and more formulaic (and not inspired by personal feeling) is Letitia Elizabeth Landon's "The Little Shroud" (1832) in which a grieving mother, having buried the last of several children, is confronted by the ghost of the dead child, who chides her for weeping at his grave. He cannot sleep, he says, because her tears have soaked his shroud. She heeds his complaint, and on another night the child visits her bedside to tell her that he now sleeps peacefully because her tears have dried. Landon was a prolific poet whose sentimental treatment of themes such as this one was popular with Victorian readers.

Romantic poets, sharing a love of childhood and a love of nature, placed their tributes to dead children in the natural world. John Clare, who wrote many of his best poems while in an asylum (between 1842 and 1864), writes in "The Dying Child" (1873) that a child cannot die in the springtime, when the world, too, is in its infancy. A sentimental evocation of the child's closeness to the natural world, Clare's poem does not approach the poignancy of poems written as a personal response to loss, such as William Wordsworth's "Surprised by Joy" (1813–1814) about the death of his daughter Catherine a few years earlier at the age of four. The joy with which the poem opens is connected with the natural world: a sudden recognition of beauty, attached to "love, faithful love," makes the poet instinctively turn to his little daughter to "share the transport," only to realize achingly that she is not beside him, but "deep buried in the silent tomb." Wordsworth wonders how the ever-present sense of her loss could even briefly have lapsed, allowing him the joy of momentarily thinking she is still there, a joy suddenly cut short by the rush of remembrance that she is gone forever. How could he have forgotten? That moment is like losing her all over again. The poem perfectly describes a habit of mind all too familiar to those who have grieved.

William Wordsworth's four "Lucy Poems" and a fifth, written at the same time (in 1899, when Wordsworth and his sister Dorothy were in

68

Germany), titled "A Slumber Did My Spirit Seal," also take up the theme of early death. The identity of Lucy, or if she was even a real woman, has never been discovered, but she is thought to be Margaret Hutchinson, the younger sister of Wordsworth's wife, Mary. Margaret died in 1796 at the age of twenty-four. "Strange Fits of Passion" details the poet's dream that as he rides toward Lucy's cottage, the moon is sinking closer and closer to it, foreshadowing her untimely death. In "She Dwelt Among the Untrodden Ways," Lucy has died, a country girl, unknown and apparently unmourned except by the poet. In her quiet and unnoticed beauty Lucy was "A violet by a mossy stone/Half hidden from the eye!" "Three Years She Grew in Sun and Shower" describes how, at the age of three, Lucy is adopted by Nature, who will form the child into a woman of the natural world, empowered by Nature's "law and impulse" and graced with an innate sympathy with animals, the sky, and storms. Lucy's life with Nature is cut short, however, and the poet is left with the "quiet scene" and only the "memory of what has been,/And never more will be."

Many of the poems on this theme achieve their power through postponing until the end the shock that the death is that of a child. One of the most moving accounts of a brother's death is Seamus Heaney's "Mid-Term Break" (1966). The title is deliberately misleading, suggesting a holiday and a release from school. But in the first stanza (seven three-line stanzas lead to the concluding single line) the poet is isolated in the sick bay at boarding school, listening for the bells that will "knell" the end of classes. He is driven home, and in the second stanza encounters his father in tears—an unusual sight, because he was usually unaffected by funerals. The reader is thus prepared for a serious death in the family. The third stanza finds the baby immune to the grief around him, cooing and laughing while visitors murmur sympathy and his mother sighs, beyond tears. Who has died? In stanza five an ambulance brings the bandaged body, still unidentified. The last two stanzas take us to the next morning and the gradual revelation of the victim. Heaney goes upstairs to the room where the body lies, surrounded by candles and snowdrops: the time of year is February, the beginning of the year; and he has not seen "him" for six weeks, since the Christmas holidays. In the last stanza we learn in the briefest of descriptions that the brother was killed—instantly and cleanly—by a car, the only mark a bruise on his head. His brother lies in a four-foot box, a detail repeated with chilling effect in the last—single—line: "A four-foot box, a foot for every year." The schoolboy's point of view—Heaney was not quite thirteen when his brother died—finely depicts his acute sense of the unique perspective of the young person, partly detached, partly intensely involved, in his family's first tragedy, both a public and private event.

THE DEATH OF POET FRIENDS

Famous among poems about the death of young adults are those by poets lamenting the loss of poet friends. John Milton's "Lycidas" (1637), an elegy for his friend Edward King, became a standard for later poets to follow. King, a fellow student of Milton's at Cambridge, had drowned on his way to Ireland in 1637. Milton distanced himself from a personal expression of grief by writing the poem as a Pastoral elegy, a classical form that placed the poet and his subject in the bucolic world of the shepherd. The form also allowed Milton to go beyond a personal tribute to King and consider the Puritan theme of temptation and the idea of rewards and punishments. The poem falls into three movements that culminate in three successive triumphs. The first begins with a simple shepherd's lament for the loss of his fellow shepherd and singer (poet), and an appeal to the Muses to sing his praises. The speaker describes their life as shepherds and the effect on the natural world of Lycidas's untimely death, when he was taken as unexpectedly as "frost to flowers that their gay wardrobe wear/When first the white-thorn blows." He chastises the deities of nature for failing to protect Lycidas, but then remembers that not even the great poet Orpheus was protected from death. The speaker then queries the point of studying and working hard as a poet when life is so uncertain; fame is the poet's only inspiration, but fame may never be achieved if an early death strikes. This temptation to renounce a poetic career and live for the day instead is resisted at the end of the first movement, however. Phoebus (or Apollo, the god of poetic inspiration) reminds the speaker that fame is earned not on earth, but in heaven. That will be the poet's reward.

In the second movement the speaker returns to the drowning and queries why Lycidas was allowed to drown when bad shepherds are still flourishing. Here we find Milton's famous attack on hypocritical, greedy clergymen, spoken by "the pilot of the Galilean lake" (usually interpreted as Saint Peter, but the reference could also be to Christ), when he compares the gentle shepherd Lycidas to those who "for their bellies' sake/ Creep and intrude and climb into the fold!" Such false clergy are "blind mouths" who steal from those they should be feeding. This section is sometimes seen as a digression that is not integrated into the elegy, but Milton here is dealing with punishment as opposed to reward. The bad shepherds will find their just desserts in heaven as surely as Lycidas will be rewarded.

The third movement seeks a more satisfying solace for the speaker than those offered in the first and second movements. Here the poem returns to the motif of water, remembering that Lycidas drowned and was therefore deprived of a Christian burial; the speaker's "frail thoughts dally with false surmise" in imagining the flowers of the field adorning his dead friend's hearse. Then he recalls that his friend's "bones are hurled" somewhere in the depths of the wild ocean. The only true consolation comes at the end of the poem, when the treacherous sea becomes redemptive and live-giving water. Just as the sun sinks into the ocean to rise again, so Lycidas, "sunk low," is "mounted high" by the power of Christ, who "walked the waves." Lycidas is not dead, but instead is transformed to become "the genius of the shore,/In thy large recompense": the true reward. The speaker is also rewarded in achieving this understanding of Lycidas's death and rebirth. The poem ends with the "uncouth" speaker's return to daily life, now that he has accepted the loss of his friend: "Tomorrow to fresh woods, and pastures new."

In "To the Memory of Mr. Oldham" (1684), John Dryden wrote about the death at the age of thirty of the poet John Oldham. Writing in the heroic couplets of the time, Dryden approaches Oldham's death in the manner of the Augustan Age in which both poets wrote. His concern is not with religious matters but with the waste of Oldham's talent. He acknowledges their similarity of interests; both were satirists, and "knaves and fools we both abhorred alike." Twenty-two years older than Oldham, Dryden ponders how the years would have improved his talent had he lived. He might have learned more about metrics and rhythm, subjects that do not come naturally, but Dryden argues that satire does not require smoothness and, in fact, is better without it. His "generous fruits" would only have mellowed and would have lost their sharp wit. Bidding farewell to him in the words of the Roman poet Catullus to his brother, Dryden recalls the opening image of "Lycidas" in placing laurels and ivy around the young poet's head. But Christian consolation evades Dryden as the poem ends with acceptance that "fate and gloomy night encompass thee around."

When John Keats died in Rome in February 1821, at the age of twenty-six, Percy Bysshe Shelley wrote "Adonais" in his memory. Like Milton in "Lycidas," Shelley distances himself from emotion by casting his subject in mythical terms, in this case Adonis, the handsome young man of Greek mythology with whom Aphrodite fell in love and who was killed by a wild boar. The poem is written in fifty-five Spenserian stanzas (nine lines rhyming ababbcbcc, the first eight lines being iambic pentameter and the ninth an alexandrine, or iambic hexameter). Shelley thought that Keats's death had been brought about by a particularly hostile review of Keats's "Endymion" in 1818 (Keats actually died of tuberculosis), and their hatred of critics is evident in the poem. It begins, as does "Lycidas," with an appeal to nature and the Muses to mourn for the dead poet. Shelley calls upon Urania, the Muse of astronomy but also another name for Venus, who had loved Adonis. In the poem, Urania is the mother (and therefore inspiration) of the poet, who failed to protect him from the deadly shaft of the critic's harsh words. After recalling the death of

Milton, Shelley likens Adonais (Keats) to a fragile flower, broken before it could fully bloom. He concentrates on the young poet's silent sleep, his voice forever mute. Stanzas nine to fourteen describe Keats's dreams, the creatures of his imagination that now gather around his dead form, weeping over it. Shelley's images here are of frost and coldness, particularly the turning of water into ice: their tears are "frozen," and a moist kiss is stilled when "the damp death/Quenched its caress upon his icy lips." Stanzas fifteen to twenty return to nature's grief, seen in the mourning of other figures from Greek mythology such as Echo, and in the return of spring, so incompatible with Adonais's death. In stanza twenty-two Shelley urges Urania to arise and bring healing to the world's grief for the lost poet, her son. Urania visits Adonais's tomb, where her presence momentarily banishes death as she speaks to Adonais and denounces the critics who, like "herded wolves," "obscene ravens," and "vultures," preyed on the innocent poet whose "godlike mind" eclipsed them as the sun brings forth but also obliterates the "ephemeral insect." Adonais is then visited by other contemporary poets, portrayed in the poem as shepherds (another echo of "Lycidas"): Byron, Thomas Moore, and Shelley himself, a "frail Form . . . A pardlike Spirit beautiful and swift." Shelley's powerlessness in the face of his grief is finely described in stanza thirty-two as "a dying lamp, a falling shower,/A breaking billow;—even while we speak/Is it not broken? On the withering flower/The killing sun smiles brightly: on a cheek/The life can burn in blood, even while the heart may break." Foremost in the group mourning the dead poet is Leigh Hunt, close friend and fellow poet of Keats and Shelley. Stanzas thirty-six to thirty-eight castigate the critic of "Endymion" again, reminding him that he will be punished by "Remorse and Self-contempt" and "Hot Shame."

Stanza thirty-nine shifts the theme from grief and anger to consolation with the words "Peace, peace! He is not dead, he doth not sleep—/He hath awakened from the dream of life." Shelley accords to Keats an immortality that has freed him from the cares and inconstancy of mortal life. Keats is now a part of the Platonic ideal, "made one with Nature," where his voice can now be heard in the nightingale's song (a reference to Keats's "Ode to a Nightingale" [1819]); he is a part of the ideal beauty of which Shelley wrote in his "Hymn to Intellectual Beauty" (1816); he has joined other poets who died young—Chatterton, Sidney, and Lucan. Finally, Shelley urges mourners to go to Rome, where Keats is buried beside Shelley's three-year-old son, William. There they will learn from Adonais (as Milton learned from the dead Lycidas) that the dead are freed from "cold mortality": "The soul of Adonais, like a star,/Beacons from the abode where the Eternal are." Ironically, the closing stanza speaks of Keats's spirit luring Shelley's soul, like a ship, out to sea, where he is "borne darkly, fearfully, afar." Just one year later, Shelley drowned in a storm off the coast of Italy and was buried near him in the cemetery in Rome.

Alfred, Lord Tennyson's most famous poem, "In Memoriam A.H.H." (1850), similarly moves from grief and pain to recognition of immortality, but Tennyson's consolation is Christian rather than Platonic. He, too, was writing about the loss of a poet friend, and there are parallels with Milton and Edward King. Arthur Henry Hallam and Tennyson were fellow students at Cambridge; they both wrote poetry and belonged to a group of young intellectuals, the Apostles. Tennyson came from a family troubled by alcoholism, poverty, and mental illness, so Hallam's enthusiastic support of him as a friend and poet was invaluable; Hallam was also engaged to Tennyson's sister Emily. When he died suddenly in Vienna, while traveling in Europe with his father, Tennyson was devastated. He began writing "In Memoriam A.H.H." almost at once, and he continued to work on it for the next seventeen years, jotting down stanzas in a butcher's account book as they came to him. The order in which the eighty sections now appear, which recreates the months and years following Hallam's death, was decided upon in 1850 when the poem was published, and was not the order in which they were written. Each of the 131 sections, framed by a prologue and an epilogue, contains a varied number of four-line stanzas—which Tennyson called "Elegies"—consisting of four lines of iambic tetrameter rhyming abba. This circular form, which opens out in the middle two lines and circles back on itself in the fourth, is characteristic of the philosophic movement of the poem's search for the meaning of life and death. Rather than moving forward in a logical argument, the poem fluctuates between hope and despair, consolation and loss. In Section 12, when Tennyson awaits the return of Hallam's body in a ship, he compares his grief to a "circle moaning in the air:/'Is this the end? Is this the end?' " The circle closes near the end of the poem when, through Christian faith, Tennyson accepts Hallam's immortality: "I prosper, circled with thy voice;/I shall not lose thee tho' I die." The ebb and flow movement of the four lines is characteristic of Tennyson and suggests the influence of the sea, a powerful metaphor in many of his poems, especially those that deal with death.

"In Memoriam A.H.H." is a complex poem that considers many themes, so discussions of it will be found in the Christmas poems section and also the Immortality section. Here we are concerned with Tennyson's response to the loss of his best friend at the age of twenty-two. Many of the images recall earlier poems about the loss of a young person. The second section, for instance, speaks movingly of the pain of contemplating Arthur's body lying in the churchyard, his bones entwined by the roots of the old yew tree growing above: "Thy fibres net the dreamless head,/Thy roots are wrapped about the bones." In Section 7, Tennyson is standing outside Hallam's house in the early morning, unable to sleep and devastated by the gulf that has formed between the living and the dead. In an echo of the angel's words at the empty tomb of Christ, Tennyson writes, "He is not here; but far away," suggesting Tennyson's acute sense of his friend's absence. In a clever enjambment, however, the second phrase is seen to refer not just to Hallam but to Tennyson's surroundings: "He is not here; but far away/The noise of life begins again. . . ." Tennyson's despair is evident in the last two lines, when "ghastly through the drizzling rain/On the bald street breaks the blank day." Sections 9 to 20 describe Hallam's body being brought home from Trieste. As Tennyson pictures the ship bringing his friend back to England, his fear of a shipwreck recalls Milton's distress that King's body was lost at sea. Tennyson fears that Hallam's hands, "so often clasped in mine,/Should toss with tangle and with shells." The body arrives safely, however, and is transported in a horse-drawn hearse across England for burial in the family vault in a small twelfth-century church at Clevedon, Avon, on the west coast.

Much of "In Memoriam A.H.H." speaks movingly of the pain of the physical loss of a loved one. Tennyson recalls the times spent with Arthur and tries to conjure up his face and his voice. Section 87, for example, describes their Cambridge days, and in Section 89 he remembers Hallam's visit to Tennyson's home at Somersby. The holding of hands becomes a motif that expresses the physical loss of his friend as the poem ebbs and flows between pain and resignation, doubt and faith. The turning point occurs in Section 95, when Tennyson describes an evening at Somersby. He is sitting alone in the middle of the night, re-reading Hallam's letters, when suddenly he has a mystical sense of Hallam's presence: "And all at once it seemed at last/The living soul was flashed on mine." After this recognition of Hallam's immortality, Tennyson begins to describe him in spiritual rather than physical terms, and in Section 129 he becomes a part of a divine love: "Known and unknown, human, divine;/Sweet human hand and lips and eye;/Dear heavenly friend that canst not die,/Mine, mine, forever, ever mine."

Not many poets have written about their own early demise. The most famous short-lived poet was Keats, whose death by tuberculosis was foreseen and lamented in many of his poems whose themes place them in other sections of this book. (See, for example, "Ode to a Nightingale," "Bright star, would I were stedfast as thou art" [1819] and "When I have fears that I may cease to be" [1818].) One poem written under peculiar circumstances was Chidiock Tichborne's "On the Eve of His Execution," written on September 19, 1586, the day before his barbarous disemboweling for conspiring to murder Queen Elizabeth I and restore Roman Catholicism. In each line of the three six-line stanzas, an antithesis is formed between hope and despair, youth and death, each stanza culminating in the line "And now I live, and now my life is done." The poignancy of Tichborne's short life (the date of his birth is uncertain, but he was probably twenty-eight when he died) is startlingly realized in his stark, monosyllabic metaphors—"My feast of joy is but a dish of pain,/ My crop of corn is but a field of tares . . . My fruit is fallen, yet my leaves are green . . . My thread is cut and yet it is not spun . . . I sought my death and found it in my womb."

From parents seeking consolation for the death of their children, to poets grieving the early loss of talented friends, or fearing their own early deaths, writers on this theme have helped many readers understand and accept these most painful of losses. They also remind us that even when the death of children was much more commonplace than it is today, it was never any easier to bear.

ᘓᘏᗀᘐᗕ

"On My First Daughter," Ben Jonson
 NAEL-1
"Upon a Child" ("Here a pretty baby lies"), Robert Herrick
 TrGrPo-1
"Requiescat," Oscar Wilde
 TrGrPo-2
"On My First Son," Ben Jonson
 NAEL-1; OAEL-1; OBEV; SB; TFi
"Epitaph on S.P., a Child of Queen Elizabeth's Chapel," Ben Jonson
 NAEL-1; OAEL-1; OBEV; TFi
"Maternity," Alice Meynell
 OxBSP
"For a Child Born Dead," Elizabeth Jennings
 AIW
"On the Death of My First and Dearest Child, Hector Philips," Katherine Philips
 NAEL-1
"The Little Shroud," Letitia Elizabeth Landon
 NAEL-2
"The Dying Child," John Clare
 TrGrPo-2
"Surprised by Joy," William Wordsworth

NAEL-2; OAEL-2; TFi

"A Slumber Did My Spirit Seal," William Wordsworth

    ImPo; NAEL-2; OAEL-2; TFi

"Strange Fits of Passion," William Wordsworth

    NAEL-2; OAEL-2; TFi

"She Dwelt Among the Untrodden Ways," William Wordsworth

    ImPo; NAEL-2; OAEL-2; TFi

"Three Years She Grew in Sun and Shower," William Wordsworth

    NAEL-2; OAEL-2; TFi

"Mid-Term Break," Seamus Heaney

    NoP

"Lycidas," John Milton

    ImPo; NAEL-1; OAEL-1; OBEV; SB; TFi; TrGrPo-1

"To the Memory of Mr. Oldham," John Dryden

    BL; NAEL-1; OAEL-1; OBEV; TFi

"Adonais," Percy Bysshe Shelley

    ImPo; NAEL-2; OAEL-2; TFi; TrGrPo-2

"In Memoriam A.H.H.," Alfred, Lord Tennyson

    BAVP; NAEL-2; OAEL-2

"On the Eve of His Execution" ("My prime of youth is but a frost of cares"), Chidiock Tichborne

    OBEV; OAEL-1; SB; TFi; TrGrPo-1

Duty

The theme of duty arises mainly in connection with war: the duty of the soldier, the sailor, or the airman to his country and his superiors who issue his orders. That dying in the line of duty is an honorable death is an ancient assumption sometimes upheld, sometimes challenged, by the poets. Duty in the more general sense of living thoughtfully and self-lessly is the subject of William Wordsworth's "Ode to Duty" (1804), a somewhat uncharacteristic poem that Wordsworth said was modeled on Thomas Gray's "Ode to Adversity" (1742), which in turn had been a translation of the Roman poet Horace's "Ode to Fortune." The poem is prefaced by a Latin quotation from the Roman writer Seneca, who said that he acted morally because he had been trained to do so, not because of conscious intent. Wordsworth addresses Duty as the "Daughter of the Voice of God," and the poem examines the relationship between the poet and his sense of duty, which he likens to conscience in calling it "a light to guide." Wordsworth maintains Duty as a general concept throughout the poem; he does not identify the object of duty as being one's family or country, but he echoes Milton in seeing the object as fulfilling the will of God, which in youth we often choose to ignore. Duty is the imposing of restrictions on the sometimes selfish freedom of youth, and he describes his own desire to curb "this unchartered freedom" in favor of the greater benefits of being guided by Duty. The poem ends with a plea for humility: "Give unto me, made lowly wise [a phrase from Milton],/The spirit of self-sacrifice." Recalling the biblical statement that the truth shall make you free, Wordsworth sees the passage from youth to maturity as an acceptance that the "Bondman," Duty, shall "in the light of truth" paradoxically give us greater freedom than we think we have when we rely only "upon the genial sense of youth."

In "Quiet Work" (1849), the Victorian poet Matthew Arnold also considers duty in its more general sense of seriousness of purpose and the living of a meaningful life. Addressing Nature, Arnold asks to learn from her one lesson about two duties: the duty of "toil unsevered from tranquillity," and the duty of "labor, that in lasting fruit outgrows/Far noisier schemes." Contrasting Nature's silent but constant work with the "fitful uproar" and "vain turmoil" that often accompanies man's labors, Arnold speaks of the serenity that accompanies true duty. The poem expresses the truth of Christ's message in Matthew 6:28: "Consider the lilies of the field, how they grow; they toil not, neither do they spin."

The theme of duty goes back to the earliest stories of human achievement and is often associated with loyalty to a cause or an ideal that takes precedence over one's own personal safety or interest. Duty as loyalty is a quality often revered in animals, and the old ballad "The Three Ravens" (known in the Scottish version as "The Twa Corbies") celebrates the loyalty of a slain knight's hounds and hawks, who guard his body against predatory birds (the ravens who narrate most of the poem as they look down from their perch). The knight is finally delivered from the ravens' clutches by a pregnant doe, who loses her own life in carrying him to a grave, where she buries him. In some versions, the deer becomes a "lady full of woe."

The ballad "Sir Patrick Spens" also celebrates duty. In this famous narrative poem, a Scottish king requests the services of a good sailor, and Sir Patrick Spens is recommended to him. Sir Patrick receives the king's letter while walking on the shore, and the impending tragedy is foretold by his response to it: at first he laughs at the folly of the order, but immediately "the tear blinded his ee" because he knows he has to fulfill the request. The simplicity of the ballad form draws attention to the conflict when Sir Patrick calls his noble men together and one of them tells him of an omen that foretells disaster. The actual loss of the ship is not recorded; we learn of the tragedy in the stark image of the sailors' hats floating on the ocean swell. The poem closes with the Scottish nobles' wives fruitlessly awaiting their return, while out at sea "there lies guid Sir Patrick Spens,/Wi' the Scots lords at his feet."

Felicia Dorothea Hemans used the ballad stanza form of "Sir Patrick Spens" (four-line stanzas alternating iambic tetrameters with iambic trimeters) in her famous poem "Casabianca" (1826). This narrative poem, which begins "The boy stood on the burning deck/Whence all but he had fled," was once a favorite recital piece for schoolchildren because of its regular rhythm, abab rhyme scheme, and dramatic story. According to Hemans, Casabianca was a thirteen-year-old boy who sailed with his father, the admiral of the *Orient*, to the Battle of the Nile, at which Nelson destroyed the French fleet in 1798. The poem tells the story of the boy's strict adherence to duty, having promised his father that he would not leave his post without permission. The ship in flames and all around him dying or dead, the boy repeatedly calls to his father for leave to quit his post, but his father, "faint in death below," does not hear his cries and is wholly "unconscious of his son." Gradually the flames engulf the ship until an explosion destroys all. The poignancy of the boy's plight is evident in Hemans's telling: she sees his devotion to the promise made to his father as both childlike and heroic, foolish but also admirable: "The noblest thing which perish'd there/Was that young faithful heart!" The poem achieves a dramatic intensity as the flames swirl around the desperate boy, whose cries are lost in the storm while he "look'd from that lone post of death/In still, yet brave despair."

Much more critical of foolish orders, such as those handed down by Sir Patrick's king and Casabianca's father, is Alfred, Lord Tennyson's famous defense of the British soldiers killed in "The Charge of the Light Brigade" (1854). During the Crimean War, a British cavalry brigade was ordered to attack what turned out to be a heavily armed Russian unit during the Battle of Balaklava. Of the "noble six hundred" sent out, only 150 returned. The mismanagement of the Crimean War was already a subject of public outcry (hundreds of British soldiers died from inadequate clothing and food during the winter of 1854–1855), so Tennyson was taking up the popular attack on the administration of the war when he glorified the loyal soldiers, sent to their deaths because of their duty as soldiers:

> Was there a man dismayed?
> Not though the soldier knew
>   Someone had blundered.
> Theirs not to make reply.
> Theirs not to reason why,
> Theirs but to do and die.

The driving dactylic meter of Tennyson's poem ("Cannon to right of them,/Cannon to left of them/Cannon behind them/Volleyed and thundered") has made it one of the most famous of poems championing the lowly private who in every war has been at the mercy of his superiors' "blunders."

Ivor Gurney, who fought in World War I, took up the theme of duty in "The Silent One" (1954). The speaker is a soldier who does not follow his comrade over the barbed wire that separates the trenches from the battlefield. The dutiful soldier, the "silent one" of the title, steps over the wires and is killed on them. But the speaker, willing to fight with his comrades but not risk death alone, accepts that the wires are intact and therefore he is not required to advance. When an upper-class voice (an officer's) invites him to crawl through a hole, he replies politely "I'm afraid not, Sir." The poem both honors the soldier who died and recognizes that sometimes choices can be made. The speaker chooses to fight in the line of duty with his fellow soldiers, rather than making a futile gesture of heroism.

In "An Irish Airman Foresees His Death" (1919), William Butler Yeats offers an even more equivocal view of duty. The pilot's statement—sixteen lines rhymed as four quatrains of abab, cdcd rhyme—rejects notions of heroism, patriotism, or the desire for glory. He is driven, he says, not by duty or law, by adulation or challenge, but rather by a "lonely impulse of delight." The airman sees his past life as "a waste of breath," so his future life and his death are also meaningless. Yeats deliberately undermines the accepted view of the heroic serviceman acting out of a strong sense of duty to his country and his neighbors. The airman is alone in the clouds, unconnected to the authorities who sent him or the people for whose protection he risks his life.

∾⌒⋀⌒∾

"Ode to Duty," William Wordsworth
    ImPo; NAEL-2; OAEL-2
"Quiet Work," Matthew Arnold
    TrGrPo-2
"The Three Ravens" ("The Twa Corbies"), anonymous
    NAEL-1; OAEL-1; OBEV; SB; TFi; TrGrPo-1
"Sir Patrick Spens," anonymous
    ImPo; NAEL-1; OAEL-1; OBEV; SB; TFi
"Casabianca," Felicia Dorothea Hemans
    BAVP; NAEL-2
"The Charge of the Light Brigade," Alfred, Lord Tennyson
    BAVP; NAEL-2; OBEV; TFi
"The Silent One," Ivor Gurney
    NAEL-2; SB
"An Irish Airman Foresees His Death," William Butler Yeats
    TFi

Fame and Ambition

❧⟡❧

The quest for fame has nearly always been seen as a double-edged sword. Ambition—the desire to better oneself, to make full use of one's talents—is surely a noble human aspiration. But uncontrolled ambition and the craving for fame has throughout history been seen as ultimately destructive. Unfortunately, simple ambition can quickly grow into an obsession for power; success breeds success, and power corrupts as it grows. Drama is the main vehicle for the study of the overly ambitious: most of Shakespeare's tragic heroes are driven by overweening ambition, and the epitome of the type is Faust, who sells his soul to obtain superhuman power. Faust's miserable end, tumbling and vainly screaming into the pit of hell, is the most graphic of the falls that await the overly ambitious. The theme is thus closely related to pride or "hubris," the first of the seven deadly sins and the most important of the vices depicted in Greek tragedy. It is also akin to vanity, against which we are warned by the preacher in Ecclesiastes. Even the quest for knowledge, Faust's original ambition, can be dangerous, as the preacher tells us: "For in much wisdom is much grief: and he that increaseth knowledge increaseth sorrow." This section discusses poems that focus on the quest for political, literary, or athletic glory.

One of the most powerful admonitions against the ambition of rulers is found in the seventeenth-century dramatist James Shirley's play *Ajax and Ulysses* (1659). "The Glories of Our Blood and State" was said to have been sung to King Charles I (who was beheaded by parliament) and served as a warning to Oliver Cromwell, the leader of the commonwealth that succeeded Charles's rule. Similar in theme to the poems that remind us that death comes to all, regardless of station, the poem warns, "there is no armor against fate;/Death lays his icy hand on kings." The proud ruler is reminded to "boast no more your mighty deeds"; only the actions of just men will "blossom in their dust." Shirley takes up the theme again in a poem from his play *Cupid and Death* (1653). "Victorious Men of Earth" addresses powerful rulers to remind them that although their "triumphs reach as far/As night or day" they will "mingle with forgotten ashes" one day. Death comes, not just through famine, plague, and war, but also through heartbreaking smiles and kisses.

Percy Bysshe Shelley's sonnet "Ozymandias" (1817) neatly encapsulates the fate of the overly ambitious Egyptian pharaoh, Ramses II, who ruled over a vast and successful empire from 1292–1225 B.C. Ramses is still renowned for restoring the Sphinx and building huge monuments and statues—empire-building that Shelley brilliantly satirizes in his sonnet. The speaker has met a traveler who has returned from Egypt and describes in his own words his finding of a statue to Ozymandias. The statue would have been imposing at one time, but now it is just two "vast . . . legs of stone." The head, shattered, lies nearby on the sand, and the expression on the face—a "frown/And wrinkled lip, and sneer of cold command"—reveals the discrepancy between Ozymandias's pride and the sculptor's disdain for his vanity. The sculptor's hand "mocked" the face it was modeling, while the proud ruler's heart "fed" on the adulation he craved. In the sestet of the sonnet, Ozymandias is allowed to speak for himself through the words on the pedestal: "My name is Ozymandias, king of kings:/Look on my works, ye Mighty, and despair!" Ozymandias's desperate desire to reign after his death, to remain the most powerful man in the world, is wonderfully mocked by the last three lines, where the proud man's boast is humbled. A short sentence— "Nothing beside remains"—starkly contrasts Ozymandias's grandiose words. The twelfth line flows seamlessly into the last two lines, depicting the empty desert on which no sign of Ozymandias's "works" can be seen: "Round the decay/Of that colossal wreck, boundless and bare/The lone and level sands stretch far away." The alliteration of soft sounds prepares for the final image of a landscape, empty of man's influence, fading into infinity. The proud pharaoh's boast is reduced to a rubble of stones.

John Keats wrote movingly about coming to terms with his impending early death and the cutting short of his poetic career in "When I have fears that I may cease to be" (1818). Like a Shakespearean sonnet, the poem moves through three quatrains, each one looking into a future that will not be realized. In the first, he likens his poetry to "full ripened grain" that will never be garnered into "high piled books." In the second he finds in the night sky "huge cloudy symbols of a high romance" that he will never be able to translate into poetry. The third quatrain addresses a lover, knowing that "the fairy power/Of unreflecting love" is not to be. As in Shakespeare's sonnets, however, the poem turns in the closing couplet. Here Keats, standing alone "on the shore/Of the wide world," escapes from personal regret to a sense of his oneness with that greater world, hinted at in the "night's starred face" of the second quatrain. In the presence of something more powerful, "love and fame to nothingness do sink."

Keats rejects ambition and the quest for fame in his "Ode on Indolence" (1819). Taking as his epigraph Christ's reminder to consider the lilies who "toil not, neither do they spin," he chooses idleness over the attractions of poetry, ambition, and love. Keats described the origin of the poem in a letter to his brother on March 19, 1819: "This morning I am in a sort of temper indolent and supremely careless. . . . Neither Poetry, nor Ambition, nor Love have any alertness of countenance as they pass by me: they seem rather like three figures on a Greek vase." In the poem the three figures appear three times before the poet's mind "like figures on a marble urn." Keats recognizes poetry, ambition, and love as the central inspirations of his life, but in his present mood, he turns them away. The only male figure is Ambition, which "springs/From a man's little heart's short fever-fit." Here Keats gives himself over to a dreamlike state (similar to that described in his "Ode to a Nightingale" [1819]), in which the poet's soul retreats from the world of fame and glory into a silent lethargy; his soul "had been a lawn besprinkled o'er/With flowers, and stirring shades, and baffled beams." In a letter written three months later, Keats speaks of this time, when he felt "averse to writing; both from the overpowering idea of our dead poets and from abatement of my love of fame." Despite this rejection of love, ambition, and poetry, however, the poet still seeks expression of his feelings in an ode.

George Gordon, Lord Byron, a contemporary of Keats, also affects to reject fame in "Stanzas Written on the Road between Florence and Pisa" (1821). Byron, like Burns, has achieved fame partly as a lover of women, and in this ironic poem he rejects fame as an empty goal. Rather than pursuing fame, we must enjoy youth, "the days of our glory." The poem is written in anapests, which give it a light-hearted tone as he explains that if he ever "took delight" in fame it was only so that a woman would find him more worthy; in the woman's admiring glance he found glory. Byron's colorful life somewhat belied these sentiments.

The pursuit of glory in athletics is the subject of A. E. Housman's "To an Athlete Dying Young" (1896). Addressing the young athlete, who is brought home shoulder-high twice—after winning a race, and then in his coffin—the poet tells him, with some irony, that he is a "smart lad" to die at the height of his fame. If he had lived, it would only have been to see his records broken and his name forgotten. Among the dead he can still be admired for his prowess. But Housman's tone is gently ironic, offering the poem as a bittersweet consolation to the young runner. Housman is also critical of the adoring townspeople, who encourage the young to be ambitious but who are quick to look for new heroes to worship.

A rather different response to the human desire for fame is offered in Philip Larkin's "At Grass" (1950). The poet is watching two race horses grazing in a field and ponders whether they remember their glory days, fifteen years ago, when crowds flocked to see them compete. But the horses "shake their heads." Their names live on in the almanacs, but the horses themselves are free from the regret that Housman's young athlete did not live to endure. The horses, untroubled by human ambition, "stand at ease." Natural creatures, they are content to be "at grass." The poem neatly contrasts the serenity of the horses with the anxiety surrounding the human competitiveness that made the horses race. The poem ends wistfully, the owners and gamblers replaced by men who truly appreciate the horses for their natural, unforced beauty: the groom and his boy who now care for them in the evening of their lives.

❧

"The Glories of our Blood and State," James Shirley
>ImPo; TrGrPo-1

"Victorious Men of Earth," James Shirley
>TrGrPo-1

"Ozymandias," Percy Bysshe Shelley
>ImPo; NAEL-2; OAEL-2; OBEV; TFi; TrGrPo-2

"When I have fears that I may cease to be," John Keats
>ImPo; NAEL-2; OAEL-2; TFi; TrGrPo-2

"Ode on Indolence," John Keats
>NAEL-2

"Stanzas Written on the Road between Florence and Pisa," Lord Byron
>NAEL-2

"To an Athlete Dying Young," A. E. Housman
>NAEL-2; TFi

"At Grass," Philip Larkin
>OBEV

Family Relations

⧉⧈⧉

Parents and children, brothers and sisters—family relations are a rich source of comedy and tragedy and are thus more often the subject of drama than of poetry. Poems that explore the complex relationship between husbands and wives will be found in this survey in the Marriage section.

The closest poetic form to drama is the ballad, particularly the ones that tell a story through dialogue such as the tragic "Edward." Here a son has to explain to his mother why his sword is dripping with blood. He evades the question at first, claiming he has killed his hawk and his horse. Finally he confesses that it is his father he has killed, and that he will have to leave his family and seek exile. The climax occurs at the end of the poem, when the boy curses his mother for ordering him to kill his father.

Not many poets have written about their children—unless they die young (a subject large enough to merit its own section in this survey). Anna Letitia Barbauld, a champion of education and a popular eighteenth-century writer for children, addresses her unborn child in "To a Little Invisible Being Who Is Expected Soon to Become Visible" (1795?). The title suggests the reverence with which Barbauld approaches the mystery of her child's being. She compares the child to a seed, ready to blossom into the world of sense and sound, and she is impatient for the fruition of much planning and waiting. The poem neatly describes the relationship between a woman and her unborn child: "part of herself, yet to herself unknown . . . the stranger guest,/Fed with her life through many a tedious moon." The baby is urged, "Haste, little captive, burst thy prison doors!" so that the woman may indulge her pent-up love for this mysterious child.

Writing in the previous century, Anne Bradstreet describes her eight children in "In Reference to Her Children, 23 June, 1656." Bradstreet's extended metaphor is of a mother bird whose five oldest chicks have flown from the nest to marry or study. The "empty nest" metaphor is commonplace now, but Bradstreet makes delightful use of it in describing her sense that mothers never cease to worry about their offspring; in fact, when they leave the nest the mother worries more. Her birds face all sorts of threats in the big world—snares, boys with stones, hawks—and their mother is powerless now to protect them. Finally, she speaks of her remaining years, when as a poet she will continue to sing. Her hope is that once she is gone her children will speak of her to the baby birds in their own nests.

Perhaps the best-loved poem written by a father for his child is Samuel Taylor Coleridge's "Frost at Midnight" (1798), discussed in this survey in the Nature section. Similar in method to Coleridge's beautiful poem is William Butler Yeats's address to his infant daughter, "A Prayer for My Daughter," written in 1919 when the poet was fifty-three and Anne was a few weeks old. As in Coleridge's poem, the poet is alone with his sleeping infant, and the weather outside (a frosty night for Coleridge, a storm for Yeats) inspires the poet to meditate on his tiny child's future. As in "The Second Coming," which Yeats had recently completed, the poet here fears that the world is descending into chaos, symbolized by the storm raging outside. The poem quickly shifts from a meditative reflection (as in Coleridge's poem) to a more cynical concern for the little girl's future. Yeats hopes that she will be beautiful, but not so beautiful that she loses innate compassion, and worse, marries a fool as happened to Helen of Troy and Aphrodite. Rather than beauty, he wishes her courtesy and charm, which will help her attract a worthier mate. If she is as cheerful as a linnet and as firmly rooted as a laurel tree, she will be much happier than intellectual women who give themselves over to hatred, like Maud Gonne, who traded her accomplishments for cynicism and rancor. Finally, he hopes that she will marry a man from the aristocracy so that she may enjoy the established privilege of the great country houses such as Yeats's beloved Coole Park, home of Lady Gregory. Whereas Coleridge returns to the fine images of the frost on the window at the end of his poem, Yeats loses touch with his opening symbol of the storm of modern life, against whose buffets he offers only marriage into a landed family.

Another view of family relations is offered in poems about parents, written by adult poets about their memories of childhood. Many of these are written in response to the death of a parent (and will therefore be found in the Death section of this survey). D. H. Lawrence wrote a series of poems specifically about his mother's death, but "Piano" (1918) is his best-known evocation of nostalgic memories of childhood, inspired by a woman playing the piano and singing as his mother used to do. Hearing the familiar sound, he is swept back to his childhood when he would sit under the piano, finding comfort in touching his mother's foot as she played. The flood of emotion that overwhelms the poet through the flood of sound from the piano is echoed in the long, flowing lines that cascade over into the next ones. Always an emotional writer, Lawrence here allows the wave of sadness for his lost mother and lost childhood to engulf him; however much he tries to resist giving in to nostalgia, the "insidious" music "betrays" him and he is swept back to winter Sundays, the piano guiding them through the hymns. Even though the pianist switches into a rousing appassionato, quite out of keeping with the poet's memories of the quiet winter parlor, Lawrence is caught up in the "glamour" of childhood. His adulthood is swept away in the memories and he "weep[s] like a child for the past."

A rather different view of parents, based in the imagination rather than in memory, is offered by Charles Causley in "Eden Rock" (1988). The poem describes a vision of the speaker's parents, in their early twenties, perhaps shortly after their marriage and not long before the birth of the child who, now an adult, is imagining them picnicking near Eden Rock. Memories from his childhood help to create the portrait—his father in his Irish tweed suit, his father's terrier, Jack, a young dog again. The poem begins with the thought that his parents are waiting for him in this idyllic spot, and after the picnic the poet appears, his position as observer now established on the other side of a river. His parents beckon to him while his father skips stones; they reassure him that crossing over to them is easier than it looks, and the poem ends with the poet's enigmatic statement that he "had not thought that it would be like this." What is "it"? What is "this"? The poem seems to be a vision of the afterlife, a reunion with his parents, who are now eternally young beneath a sunlit sky.

Philip Larkin writes poignantly of the passing of family life in "Home Is So Sad" (1958). The house he describes is personified as withered and bereft, now that its owners have grown up and moved away. The house remains as it was when they last lived in it, a silent witness to what might have been. It has no one to please, no will to return to its original glory when the youthful hopes of its owners enlivened it. In an implied metaphor from a child's game, the hopes that were thrown so optimistically have all long ago missed their mark. The past of the house and its owners are movingly rendered in the contents of the still house: "The music in the piano stool. That vase."

❧❧❧

"Edward," anonymous
    OBEV; TFi; TrGrPo-1

"To a Little Invisible Being Who Is Expected Soon to Become Visible," Anna Letitia Barbauld

    ECP; NAEL-2

"In Reference to Her Children, 23 June, 1656," Anne Bradstreet

    SB

"A Prayer for My Daughter," William Butler Yeats

    NAEL-2; TFi

"Piano," D. H. Lawrence

    NAEL-2; OAEL-2; TFi

"Eden Rock," Charles Causley

    SB

"Home Is So Sad," Philip Larkin

    OxBSP

Freedom and Captivity

ברויינטם

The earliest poem by a known author in the English language on the theme of freedom is the sixteen-line poem titled "Freedom" from "The Bruce," a fourteenth-century epic by the Scottish poet and archdeacon John Barbour. Without defining it, Barbour succinctly and elegantly describes freedom as the condition without which no other comforts can be possible; freedom "all solace to man gives,/He lives at ease that freely lives."

Later poems take up the theme in terms of prison rather than feudalism. One of the best loved of the Cavalier poems is Richard Lovelace's "To Althea from Prison," written when Lovelace was imprisoned in 1642 for supporting the traditional powers of the monarchy rather than parliament. His witty response to captivity juxtaposes three forms of enslavement to freedom, but each is a paradox. He is captivated by Althea, but as he lies "tangled in her hair/And fetter'd to her eye" he actually enjoys more liberty than the birds. Stanza two accords more freedom to the wine drinker than to the "fishes that tipple in the deep." In the third, the Cavalier finds liberty in outspokenly singing the virtues of his king—the cause of his imprisonment in the first place—liberty greater than that of the "enlarged winds that curl the flood." The fourth stanza begins with the now-famous lines, "Stone walls do not a prison make,/Nor iron bars a cage." If his heart and soul have liberty, only an angel has more freedom than he.

Emily Brontë was drawn to the same notion of the freeing of the soul while the body is held captive in "The Prisoner: A Fragment" (1845), from the poems written by Emily and her sister Anne about an imaginary land called Gondal. The poem is a conversation between the narrator, in whose father's dungeon they are speaking, the jailer, and the prisoner, a beautiful woman. When she tells them that their chains will not long hold her, the jailer presumes she is expecting mercy from his master and laughingly tells her that while the master may appear mild, his soul is "hard as hardest flint." The prisoner replies scornfully that she will be freed by death, a freedom that she already enjoys every night in a spiritual vision in which "the invisible, The Unseen its truth reveals." The most effective section of the poem describes the woman's despair each morning as the recognition of her captive state gradually returns:

> Oh, dreadful is the check—intense the agony
> When the ear begins to hear and the eye begins to see;
> When the pulse begins to throb, the brain to think again,
> The soul to feel the flesh and the flesh to feel the chain!

The poem concludes with the speaker's sense that death will soon free the woman from his father's fetters.

In 1895 Oscar Wilde was sentenced to two years of hard labor for homosexual offenses, and he described his impressions of prison in "The Ballad of Reading Gaol," written in France in 1898. The poem centers on a man sentenced to hanging, whom Wilde saw regularly in the prison compound until the man's sentence was carried out. Although he never spoke to the condemned man, the poem suggests that he felt an affinity with him. "Yet each man kills the thing he loves," declares Wilde, but those who kill by look, word, or kiss do not die for it even though their crime is just as great. Isolated from Wilde and the others, who watch him with fascination, the condemned man still finds solace and comfort in the living world of sky, air, and tree within the prison yard: "With open mouth he drank the sun/As though it had been wine!" After he has gone, Wilde thinks of himself and the dead man as "two doomed ships that pass in storm," unable to speak to each other but united in their transgressions. "A prison wall was round us both,/Two outcast men we were:/The world had thrust us from its heart,/And God from out His care." Wilde adopts the rhythm of the traditional ballad (alternating iambic tetrameter and iambic trimeter lines), creating a driving, forceful cadence that contributes to his sense of the alienation of all convicts from human society.

Political rather than personal freedom was the subject of many poems of the Romantic movement, inspired by the democratic ideals of the French Revolution of 1789. An earlier influence on the movement was Thomas Chatterton, best known now as the "marvellous Boy" of Wordsworth's poem "Resolution and Independence" (1802). The Romantic poets recognized his genius and lamented the short, destitute life of this obscure poet who committed suicide in 1770 at the age of seventeen. Chatterton's "Ode to Liberty" (from *Goddwyn* [1769]) personifies Freedom as a frightening female warrior, who, unmoved by fear or grief, engages in a bloody battle with Power and overcomes him. The poem ends with the figure of War, armed by Envy, unvanquished and brandishing "ten bloody arrows in his straining fist."

Shelley also personified Freedom in an "Ode to Liberty," written in 1820 in response to a Spanish uprising against Ferdinand VII, who had overturned the democratic reforms of 1812. Shelley, speaking the words of a voice that comes to him "out of the Deep," traces the development of liberty (which he identifies with the democratic movement) in human history, beginning with chaos, when anarchy reigned and no species knew freedom. Liberty first flourished in ancient Greece and Rome, to be banished by a thousand years of Christianity ("The Galilean serpent forth did creep,/And made thy world an undistinguishable heap"). Stanza nine sees the gradual return of liberty with "Saxon Alfred" in England and then the Renaissance in Italy, where "Art, which cannot die,/With divine wand traced on our earthly home/Fit imagery to pave heaven's everlasting dome." Martin Luther and John Milton take up the call of Liberty, now personified as a huntress whose "sunlike" arrows pierce the cloudy darkness of Error. Shelley elaborates this metaphor of battle, culminating in the violent overthrow of church and monarchy in the French Revolution and the rise of Napoleon, "The Anarch of thine own bewildered powers." Stanza thirteen finds England and Spain still seeking democracy. England, with a parliamentary system, can avoid revolution: "Her chains are threads of gold, she need but smile/And they dissolve." Spain's were "links of steel," but both will eventually throw off the yoke of tyranny. Germany, too, Shelley sees on the verge of revolution. The poem ends with a fierce attack on king and church—tyrants that make "life foul, cankerous, and abhorred." Once priests are vanquished, "human thoughts might kneel alone,/Each before the judgement-throne/Of its own aweless soul, or of the power unknown!" Art and science will be able to flourish, because liberty will always bring wisdom, justice, and love.

Lord Byron, a contemporary of Shelley, was also passionate about liberty, and he became a champion for freedom across the English Channel rather than at home. His long poem "The Prisoner of Chillon" (1816), a greatly embellished tribute to a Swiss patriot, Francois de Bonnivard (1496–?1570), was prefaced by the famous "Sonnet on Chillon." In the sonnet, Byron, like Lovelace, contrasts the "dayless gloom" and "cold pavement" of the famous prison on the shores of Lake Geneva with the unfettered thoughts of the prisoner. Liberty, the "eternal spirit of the chainless Mind" is "brightest in dungeons" because Bonnivard's martyrdom inspires his countrymen to fight for freedom. Byron takes a more ironic view of fighting for freedom in his eight-line epigram "When a man hath no freedom to fight for at home" (1810). The altruistic soldier who volunteers to fight for another country gets "knocked on the head for his labors." All the same, he argues, it is noble to "battle for Freedom wherever you can,/And, if not shot or hanged, you'll get knighted." Sadly, Byron did not heed his own satirical advice: he joined a movement that was fighting for Greek independence and died of illness brought on by the harsh conditions in 1823. The Greeks still consider him a hero.

❦

"Freedom," John Barbour
> TrGrPo-1

"To Althea from Prison," Richard Lovelace
> BL; ImPo; NAEL-1; OBEV; TFi; TrGrPo-1

"The Prisoner: A Fragment," Emily Brontë
> BAVP; NAEL-2

"The Ballad of Reading Gaol," Oscar Wilde
> OAEL-2; OBEV; SB; TFi

"Ode to Liberty," Thomas Chatterton
> TrGrPo-1

"Ode to Liberty," Percy Bysshe Shelley
> not anthologized; available in editions of Shelley's poetry

"Sonnet on Chillon," Lord Byron
> TrGrPo-2

"When a man hath no freedom to fight for at home," Lord Byron
> NAEL-2; TrGrPo-2

The Golden Mean

◦━◠◠△◠◠━◦

The "golden mean" signifies the middle course between extremes, or moderation. As a principle to live by it was made popular by the Roman poet Horace in *Ode*, II. x, in which Horace advises us to make the golden mean (*aurea mediocritas*) our guide: do not seek great wealth because it is as prone to disaster as the tall pine and the high mountain (which suffer the severest weather). The Renaissance playwright Philip Massinger in *The Great Duke of Florence* (1627) urges us to avoid greatness. His duke, bemoaning his apparently favored state, declares, "Happy the golden mean!" In English poetry it was a favorite theme of the Renaissance and seventeenth century, where it was described as an educated, civilized way of life. Like the poems that favored the contemplative rather than the active life, these poems praise a life of seclusion in the country, surrounded by good books, fine wine, and congenial friends. John Pomfret's poem "The Choice" (1700) is the longest expression of the theme. Samuel Johnson in his *Lives of the English Poets* (1779–1781) praised Pomfret's portrait of the golden mean as "such a state as affords plenty and tranquillity, without exclusion of intellectual pleasures." The poems included in this section deal exclusively with describing such a moderate life, whereas poems in the Active and Contemplative Lives section contrast different ways of living that are often complemented by mood or personality.

The Renaissance poet Henry Howard, earl of Surrey, describes the golden mean in "My Friend, the Things That Do Attain" (1548), a translation of an epigram by the Latin poet Martial. The poem, four stanzas of four lines each, is arranged formally with a statement of intent, a colon, and a list of the requirements for a happy life, each item separated by semicolons so that the whole poem is actually one sentence. Surrey neatly dramatizes the balance required by the theme in the arrangement of ideas. Many lines are broken in half, balancing equal requirements of the happy life: "The fruitful ground; the quiet mind; . . . Without disease, the healthy life; . . . The mean diet, no dainty fare; . . . The faithful wife, without debate; . . . Neither wish death, nor fear his might." The keynote is contentment, neither striving for more nor living in want.

Moderation is the advice offered by another Renaissance poet, Sir Henry Wotton, in his "Character of a Happy Life" (1557). Like Surrey's poem, Wotton's exemplifies balance and good sense in its form, six four-line stanzas of regular iambic tetrameter, rhyming abab. Wotton had an active political career as an ambassador and diplomat, but his most famous poem rejects such a life in favor of retirement. True happiness, he says, comes from virtue—"honest thought . . . simple truth . . . rules of good . . . conscience"—not from the flattery of the world. The happy man prays for grace, not gifts, and finds contentment in "the harmless day/ With a well-chosen book or friend." Free from ambition and the fear of failure that accompanies it, the moderate man "having nothing, yet hath all."

Ben Jonson takes a different approach to the theme in a short poem, "Oak and Lily," from a collection entitled *Underwoods* (1740). Jonson compares ways of living to the growth of an oak tree or a lily, finding in the short-lived and delicate lily a better model than the bulky, long-lived oak. This delightful short lyric recommends the golden mean in its close, when Jonson suggests that "In small proportions we just beauties see;/ And in short measures life may perfect be." While he argues for smallness rather than moderation ("It is not growing like a tree/In bulk, doth make man better be;"), the poem reminds us of Horace's warning that the tall pine is prone to storms. Both poets resist the worldly admiration of size, strength, and might.

Richard Corbet, bishop of Oxford and Norwich, was a friend of Ben Jonson who, while not well known now, wrote a few memorable poems. "To His Son, Vincent" (1648), written for his three-year-old son, offers advice on living a moderate life. The tone is humorous ("Nor too much wealth, nor wit, come to thee,/So much of either may undo thee"), but the sentiments are genuine. He wishes the boy health rather than wealth, learning for its own sake, not for show, a friend at court to protect him rather than promote him, and peace rather than idleness. Finally, the father hopes that the three-year-old will retain his child's innocence.

Anne Finch's twelve-line poem "On Myself" (1769) answers those who call women the "weaker" sex. Finch replies that if God's design made her weaker, it also made her soul temperate, not attracted by extremes: "Pleasures, and praise, and plenty have with me/But their just value." She will seek them within the bounds of religion and reason; if they are denied, she is self-sufficient. The moderate soul is not buffeted by the winds of adversity that bring down the ambitious and mighty; rather, it finds contentment in all fortunes: "When in the sun, my wings can be displayed,/And in retirement, I can bless the shade." Anne Finch's "The Petition for an Absolute Retreat" (1713), discussed in the Active and Contemplative Lives section, also argues for the golden mean in modest living and congenial company.

"My Friend, the Things That Do Attain," Henry Howard, earl of Surrey
TrGrPo-1

"Character of a Happy Life," Sir Henry Wotton
OBEV; TrGrPo-1

"Oak and Lily" ("It is not growing like a tree"), Ben Jonson
ImPo; TrGrPo-1

"To His Son, Vincent," Richard Corbet
TrGrPo-1

"On Myself," Anne Finch
TrGrPo-1

Immortality

❧❦❧

Immortality is often a religious question, and the religious poems considered in this section (rather than the ones in "Religion") are those that are concerned specifically with immortality. The poems in "Time and Change" are also closely connected with this theme. But many other fine poems consider other ways of achieving immortality apart from the notion of eternal life with a creator. Most famous of these are Shakespeare's sonnets, many of which offer immortality to a loved one through the sonnet itself.

Shakespeare's Sonnet 18, the well-loved "Shall I compare thee to a summer's day?" (1609) turns on the perfect moderation of the loved one in comparison to the vagaries of summer weather, which is often too windy, too hot, or too fleeting. In the "eternal lines" of the poem, the beloved's beauty is offered a permanence not found in the seasons: "So long as men can breathe or eyes can see/So long lives this, and this gives life to thee." Sonnet 19, "Devouring Time, blunt thou the lion's paws," concludes in the same way but the poem is addressed to Time rather than the loved one, and the images are much more violent. The cruelty of Time's inexorable passing is reflected in the images Shakespeare chooses to be devoured: Time blunts the lion's paws and makes the earth, like a lioness, "devour her own sweet brood." Time causes the "fierce tiger's jaws" to give up the beast's "keen teeth," and even the phoenix, promised a life of 500 years according to legend, is "burn[ed] . . . in her blood" by all-devouring Time. From these images of destruction, all associated with violent death, the poem moves in the second quatrain to milder images of Time as "swift-footed," bringing about the short-lived seasons and the "fading sweets" of the world. In the third quatrain Time is seen at work on human life, and the image is of the wielder of a pen that is more like a knife as it carves wrinkles and lines into the beloved's face. Shakespeare forbids it this "heinous crime" because the handsome young man's face must become a pattern for later men (the "type" of biblical belief found in Sonnet 106). By the final couplet, Time, no longer "devouring," is reduced to "old," because even Time cannot prevent the sonnet from giving the young man eternal youth.

In Sonnet 55, "Not marble, nor the gilded monuments" (1609), the immortality of the poem becomes the topic from the first two lines. Contrasting the more obvious permanence of buildings and statues, erected to give immortality to the "princes" they memorialize, the sonnet declares that such marble will, in fact, not live as long as "this powerful rhyme." The next two lines reveal the audience to be the beloved who will be immortalized in the poem. While buildings decay and become ugly, "besmeared with sluttish time," the beloved will actually shine "more bright" in the sonnet, as time goes by. In the second quatrain, the stone monuments are beset not just by dirt but by war, and again the beloved is spared this fate because "the living record of your memory" is held fast in the poem. The third quatrain extends the immortality of the beloved to the readers of the poem; just as in Sonnet 18 immortality lasted only so long as "men can breathe or eyes can see," in Sonnet 55 Shakespeare imagines readers praising his beloved and therefore giving him life until the final judgment, when the beloved will be raised into new life. Again, the sonnet links immortality with typology when the beloved becomes a model for later lovers: "You live in this, and dwell in lovers' eyes."

Sonnet 65, "Since brass, nor stone, nor earth, nor boundless sea" (1609), takes up the same comparison of seemingly long-lasting things with fragile and mutable beauty, "whose action is no stronger than a flower." Each quatrain asks a variation of the same question: How can something as delicate as beauty withstand the ravages of time if rocks and "gates of steel" cannot? The couplet as usual supplies the answer: only the "miracle" of black ink on paper—the poem itself—can allow his love to "still shine bright."

In Sonnet 74, "But be contented when that fell arrest" (1609), Shakespeare talks to his beloved about his own death, and again, his immortality is assured through the poem. When death claims Shakespeare, like a bailiff arresting him with no chance of bail, the earth will receive his body but his spirit, "the better part," will be found in the poem. The third quatrain concentrates on the death of the body, the "dregs of life" that go to the worms and are not worth remembering. The couplet reminds the beloved that what is worthwhile is the spirit contained in the body, and that spirit is now contained in the poem and therefore "remains" with the reader.

Shakespeare's notion of immortality is founded in the immutability of art, and yet in *The Tempest* (c. 1610), a play often seen as his farewell to the stage and playwrighting, he speaks movingly of the fragility of human invention. Just as Prospero's masque, conjured up out of the mind of the magician, is suddenly "melted into air, into thin air," so the play itself is just a figment of Shakespeare's own imagination: the whole vision "shall dissolve,/And, like this insubstantial pageant faded,/Leave not a rack behind." The sonnets suggest that Shakespeare was acutely aware that the immortality of his poems and their subjects was dependent upon the vagaries of parchment and ink, and the preservation of those flimsy man-made articles. Prospero goes on to describe the fragility of human life: "We are such stuff/As dreams are made on, and our little life/Is rounded with a sleep." Where in a universe characterized by change can immortality be found?

Henry Vaughan supplies the answer to this question in his hauntingly beautiful visionary poems "The World" (1650) and "They Are All Gone into the World of Light!" (1655). "The World" opens with the famous lines, "I saw eternity the other night,/Like a great ring of pure and endless light,/All calm as it was bright." The rest of the poem elaborates the temporal world in which man dwells, the "vast shadow" of the lover, the statesman, and the miser who cherish the material pleasures of earthly existence. Like moles, we stumble about in a dark world that sharply contrasts the light of eternity. The statesman is "hung with weights and woe/Like a thick midnight fog." The poem takes up the theme of vanity as each of the lovers of earthly pleasures strives to make meaningful his shadowy world of temporal pleasures. In the final stanza the poet sees a few soaring up into the ring of eternity, and he wonders why most "prefer dark night/Before true light!" The answer comes with a reference to Revelation, that eternal life belongs to those who accept Christ as their savior. Finally, Vaughan quotes John 2:16–17, "the world passeth away, and the lusts thereof, but he that doth the will of God abideth forever."

In "They Are All Gone into the World of Light!" Vaughan again contrasts the dark world with the light of eternal life as he, left behind in the shadows, imagines those who have died before him inhabiting a world of bright, glittering air. A series of images describes the earth-bound poet's apprehension of the eternal world, coming to him in the memory of the dead, which "glows and glitters in [his] cloudy breast/Like stars upon some gloomy grove." The poet asks God, the "Father of eternal life," to "disperse these mists" that prevent him from fully seeing the eternal world: like an empty bird's nest, the world is the shell that tells him that the dead have flown to another, glorious realm.

Vaughan's contemporary Thomas Traherne, a clergyman, was never published in his lifetime, and when his manuscripts turned up 200 years later, the poems were at first thought to be by Vaughan. Like Vaughan's,

Traherne's poems express a mystical Christianity in which the poet makes concrete his childhood sense of the divine in the world. Perhaps most striking of Traherne's poems is "Shadows in the Water" (c. 1660–1670). Here he remembers how in "unexperienc'd Infancy" he would look into a stream and think that he was looking into a whole other world. The poem beautifully elaborates this watery vision of upside-down people, a parallel world to his own that he recognizes but cannot communicate with. But the child's mistake is "sweet" and the image of the child gazing into the pond becomes a metaphor for the biblical "looking through a glass darkly." The child's sense of closeness to this other world, recognition that the people in it are like him, as well as his knowledge that a thin barrier separates him utterly from it, is an emblem of our earthly apprehension of eternity:

> What can it mean?
> But that below the purling Stream
> Some unknown Joys there be
> Laid up in store for me;

William Wordsworth was one of many poets to see the child as having a clearer vision of the eternal world. "We Are Seven" (1798) describes a conversation the poet held with a small girl who includes her dead sister and brother in her family, even though they lie in the churchyard. The child includes them in her day and makes no distinction between these two, two others who are at sea, and two more who have moved away. No matter how much the poet wishes the child to count only her living siblings, she continues to reiterate "we are seven." Wordsworth more fully examines the child's unshakable sense of immortality in his famous "Ode: Intimations of Immortality from Recollections of Early Childhood" (1802–1804), in which he laments the loss of his childhood awareness of his connection to the divine. In a famous letter, written in 1843, Wordsworth described to a friend how as a child he would sometimes have to grab hold of a tree or wall to keep himself centered in the real world.

"Ode: Intimations of Immortality" embodies the central tenets of Romanticism in its championing of the child's innate closeness to the natural world through the imagination, and the loss of that closeness as the poet ages. But Wordsworth's theme is specifically his lifelong belief that this closeness is derived from the child's innate memory of a prior existence. In the first stanza, he describes how for the young Wordsworth the world "did seem/Apparelled in celestial light,/The glory and the freshness of a dream." The long last line—echoed in the tone of the concluding line of each of the eleven stanzas—regrets that the adult poet is no longer able to apprehend the light. Despite the adult's appreciation of the natural world, the poet is still painfully conscious that something is missing. At the end of stanza four he asks, "Whither is fled the visionary gleam?/Where is it now, the glory and the dream?" In stanza five, Wordsworth lays out his concept of the immortality of the soul from before birth (an idea that in his letter he notes is derived from Plato, but which he does not see as being at variance with Christian belief). The stanza has become one of the most famous literary statements in support of children at a time when the Puritanical view considered them as more prone to evil than adults ("Naturally vicious!" as Mr. Wopsle tells Pip in Charles Dickens's *Great Expectations*) and the Utilitarian view considered them as possessing no innate perceptions. The poem tells us that "trailing clouds of glory do we come/From God, who is our home." The stanza then describes the loss of this early memory of a prior existence: "Heaven lies about us in our infancy!" But soon "shades of the prisonhouse" close around the growing child; his imaginative connection with the natural world is gradually severed by real life and its responsibilities. The youth is still "Nature's Priest," capable of apprehending the divine in the world; but by adulthood he sees the vision "fade into the light of common day."

Wordsworth's tone is regretful as he moves from a recollection of his childhood vision of an immortal world to an adult's sense of the loss of that power. But it is not completely lost; "Though inland far we be,/Our Souls have sight of that immortal sea/Which brought us hither." The natural joy of the child has gone ("Though nothing can bring back the hour/Of splendour in the grass, of glory in the flower"), but it is replaced by a wiser and calmer adult sense of compassion for the suffering and pain of the real world. The "clouds of glory," though now only dimly remembered, still provide "the faith that looks through death,/In years that bring the philosophic mind." No other poem so succinctly contains the themes associated with the Romantic movement as Wordsworth's "Ode." While its subject is immortality, it is equally important as a poem about nature, children, and the imagination.

Another Romantic poet, John Keats, wrote about immortality in his sonnet "Bright star, would I were steadfast as thou art"(1819). Ever conscious that he had only a short time to live (his brother had already died of tuberculosis), Keats envies the immutability of the star, but he does not seek its lonely, distant, and eternal watching of the earth; rather, he wants to share its immortality while in the arms of his beloved. Keats lived for only one more year.

Emily Brontë also died of tuberculosis (at the age of thirty), and her last poem, "No Coward Soul is Mine" (1846) unequivocally demonstrates her strong faith in an afterlife. Bronte has no time for doubters, for the "unalterably vain" whose feeble creeds are "worthless as withered weeds,/Or idlest froth amid the boundless main." They have no sway with one whose faith is "anchored on/The steadfast rock of immortality." In the poem Brontë addresses the God within her heart who is eternal and thus gives her immortality also. Just as her mortal life has contained God, so "I, undying Life, have power in thee!"

Alfred, Lord Tennyson's long poem "In Memoriam A.H.H." is discussed in the Christmas, Death of the Young, and Religion sections, but its central concern is with the immortality of the soul. When Tennyson's college friend, fellow poet, and soul mate, Arthur Henry Hallam, suddenly died while traveling on the European continent, Tennyson was devastated. He wrote "Ulysses" (1833) as his immediate response to the loss (see "Active and Contemplative Lives"), but shortly after he began to write stanzas that over seventeen years became "In Memoriam A.H.H." Each stanza contains four lines rhymed abba, but the sections vary in the number of stanzas they contain. When Tennyson published the whole series in 1850, he reordered the stanzas into an elegy that moves through grief, black despair and loss, doubt, and questioning to a strong sense of Hallam's immortality through Christian belief. Doubt enters because of the scientific discoveries of the day, described in the well-known stanzas fifty-four to fifty-six. How is the immortality of the soul to be found when "Nature, red in tooth and claw" is "so careless of the single life"? How could he trust that love is "Creation's final law" when the recent findings of geologists have shown that the biblical account of time is incorrect and that species had once lived and had died out? What hope is there for the immortality of Hallam's "single life"? Tennyson's answer comes in stanza ninety-five, when after a family party he sits alone in the night, re-reading Hallam's letters. Suddenly, in a mystical experience he feels that Hallam is there: "And all at once it seemed at last/The living soul was flashed on mine." Although doubts followed, he felt that his own soul had entered an immortal world, and the poem then proceeds gently to replace the mortal Hallam, whose loss was so painful, with an immortal Hallam, who at the end of the poem "lives in God." Tennyson wrote of his experience in the garden as a trancelike state that affirmed for him that his "liebes Ich" (dear self) "will last for aeons of aeons."

Unwanted immortality is the subject of Tennyson's memorable dramatic monologue "Tithonus" (1833, revised in 1860), based on the harrowing Greek myth about a handsome Trojan prince. Eos, the goddess of the dawn, falls in love with Tithonus and persuades Zeus to grant him eternal life, but she forgets to request eternal youth as well. An ancient man, he shrivels and withers until, praying for release from his misery, he is turned into a grasshopper. The story particularly suited Tennyson's keen ear for the sounds of regret and loss, evident in so many of his poems. Tithonus, the speaker, is addressing Eos after all hope of reversing the gift is lost. The poem opens with a powerful contrast between the mortal world and Tithonus's plight:

The woods decay, the woods decay and fall,
The vapors weep their burthen to the ground.
Man comes and tills the field and lies beneath,
And after many a summer dies the swan.
Me only cruel immortality
Consumes; I wither slowly in thine arms,
Here at the quiet limit of the world.

The tone is quietly resigned, subdued, and muted like the old, old man who speaks of their past love and contrasts his shriveled, wrinkled form with her dewy freshness, which is renewed every morning as she wakes the earth. Many of Tennyson's poems share Tithonus's sense of a life that is not really life at all, of "Death in Life," as he describes it in "Tears, Idle Tears" (1847). Tithonus is as enclosed in his miserable state as Mariana in her moated grange or the Lady of Shalott in her tower. All are suspended in an eternal and hopeless present, longing for the end. Life without death is a tragic desire, wholly unlike life after death, the real meaning of immortality.

ʚↄ᷍ᔰↄɞ

Sonnet 18, "Shall I compare thee to a summer's day?" William Shakespeare

ImPo; NAEL-1; OAEL-1; OBEV; TFi; TrGrPo-1

Sonnet 19, "Devouring Time, blunt thou the lion's paws," William Shakespeare

ImPo; NAEL-1; OAEL-1; TrGrPo-1

Sonnet 55, "Not marble, nor the gilded monuments," William Shakespeare

ImPo; NAEL-1; OAEL-1; OBEV; TrGrPo-1

Sonnet 65, "Since brass, nor stone, nor earth, nor boundless sea," William Shakespeare

ImPo; NAEL-1; TFi

Sonnet 74, "But be contented when that fell arrest," William Shakespeare

NAEL-1

"The World," Henry Vaughan

ImPo; NAEL-1; OAEL-1; OBEV; TFi; TrGrPo-1

"They Are All Gone into the World of Light!" Henry Vaughan

BL; ImPo; NAEL-1; OAEL-1; OBEV; SB; TFi

"Shadows in the Water," Thomas Traherne

OAEL-1; SB

"We Are Seven," William Wordsworth

NAEL-2

"Ode: Intimations of Immortality from Recollections of Early Childhood," William Wordsworth

ImPo; NAEL-2; OAEL-2; OBEV; TFi; TrGrPo-2

"Bright star, would I were steadfast as thou art," John Keats

ImPo; NAEL-2; OAEL-2; TFi; TrGrPo-2

"No Coward Soul is Mine," Emily Brontë

BAVP; NAEL-2; OAEL-2

"In Memoriam A.H.H.," Alfred, Lord Tennyson

BAVP; NAEL-2

"Tithonus," Alfred, Lord Tennyson

BAVP; ImPo; NAEL-2; OAEL-2; OBEV

Industrialism and the City

෴

The distinction between peaceful, expansive, and settled country life and bustling, crowded city life has been the subject of literature from the time of the ancients (exemplified in Aesop's tale of the town mouse and the country mouse), long before the Industrial Revolution of the late eighteenth and nineteenth centuries gave rise to the modern city and its unique character. The contrast between city life and country life is one aspect of the Active and Contemplative Lives theme, as writers usually associated the active, social life with the city, and the solitary, contemplative life with the country. Playwrights loved to contrast the sophisticated city dweller and the country bumpkin, who would visit the town with mud still on his boots and lay himself open to ridicule for his coarse, rustic ways. The poets of the eighteenth century usually regarded the city as the source of inspiration and ideas; they loved the social exchange of the coffeehouses and salons. The country was pleasant for a brief retreat (and well-to-do Londoners all fled to Bath or their country estates from time to time), but life was lived in the bustle of the city. The Romantic poets, writing at the beginning of the Industrial Revolution, began the modern rejection of city life that Aesop's country mouse had exemplified so many centuries ago.

Long before the Industrial Revolution gave rise to the overcrowded, smoky cities of northern England, the brilliant eighteenth-century satirist Jonathan Swift revealed the ugly underside of sophisticated London in his apparent tribute to the city, "A Description of a City Shower" (1710). The title suggests a pleasant, refreshing interlude, but from the opening heroic couplet we are warned to "dread" this particular shower because, unlike its country counterpart, the city shower amplifies the dirt and squalor of the town. Always quick to notice the seedier side of life, Swift begins to catalog the inhabitants—animal and human—of London, and relates their miseries as the rain begins to fall. The shower is forecast in a general feeling of bad temper ("spleen") and aches and pains. Swift builds up his portrait in mock heroic terms, as though describing a battle, to make fun of his lowly subject. As the rain begins to fall, the poet is buffeted by wind and showered by dust from a careless maid's mop. As the rain increases so does the intensity of the imagery; a "flood comes down,/Threatening with deluge this devoted town." Londoners of all classes scurry for cover, from the "tucked-up semptstress" to the members of parliament, who forget their differences in their hurry to "save their wigs." The poem sweeps along with the rain as it courses down the overflowing kennels, or open gutters, taking the detritus of London with it: "Sweepings from butchers' stalls, dung, guts, and blood,/Drowned puppies, stinking sprats, all drenched in mud,/Dead cats, and turnip tops, come tumbling down the flood." The final vision suggests an apocalyptic sweeping away of the dirt and decay of a fallen human world, whose imperfections were always Swift's chief object of satire.

A companion piece to Swift's satiric "Description" is Mary Robinson's "London's Summer Morning" (c. 1795). One of the earliest of the Romantic poems to describe the sootiness and grime of London streets, Robinson's poem (forty-two lines of blank verse) recounts the coming to life of the city in the morning through the actions of the inhabitants: the "sooty chimney-boy, with dingy face," the "sleepy housemaid," the milkman, and the dustman. Like Swift, Robinson builds on the activities and noise as the city comes to life, piling up images of street traders, craftsmen, carriages, wagons—all the bustle and fever of the city. As in Swift's description, here a housemaid also "twirls the busy mop," throwing dust over the passersby. But as the sun rises, Robinson's city begins to glow rather than decay as shops open to display "gay merchandise," as alluring to the passersby as the pastries are to passing insects. As the morning sun heats the "sultry pavement," a hint of London's underside is seen in the old-clothes-man, shuffling along with his pilfered loot—all worthy to be painted in verse by the "poor poet" who "wakes from busy dreams" to this scene.

London just a year or two later is described by William Wordsworth in his sonnet "Composed upon Westminster Bridge, September 3, 1802," but Wordsworth's city is beautiful because it is very early morning, before the residents are astir. As a Romantic poet, Wordsworth rejected city life in favor of the wild beauty of the Lake District, but here he sees the sleeping city as a part of the natural world. He personifies it as a "mighty heart . . . lying still." From the bridge he sees the skyline of the city "all bright and glittering in the smokeless air." As the rising sun steeps the roofs in a golden glow, Wordsworth finds the city as calmly beautiful as any country scene. Only in the early dawn before the inhabitants emerge can the city be illumined as a living part of creation.

The Romantic poets more typically saw the city as exemplifying the misery and want that urban life and the Industrial Revolution brought to the working poor. William Blake was one of the first poets to draw attention to their plight. In "London" (1794), written about the same time as Robinson's and Wordsworth's descriptions, Blake paints a much more chilling portrait of the inhabitants of the city. As the poet "wander[s]" through the city streets, he sees in every face "marks of weakness, marks of woe." From the faces, the poet moves to the sounds of the city, and again the misery of the people is the subject of his startling images of an un-Christian world where the poor are neglected, exploited, and despised. The chimney-sweeper's cry "appalls" the "blackning Church," while the soldier's sigh "runs in blood down Palace walls." Most violent of all these perversions of human nature, twisted in the "mind-forg'd manacles" of modern city life, is the harlot's curse (venereal disease) that destroys both infant and marriage.

The best known of Blake's poems about the spiritual death of England through the Industrial Revolution appeared as the preface to his long poem *Milton* (c. 1804–1810) and is now known as "Jerusalem." As a song, set to music by Sir Hubert Parry, the poem has become famous as prom-goers thunder it out every year at the last night of the Promenade concerts in London. In the poem, Blake ponders the old legend that Christ and Joseph of Arimathea actually visited the "pleasant pastures" that formed the green north of ancient England. Could it be possible that Jerusalem had once stood on the site of the Industrial Revolution's new "dark satanic mills"? This image has become the keynote of protests against the ugliness and spiritual torture of industrial life, representing as it does both the factory mills and the atheistic, utilitarian view of human affairs that drove the early days of industrialism. Thomas Carlyle and Charles Dickens both took up the notion of industrial workers being ground in mills. Calling for weapons to fight the darkness (his sword will be his pen), the poet pledges to build Jerusalem again, "In England's green and pleasant land."

Blake's apocalyptic vision was not to be; instead, the mills of England spread over the northern landscape, blackening the air and grinding down the men, women, and children who labored long hours in the noise and gloom. We think of the "industrial novels" such as Dickens's *Hard Times* (1854) and Elizabeth Gaskell's *North and South* (1854–1855) as bringing to public attention the working conditions of factory hands in the mid-nineteenth century. But poets also turned their attention to the plight of the urban poor, as Blake did. The subject of Letitia E. Landon's "The Factory" (1835) is child labor. Landon sees the black cloud of industrial smoke hanging over the town, a symbol of the ungodly activities going on beneath it (John Ruskin was to pursue this symbol in his 1884 lecture "The Storm-Cloud of the Nineteenth Century"). The poem shares the theme of innocence and experience in its attack on the sacrifice of children on the altar of Gain. Landon decries the loss of childhood and its innocent joys as children's bodies and souls are crippled by factory work: "And here the order is reversed,/And infancy, like age,/Knows of existence but its worst,/One dull and darken'd page." England is cursed, she concludes, as long as its prosperity is founded upon the slavery of small children.

Landon's war cry was taken up in 1843, not just in Dickens's *A Christmas Carol* but also in Elizabeth Barrett Browning's "The Cry of the Children" and Thomas Hood's "The Song of the Shirt." Like Dickens, Browning was inspired by recent parliamentary reports on the appalling conditions under which young children worked in mines and factories. Addressing her "brothers" (recalling the "brotherhood of man" and her readers' responsibility as a society, especially for its weakest members), the poet draws their attention to the children who are dying every day in the country's mills, mines, and factories. The children speak for themselves in the poem, eloquently pleading their miserable existence that is such a perversion of natural childhood. The main metaphor, akin to the grinding of Blake's dark, satanic mills, is of the wheels of iron that move the coal and turn the factory machines, but that also mechanically destroy the bodies and souls of the young workers that operate them:

> Still, all day, the iron wheels go onward,
>   Grinding life down from its mark;
> And the children's souls, which God is calling sunward,
>   Spin on blindly in the dark.

Browning emphasizes the immense gulf between Christian principles and her "brothers' " practices, and the poem ends with a chilling reminder that England was becoming rich on the blood of its own children.

Thomas Hood's "The Song of the Shirt" was also based on contemporary reports that revealed the wholly inadequate wages and long working hours of women who took in sewing in London. Hood's work-worn woman sings "The Song of the Shirt" as she sews, and sews, and sews, all through the long night in her poor room, trying to earn enough money to feed herself and her children. Like the cries of the children in Browning's poem, the woman's song is a cry for justice in a supposedly Christian land. Like the children, she is separated from the natural world of clean air, flowers, and sunshine; like them, she is caught up in a mechanical process (the rhythm of the poem echoes the repetition of her needle) that is destroying her for someone else's gain:

> Work, work, work,
>   Like the Engine that works by Steam!

> A mere machine of iron and wood
> That toils for Mammon's sake—
> Without a brain to ponder and craze
> Or a heart to feel—and break!

A very different expression of the ugliness of industrial life is found in John Masefield's much-loved poem "Cargoes" (1910). Three stanzas center on three different times in history and list the cargoes carried by the ships of the time. The first two stanzas are exotic and wonderful, rich and evocative as ancient ships from faraway, palm-strewn lands bring luxurious woods, wines, coins, and gold. But in the last stanza, the ship of the Industrial Revolution is a "dirty British coaster." Far from exotic, its cargo is dull and ugly, containing both the raw materials of the factory age—coal, lead, railway ties—and its mundane products: "ironware, and cheap tin trays."

❦

"A Description of a City Shower," Jonathan Swift
    BL; ECP; NAEL-1; OAEL-1

"London's Summer Morning," Mary Robinson
    ECP; NAEL-2

"Composed upon Westminster Bridge, September 3, 1802," William Wordsworth
    ImPo; NAEL-2; OAEL-2; OBEV; TFi; TrGrPo-2

"London," William Blake
    NAEL-2; OAEL-2; OBEV; TFi

"Jerusalem" ("And did those feet in ancient time"), William Blake
    ImPo; NAEL-2; OAEL-2; OBEV; TFi; TrGrPo-1

"The Factory," Letitia E. Landon
    BAVP

"The Cry of the Children," Elizabeth Barrett Browning
    BAVP; NAEL-2

"The Song of the Shirt," Thomas Hood
    BAVP

"Cargoes," John Masefield
    SB; TFi

Innocence and Experience

තිරිරිර

The contrasting ideas of innocence and experience are most commonly associated with the Romantic movement—William Blake and William Wordsworth in particular. The Romantic poets believed that children were more spiritually aware and more simply moral than adults because their imaginations had not been curbed by institutional thinking. The Romantics were responding to two views of children that were widely held in the eighteenth century, both antithetical to them. Rationalists like John Locke held that we come into the world with no innate perceptions (what the Romantics would call imagination), and thus education was all important. Until the child is educated and experienced, he has no contribution to make. Equally critical of children but from a different perspective were Puritanical Christians, whose belief in Original Sin led to the conviction that children come into the world in a state of sin and have to be educated (and disciplined) into righteousness. Romanticism, in response, held that experience (living in the everyday world, beset by human rules and narrow-minded conformity) deprives us of our imaginative, creative impulses and hardens us, if not into realists and cynics, at least into disappointed, materialistic adults too busy with "life" to appreciate the natural world and experience wonder and joy. The Romantics brought innocence as a virtue back into the real world. Christian belief had placed innocence in the Garden of Eden; Adam and Eve lost their innocence and were driven out of the Garden into the real world (of experience) because they desired (and received—by eating from the forbidden tree) knowledge of good and evil. The ancients also saw innocence as an early stage in mankind's development, a "Golden Age" long ago when men lived in harmony with nature and there was no evil. Such an innocent, utopian world is no longer attainable in these systems, but for many poets, childhood is a spiritual stage that resembles a pre-lapsarian world.

For some poets, childhood innocence implies a prior existence with God, a former blessed state that is remembered by the child and accounts for his recognition of the divine in the world. Wordsworth's "Ode: Intimations of Immortality" (1802–1804) describes the gradual loss of this innocence in the real world of experience, described as the "prison-house" that closes around the growing child. Because Wordsworth saw immortality as the central idea in his poem, it is discussed in that section of this survey although it is equally concerned with the shift from innocence to experience. The notion of pre-existence was described earlier, however, in Henry Vaughan's "The Retreat." Vaughan, a doctor, devotional poet, and follower of George Herbert, sees his childhood as heaven on earth, when he still could see God's face. As a child, he saw "shadows of eternity" in the natural world. Now in his "second race," or the world of adult experience, his innocent senses have been damaged by a willful desire to sin; he "taught" his tongue to belie his conscience, separating him from the divine world he once knew. He yearns to return to his earlier innocent state, where he recognized a union with God, but his "soul with too much stay/Is drunk, and staggers in the way." Only in death will he be able to return to the "white, celestial thought" of his unblemished birth.

Vaughan's contemporary, Thomas Traherne, a clergyman, wrote many poems that contrast the innocence of his childish understanding with his later knowledge of evil and suffering. "Wonder" (1903) depicts the child as an angel, whose understanding of the world is colored by an innocence that does not see "harsh, ragged objects . . . Oppressions, tears, and cries,/Sins, griefs, complaints, dissensions, weeping eyes. . . ." The child knows no envy or jealousy because others' wealth seems to belong to him. In the poem "Eden" (1903) it is "a learned and happy ignorance" that keeps the child from a knowledge of sin. To him, "all were brisk and living things . . . Yea, pure, and full of immortality." He compares the child's innocent state to that of Adam in the Garden of Eden. In "Childhood" (1903) he prefigures Wordsworth in finding that as an adult he can recapture the visions of his child's imagination.

The poet most often associated with innocence and experience is William Blake because he wrote a series of contrasting poems under those headings. In 1789 he published "Songs of Innocence," and in 1794 he reissued them with a complementary set of songs, titling the collection "Songs of Innocence and of Experience Showing the Two Contrary States of the Human Soul." Blake, therefore, was not associating innocence necessarily with childhood and experience with adulthood, as earlier poets had. Neither did he see innocence as an unqualifiedly better state; rather, he seemed to incorporate the biblical injunction "When I was a child, I spoke as a child, I understood as a child, I thought as a child: but when I became a man, I put away childish things." In a poem that he wrote as a preface to the "Songs" he suggests that childhood innocence is also a kind of ignorance that leads the child into following blindly the thoughts of others. Experience, he says, can sometimes teach us to free ourselves from restrictions and think imaginatively.

The "Songs of Innocence" are prefaced by a short poem, "Introduction," explaining how they were inspired by the request of a child. The poet is "Piping down the valleys wild/Piping songs of pleasant glee," when he encounters the child sitting on a cloud, who asks him to write the songs down "in a book that all may read." The act of doing so is contrasted with the simplicity of the child because in turning his reed into a pen, the poet "stain'd the water clear." The songs are, thus, intended for children, as are the "Songs of Experience," and many of them are narrated by children or echo the rhythms of nursery rhymes. This simplicity has not prevented them from becoming some of the most written-about poems in the English language. Like the poems of Robert Frost, many of the songs are deceptively simple, and critics have weighted them with meaning in response to Blake's own complex theological beliefs. There is only time in this study to draw attention to the best known of the songs, in particular those ones that have a counterpart in each section.

"The Lamb" is the most representative of innocence, and its counterpart is "The Tyger" in "Songs of Experience." The speaker of "The Lamb" is a child, addressing the lamb and asking it, like the child's catechism, if it knows its creator. The child answers the question for the lamb by telling it that both the child and the lamb are created by Christ, the Lamb of God, after whom both child and sheep are named. The poem very simply reminds the reader that Christ valued children for their innocence and vulnerability. One of the main themes of the "Songs of Innocence and of Experience" is that children are often the victims of adult neglect, and, even worse, religious hypocrisy. "The Lamb" emphatically identifies the innocent child with Christ as scapegoats (sacrificial victims) in societies driven by adult greed and ambition: "He is meek and he is mild,/He became a little child;/I a child and thou a lamb,/We are called by his name."

"The Tyger" is the companion poem in "Songs of Experience." Now the child's firm belief in Christ's compassion and love (the lamb recalling also the Twenty-third Psalm, and the idea of God as the shepherd who protects his flock) is replaced by a series of questions leading up to the eternal question: "Did he who made the Lamb make thee?" Just as the lamb embodies Christ's compassion, so the tiger represents a world that is not innocent, a world that is dangerous and arbitrarily cruel. Addressing the tiger, the speaker puts into words the thoughts of all who look at "nature red in tooth and claw" (as Tennyson phrased it in "In Memoriam: A.H.H" [1850]) and wonder how a loving God could create such ruthless cruelty: "Tyger! Tyger! burning bright,/In the forests of the night,/What immortal hand or eye/Could frame thy fearful symmetry?" Blake's fear of the mechanization brought about by the Industrial Revolution is evident in the language he uses about the tiger. The tiger is created from fire by a blacksmith god (like Haephestus), working with hammer, anvil, and furnace. The tiger is frightening but he is also vital and fascinating; he *is* created by the God who made the gentle lamb, and the counterpoise of the two poems is typical of Blake's sense that life is composed of such seemingly antithetical forces, the submissive and the aggressive. The illustrations that Blake drew for the poems points to this harmony of opposites: his view of "The Lamb" depicts the surrounding trees as somewhat forbidding and restrictive, whereas his tiger is a big, friendly pussy cat. Both are states of consciousness and both are necessary to a complete understanding of the divine.

"Holy Thursday" appears in both series of songs. In the "Songs of Innocence" version, the poem describes children from a charity school attending an Ascension Day service (thirty-nine days after Easter, and thus always a Thursday) at St. Paul's Cathedral in London. They are led by "grey headed beadles . . . with wands as white as snow," suggesting the authority and self-righteousness of the elders who were responsible for the welfare of orphan children. The children are "flowers," sitting "with radiance all their own," and "raising their innocent hands" as they raise their voices in thanksgiving while the "aged men, wise guardians" sit "beneath them" (the image suggesting the angelic purity of the children). The last line can be taken innocently, as the children would understand it, or ironically, as a comment on the self-righteous guardians: "Then cherish pity, lest you drive an angel from your door." Ironic or not, the last line suggests that the beadles look after the children out of self-interest. The long flowing lines of the "Songs of Innocence" version contrast strongly with the terse, abrupt lines of the counterpart in "Songs of Experience," also called "Holy Thursday." Like "The Tyger," the response depends on unanswered questions: how can so many children be poor in a land of plenty? How can Christians—at a church service—ignore the words of Christ himself and allow children to be fed "with cold and usurous hand"? In a "rich and fruitful land," why is it "eternal winter" for the children? How can English life be so contradictory, with poverty existing side by side with plenty?

"The Chimney Sweeper" also appears in both the "Innocence" and "Experience" sections. The narrator of the first is the little chimney sweeper himself, a boy whose mother has died and whose father has "sold" him into the slavery of chimney sweeping. As in the companion poems of the lamb and the tiger, the poem depends upon the contrast between whiteness and blackness to juxtapose the child sweep's innocence with the evil of the adults who exploit him. The child describes his friend, Tom Dacre, whose white lamblike curls are shaved off. The narrator comforts him with the thought that now at least his innocent head will not be spoiled by the chimney soot. The boy then tells the story of Tom's dream in which a multitude of young sweeps are released from their "coffins of black" by an angel, who leads them to a green place where they "wash in a river and shine in the Sun." The poem ends with the children's response to the angel's message that if they are good they will "have God for a father and never want joy." Tom awakes feeling "happy and warm," and the young narrator concludes with a homily that he would have heard often from the adults who exploit him in the name of Christianity: "So if all do their duty, they need not fear harm." The poem poignantly draws attention to the vulnerability of children. Even though the message comes to the child from an angel and not from an adult, the language is that of the religious hypocrite who used "duty" as a way of keeping the poor and dependent in their places. The poem thus suggests Blake's qualification that "innocence" can sometimes be a blind adherence to doctrines preached by those in power. The little sweeps had every need to "fear harm" when the adults responsible for them neglected their own duty.

The companion poem in "Songs of Experience" is shorter. As in the first poem, Blake plays on the childish lisping of the word "sweep," which becomes the poignant cry, " 'weep" in the child's mouth. And again, black and white are juxtaposed as the speaker encounters the child sweep—"a little black thing among the snow"—and converses with him. The child's response offers another view of the sweep's resignation to duty in the "Innocence" poem. His parents are at church, congratulating themselves on their child's happiness because he has made the best of his miserable state. Now they have "gone to praise God and his Priest and King,/Who made up a heaven of our misery." Blake's targets are frequently the established church (priest) and government (king), institutions that he condemned because they not only sanctioned the exploitation of children but even gloried in it, exemplifying it as God's will. This child, the child of experience, is much more conscious of adult hypocrisy. Whereas the innocent child accepted his servitude as duty, this child notes that the parents "think they have done me no injury." But his clothes are the "clothes of death," and his song "the notes of woe." Blake was ahead of his time in recognizing the death of the spirit of Christianity in the very idea of child labor. His war cry on their behalf would continue to echo throughout the nineteenth century in the poetry of Thomas Hood, Elizabeth Barrett Browning, and Letitia E. Landon (discussed in the Industrialism and the City section) and in the prose writings of Charles Dickens, Elizabeth Gaskell, Thomas Carlyle, and John Ruskin.

Like Blake, William Wordsworth is always associated with the theme of innocence and experience because he idealized childhood as a time of powerful imagination and natural spirituality. His "Ode: Intimations of Immortality" (1802–1804) has already been discussed as explaining his belief in the preexistence of the soul, thus accounting for the child's superior powers of intuition and perception. The short lyric "My Heart Leaps Up" (1802) also exemplifies Wordsworth's faith in the child. Although as an adult he is still stirred by the sight of a rainbow, his innate early response to it makes this later response possible. "The child is father of the man," he argues, because the child's intuition gives rise to any sense of the divine that the adult may have. "Natural piety" binds the adult to the child; the adult thus learns, not from experience, but from retaining childhood innocence. Wordworth's long autobiographical poem "The Prelude, or Growth of a Poet's Mind" (1850) worked on over many years, attempts to describe in "Book First" the rapture he felt as a child whose first consciousness dawned in the beautiful countryside of the Lake District. The poem seeks to explain how "natural piety" has bound the adult to this child and allowed him to retain the child's innocence, even though "so wide appears/The vacancy between me and those days. . . ." Wordsworth often wrote about the innocence of other children besides himself. In the sonnet "It is a beauteous evening, calm and free" (1802), for example, he describes walking by the sea at dusk with his young daughter Caroline. While the adult rhapsodizes over the beauty of the evening, the child seems "untouch'd by solemn thought." Wordsworth sees this as evidence that she does not need consciously to think of nature as containing God's spirit (the poet even has to use similes—the evening time is "quiet as a Nun/Breathless with adoration"). Rather, the child is at one with the divine spirit and lives within it.

A very popular evocation of childhood innocence is Dylan Thomas's "Fern Hill" (1946), a recollection of his summer holidays spent at his aunt's farm. Thomas captures more vividly than does Wordsworth the child's way of speaking (as he also does in his essay "A Child's Christmas in Wales" [1945]). The poem is songlike, with a lilting rhythm that brings to life the carefree summer days of childhood. Thomas fills the poem with concrete images that recreate the sights and sounds of the farm as they would appear to a child—a green child in a green and golden world of apple trees and sunshine. Quotations cannot do justice to the overall impression of this lyrical evocation of a child's world, so seamlessly does it flow from image to image, capturing the child's sense of timelessness and also connection to the natural world. As for Wordsworth and Blake, the memory for Thomas is of a time when the child sensed the divinity of the world in the pebbles of a stream, quite apart from the ritual and formality of adult religion. Only at the end of the poem do the "heedless ways" of the child give way to experience, when time overtakes him and leads him "out of grace." Thomas's metaphors for the world of experience are equally vivid, however: the shadowy haunt of swallows in the hayloft; the moon in the darkened sky. As an adult he recognizes how fleeting was the child's sense of freedom. The prison-house that Wordsworth saw closing around his boyhood (in "Intimations of Immortality") appears in "Fern Hill" as time's chains that held Thomas while he was both "green" but also "dying." The image finely encapsulates the poignancy of innocence and experience: only later, with the knowledge provided by experience, does the poet appreciate the gift of innocence.

໑ມໂຊ

"The Retreat," Henry Vaughan

   ImPo; NAEL-1; OAEL-1; OBEV; TFi; TrGrPo-1

"Wonder," Thomas Traherne

   ImPo; NAEL-1; OBEV; TrGrPo-1

"Eden," Thomas Traherne

   TrGrPo-1

"Childhood," Thomas Traherne

   TrGrPo-1

"The Lamb," William Blake

   ImPo; OAEL-2; NAEL-2; TFi; TrGrPo-1

"The Tyger," William Blake

   ImPo; NAEL-2; OAEL-2; OBEV; TFi; TrGrPo-1

"Holy Thursday" (two poems), William Blake

   NAEL-2; OAEL-2; TFi

"The Chimney Sweeper" (two poems), William Blake

   NAEL-2; OAEL-2; TFi

"My Heart Leaps Up," William Wordsworth

   ImPo; NAEL-2; OAEL-2; TFi; TrGrPo-2

"The Prelude or Growth of a Poet's Mind," "Book First," William Wordsworth

   NAEL-2; OAEL-2

"It is a beauteous evening, calm and free," William Wordsworth
ImPo; NAEl-2; OAEL-2; TFi; TrGrPo-2

"Fern Hill," Dylan Thomas
ImPo; NAEL-2; OAEL-2; SB; TFi; TrGrPo-2

Love

⊙ᢒᢙᢙᏐᠲᠣᢀ

Poetry is often called the language of love. More poems have been written on this theme than on any other, and many of the poems discussed under other themes in this survey—"Death," "Time," "*Carpe Diem*," and "Beauty," for example—are also love poems because poets are often concerned with these ideas because they love someone. Love, of course, is central to the Family Relations theme. The poems discussed in this section, however, are all expressions of what is often referred to as "romantic love," a theme that in British poetry has been strongly influenced by the erotic poetry of the Roman poet Ovid, the sonnets to Laura of the Italian poet Petrarch, and the courtly love tradition that began in eleventh-century France. In courtly love poems, a knight idealizes—in fact, worships—a beautiful but unattainable woman. He fights his battles as much to win her favor as to serve his king; he sees himself as her servant or slave, and he suffers agonies of body and soul (the "lovesick" hero) in his unrequited love for her. In contrast to centuries of marriage, where the husband was legally his wife's master, courtly love poems introduced the notion that the lover was slave to his mistress. Many love poems and songs follow such conventions, but others, especially in the last two centuries, have offered complex and powerful responses to "the battle of the sexes."

SEDUCTION POEMS

Poetry and song have traditionally been in the arsenal of the young man wanting to attract the attention of his intended. The language of poetry is often the language of seduction, glossing over the harsh realities of passion and steeping the man's intentions in the rosy glow of flattery and artifice. Sir John Suckling's "Why so pale and wan" (1638) is an ironic comment on the would-be seducer that pokes fun at the traditional view of the lover as pale and tongue-tied. The speaker chastises his audience, the nervous young man, reminding him that if healthy looks and a smooth tongue failed to win the lady, why does he think this show of misery will do so? Finally the speaker advises him to give up: "If of herself she will not love,/Nothing can make her:/The devil take her!"

Much more appealing to the female reader is Ben Jonson's delightful song, "To Celia" (1616). Addressing Celia herself, the poet opens with the justly famous

> Drink to me only with thine eyes,
>   And I will pledge with mine;
> Or leave a kiss but in the cup,
>   And I'll not look for wine.

The metaphor is elaborated in the next four lines, as the poet finds Celia's charms a more delightful drink for the soul than the nectar of the gods. The eroticism of the opening images continues in the second stanza when the poet tells Celia that he sent her a wreath of roses in the hope that her perfect nature would prevent it from withering. But when she returned it, it was infused not with the scent of roses but with the essence of Celia's incomparable perfume. Jonson neatly overturns the usual winning of the lady with a rose; now the lady wins the poet by sending him herself in place of the rose.

One of the most famous seduction or invitation poems is Christopher Marlowe's "The Passionate Shepherd to His Love" (1599). Based on the ancient Greek idea of the Golden Age, the poem (often set to music) recreates a pastoral paradise similar to the portrayals of innocence in the Innocence and Experience section. "Come live with me and be my love" is the celebrated opening line of the poem, which then paints an idyllic picture of the lovers enjoying a perfect life on a hillside, in perpetual Spring, surrounded by peaceful country life. "I will make thee beds of roses," promises the shepherd; she will be adorned with beautiful clothes fashioned from lambs' wool and "fair lined slippers," should winter intrude on their bliss. The poem ends where it began, importuning the lady that if she finds her mind moved by "these delights," "Then live with me and be my love."

The poem begged a response from the shepherdess, the most famous of which is Sir Walter Ralegh's "The Nymph's Reply to the Shepherd" (1600). Ralegh's speaker cleverly responds to each of the shepherd's promises, reminding him that we no longer live in the Golden Age where time stood still. "If all the world and love were young," she begins, referring to the notion that an idyllic world existed in the distant past (before the Fall in Christian terms). In our fallen world, where man is mortal, such a life is impossible. "Time drives the flocks from field to fold,/When rivers rage, and rocks grow cold." His "honey tongue" belongs to "fancy's spring," but inevitable is the coming of "sorrow's fall." Only if they could live in a world untouched by time might she be moved by the shepherd's invitation.

Another response to Marlowe's poem is John Donne's brilliant invitation poem "The Bait" (1633). As dean of St. Paul's Cathedral, Donne wrote many famous sermons and religious verses. But he is equally admired for his often erotic love poetry. As a metaphysical Donne delighted in describing physical love in spiritual terms. He also rejected the traditional metaphors for love (birds, roses, stars) for unconventional, often earthy ones. Donne's speaker borrows the shepherd's opening line, but then promises some "new" pleasures. The speaker imagines the woman swimming in a river, such a beautiful fish herself that the real fish will want to be caught by her. The metaphor expands through the poem as the speaker comically compares himself to bungling, coarse anglers, beset by cold water, sharp stones, and slimy weeds in their pursuit of fish. As they cast their artificial flies, the deceived fish rise to the bait. Here the poem shifts from the speaker as fisherman to the woman as fisherwoman; she needs no bait to attract fish (and the speaker), because she herself is alluring enough to catch them all. The woman is thus fishing for him, while she swims "amorously" in the "live bath" of the river.

John Donne's most ingenious seduction poem is "The Flea" (1633), a dramatic monologue in which we hear only the speaker's side of a conversation. But the setting is evident: the speaker and his intended are sitting together on a settee. A flea has bitten both of them, and the speaker sees in the bite a crafty way of seducing the lady. Look, he says, our blood is mingled in the flea's body and no harm has come from it—no "sin, or shame, or loss of maidenhead." Between the first and second stanzas the woman attempts to kill the flea, but the speaker stops her hand, ingeniously arguing that she would be killing all three of them. He elaborates his flea metaphor, finding its body now "our marriage bed and marriage temple." Despite the objections of her parents and herself, she is as good as married to him because her blood is mixed with his in the flea. Not falling for this line of reasoning, the woman kills the flea between the second and third stanzas, causing the man to pursue a new argument. She has claimed that killing the flea has done no harm to either of them, and the man turns this to advantage: just as she did not lose her life in killing the flea, she will lose no honor in yielding her virtue to him. An ingenious argument, but although we never hear from the woman directly, we know only too well what her response to his proposal will be.

Other seduction poems can be found in the *Carpe Diem* section of this survey, in which would-be lovers argue the brevity of life in seeking to persuade their "coy mistresses."

EROTIC LOVE

Erotic poems speak of love requited, desire fulfilled. While sexual desire is hinted at in many love poems, often love poetry (especially in the courtly love tradition) distances itself from the physical, praising the woman for her purity, or lamenting her firm refusal of sexual advances. Usually written by men, erotic poems indulge in lengthy and sensuous descriptions of the woman's body and the consummation of their love. They are often witty and ironic, following in the tradition of the Roman poet Ovid. Christopher Marlowe's "Hero and Leander" (1598) takes some liberties with the classic story about Leander's swimming of the Hellespont to visit his beloved Hero. John Donne's "Elegy 19. To His Mistress Going to Bed" (1669) is based upon Ovid's *Amores* (43 B.C.–A.D. 18) and is a famous address to a woman about to join the speaker in bed. The poem describes the removal of the woman's clothes and, when she is in bed, expresses his pleasure in "discovering" her body much as an explorer discovers a new continent. The speaker wittily describes her as "my America! My new-found-land." Thomas Carew's "A Rapture" (1640) is a similar address by an ardent young man to his lover, Celia. Carew takes up many of the images in Christopher Marlowe's "The Passionate Shepherd to His Love" (1600) and gives them the sexual connotation that is lacking in Marlowe's prelapsarian vision. The idyllic hillside with its sweet-smelling myrtle and bed of roses becomes the setting for the consummation of the lovers' desire. The idea of the lovers existing in an ideal natural world is employed to justify the relationship. There, "the hated name/Of husband, wife, lust, modest, chaste, or shame" are unknown; sex is glorified as natural and free, and the concept of "honor" is rejected as unnecessary and unnatural.

John Keats went to the stories of myth and fairy tale for his love poetry, which was written along with almost all his poetry in 1819. The previous year he had fallen in love with eighteen-year-old Fanny Brawne (Keats was twenty-four) and had become engaged to her; he had also lost his brother to tuberculosis and knew he was threatened with an early death. "The Eve of St. Agnes" is much more than just an erotic poem, being also a richly symbolic narrative set in medieval times. But its story line and imagery is of desire fulfilled. It was based upon the old legend that a young girl could dream of her future husband on January 20, the eve of the day celebrating Saint Agnes, patron saint of virgins who was martyred at the age of thirteen. Keats's poem tells the story of Madeline, who follows all the instructions handed down by old wives as she prepares for bed on St. Agnes' Eve. Unbeknownst to her, Porphyro, the man she loves (like Romeo and Juliet they belong to hostile families), knows the old story and plans to make use of it to seduce her. With the aid of Angela, an old retainer whom he cons into helping him, he hides in Madeline's room to watch her get ready for bed.

The poem depends for its effect on the use of strong contrasts, which reach a climax in the bedroom scene. Outside, the night is "bitter chill," and the old beadsman who is praying for the souls of the residents of the castle (his presence frames the poem) is numb with cold as he paces the freezing chapel with its statues of knights and ladies, who "may ache in icy hoods and mails." The old beadsman spends the night in frosty penance, awaiting his death. In the bedroom, in contrast, the lovers are only too warm and alive, shut out against the cold and the noise of the party in their isolated bower that is rich with sensuous detail. Porphyro covers a table with a red, gold, and black cloth and heaps succulent fruit and sweetmeats in silver dishes upon it to perfume the room as he sinks down beside Madeline's sleeping form. When at his urging she suddenly wakens from her dream of him and sees him in real life, she is for a moment suspended in a state between the two, and she finds the dream preferable because it suggests the immortality of art. The real Porphyro is "pallid, chill, and drear," and she fears he will die and leave her, whereas the dream Porphyro has "spiritual and clear" eyes and "looks immortal." Taking advantage of her innocence, Porphyro, "impassion'dfar/At these voluptuous accents," rapes Madeline by taking advantage of her girlish faith in the old legend. The consummation of their love occurs in this half-waking state, when "into her dream he melted, as the rose/Blendeth its odour with the violet." After this "solution sweet," Madeline fears that her lover will now desert her, but she flees with him into the storm, leaving behind the drunken revelers who have been carousing in the castle all night, a porter (asleep), a bloodhound (awake), and Angela and the beadsman, who both sink into their last sleep among the "ashes cold." The poem is rich in symbolism and it has attracted many interpretations, but the story line builds to the climax in Madeline's bedroom, which is one of the most sensual descriptions of seduction in English poetry.

The influence of Keats's poem can perhaps be traced in Alfred, Lord Tennyson's equally beautiful lyric "Now Sleeps the Crimson Petal" from "The Princess" (1847). Again, while not strictly an erotic poem (because it can be interpreted in different ways), the setting is a palace rich in sensual detail (and recalling also the story of the sleeping beauty) as the speaker and his lover awake to love. As the palace sinks into sleep ("Now sleeps the crimson petal, now the white"), the firefly and the lovers awake unto each other, in body and soul. The sexual imagery of the earth receiving the stars, as Danae received Zeus in a shower of gold, and a meteor sliding through the sky, a "shining furrow," is continued in the last stanza when a lily "folds . . . all her sweetness up,/And slips into the bosom of the lake." These images recall Keats's lover, Porphyro, who "arose,/Ethereal, flush'd, and like a throbbing star" and melted into Madeline's dream "as the rose/Blendeth its odour with the violet." Even the name Porphryo is repeated in Tennyson's lyric in the "porphyry font" that holds the sleeping goldfish. Finally, the speaker entreats the lover thus to "slip/Into my bosom and be lost in me." Like Madeline and Porphyro, Tennyson's lovers are united in a dream state that is neither sleeping nor waking. Few English poems have so successfully evoked the sensation of sleep overcoming consciousness, of the mind slipping away into dream. Tennyson's lyric seems to reenact Madeline's drifting off to sleep, ready to dream of her lover on St. Agnes' Eve.

THE CONSTANCY AND INCONSTANCY OF LOVERS

This favorite theme, especially of male poets, is mentioned by Captain Harville in Jane Austen's *Persuasion* (1818) as being the subject of every book he ever opened. "Songs and proverbs all talk of woman's fickleness," he declares to the heroine, Anne Elliot, who replies that as these works were all written by men, literature is an unreliable indication of female behavior. Certainly, Captain Harville is correct in finding many complaints about female inconstancy in British poetry, but the complaint is usually light-hearted, a recognized convention that is as much a practice piece as a serious statement of the poet's own situation. A companion theme is the constancy of the (usually male) lover, as in George Gascoigne's Renaissance sonnet "The Constancy of a Lover" (c. 1575). Here the poet tells the woman who rejected him that he will continue to love her. The poem moves through the constancy of his tongue, hand, and heart, all of which will remain faithful to his love. The poet does not berate the woman's fickleness; rather, he asserts his own constancy, body and soul.

Sir Thomas Wyatt was a courtier and diplomat in the court of Henry VIII who wrote many poems on this theme. In his sonnet "Divers doth use, as I have heard and know" (c. 1557) he compares his own sensible reaction to being rejected with the extreme emotions of other men in that sad position. The men of the first quatrain "mourn and wail"; those in the second hope to win over their fickle mistresses with words. In the third quatrain the speaker asserts that he will just accept that women often flirt and pretend a love they do not feel. Like Mozart, who declares in his opera *Così fan tutte* that "women are like that," the speaker declares "that often change does please a woman's mind." In "Madam, withouten many words," a similar speaker asks his mistress to be honest with him: if she seeks another man, fine—he will then be free to become his own man again.

One of Sir Thomas Wyatt's finest poems, "They Flee from Me," uses an extended but implied metaphor that compares fickle lovers to timid deer, a comparison that became popular in poetry for the poet's sense of women as skittish, nervous, and easily scared away. The first stanza refers to more than one creature who had approached the poet meekly, seeking "bread at my hand," but who now "range, . . . Busily seeking with a continual change." The second stanza speaks of one woman in particular who seduced the poet with her beauty and her wiles, only to leave him in the third stanza. His "gentleness" led only to her "strange fashion of forsaking." The poem charges the women with the cruelty that is traditionally associated with men. Here the women turn out not to be nervous and sensitive at all; rather, they pretend to be so in order to get the upper hand. The poet's gentility and good manners are returned with cruel deception. Wyatt lived at a time of considerable intrigue, plotting, and personal danger, and the poem has often been interpreted as referring generally to the backstabbing of court life rather than to the poet's relationships with women.

Wyatt wrote many other poems on the subject of unrequited or inconstant love. "Farewell, Love" (c. 1557) is a sonnet addressed to Love itself rather than to a mistress, renouncing its "baited hooks" that will no longer "tangle him." Rather, he will seek happiness in more steadfast and reliable occupations of the mind, as recommended by Plato and Seneca. Whereas he stumbled about "in blind error," loving where it was not returned, now he is renouncing love and tells it to "go trouble younger hearts." His final metaphor is a surprising one: no longer does he desire "rotten boughs to climb." The image suggests the often unexpected and painful shock of unrequited love, the disappointment as sharp and distressing as plunging to the ground while climbing a tree.

The metaphysical poet John Donne's love poetry is characterized by unusual, sometimes violent imagery and technique. In "Song" (1633) ("Go and catch a falling star"), a disappointed lover, urging his listener to accomplish various impossibilities and to travel for "ten thousand days and nights," dares the man to find in that time "a woman true, and fair." In the last stanza the cynical speaker tells his listener that even if he should find such a creature, by the time he has written to the speaker to tell him about her, she will have been unfaithful "to two, or three."

The speaker of John Donne's "The Indifferent" (1633) tells a woman that he loves all women so long as they are inconstant, as he is. He teases the woman, urging her to fickleness so that he may be fickle also. In the last stanza he tells the woman that Venus (the goddess of love) heard his argument and went in search of a constant lover. She found only a few "poor heretics," and told them that even if they are true, their lovers will not be. A similar view is found in Donne's "Woman's Constancy" (1633). Having berated his mistress for loving him for only one day, the speaker poses various clever questions by which the woman may try to acquit herself. At the end of the poem, however, he declares that he is as fickle as she; tomorrow will find him out of love as well.

Ben Jonson, whose range of topics is immense, wrote on this theme in a song, "In Defence of Their Inconstancy" (1640). Written from the point of view of a woman, the poem wittily argues that it is wise of women not to attach themselves to one man before marriage takes away their freedom. Just as men become more valorous when they fight different foes, so women become expert in love when they change their partners. Finally, the speaker argues that change is not inconstancy if it results in discernment, allowing the woman to compare her lover with other men and find the most deserving. Most importantly, inconstancy ensures that the woman will be valued. Men are more faithful to experienced women than to worthy ones.

In "To My Inconstant Mistress" (1640) by Ben Jonson's friend Thomas Carew, the speaker uses religious terms (as in much metaphysical poetry) to describe the love affair that has ended because of the woman's inconstancy. She is now "excommunicate" from "the joys of love," which belong to him because of his "strong faith" in true love. A fairer hand than hers will heal the heart she broke; the new couple's souls shall be "with equal glory crown'd." The fickle former mistress will be left weeping and complaining but to no avail, "damned for thy false apostasy."

Lady Mary Wroth, a Jacobean poet and niece of Sir Philip Sidney, argues for the virtue of constancy—and criticizes men's inconstancy in particular—in her prose romance *Urania* (1621). In a song at the end of Book 1, a shepherd laments the fickleness and transience of love in a series of answers to the repeated question "Love what are thou?" Created by "idle smiles," love is just a "vain thought"; a transient fantasy; a brief day; a flower that blooms briefly and dies; "bubbles made by rain."

Sir John Suckling was a wealthy, flamboyant Cavalier, or supporter of Charles I, who is famous for his witty songs and lyrics that often made fun of conventional love poems. "The Constant Lover" ("Out upon It!") (1659) exclaims in four stanzas the poet's amazement that he has been constant for "three whole days together." He promises to continue for three more, "If it prove fair weather," thus proving himself the most constant of lovers. In the last two stanzas he disclaims any credit for such devotion; the credit should go to his fair mistress. Had it not been for her beautiful face, "There had been at least ere this/A dozen dozen in her place."

The most sustained and artistic expression of frustration over a fickle woman is Sir Philip Sidney's sonnet cycle *Astrophil and Stella* (1582?). Several of the sonnets are discussed in the Art, Imagination, and Inspiration section of this survey, because they take up the subject of Stella as the poet's Muse. The whole sequence, however, turns on the vicissitudes of love from the male point of view: the woman's beauty that lures the man into hopeless devotion; her power over him that keeps him constantly enthralled, never knowing if she returns his love; the sleepless nights and miserable days. Although the ideas and images are often Petrarchan, Sidney's sonnets are brilliantly original and compelling. In Sonnet 31, for example, "With how sad steps, O Moon, thou climb'st the skies," the speaker gazes on the "wan" face of the moon and presumes that it, too, must have been the victim of Cupid's arrows. Sensing a fellow sufferer, he asks the moon if the politics of love are as unfair on the moon as they are on earth, where constancy is regarded as "want of wit" and beautiful women delight in attracting attention only to scorn those attracted. On earth, he moans, the woman's ingratitude is praised, while the man's devotion is discounted. In Sonnet 45, the speaker compares his "face of woe" to a stormy sky and wonders why Stella can fail to pity him when stories about unhappy lovers cause her to weep. If she is so moved by imaginary despair, perhaps she can look at his miserable face and pity him as though he were a storybook hero.

Anne Elliot's dismissal of poems about lovers' constancy seems to be justified: this theme is predominantly a male poet's complaint about his mistress's teasing ways. But the poems approach the theme with irony and wit. The truly heartbroken lover's lament will be found in the Unrequited Love section.

UNREQUITED LOVE

Poems about unrequited love, or love that is not returned, have much in common with poems about inconstant lovers. Here, though, the object of desire has never shown any interest in the lover (usually the speaker); he or she is not so much inconstant as indifferent. The theme finds its purest expression in the old ballad of "Bonny Barbara Allan." There are many versions of this tragic tale: in some, the young man, dying for love of bonny Barbara, is a nobleman, Sir John Graeme; in others he is a village boy, young Jemmy Grove. Barbara is called to the deathbed, where she accuses the young man of having slighted her when the toasts to the ladies were given at the tavern. Returning home, she hears the bells toll his death, and repentance overcomes her. The poem ends with Barbara's bitter request to her mother to prepare her grave; since her lover died for her today, she will "die for him tomorrow."

The metaphor of the chase is a favorite one in love poetry, the woman being represented as the beautiful but skittish prey, and the man the hunter. It was a popular metaphor in classical literature and also in Petrarch's love poetry, from whom it came to the Renaissance poet Sir Thomas Wyatt. The speaker of his sonnet "Whoso list to hunt" (c. 1557) regrets that he is too tired to keep up his pursuit of his beautiful prey, even though his "wearied mind" continues to seek her: ". . . as she fleeth afore,/Fainting I follow." The speaker warns other hunters that their pursuit is in vain; the metaphor of the hunt reaches a climax when he tells them that the deer wears a collar engraved with the words "*Noli me tangere* [do not touch me] for Caesar's I am," an inscription that was apparently found on Caesar's hinds to warn off hunters. The plight of the unrequited lover is also charmingly expressed in another metaphor. The speaker says he is giving up the hunt because "in a net I seek to hold the wind."

Edmund Spenser turned the futile chase metaphor around in Sonnet 67 of his sonnet cycle *Amoretti* ("little loves") (1595), written for his wife Elizabeth. "Lyke as a huntsman after weary chace" describes the lover and his hounds giving up their pursuit of the elusive deer. But while he rests in the shade, the deer inexplicably returns, seeking a drink from the nearby stream. Unafraid of the hunter, she allows him to come up to her and capture her. The poem ends with the delightful twist that "with her own goodwill" she is finally caught: "Strange thing me seemed to see a beast so wild,/So goodly won with her own will beguiled." Unrequited love happily finds its fulfillment.

The Christian poet Christina Rossetti (1830–1894) rejected two proposals of marriage, possibly because neither suitor shared her Anglican faith, but more likely because, like her sister who had become a nun, she considered herself wedded to Christ. She was able to write with some humor about her rejections, however. In "No, Thank You, John" (1860) the speaker addresses her would-be lover, reminding him that she never encouraged his advances and making fun of his ardent pursuit: "Why will you haunt me with a face as wan/As shows an hour-old ghost?"

A twentieth-century poem on this theme is Thomas Hardy's "A Broken Appointment" (1902). Addressing the woman who stood him up, the speaker faults her less for not loving him than for her lack of basic human kindness in failing to spend an hour "to soothe a time-torn man." Such a kindness, he says, would be a more "divine" human act than loving him.

LOST LOVE

Poems about lost love are often less playful than those about unrequited love. Although Tennyson tells us in "In Memoriam A.H.H." (1850), " 'Tis better to have love and lost than never to have loved at all," many poets express bitter pain that cannot be easily assuaged or rationalized. The old ballad "Lord Randal" paints a tragic history of a failed love affair in a brief dialogue between the heartbroken young man and his mother. The story gradually emerges, couched in the hunting metaphor traditionally used in love poetry. The young man dined with his "true love," when he and his bloodhounds were poisoned by her, and he "fain would lie down." The last line makes the connection between the poisoned man and the poisoned love affair, for he is "sick at the heart." Many a lover feels that rejection is, without doubt, a fatal blow.

Sir Philip Sidney's "The Nightingale" (c. 1581) builds on the old idea that spring is traditionally the time when people as well as birds and animals seek a soul mate. The nightingale's beautiful song is heard only in spring in England, and according to tradition, lovers who heard the nightingale would be blessed (whereas the lark's song was a bad omen, as Romeo and Juliet discovered). The poem also employs the Greek myth of Philomel, who was raped by her brother-in-law Tereus and was turned into a nightingale (for a discussion of this story see the Art, Imagination, and Inspiration section). Sidney plays upon the legend that Philomel pressed her breast against a thorn to remind her of the pain of the rape, thus making her song more poignant. The poet finds his own grief at losing his love much more painful than Philomel's, because his is ongoing, whereas hers is in the past: "Thine earth now springs, mine fadeth;/Thy thorn without, my thorn my heart invadeth." She has the new season to enjoy, whereas he can see only sorrow ahead. In the second stanza he again finds the nightingale luckier than he because she suffered from too much desire (the rape), whereas "I who daily craving,/Cannot have to content me,/Have more cause to lament me,/Since wanting is more woe than too much having."

Michael Drayton, an Elizabethan poet and contemporary of Shakespeare, wrote a sonnet sequence entitled "Idea" (1619). In his opening sonnet he tells the readers that they can expect the truth from him, not the tears and sighs of conventional love poetry. One of the most delightful of the series is Sonnet 61, "Since there's no help, come, let us kiss and part." The octave of the sonnet is a sensible plea from the speaker to his girlfriend, agreeing that their love affair is over: let's shake hands on it and go our separate ways. When we meet again by chance, there will be no hint at all that we had once been lovers. The sestet opens with the personification of their passion, which is even now breathing its last. With "faith" and "innocence" attending at the deathbed, all seems to be over. But in the closing couplet, the poet (like many lovers) reverses all his sensible thoughts: please, can she possibly bring their dead love back to life?

After the Renaissance poets of the sixteenth century and the Cavalier poets of the seventeenth century, the next poet to make his name as a poet of love did not appear until the end of the eighteenth century. While many of the earlier poets wrote in a tradition of love poetry that did not necessarily reflect their own emotional life, Robert Burns's poems emerged from his own incorrigible liking for the "lasses" on the Ayrshire farms where he lived and worked. Many of his lyrics were based on traditional songs, but he gave them new expression and color. Now often set to music, they have become a part of the language of love for English speakers. (Burns's song "A Red, Red Rose" [1799] takes up the medieval symbol for love in a simple lyric that has become as central to modern expressions of love as St. Valentine's Day.) In Burns's "The Banks o' Doon" (1808), the speaker may be the woman, whose lover has deserted her. She listens enviously to a bird singing to its mate, remembering happier days before she knew of her lover's treachery. In innocence and singing like the bird, she plucked a rose (always symbolic of love). The concluding lines are ambiguous, as the woman says her "false lover stole the rose/But left the thorn wi' me." Is the thorn a pregnancy, cause of the man's sudden departure, or just the pain of the deserted, faithful woman?

Two poems by the Romantic poet Percy Bysshe Shelley speak eloquently of lost love. The eight-line lyric, "Music, when soft voices die" (1821), compares the poet's memories of the departed lover to the lingering sounds of music, odors of violets, and sight of rose leaves. Each image suggests the ambiguity of remembered pleasure, tender and free from bitterness or pain: "And so thy thoughts, when thou art gone,/Love itself shall slumber on." Similarly elegiac in tone is Shelley's "When the lamp is shattered" (1822), but now no lingering memory remains to comfort the speaker. A series of fine images—"When the lamp is shattered/The light in the dust lies dead—When the cloud is scattered/The rainbow's glory is shed"—are compared to the deserted lover's soul. Then images of mourning ("sad dirges/Like the wind through a ruined cell") convey the speaker's emptiness of spirit. In the last two stanzas the poet focuses on the couple that has fallen out of love. Why, he asks, is it always the stronger heart that breaks the attachment, leaving the weaker one still loving in vain. Why, he asks Love, do you choose the frailer heart "for your cradle, your home and your bier?" The metaphor in the last two stanzas compares the lovers' hearts to birds' nests. The heart, or nest, of the deserted lover, who continues to hold onto love, will be rocked with the storms of passion, mocked with the sun of reason, and finally torn open and exposed "when leaves fall and cold winds come." The images in the poem vividly convey the hopeless desolation of the abandoned lover.

John Keats's "La Belle Dame sans Merci: A Ballad" (1819) is often interpreted allegorically because it is written in highly symbolic language. But on one level it is a tale of lost love. The hero is a "knight at arms,/Alone and palely loitering," who meets the narrator and tells him why he looks so miserable; in fact, he is clearly dying. The knight tells an old, old story: he was seduced by a beautiful, supernatural woman, a "fairy's child," who lured him to her "elfin grot" and lulled him to sleep. His dream brought him a warning from other lost men who had been seduced by the beautiful lady, who has no mercy; bloodless and starving, they exist in a living death, where he, too, now roams, "though the sedge is wither'd from the lake,/And no birds sing." Who is the lady? She has been variously interpreted as Death, Love, Poetry, and Imagination, but the poem can be enjoyed just for its poignant expression of love, which is irresistible and seems real, but which turns out to be a cruel deception.

Another poem famous for its depiction of abandonment through natural images is Alfred, Lord Tennyson's "Mariana" (1830). Based upon that character in Shakespeare's *Measure for Measure* (1623), Mariana has been jilted by her lover and waits, forlorn and hopeless, in her "moated grange." This beautiful poem relies upon what T. S. Eliot called the "objective correlative," or the embodying of Mariana's emotional state in her surroundings. The reader thus understands Mariana's suffering through the detailed and evocative description of the grange. Like so many of Tennyson's subjects, Mariana is trapped, suspended in a life that is really more like death. The opening stanza depicts this stagnation, where movement and change is either imperceptible or notable for its absence. The "flower-plots" are encrusted with "blackest moss," and the "rusted nails fell from the knots/That held the pear to the gable wall." Onomatopoeia in the line "Unlifted was the clinking latch" reminds us that the latch is *not* clinking, because no one comes. The sounds in the stanza, emphasized by alliteration in "sad and strange" and "weeded and worn," draw attention to Mariana's desolation of spirit. Each of the seven stanzas closes with variations on Mariana's mournful refrain, "He cometh not . . . I am aweary, aweary,/I would that I were dead!"

The poem follows Mariana's unchanging mood as day fades to night and night fades to day. The only movement in the second stanza is the "flitting of the bats" and Mariana's hopeless search of the landscape for her lover's return: "She drew her casement curtain by,/And glanced athwart the glooming flats." In stanza three, the cock wakes her before dawn, perhaps reminding the reader of betrayal (Christ told Peter that he would deny Jesus three times before the cock crowed). Even in sleep "she seemed to walk forlorn,/Till cold winds woke the gray-eyed morn. . . ." Stanza four introduces the possibility that Mariana is contemplating suicide, for near the grange "a sluice with blackened waters slept,/And o'er it many, round and small,/The clustered marish-mosses crept." That she is longing for death begins to pervade the images of the poem. A poplar tree, associated with the underworld, is the only tree on "the level waste, the rounding gray," and even it resembles the elderly, with its "gnarled bark" and palsied shaking. Like an omen, the shadow of the poplar falls across the lank form of Mariana as she lies on her bed, watching the outside world begin to close in upon her. In stanza six the sense of enclosure and suffocation becomes intense in a memorable description of the interior of the house:

> All day within the dreamy house,
>   The door upon its hinges creaked;
> The blue fly sung in the pane; the mouse
>   Behind the moldering wainscot shrieked.

Trapped in her own grief, Mariana is retreating from the world into a mental and physical prison in which she is acutely conscious of sounds in the house, as though they were contained within her own head. The real world starts to fade, and she sinks into memory, beset by ghosts of the dead: "Old faces glimmered through the doors . . . Old voices called her from without." In the last stanza, Mariana's grip on the present is loosening, and Tennyson's mastery of sound and image is evident (even in this early poem) in his description of the house that echoes her utter desolation:

> The slow clock ticking, and the sound
> Which to the wooing wind aloof
>   The poplar made, did all confound
> Her sense; but most she loathed the hour
>   When the thick-moted sunbeam lay
>   Athwart the chambers, and the day
> Was sloping toward his western bower.

In her final refrain, she has lost all hope, and death seems to be near. "He cometh not" is replaced by "He will not come," and her conditional statement, "I would that I were dead!" is now a prayer for release from her suffering: "Oh God, that I were dead!"

The Irish poet William Butler Yeats's poem "When You Are Old" (1891) shares the elegiac tone of Shelley's and Tennyson's poems about lost love. The poet is addressing Maud Gonne, a woman he loved, reminding her that when she is old she will regret the loss of a man who loved her for all the qualities that would make her still lovable in old age. When she is old and nodding at the fire, she will realize that this man, alone of her admirers, would have loved her now as he did when she was young and beautiful. She will realize

> . . . how Love fled
> And paced upon the mountains overhead
> And hid his face amid a crowd of stars.

Sir John Betjeman's poem "Pershore Station, or a Liverish Journey First Class" (1954) is a love poem that speaks eloquently of regret for a lost opportunity. The speaker is traveling by train one winter night, and the juxtaposition of modern train, lit by electric light, and the platform of the old station, lit by gas light, reminds him of the passage of time. Pershore, a twelfth-century abbey town near Stratford-on-Avon, conjures up long ago days for him, and he begins to recollect an old love affair that ended unhappily when a vulnerable woman retreated from his cruel hardness. Regret and guilt fill his heart as he goes over that sad time, and, self-pityingly, he imagines what their life could have been like, with the "freckled faces" of children taking the place of the void that he deliberately chose: One word would have brought her back, but he refused to say it. The contrast between new and old, this life and the life that could have been, and the one that belongs to the past that is Pershore recurs at the end, when he suggests that the comfortable, cushioned carriage in which he is akin to the cocoon in which he barricaded himself against a loving relationship. Enveloped by the carriage and cut off from the warmer, more human time when Christian faith (the abbey) brought a closer human bond, he has carried "a deadweight" in his heart all his life.

IN PRAISE OF TRUE LOVE

Many of the finest love poems in English seek to define true love, or to express the deepest and most inexplicable feelings of the human heart. While conventional love lyrics about inconstancy are often witty or even cynical, poems about true love are usually heartfelt and sincere. Shakespeare's sonnets, like his plays, consider love in all its aspects. Many of the sonnets take up several themes at once—a sonnet about time or death often becomes in the final couplet a poem about love. Shakespeare's sonnets about immortality are also often love poems. So many and varied are they that this survey cannot possibly do justice to Shakespeare's remarkable variations on the theme. Central to any discussion of love in poetry, however, is Sonnet 116, "Let me not to the marriage of true minds" (1609). Here Shakespeare's tone is authoritative, his language legal, as he defines love objectively, rather than writing for a particular person. The reference to marriage is echoed throughout the sonnet, suggesting that Shakespeare's legal language is based upon the marriage service. He will not "admit impediments" to this marriage of true minds, just as a couple about to be married must declare if they know of any impediments to their union. In the first quatrain Shakespeare defines love by what it is not: love is not the kind of infatuation "which alters when it alteration finds"—which comes and goes according to circumstance. "Oh no!" he declares at the beginning of the second quatrain, which contains two metaphors for true love's constancy. It is "an ever-fixed mark/That looks on tempests, and is never shaken." True love is like a lighthouse that keeps the lovers safe throughout life's trials and vicissitudes. It is "the star to every wandering bark." True love, like a star, is eternal, beautiful, and priceless. Like the "ever-fixed mark," the star metaphor also suggests love as a guide, a safeguard against danger and a source of strength in troubled times. The third stanza returns to a definition of love by negation. It is "not Time's fool," even though we grow old. Love endures "even to the edge of doom," or "till death do us part" as the marriage service requires. The closing couplet sets the legal seal on Shakespeare's definition: "If this be error and upon me proved/I never writ, nor no man ever loved."

Shakespeare's Sonnet 29 (1609) opens with the speaker in the depths of self-pity, bemoaning his bad luck and failure in society: "When, in disgrace with fortune and men's eyes, I all alone beweep my outcast state." Even his prayers are not heard for heaven is "deaf." In the second quatrain he wishes he were more like his successful acquaintances—as handsome as one, as popular as another, as talented as a third. In the third quatrain, however, he drags himself out of his sorry state in a fine image that has become well known. Thinking of his lover instead of himself, he finds his

> . . . state
> (Like to the lark at break of day arising
> From sullen earth) sings hymns at heaven's gate.

The couplet reinforces the power of love to dispel material wants. Love brings such "wealth" that he would "scorn to change [his] state with kings." In finding true wealth in the spiritual realm of love rather than in the material world of status and possessions, the sonnet is also in the tradition of poems that favor the contemplative rather than the active life.

Many of John Donne's love poems celebrate true love, but not in the Petrarchan tradition esteemed by the Renaissance poets or the Cavalier poets of his own time. Donne's poems often shock with their abrupt tone and sometimes jarring imagery. He liked to link the physical with the spiritual, seeing human, sexual love as an expression of divine love. This "metaphysical" linking of apparent opposites was disliked in the eighteenth century, and Donne was little read until he was rediscovered by T. S. Eliot in the twentieth century. Donne's poems in praise of true love usually describe the absolute union—body and soul—of the lovers. "The Good-Morrow" appears first in most selections of Donne's *Songs and Sonnets* (1633) because in it the speaker tells his mistress that their newfound love is an awakening into perfect union. He dismisses the need for the outside world, for love "makes one little room an everywhere." The speaker plays on the notion of world exploration and mapmaking, finding in their love two halves that make a new world. Their eyes are windows to the soul and reflectors of the outside world, and the strength of their union depends upon their equal love for each other. "Whatever dies was not mix'd equally," so their perfect love gives them immortality.

These ideas are realized also in Donne's "The Canonization" (1633), which, like Shakespeare's Sonnet 29, prefers the contemplative, private life of two lovers to the active, social life of court and town. The speaker begins in anger, shouting at his listener (who represents the busy world), "For God's sake hold your tongue, and let me love." Criticize my age, my illnesses, and my lack of public success, he grumbles; go and busy yourself in the world of money and society; just leave me alone with my love. In the second stanza he points out that no one has been injured by the love affair and makes fun of the traditional emotions of the love poet—sighs and tears—by asking who has been drowned by them. Soldiers and lawyers are still fighting real and legal battles; the secular world continues to pursue its materialistic, litigious way, despite his love. The third stanza moves to the lovers and begins the poem's shift from the insignificance of the lovers in the world to their vital importance in another realm altogether. The speaker describes the loving couple in metaphors of flies to a candle, and the phoenix. Donne loved paradox, and here he finds the lovers to be both fly and candle, while hinting at their sexual relationship when the flies "die" in the candle flame. As phoenix also they "die and rise the same," just as the legendary bird erupts into flames every 500 years and then rises from the ashes. The sexuality of the couple is purified by the image; they are both contained in "one neutral thing" (the phoenix) and thus transcend male and female and become one. They "prove/Mysterious by this love." This purity is extended in the fourth stanza. "We can die by it, if not live by love," he says, referring to the biblical saying that man cannot live by bread alone, and thus introducing the poem's identification of human love with spiritual love. In renouncing the material world of money and bread (as real saints do), the lovers give themselves up to death. But in doing so they will be transformed into saints of love. Their legend, rather than appearing on tombs, will be immortalized in verse—small, humble poems that, like the "well-wrought urn" (rather than the ostentatious "half-acre tomb"), can contain "the greatest ashes." The final stanza contains the hymn that other lovers will invoke for the lovers who have died for love. Here, too, love as a retreat from the material, active world is favored over that world and paradoxically becomes it. Other lovers will say to them that their "reverend love/Made one another's hermitage"; in each other they find not only a retreat but also the world of "countries, towns, courts" that they rejected in life. The lovers saw "the whole world's soul" in each other's eyes, which reflected the world back, like a mirror. The lovers will become a "pattern" for other lovers to follow, just as a saint exemplifies a model life.

Donne may have been writing to his wife in "A Valediction: Forbidding Mourning" (1633), to reassure her of his love for her when he was away in France. Again, the speaker makes fun of the Petrarchan convention of love poetry that finds the lovers sighing and weeping publicly. Their love is a private matter, all the more important for its lack of fanfare. He then compares their love to that of ordinary couples, which cannot survive absence because it exists only on a physical level. His argument recalls Shakespeare's Sonnet 116, which declares love not to be true love if it "alters when it alteration finds." He is able to reassure his wife that because their souls are united, they really do not part at all, even though they are physically separated. His metaphor for their relationship is ingenious and unusual (such a striking metaphor is known as a "metaphysical conceit"). They are like a pair of compasses, with his wife the fixed foot, remaining at home, and he the traveling foot, inscribing a circle (symbol of union) around her. Because they truly love each other they are joined together as the two feet of the pair of compasses are joined. As he moves away, she leans over too:

> And though [her soul] in the center sit,
>   Yet when the other far doth roam,
> It leans and hearkens after it,
>   And grows erect, as that comes home.

Her "firmness" makes his circle "just," and "makes me end where I begun." True love is a union, the alpha and omega that is complete and cannot be severed, even by physical separation.

Lady Mary Wortley Montagu lays out a woman's requirements in a lover (or husband) in "The Lover: A Ballad" (1721–1725). The anapestic rhythm and rhyming couplets add to the humor of the speaker's exasperation with men who think she is coy or fickle or indifferent, as so many of the male poets describe women. She is not afraid of love, nor does she overvalue chastity. And she knows as well as they do that time flies and we must seize the day (*carpe diem*). No, she asserts, the problem is this: Where can she find a man with "good sense and good nature equally joined"? The speaker's description of a good husband is similar to Millimant's famous "proviso" speech in Congreve's play *The Way of the World* (1700), and it is typical of the eighteenth-century emphasis on common sense, civility, and moderation. But Montagu allows for more pleasure in marriage than does Millimant. In the privacy of their home, "let the friend and the lover be handsomely mixed." Until such a rare bird can be found, she will continue to be unmoved by the foolish importunings of witless lovers.

The best-known woman writer of love poems is Elizabeth Barrett Browning, who wrote of her courtship with and marriage to Robert Browning in the forty-four sonnets that comprise *Sonnets from the Portuguese* (1845–1847). Elizabeth Barrett was already an established and admired poet (although an invalid confined to her bedroom in her father's house in London) when Robert Browning, a lesser-known poet, began to call. The sonnets, which she pretended at first were translations of Portuguese poems, finely describe the turmoil of emotions that she felt: deepening love for Robert, fear that his love for her would not last, and finally joy in their decision to be married (they had to elope because of her father's opposition to the marriage). Sonnet 22, "When our two souls stand up erect and strong," resembles Donne's metaphysical poetry in portraying the lovers' souls as almost corporeal. Barrett Browning imagines their souls flying together heavenward, until an angel would attempt to "drop some golden orb of perfect song/Into our deep, dear silence." Again, like Donne, she prefers to think of their love in the busy world, where "the unfit/Contrarious moods of men recoil away," leaving them happily isolated in their love.

In Sonnet 14, "If thou must love me, let it be for nought," Elizabeth Barrett Browning expresses her fear—understandable in an invalid—that Robert loves her only out of pity, or for transitory attractions like her smile or a manner of speaking. Like Shakespeare in Sonnet 116, she differentiates such transient affection from true love: "But love me for love's sake, that evermore/Thou may'st love on, through love's eternity." Most famous of Elizabeth Barrett Browning's sonnets is number 43, "How do I love thee? Let me count the ways." Its directness and balance endear it to many readers and make it trite to others (Virginia Woolf disliked it intensely—but Woolf was out of sympathy with Barrett Browning's strong religious faith), but it has survived as one of the most popular and sincere expressions of romantic love, rooted as it is in the poet's emotion rather than in the allegorical traditions of courtly love. In its repetition of "I love thee . . ." ("I love thee freely, as men strive for Right;/I love thee purely, as they turn from Praise./I love thee with the passion put to use/In my old griefs, and with my childhood's faith"), the sonnet sounds almost like a childhood catechism and has the power of that familiar form for many readers. It is also strongly reminiscent of Shakespeare's love sonnets, closing on a hope for immortality as so many love poems do: "and, if God choose,/I shall but love thee better after death." Although male poets dominated the writing of love poetry for centuries, Elizabeth Barrett Browning's sonnets have established the female voice in this most universal of themes.

❦❧

"Song" ("Why so pale and wan, fond lover?"), Sir John Suckling
  OBEV; TFi; TrGrPo-1
"To Celia," Ben Jonson
  ImPo; NAEL-1; OAEL-1; OBEV; TFi; TrGrPo-1
"The Passionate Shepherd to His Love," Christopher Marlowe
  ImPo; NAEL-1; OAEL-1; OBEV; TFi; TrGrPo-1
"The Nymph's Reply to the Shepherd," Sir Walter Ralegh
  ImPo; NAEL-1; TFi; TrGrPo-1
"The Bait," John Donne
  NAEL-1; OAEL-1
"The Flea," John Donne
  ImPo; NAEL-1; OAEL-1; TFi; TrGrPo-1
"Elegy 19. To His Mistress Going to Bed," John Donne
  NAEL-1; OBEV
"A Rapture," Thomas Carew
  NAEL-1
"The Eve of Saint Agnes," John Keats
  ImPo; NAEL-2; OAEL-2; OBEV; TFi; TrGrPo-2
"Now Sleeps the Crimson Petal," Alfred, Lord Tennyson
  NAEL-2; OBEV; TFi; TrGrPo-2
"The Constancy of a Lover," George Gascoigne
  EnRePo
"Divers doth use, as I have heard and know," Sir Thomas Wyatt
  NAEL-1
"They Flee from Me," Sir Thomas Wyatt
  ImPo; NAEL-1; OAEL-1; OBEV; SB; TFi
"Farewell, Love," Sir Thomas Wyatt
  NAEL-1; OAEL-1; OBEV; TrGrPo-1
"Song" ("Go and catch a falling star"), John Donne
  ImPo; NAEL-1; OBEV; TFi; TrGrPo-1
"The Indifferent," John Donne
  NAEL-1
"Woman's Constancy," John Donne

NBLV; NoP

"In Defence of their Inconstancy" ("Hang up those dull, and envious fools"), Ben Jonson

    NAEL-1 (5th ed., 1986)

"To My Inconstant Mistress," Thomas Carew

    TFi; TrGrPo-1

"Song," from *Urania*, Lady Mary Wroth

    NAEL-1

"The Constant Lover" ("Out upon It!"), Sir John Suckling

    ImPo; NAEL-1; OBEV; TrGrPo-1

Sonnet 31, *Astrophil and Stella* ("With how sad steps, O Moon, thou climb'st the skies"), Sir Philip Sidney

    NAEL-1; OBEV; SB; TFi; TrGrPo-1

"Bonny Barbara Allan," anonymous

    NAEL-1; TrGrPo-1

"Whoso list to hunt," Sir Thomas Wyatt

    NAEL-1; OAEL-1; OBEV; TFi; TrGrPo-1

Sonnet 67, *Amoretti* ("Lyke as a huntsman after weary chace"), Edmund Spenser

    NAEL-1; TrGrPo-1

"No, Thank You, John," Christina Rossetti

    BAVP; NAEL-2

"A Broken Appointment," Thomas Hardy

    BAVP; NAEL-2

"Lord Randal," anonymous

    ImPo; NAEL-1; OBEV; SB; TFi; TrGrPo-1

"The Nightingale," Sir Philip Sidney

    NAEL-1

from "Idea" ("Since there's no help, come, let us kiss and part"), Michael Drayton

    ImPo; NAEL-1; OBEV; SB; TFi; TrGrPo-1

"A Red, Red Rose," Robert Burns

    ImPo; NAEL-2; TFi; TrGrPo-1

"The Banks o' Doon," Robert Burns

    TFi; TrGrPo-1

"Music, when soft voices die," Percy Bysshe Shelley

ImPo; NAEL-2; OBEV; TFi; TrGrPo-2

"When the lamp is shattered," Percy Bysshe Shelley

ImPo; NAEL-2; OBEV; TrGrPo-2

"La Belle Dame Sans Merci: A Ballad," John Keats

ImPo; NAEL-2; OAEL-2; OBEV; SB; TFi

"Mariana," Alfred, Lord Tennyson

BAVP; NAEL-2; TFi; TrGrPo-2

"When You Are Old," William Butler Yeats

NAEL-2; OBEV; TFi

"Pershore Station, or a Liverish Journey First Class," Sir John Betjeman

not anthologized; available in editions of Betjeman's poetry

Sonnet 116, "Let me not to the marriage of true minds," William Shakespeare

ImPo; NAEL-1; OAEL-1; OBEV; TFi; TrGrPo-1

Sonnet 29, "When, in disgrace with Fortune and men's eyes," William Shakespeare

ImPo; NAEL-1; OAEL-1; TFi; TrGrPo-1

"The Good-Morrow," John Donne

ImPo; NAEL-1; OAEL-1; OBEV; TFi; TrGPo-1

"The Canonization," John Donne

NAEL-1; OAEL-1; TFi; TrGrPo-1

"A Valediction: Forbidding Mourning," John Donne

ImPo; NAEL-1; OAEL-1; SB; TFi

"The Lover: A Ballad," Lady Mary Wortley Montagu

BL; ECP; NAEL-1; OBEV

Sonnet 22, *Sonnets from the Portuguese* ("When our two souls stand up erect and strong"), Elizabeth Barrett Browning

BAVP; NAEL-2; TrGrPo-2

Sonnet 14, *Sonnets from the Portuguese* ("If thou must love me, let it be for nought"), Elizabeth Barrett Browning

TrGrPo-2

Sonnet 43, *Sonnets from the Portuguese* ("How do I love thee? Let me count the ways"), Elizabeth Barrett Browning

BAVP; ImPo; NAEL-2; TFi; TrGrPo-2

Marriage

❦◠◠◠❦

The theme of marriage lends itself to a variety of poetic approaches. The ancient Greeks and Romans established a tradition of songs written to celebrate the wedding ceremony and to request a blessing on the new marriage. Other poets have paid tribute to their spouses in verse, or complained about the bonds that sometimes become chains. Modern poets look at the ritual of the wedding as a way of understanding how attitudes to marriage and love have changed, and what remains the same.

The first English poet to debate the vexed subject of marriage was Geoffrey Chaucer, who in his *Canterbury Tales* (c. 1387) offers lively and diverse views from the perspective of both women and men. Seven of the tales comprise what has become known as the "marriage group" because they take up the topic of authority in marriage. Best known of the debaters is the Wife of Bath, five-times married and widowed, and now on the lookout for a sixth husband as she travels to Canterbury with the other pilgrims. In the prologue to her tale, the Wife of Bath is an outspoken proponent of women's rights within marriage. She defends herself vigorously against those who criticize her many marriages, arguing that despite the dictates of the church, God intended us to marry and enjoy sexual love; chastity, she says, is unnatural. Chaucer's portrait of the Wife in the "General Prologue" establishes her lusty nature, and also introduces a central topic of the marriage theme: does one marry for money, or for status, or for security, or for love? The Wife of Bath chose her first three husbands because they were rich and old; thus, they gave her status in society and she easily gained mastery over them through her willingness to please them in bed. She calls her three rich husbands her "good" husbands, because they so readily submitted to her authority. But the only husband she actually loved, Jankyn, her fifth, and twenty years her junior, was the one she could not control, and the Wife admits that women most desire what they cannot easily acquire. After a turbulent battle for mastery, one night the Wife rips three pages out of his favorite book—a catalog of stories about disobedient wives—and Jankyn beats her, leaving her deaf in one ear. Contrite, he accepts her sovereignty in the home, and they live peacefully and happily from then on.

The Wife's tale exemplifies her experience. When a young knight rapes a beautiful young girl, he is sentenced to death unless he can discover what women truly want. He roams the world, asking every woman he meets, but every one has a different answer. Finally, as he nears the castle he meets an ugly old hag who assures him she knows the right answer. She accompanies him to court and declares that women want sovereignty in marriage, an answer that all the women present agree is correct. The hag makes the knight marry her, which he does, unwillingly. When he complains of her ugliness and humble background, she replies that he has a choice: she can remain as she is, ugly but faithful and loving; or she can become young and beautiful, but also unfaithful and capricious. The knight replies that he will leave it to her "wise governance"; whatever she chooses he will accept as right. This answer, of course, is the correct one, and she is transformed into a faithful, beautiful wife. This wife, like the Wife of Bath herself, has the upper hand in the marriage through subtle, sometimes devious means in the age-old battle of the sexes. In law, there was no question of who was sovereign: women were their husband's "property," and they had no legal rights. The church and the law upheld the husband's right to punish his wife. Subtle means were thus essential if a wife was to undermine the accepted relationship between husband and wife.

Exemplifying this view of the husband as sovereign, whose word was to be obeyed absolutely, is the Clerk's tale of patient Griselda, an often-repeated story first found in Boccaccio's *The Decameron* (1348–1353) and translated from there into Latin by Petrarch, Chaucer's source. A wealthy young lord, Walter, chooses for his wife a village girl noted for her virtue and sweet temper. Despite her devotion to him, he decides to test it even further by taking first her baby daughter and then her young son from her, pretending that they are to be killed because his people resent her lowly birth. Finally, he tells her that he is divorcing her in order to marry a woman more pleasing to his people. Griselda accepts all of these trials without complaint, even gladly, assuring him always that her place is to obey him willingly, no matter what he may require. Her patient suffering is rewarded when Walter breaks down, admits the plot, returns her children to her, and reinstates her as his wife. The Clerk tempers his tale at the end by telling his audience that he did not intend that wives should emulate Griselda; rather, he meant that we should all suffer with patience and thankfulness the tests God similarly imposes on us because he wants to strengthen our virtue, not to punish us. The Clerk has also stressed that part of Griselda's submissiveness is not just that of a wife, but is, more importantly, that of a villager to the lord in a feudal society. Griselda feels she has no choice but to obey her "lord," and if his nobles require these sacrifices of her it is her duty to obey as a humble peasant girl. Chaucer, who is one of the pilgrims on the journey and who narrates the "General Prologue" and linking passages about the pilgrims, comments on the story in a concluding "envoy," which strongly warns women against being Griseldas. Copy Echo, he says, and answer back to your husband; defend your home; speak up—even though he seems armed in mail, your "crabbed eloquence" can pierce him to the quick. The Wife of Bath is allowed the last word, through Chaucer's humorous defense of strong-willed wives.

The Merchant's tale follows the Clerk's and tells of another well-known marriage, that of an old husband, January (white-haired, like the snows of winter), and a young wife, May (as fresh as the spring). In his brief prologue, the Merchant warns his audience against marriage, his own wife (of only two months, we hear) being a shrew who is making his life unbearable. January is an elderly bachelor who believes that marriage is the ideal state because women are a man's helpmate and support. He rejects Theophrastus, who thinks servants are more useful and less trouble than wives, and goes on to take the Wife of Bath's position that women should be heeded, citing several biblical examples of their wisdom. His choice of a wife, however, is limited: she must be very young, so that he can enjoy her body and form her mind. His friends argue over the wisdom of his decision, but January goes ahead with his marriage to May, much to the distress of her young admirer, Damyan, who pines pathetically for her. Love is blind, and when January goes blind too he is violently afraid that May will be unfaithful to him. She is, in her husband's orchard, where she entertains Damyan in a pear tree. Pluto, god of the underworld, and his wife Proserpine, enter the garden. Pluto vows to give January his sight so that he may see his faithless wife, but Proserpine replies that she will give May (and all other wives afterward) the gift of golden words, so that she may talk her way out of her predicament. As the Wife of Bath declared, women gain authority through wheedling and verbal dexterity. And so when January sees his wife in the arms of Damyan, May deftly replies that she had been told that struggling with a young man in a tree would restore his sight. When January questions the "struggle," she convinces him that his newly recovered sight must have deceived him. January happily accepts her explanation and becomes one in a long line of foolish elderly husbands whose young wives easily get the better of them.

"The Franklin's Tale" completes the marriage group in *The Canterbury*

Tales by offering a balanced answer to the question of authority in marriage. The Franklin begins by saying that love in marriage can only thrive when husband and wife are equal and neither has sovereignty. The tale he tells is of the faithful Dorigen and her noble husband Arveragus, who exemplify this trusting balance. When Arveragus goes overseas for two years, Dorigen is pursued by the equally noble Aurelius, whom she tries to avoid by promising to be his if he performs the apparently impossible task of removing the dangerous rocks on the coast of Brittany, where she lives. When Aurelius accomplishes the task with the help of a magician, Dorigen wishes to die, but her husband says he will give her up rather than have her break her promise. Aurelius generously frees her from the bargain, and in turn the magician frees him from having to pay for the service. The loyalty and honor of all three is rewarded, and married love is seen to be dependent upon mutual love and respect.

Several early poems look at marriage with some humor. Thomas Campion's "Fain Would I Wed" (1617) is spoken by a young maid who regrets the fickleness that prevents her from loving one man for long. Faced with only the convent, she still hopes that, like her mother, she will become a wife. The form of the poem, twelve lines of fourteen syllables each, rhyming in couplets, adds to the comic effect of the maid's lament.

Another comic poem on the subject of marriage is Ben Jonson's "On Giles and Joan" (1616). Beginning with the premise that this husband and wife always agree, the poem moves through Giles's opinions, with which Joan is always found to concur. Unfortunately, Giles's views are all based on his regret that he married—but each regret is shared, as a kind of refrain, by Joan, which neatly undercuts Giles's evident sense that only he is dissatisfied with the marriage:

> Giles riseth early,
> And having got him out of door is glad;
> The like is Joan. But turning home is sad,
> And so is Joan.

The crowning irony is Giles's firm belief that their children are not his; Joan agrees with this too. What a harmonious couple.

John Dryden's comic song "Why should a foolish marriage vow" from his tragicomedy *Marriage a-la-Mode* (1673) reflects the more flippant attitude to marriage adopted by the upper classes of Restoration England, as compared to the devout, perhaps idealized, view of Spenser and other Renaissance writers. The court of the "Merry Monarch" King Charles II, restored to the throne in 1660, was well known for its openly promiscuous behavior. Dryden himself unhappily married (his epitaph for his wife, written before her death, read succinctly, "Here lies my wife: here let her lie!/Now she's at rest. And so am I.") had several mistresses, and he no doubt sympathized with the sentiments sung by a female character in the play. Sexual pleasure leads to the taking of marriage vows, she argues, so once those pleasures have "decayed" there is no need to remain tied to each other. Better for both people to move on to new lovers and new pleasures. "A la mode" suggests the type of society marriage that the artist William Hogarth had caricatured in his series of pictures of the same name from 1743 to 1745: a marriage based on the materialistic desire for a name or for wealth can have only a tragic end.

Kathleen Philips rejected marriage succinctly, unequivocally, and humorously in her short poem "A Married State" (1646). Even the title suggests marriage as an impediment to freedom for women, and Philips takes issue with the traditional view that women are incomplete and unfulfilled if they do not marry. "The best of husbands are so hard to please," she writes, and this burden can be seen in the faces of married women, however hard they may try to disguise it. Spinsterhood, on the other hand, is free from the worries of "blustering husbands," painful childbirth, and troublesome children. Taking up John Donne's metaphor of lovers as saints (in "The Canonization" [1633]), Philips urges women to "turn apostate to love's levity" and "suppress" any instincts in favor of marriage. Philips was probably only fifteen when she wrote this impassioned plea; she married a man thirty-eight years her senior just two years later.

A more sustained and bitter condemnation of the double standard surrounding married love is found in Lady Mary Wortley Montagu's "Epistle from Mrs. Yonge to Her Husband," written in 1724 but not published until the 1970s. Mrs. Yonge's husband, well known for his affairs, separated from her and then sued for divorce on the grounds of her adultery. He was successful, and as well as receiving damages from her lover, he also was awarded her dowry and a large part of her personal fortune. The case dragged Mrs. Yonge through the courts, where her affair was made embarrassingly public. The poem is intended as a defense of Mrs. Yonge and a critique of the injustice of a system that allowed married men to have affairs while condemning adulterous women regardless of the circumstances. In her letter, Mrs. Yonge points out that the wife of an unfaithful husband has no redress. Unlike defrauded servants, who can quit their employment, wives are expected to remain constant, "to daily racks condemned, and to eternal chains." After years of her husband's abuse and after his separation from her, she found kindness and support in another man's arms, a relationship that she kept out of the public eye until her husband took her to court, using his power as a man to humiliate and ruin her. Her only consolation is that fair-minded people will acquit her of all wrongdoing and recognize the injustice of the patriarchal system of "old boys" that protected her husband while exposing her to public shame.

Matthew Prior's "An Epitaph" (1718) similarly reveals a marriage that is far from satisfying. Parodying poems written in praise of someone now dead, Prior's epitaph commemorates a couple whose long married life was unremittingly dull. "Sauntering Jack and idle Joan" knew no passion or even interest in life; their adherence to the moderation urged by philosophers was so complete that they hardly lived at all. Indifferent to everything except their own limited marriage, they ignored their servants, their children, their parish, and their religion. And so they lived and died, well suited to each other:

> If human things went ill or well;
> If changing empires rose or fell;
> The morning passed, the evening came,
> And found this couple still the same.

One of the most chilling poems about a marriage is Robert Browning's dramatic monologue "My Last Duchess" (1842). We find ourselves overhearing a conversation between the speaker, a duke, who is showing a picture of his late wife to a visitor, who does not speak but whose reaction to the Duke's story is evident in the poem. In a dramatic monologue the speaker unconsciously reveals his true nature while thinking he is making a different impression on his implied audience. The Duke's egotistical need to control is evident from the beginning of the poem, when he draws back a curtain that covers the Duchess's portrait: "none puts by/The curtain I have drawn for you, but I." As he gazes again on his late wife's face, revealed now to the visiting agent, his possessiveness begins to bubble up from beneath his calm, measured exterior. Browning's lines deftly reveal the pent-up emotions just below the surface of the Duke's apparent composure. Pointing out a slight blush on the Duchess's cheek, the Duke notes that she blushed not just in her husband's presence; perhaps the painter had flirted a little with her.

> She had
> A heart—how shall I say?—too soon made glad,
> Too easily impressed; she liked whate'er
> She looked on, and her looks went everywhere.

As the Duke's complaints against his wife begin to emerge, the reader is already suspicious of him and sympathetic to the Duchess. When we hear that she was equally kind to the servants and her white mule, we begin to suspect that here was a kind-hearted woman kept under strict control by her husband. As his resentment against her grows with the telling, we begin to see that his enormous pride has been wounded by her failure to pay attention to only him:

> She thanked men—good! But thanked
> Somehow—I know not how—as if she ranked
> My gift of a nine-hundred-years-old name
> With anybody's gift.

But to correct her would be "some stooping; and I choose/Never to stoop."

The Duke has worked himself up into a state of barely concealed rage as he remembers his Duchess's slights. But he maintains his cool exterior, and the revelation when it comes is all the more horrifying. "This grew; I gave commands;/Then all smiles stopped together./There she stands/ As if alive." Unable to control his wife in life, now he has utter control of her in death; she is a painted version of herself, free to bestow smiles only when he opens the curtain. Inviting the visitor to accompany him downstairs, the Duke now reveals the purpose of the visit. The man is an agent for a count who wishes his daughter to marry the Duke. The agent has been sent to arrange the financial terms of the marriage. The Duke tells him that the Count is well known for his generosity and the Duke's requirements in a dowry will be met. Tellingly, though, he assures the agent that the "fair daughter's self" is his "object." The monologue has made only too clear how much of an "object" the Duke considers his wives to be. The agent does not speak in the poem, but his actions are revealing. When the Duke now blurts out, "Nay, we'll go/ Together down, sir," the reader realizes that the agent, horrified at what he has just heard, is hurrying away, but the Duke puts a large hand on his shoulder. As they move away together toward the staircase, the Duke points out another "object" that he owns, just as he wanted to "own" the Duchess:

> Notice Neptune, though,
> Taming a sea horse, thought a rarity,
> Which Claus of Innsbruck cast in bronze for me!

The parallel between the bronze Neptune and the Duke has many ramifications for the poem. The Duke intends merely to show his power—the statue was custom-made for him. But the words "for me" imply "as an emblem of me." The Duke failed to tame his Duchess, and his nature is rigid and unforgiving, his pride in his position and name as unassailable as a bronze cast. But the Duke is "cast in bronze" in a way of which he is unaware (central to the effect of the dramatic monologue form): he thinks that in having his Duchess killed and turning her into a painting, he has finally gained complete control of her. But the poem reveals all too clearly that he is still obsessed with his failure to "own" her; he is still controlled by his jealousy and impotent rage against her, emotions that control him utterly, however hard he may try to pretend otherwise. Browning's poem subtly and powerfully reveals the Duke's seething resentment and hurt pride, breaking through the calm exterior of his smooth, even contemptuous demeanor. The power struggle described by the Wife of Bath poignantly forms the backdrop to the Duke's monologue, which was based on the marriage of the Duke of Ferrara and his first wife, Lucrezia, who died in 1561.

Many poets have written in praise of their marriages. More traditional than Lady Mary Wortley Montagu's defense of Mrs. Yonge is Anne Bradstreet's gentle twelve-line poem "To My Dear and Loving Husband," first published in 1678. Like the Victorian poet Elizabeth Barrett Browning's sonnets to her future husband, Robert, Bradstreet's poem uses conventional comparisons to assure her husband of the depth of her love for him and her gratitude for his love for her. Because not everyone agrees with Isaac Walton that John Donne wrote "A Valediction: Forbidding Mourning" for his wife, when he traveled to the Continent in 1611, the poem is discussed in the Love section of this survey. The poem does, however, strongly suggest married love. John Milton and Thomas Hardy also wrote moving poems about their wives, but since in both cases the poems were written after their wife's death, they are included in this survey in the Death section.

WEDDING POEMS

Chaucer's tale of January and May describes their wedding in some detail, in the tradition of the classical poem in praise of marriage, or epithalamium (from the Greek *epithalamion*, meaning "at the bridal door," because originally the song would be sung outside the bedroom of the new bride and groom). The wedding ode was intended as a blessing on the couple's union and was thus associated with ancient prayers for fertility and the healthy bearing of children. The masque in Shakespeare's *The Tempest* (c. 1611) is one of many such celebrations of marriage. The epithalamium was popular in Greek and Roman literature, but its most famous English example is Edmund Spenser's "Epithalamion," celebrating his marriage to Elizabeth Boyle in 1594. Spenser's poem follows the format of the traditional marriage ode, with an appeal to the Muses for inspiration and then a description of the wedding day, from his bride's awakening and dressing, the procession to the church, the wedding itself, and finally the coming of darkness as the couple retire to bed. The poem, a gift from the poet to his wife, celebrates the bride's virginity and seeks a blessing on their union. The form of the poem is complex, consisting of twenty-four stanzas and 365 lines, coinciding with the hours in a day and days in a year. The first sixteen stanzas, recounting the hours from early morning to late evening, all end with some variation of a couplet declaring that someone will sing, so "That all the woods may answere and your Eccho ring." Once the couple has retired, the public celebration of their marriage gives way to the couple's private lovemaking, signaled by the shift to the absence of song, to which "the woods no more shall answere, nor your Eccho ring." The poem, ornate in style and complex in its many allusions to classical literature and the Bible, is richly allusive and surprisingly emotional despite its formal elements.

Spenser's "Prothalamion" (1596) celebrates the dual wedding of two sisters, Lady Elizabeth and Lady Katherine Somerset, daughters of the earl of Worcester. The poem employs the classical setting of a sylvan scene (the river Thames), the picking of flowers for their bridal day, and the marriage of two swans on the river to lead the brides to their waiting knights. Each stanza ends with the fine line (borrowed by T. S. Eliot in his "The Waste Land" [1922]), "Sweet Thames! Run softly, till I end my song."

The Cavalier poet Sir John Suckling parodied Spenser's formal and celebratory marriage odes in "A Ballad upon a Wedding" (1646). The scene is now the seamier side of London, the bride and groom an uncultured pair, the wedding banquet a pub, and the bride's desires as lusty as the groom's. In form, too, Suckling upsets Spenser's elaborate, long verses, telling his version of the wedding story in abrupt, comic rhythm and plain, colloquial language suited to the setting.

Several twentieth-century poems are concerned with weddings and their consequences. Philip Larkin's "The Whitsun Weddings" (1958) offers an unusual and moving comment on attitudes to marriage among the ordinary people of central England. The poet is traveling by train up to London on the Saturday afternoon of the "Whit weekend," a holiday time in England—founded in the Anglican church's celebration of Pentecost, seven weeks after Easter and the commemoration of the Holy Spirit's descent on the Apostles as they celebrated Shabuoth. Whit Sunday was traditionally a day for baptisms, but the Saturday of that weekend has become a popular day for weddings. Larkin powerfully evokes the mood of the day: the train is hot and stuffy, the countryside outside the window sleepy in the strong sunlight. There is little to interest him in the landscape that, typical of crowded England, overflows with signs of human habitation even in the country.

At first, he says, he did not notice that at every station a wedding party is assembled to see the bride and groom off on the train to their new life in London. This is the closest Larkin gets to the wedding ceremony itself. The poem, like his "Church Going" (1954) seems to suggest the absence of meaning in church ceremonies; people still enjoy the ritual of the building, the white dress, and the cheap, artificial jewelry, but they are modern inventions, devoid of substance. Just as the Whitsun wedding takes place on Saturday, not on Whit Sunday, official Pentecost, so the secular has taken over the old ceremonies of baptism, marriage, and funeral. The train journey itself symbolizes the movement into the modern secular age as the poet and the newly married couples leave the country for the big city. And yet the marriages seem to offer some consolation in the loss of meaningful ceremony. Those left behind wave farewell "to something that survived" the wedding. Recognizing something important, the poet gives up his book and becomes involved in the couples who have joined the train, referring to them now as "we." Together they are separated from the wedding parties on the platforms, where other young women consider the event a "religious wounding." This line is followed by the words "Free at last," which at first seems to refer to the girls left behind, suggesting their fear of marriage. But as the poem continues, it is the married couples and the poet who are free from the expectations of the parents and guests at the wedding, although burdened with the wedding itself (the guests' final assessment of the couple as representative of a central human event). Time has passed; the short shadows cast by the cattle at the beginning of the poem are replaced by longer shadows cast by poplar trees over the roads. Nearing London, modern, secular life impinges more and more on the poet and the marriages that have just begun. A transformation has occurred in the afternoon ceremonies; the brides declare "I nearly died," an ironic comment on their rebirth into a new life as wives. Are they "free at last," or is their world now enclosed, cut off? They do not let themselves think about the relationships that are now barred to them as married couples. This sense of marriage as entrapment seems to be suggested by the poet's image of London as divided into neat squares in opposition to the open farms at the beginning of the journey.

As the train enters the station the images suggest both entrapment and freedom. The walls of the tunnel encroach on them, with "blackened moss" (recalling perhaps Tennyson's broken-hearted Mariana, who yearns for death. The shadow of the poplars is also an echo of Mariana's plight). But the poet also sees the couples' new lives as full of the potential that change brings. The final stanza contains a metaphor of the train and its occupants as arrows in a powerful bow. They are "aimed" at London, and as the train slows, Larkin compares the emotions of the couples to a shower of arrows that will, somewhere, become rain. The final lines suggest that the wedding ceremonies, while secular and artificial, still produce something of human value and worth. The rain is clearly a symbol for fertility, for life going on for the couples on the train, however soulless the rituals of modern life have become.

Seamus Heaney's short poem "Mother of the Groom" (1966) deftly conveys the contradictory sense of pleasure and regret that a mother feels on seeing her children become independent. Watching her son's wedding, the mother remembers him as a small and vulnerable child, and the introduction of his wife into their lives is as though he had "kicked" and slipped from her soapy arms at bath time. A consolation is offered to the mother in the last stanza with the reminder that her wedding ring, which once slipped off so easily with soap, is now "bedded forever" on her finger. This mother is always a mother; but she is also a wife, as this new young woman has just become. The new bride's ring, acquired in the moment captured in the poem, will come to signify for her a lifetime of devotion as first wife and then mother, when she will share this mother's complex and deeply felt joy and pain. The speaker in Heaney's "Wedding Day" is the groom, addressing his bride and admitting in the first line to fear. Why are people crying as they wave goodbye? Why does the face of the father of the bride show "wild grief"? As his new wife sings behind the cake, she seems "demented," merely going through the motions of the day. But in the last stanza, the groom sees an ancient and modern symbol of love: a heart with an arrow through it, scratched on the washroom wall. As in "Whitsun Weddings," the poem finds love beneath the ceremony that in modern life sometimes seems devoid of meaning. As the couple drives away in the taxi, the groom frees himself from the ritual; like a child, he asks to sleep on his wife's breast. Marriage continues to be celebrated as the fullest expression of human love.

꧁꧂

"The Wife of Bath's Prologue and Tale," "The Clerk's Tale," "The Merchant's Tale," "The Franklin's Tale," from *The Canterbury Tales*, Geoffrey Chaucer

    NAEL-1

"Fain Would I Wed," Thomas Campion

    NAEL-1

"On Giles and Joan," Ben Jonson

    NAEl-1

"Why should a foolish marriage vow," from *Marriage a-la-Mode*, John Dryden

    NAEL-1

"A Married State," Kathleen Philips

    NAEL-1

"Epistle from Mrs. Yonge to Her Husband," Lady Mary Wortley Montagu

    NAEL-1

"An Epitaph," Matthew Prior
    ECP; NAEL-1; OAEL-1
"My Last Duchess," Robert Browning
    BAVP; ImPo; NAEL-2; OAEL-2; OBEV; TFi; TrGrPo-2
"To My Dear and Loving Husband," Anne Bradstreet
    OBEV; TFi
"Epithalamion," Sir Edmund Spenser
    NAEL-1; OAEL-1; TrGrPo-1
"Prothalamion," Sir Edmund Spenser
    ImPo; NAEL-1; OBEV; SB; TFi; TrGrPo-1
"A Ballad upon a Wedding," Sir John Suckling
    NAEL-1
"The Whitsun Weddings," Philip Larkin
    NoP; OxBTC
"Mother of the Groom," Seamus Heaney
    OxBSP
"Wedding Day," Seamus Heaney
    OxAEP-2

Music

Music and poetry have always been closely linked. Most poetry is considered "lyric" poetry (rather than dramatic or narrative poetry), taking its name from the lyre, a musical instrument originally used to accompany poetry. In ancient times, all poetry would have been sung, but songs are now usually considered inferior poetry. The great age of the poem set to music was the Renaissance, especially the reign of Elizabeth I, when music as entertainment was highly prized, and secular rather than religious songs became popular with contemporary poets and musicians. Thomas Campion was both, and he wrote many fine songs, such as "When to her lute Corinna sings" (1601), which neatly captures the relationship between the player and the song. Intended also as a love song, the poem credits Corinna's voice with bringing to life the sound of the lute. When she sings of happy things, the strings revive; when her song is sad, "ev'n with her sighs the strings do break." In the second stanza the poet compares himself to the lute; as Corinna plays upon the lute and governs its moods with her own, so she plays upon the emotions of the poet. "If she doth of sorrow speak,/Ev'n from my heart the strings do break." We do not need a musical setting to appreciate the deftness of Campion's comparison as he plays upon the idea of lute strings and heart strings breaking.

More usual in poetry about a woman playing a musical instrument is the poet's identification of his body with the instrument, rather than his mood. The poet envies the lute or harp whose strings are being so gently caressed by delicate fingers. Shakespeare's Sonnet 128, "How oft, when thou my music, music play'st" (1609) addresses a woman playing a harpsichord rather than a lute. The poet envies the keys "that nimble leap/ To kiss the tender inward of thy hand." He would exchange his lips for the fortunate jacks, but in the closing couplet, concedes her fingers to them if he can have her lips to kiss.

Sir Thomas Wyatt's "My Lute, Awake!" (c. 1557) is one of many love songs from the Renaissance. Here, Wyatt addresses the lute on which he is composing his lament for his unrequited love. Unable to speak directly to his cruel mistress, he addresses the lute instead, knowing that even if she could hear his complaint she would be unmoved by it. When the song is over, he says, he will stop grieving over his lost love, having used his verse to remind her that she will be punished for the pain she has dealt to her futile admirers. Finding herself old, she will regret that she rejected so many offers of love, for then it will be too late. Each stanza ends, hauntingly, with a variation on the line "My lute, be still, for I have done."

John Dryden wrote two poems for St. Cecilia's Day. St. Cecilia, an early Christian martyr in second- or third-century Rome, and the patron saint of music, was celebrated in England on her feast day, November 22, with a concert and religious service. Dryden's commissioned poems appeared in 1687 ("A Song for St. Cecilia's Day" with music by Giovanni Baptista Draghi) and 1697 ("Alexander's Feast"). "A Song for St. Cecilia's Day" honors St. Cecilia as the inventor of the organ, but it also ingeniously evokes different instruments as it celebrates the power of music as the divine harmony of the universe. The poem begins with the creation of the world, seeing music as the "heavenly harmony" that brought order out of chaos and created the Great Chain of Being, culminating in the creation of mankind. The poem is both musically lyrical in rhythm and complex in metaphor, blending the poetic and the musical. The sounds of the poem imitate the instrument (the "double double double beat/Of the thundering drum" and the "soft complaining flute"), but the creation of mankind brings woes into the world, which are also represented by the instruments. The trumpet calls us to war "with shrill notes of anger,/ And mortal alarms." The drum tells us that retreat is hopeless. The "dying notes" of the flute speak a dirge to "hopeless lovers." Violins, in contrast, proclaim a wilder misery of unrequited love:

> Their jealous pangs, and desperation,
> Fury, frantic indignation,
> Depths of pains, and height of passion,
>   For the fair, disdainful dame.

The chorus takes Creation to "the last and dreadful hour" when Music, the instrument of the Creator, shall "untune the sky" on the Day of Judgment.

"Alexander's Feast, or the Power of Music" was originally set to music by Jeremiah Clarke, but Handel also composed a score for it in 1736.

Taking the form of a Pindaric ode, the poem tells the legend of Timotheus, musician to Alexander the Great, who could inspire different passions in his master through his music. The setting is a celebratory feast in Alexander's court after his defeat of the Persian emperor Darius III at Persepolis in 331 B.C. Seated with his mistress, Thais, Alexander is feted by the famous chorus, "None but the brave deserves the fair." Timotheus uses his music to manipulate the great Alexander, first depicting him as the son of Olympia and Jove, the chief gods, in the form of a dragon. In stanza three, the musician sings in praise of Bacchus, the Roman god of wine, luring Alexander into a drunken revery about his past heroic victories. Timotheus's music has urged Alexander into a frenzied state, where in his mind "thrice he routed all his foes, and thrice he slew the slain." Seeing his master's "madness rise," Timotheus switches moods by reminding Alexander of his enemy Darius, who was assassinated by his own men after Alexander's victory: "Fallen, fallen, fallen, fallen,/ Fallen from his high estate,/And weltering in his blood." The portrait of such treachery reverses Alexander's exultant mood, casting him into a gloomy contemplation of the vagaries of fortune. In stanza five the music switches Alexander's moods once again, this time to love, easily following from pity. Now Alexander finds only folly in war as Timotheus sings, "War . . . is toil and trouble;/Honor, but an empty bubble." The legend of Alexander as told by Plutarch claims that Thais persuaded Alexander to set fire to the royal place at Persepolis in exchange for Xerxes' burning of Athens in 480 B.C. In the poem, Alexander "gazed on the fair/Who caused his care," but "with love and wine at once oppressed" he succumbs to her beauty and sinks against her, a "vanquished victor." But in stanza six the musician again manipulates the great hero, awakening him with a burst of noise that rouses him to avenge the deaths of his Greek warriors.

In stanza seven, Dryden's tribute to Saint Cecilia emerges. Timotheus with his flute and lyre "could swell the soul to rage, or kindle soft desire," but he is eclipsed by "divine" Cecilia, a Christian rather than a pagan, who invented the organ and "from her sacred store" added a spiritual dimension to Timotheus's power to influence the emotions: "He raised a mortal to the skies;/She drew an angel down."

William Wordsworth's "The Solitary Reaper" (1805) exemplifies many elements of romanticism: a new interest in ordinary rural people, a concern with individual personalities rather than "man" in general (the chief interest of the eighteenth century), and a new desire to write in the language of the common man. The poet describes coming upon a Highland lass, reaping and singing in Gaelic. Her song, more beautiful than that of the nightingale or the cuckoo, reaches across the landscape and into the poet's heart. He does not understand the words, which frees him to hear the song as belonging to the ancient world, as so many bird songs do. Even when the song is gone from the physical world of hearing, it remains with him, a part of his imagination:

> The music in my heart I bore,
> Long after it was heard no more.

One of the most haunting of poems about music is Alfred, Lord Tennyson's "The Splendour Falls" from "The Princess" (1850). The poem describes an ancient Irish castle at sunset, isolated amid wild cataracts and purple glens (Tennyson wrote the poem after visiting Killarney in 1848, where he heard eight distinct echoes of a bugle's call). The setting is merged with the sound of the bugle calling across the lake: "Blow bugle, blow, set the wild echoes flying,/Blow, bugle; answer, echoes, dying, dying, dying." The tone of lament and regret—of far-off times merged with personal losses—is typical of Tennyson's poetry, as is the poem's brilliant echoing of sound in the rhythm and language. A hint of solace appears in the third stanza, when Tennyson compares the dying of the bugle's echoes with the immortality of human communication: "Our echoes roll from soul to soul,/And grow for ever and for ever." These lines connect the poem to "In Memoriam A.H.H." (1850), but the general effect of "The Splendour Falls" is the re-creation of the sound of a bugle's call on a lonely lakeside in a faraway land, long ago. It is one of many poems that testify to the musical quality of the English language in the hands of the great poets.

❧⌣❧

"When to her lute Corinna sings," Thomas Campion
    NAEL-1; OAEL-1; TrGrPo-1
Sonnet 128, "How oft, when thou my music, music play'st," William Shakespeare
    NAEL-1
"My Lute, Awake!" Sir Thomas Wyatt
    NAEL-1; OAEL-1; OBEV; TrGrPo-1
"A Song for St. Cecilia's Day," John Dryden
    BL; ImPo; OAEL-1; NAEl-1; TFi; TrGrPo-1
"Alexander's Feast, or the Power of Music," John Dryden
    NAEL-1; OAEL-1; TFi; TrGrPo-1

"The Solitary Reaper," William Wordsworth
  ImPo; NAEL-2; OAEL-2; OBEV; TFi; TrGrPo-2
"The Splendour Falls," Alfred, Lord Tennyson
  NAEL-2; OAEL-2; TFi; TrGrPo-2

Nature and Country Life

❧

Nature, in the tangible sense of landscape—sky, rivers, oceans, land, plants, and animals—is a golden thread running through nearly all the themes of this survey, for mankind's relationship with the natural world affects almost every other relationship. What is our place in the universe, and what are our responsibilities, especially with regard to the animal kingdom? How does nature affect us personally? To what extent are our moods and thoughts—our very beings—influenced by the seasons, by weather, by the beauty of our surroundings? Why is the culture and religion of northern Europe, where the climate is severe and the land rugged and deeply forested, so different from the culture and religion of southern Europe, where the sun shines year round and the landscape encompasses a brilliantly blue sea, terraces of grapes, and sun-baked fields of olives and tomatoes? These questions have vexed all nationalities and are at the heart of religious belief also, appearing in the creation stories that account for the origins of nature and man.

British poetry offers a particularly rich appreciation of landscape because the countryside of Britain is both varied and beautiful, lush with the heavily scented greenery that a temperate climate provides. It is also a countryside that has been settled and cultivated since literature began, unlike North America, where the literature of the early settlers was deeply concerned with the taming of the wilderness. Although there are still remote and wild areas in northern Scotland and Wales, much of the British landscape has for centuries been composed of peaceful, orderly rivers and canals, neat fields, and flower-laden hedgerows. It was not until travel abroad became more commonplace in the eighteenth century that poetry about untamed nature—treacherous mountains, vast waterfalls, and fast-flowing rivers—came to be written. And although earlier poets such as Edmund Spenser, John Milton, and William Shakespeare wrote evocative descriptions of England, (often as celebrations of God's creation, found also in the poetry of Gerard Manley Hopkins in the nineteenth century), a deep appreciation of the loveliness of the British countryside did not fully enter British poetry until the end of the eighteenth century with the Romantic poets. Most earlier poets wrote in a tradition that once again went back to the ancient Greeks and Romans, and was called "Pastoral," from the Latin word for "feed" (hence a pastor was a shepherd, responsible for the feeding of his flock).

Pastoral poetry came to the British poets partly through the Greek writer Theocritus (third century B.C.) but more strongly through the Roman writer Virgil (first century B.C.). As soon as the ancient world became dominated by city-states, poets hankered after a lost countryside where life was simpler and more rewarding. This ideal, pastoral world, had been depicted by an earlier Greek farmer and poet, Hesiod, in his eighth century B.C. *Works and Days*. Hesiod describes the five ages of mankind, the oldest being the Golden Age, when country folk—shepherds and shepherdesses—knew no evil and lived in perfect harmony with nature, which supplied food in abundance. Work was unnecessary, and these innocent country shepherds and shepherdesses ("rustics") enjoyed perfect summer, courting and engaging in music competitions. With the coming of evil into man's nature, this ideal world was lost. The biblical equivalent is the Fall of man and the loss of the Garden of Eden, caused by man's desire for the knowledge of good and evil. The Fall affected the natural world also, bringing into it seasons, harsh weather, and a cycle of birth and death. The nostalgic longing for a lost Golden Age set in beautiful countryside is one aspect of Pastoral poetry that remains with us and has influenced a huge body of poetry, including poems about the active (city) and contemplative (country) lives, innocence (country) and experience (city), and the poems of the Industrial Revolution.

The idealized portrait of a Golden Age gradually altered, however, as early as in the poetry of Virgil, whose *Eclogues* (c. 40 B.C.) described a rustic paradise but also referred to contemporary events. Another strand of pastoral poetry emerged through Virgil's *Georgics* (c. 35 B.C.). Hesiod's *Works and Days* had included a farmer's calendar, giving practical advice on agriculture based on the seasons. Virgil's *Georgics* ("agricultural poems") were intended to renew the old love for the land and respect for nature and the value of working in harmony with it. Many British poets have continued in this tradition, especially after the more idealistic Pastoral poetry began to die out after its great popularity in the Renaissance. Poems about the seasons, the passing of a day and night in the country, and the rewards of working on the land have all entered British poetry in a blending of the idealized, classical Pastoral, and the more realistic native tradition. If novelists have helped to create our understanding and imaginative vision of cities—Dickens's London, James Joyce's Dublin, Sir Walter Scott's Edinburgh—the poets have brought alive Britain's beautiful countryside and the birds and animals that inhabit it. This section discusses those poems whose main theme is man's view of his relationship with nature, but it can only touch upon the wealth of poems about the natural world, and introduce readers to the poets best known for their concern with nature and its connection with human affairs.

THE SEASONS

Anyone connected with the land watches the sky and follows a calendar throughout the year, for the cycle of planting, nurturing, and harvesting is so closely tied to the seasons. As a predominantly rural land until the eighteenth century, and as a land affected by seasons, each with its own joys, Britain naturally has produced many fine poems about the changing year. Many seasonal poems are not just descriptions of the countryside but evocations of the poet's mood, either in or out of sympathy with the time of year. Ovid in the *Metamorphoses* (43 B.C.–A.D. 18) draws attention to the similarities between the seasons in nature and the seasons in a human life, as does John Keats in his sonnet "The Human Seasons" (1818). The soul moves from "lusty Spring" to dreamy Summer, when the observations made in the Spring of life are chewed upon, like a cow ruminating. Autumn brings idleness, when the soul is content to "let fair things/Pass by unheeded." Finally Winter comes, without comment, the inevitable end of "mortal nature." For Shakespeare, also, the seasons were a favorite metaphor for human life, as in *Richard III*'s (1591) famous opening line, "Now is the winter of our discontent/Made glorious summer by this sun of York."

A more profound comparison between the seasons and man's life is made by the seventeenth-century devotional George Herbert in his lovely spring poem "The Flower" (1633). Each of the seven stanzas is shaped like a flower on a stem, and the central metaphor praises God for continually bringing spiritual renewal to the poet just as he brings the world to life again in the spring:

> Who would have thought my shriveled heart
> Could have recovered greenness? It was gone
>   Quite underground; as flowers depart
> To see their mother-root, when they have blown.

While reveling in his return to full bloom, Herbert also looks forward to blossoming in God's eternal garden.

Spring is always associated with youthful vigor and restlessness; the birds and animals are courting, and so are we: "Sweet lovers love the spring," sing the pages in Shakespeare's *As You Like It* (c. 1599), and in "Locksley Hall" (1837–1838) Tennyson reminds us that "In the spring a young man's fancy lightly turns to thoughts of love." One of the earliest lyrics in English poetry is the anonymous "Cuckoo Song," a delightful song to be sung in a round as a lusty reminder of spring's return: "Sumer is ycomen in,/Loude sing cuckou!" The cuckoo returns to England in April, so every year people compete to be the first to record hearing it, therefore marking the official end of winter. Spring is wonderfully evoked by Geoffrey Chaucer in the opening lines of his *Canterbury Tales* (c. 1387) where the birds, and the young Squire, are unable to sleep, and all of nature is awakening to sexual activity after the winter: April's sweet showers have pierced dry March to the root, and brought life back to the flowers and the pilgrims. Chaucer brilliantly turns pagan aspects of country lore (such as astrology and fertility rites) into Christian imagery associated with Easter as the pilgrims set off on their religious journey to Canterbury. Another famous evocation of spring is Thomas Nashe's Elizabethan lyric "Spring, the sweet Spring, is the year's pleasant king" (1592). Each stanza ends with the sound of the cuckoo and the other birds whose mating songs are a clarion call of life returning to the land—"Cuckoo, jug-jug, pu-we, to-witta-woo!"

Many seasonal and diurnal poems find a parallel between the mood of the natural world and the mood of the poet, but the discrepancy between the two can also be a source of comment. The earl of Surrey's "The Soote [sweet] Season" (1557) is a sonnet about spring (he calls it summer, but such mixing of terms was not unusual) that unusually contains only two rhymes. Based on a sonnet by Petrarch, it employs the traditional signs of spring in the activities of the animals and birds as new life burgeons after the winter. All of nature is busy mating, feeding, sloughing off old skins, and enjoying rebirth after the harm of winter. But the couplet draws the painful contrast between nature's state of mind and the poet's. For nature, spring means the end of worry, but for him it brings only sorrow. Many Renaissance poems contrasted the happiness of birds in courtship with the misery of the lovelorn speaker.

William Wordsworth (1770–1850) is of all British poets the one most readily associated with nature (Shelley called him "Poet of Nature" in his sonnet to him). Like the earl of Surrey's poem, Wordsworth's spring poem, "Lines Written in Early Spring" (1798), contrasts nature's bountiful joy with the poet's sadness. The rejuvenation of spring in nature reminds the poet that such rebirth is harder to achieve in the human world. Whereas the earl of Surrey is made more aware of his own sadness, Wordsworth grieves the unnatural cruelty of the world created by man. He is not specific about the wrongs, lamenting generally "what man has made of man," but at this stage in his life Wordsworth was a

radical, acutely conscious of class oppression and the injustices perpe-
trated by human systems and institutions. Man has somehow transgressed "Nature's holy plan" in causing such suffering.

Sir Edmund Spenser's "The Shepeardes Calender" (1579) was the first
extended Pastoral poem based on the classical models of Theocritus and
Virgil. It contained twelve eclogues, for the months of the year, illustrated by woodcuts. As "Colin Clout," Spenser narrates the first and last
month, and the others contain conversations between shepherds on topics such as love, religion, morality, and the importance of poetry. The
landscape in "The Shepeardes Calender" is partly classical Pastoral,
partly England, partly a representation of the shepherds' moods as the
seasons pass. The relationship between the shepherds and their natural
surroundings is complex—sometimes nature governs their moods and
activities, sometimes it seems to be in sympathy with them, and sometimes it is quite independent, a beautiful but separate world from the
human world.

Another sustained poem about the seasons is James Thomson's four-
book poem in blank verse entitled "The Seasons," written between 1726
and 1730. "Winter" is followed by "Summer," then "Spring," and "Autumn." Each section is marked by acute observations of nature and country people whose lives are closely bound up with the land. It was an
extremely popular series of poems for two centuries, and it is still published in extracts, partly because Thomson is now considered a forerun-
ner of some of the Romantic poets of the early nineteenth century in his
interest in simple country people and the countryside rather than the
more sophisticated, urban topics of the Augustan poets with whom he
was a contemporary.

The early Romantic poet William Blake turned his attention to the seasons when he first began to publish poetry in 1783. Blake addresses the
seasons directly in "To Spring," "To Summer," "To Autumn," and "To
Winter." The speaker depicts Spring as the lover for whom the "love-sick
land" has been anxiously preparing; "To Summer" is spoken by England
to the lusty god that takes up residence under a tent during the hot season;
in "To Autumn" the English landscape invites the season to stay while
the harvest is gathered; "jolly Autumn" is happy to do so, but at last "fled
from our sight, but left his golden load." Finally, Winter comes as a "dire-
ful monster" bringing blight and destruction that "freezes up frail life."

The quintessential autumn poem is Keats's "To Autumn" (1819), whose
opening line—"Season of mists and mellow fruitfulness"—rises to many
English minds when the leaves start to turn and a chill is in the air. In
a letter, Keats wrote that the poem was inspired by a favorite walk near
Winchester, Hampshire, on a day when the view of the fields and river
was "warm." He intended to capture that sense of the landscape steeped

in the afterglow of a summer of sunshine. The poem, addressed through-out to the personification of Autumn, contains three stanzas. In the first, Autumn has "conspired" with the "maturing sun" to "load and bless" the land with a heavy harvest of ripe fruit. The sexual imagery associ-ated with spring here finds fruition in images of pregnancy and birth: Autumn, "close bosom-friend" of the sun, will "swell the gourd, and plump the hazel shells/With a sweet kernel. . . ." The bees will be lulled into thinking that summer will never end, finding the flowers still awash with nectar. The flowers, too, seem to be caught in a summer that cannot end. Keats emphasizes that they are "set budding more,/And still more, later flowers. . . ." Autumn is benevolent, rewarding man's labor with na-ture's seemingly endless gifts. For man's presence is there in the "moss'd cottage-trees" and the "thatch-eaves" burdened with heavy vines.

The mood of languid, passive rest after the activity of spring and sum-mer continues in the second stanza, when Autumn rather than the farmer is inside the granary. But rather than busily reaping and storing, Autumn again appears as a pregnant figure, "sitting careless on a granary floor," the wind gently ruffling her hair, or asleep "on a half-reap'd furrow," drugged with poppies and unable to finish the scything. Or she is a gleaner crossing a stream, head held steady with its load of grain, or a patient minder of a cider press, languidly watching "the last oozings hours by hours." Although Autumn is often personified as male, in this poem the image of immanent birth is strong, and the personification suggests the full, rather awkward form of the pregnant woman who is patiently absorbed in her surroundings while curiously detached from them, both sitting "careless" and watching hour after hour. The person-ification of Autumn perfectly captures the poignancy of the moment just before birth, when the long wait is over and the "mellow fruitfulness" is at the point of dropping to earth, like the fruit of the vines and apple trees of the opening stanza. The image of crossing a brook suggests the moment of birth, and recalls the same image in Keats's earlier sonnet "The Human Seasons" (1818), in which the mind in Autumn is content just to watch "fair things/Pass by unheeded as a threshold brook." The threshold marks the passage from Autumn's rich harvest to the death of winter.

The third stanza recalls spring, the season that brought about this har-vest. Where are the songs, he asks, the bird songs that heralded sexual activity, to culminate now in birth? They are replaced by the sadder songs of the cycle of nature completed. Autumn has her music too, but it is the subdued sounds of the "soft-dying day." The poem has moved beyond the harvest into the cycle of nature that sees death follow pro-creation and birth. The "small gnats mourn" as they are "borne aloft/ Or sinking as the light wind lives or dies." "Full-grown lambs loud bleat" in a reminder that their life cycle is also coming to an end. Finally, "gathering swallows" prepare to fly south as nothing now is left but the coming of winter. In its movement from late summer—the fruit still hanging on the vine—to the harvest, and finally the aftermath, where stubble has taken the place of the waving grain, and the natural cycle prepares for death, "To Autumn" has never been bettered as an evocation of an English autumn.

The influence of Keats's uncertain future—he knew in 1819 that tuberculosis was likely to cut his life short, and that he would never enjoy the winter of his life—adds poignancy to this picture of a rich harvest being garnered, just as in his sonnet about his early death, "When I have fears that I may cease to be" (1818), he laments that the books he will not have time to write will never "hold like rich garners the full ripen'd grain." Just after Keats wrote "To Autumn" he mentioned in a letter to a friend that autumn always reminded him of Thomas Chatterton, a poet much admired by the Romantics who took his own life at the age of eighteen.

An earlier sonnet, "On the Grasshopper and the Cricket" (1816), takes a more cheerful view of insect life than is found at the end of "To Autumn." The cheerful sound of grasshopper and cricket is immortal, Keats says. The first line of the octave declares that "the poetry of earth is never dead" because the grasshopper keeps singing all summer, when the birds take to the trees to avoid the heat. In the sestet "the poetry of earth is ceasing never" because in the winter the cricket's song shrills from the stove while the frost holds the world in icy silence outside. Hearing the cricket, the drowsy listener seems also to hear the voice of the grasshopper "among some grassy hills."

NIGHTTIME

If spring and autumn are the poets' favorite seasons, night is often their favorite time, at least for the Romantics and a few eighteenth-century poets who looked ahead to the Gothic, mysterious interests of the Romantics rather than the sensible, rational interests of most eighteenth-century poets. Anne Finch was one of the earliest poets to appreciate nighttime in "A Nocturnal Reverie" (1713), but she loves it as a peaceful, meditative time, away from the cares of the day, rather than for its horrors (such as are found in Coleridge's "The Pains of Sleep" [1802], for example). Fifty lines follow in one sentence from the opening introduction "In such a night, when every louder wind/Is to its distant cavern safe confined . . . ," with the details of the poem arising from a series of "when" or "whilst" clauses. The evening winds are gentle, and the wanderer is guided by the soft sounds of the nightingale. Some fine details bring the scene before the reader's eyes, such as the vision of the river, "overhung with green," upon which "the waving moon and trembling leaves are seen." Nature is transformed on such a night into a more peaceful state; the air is more fragrant than in the "repelling day," and the animals are free to enjoy a quiet meal—the horse is "loosed," the cattle "unmolested," and the partridge out of danger from men with nets. The poet seems to feel a greater kinship with nature at this quiet time, when she can be a part of the scene rather than a part of "tyrant man." For the poet, night brings a freeing of the soul from the burdens of the day, just as the animals are free from the interference of man.

William Collins (1721–1759) seemed destined for a distinguished literary career after attending Winchester School and Oxford University, and joining a literary set in London that included James Thomson, with whom he shared an interest in nature. Collins gradually went mad and died young, but his interests aligned him with the eighteenth-century poets who influenced the Romantic poets at the beginning of the next century. Collins, Thomson, and others preferred the darker side of nature and human nature to the hearty faith in common sense and civilized, urban life of the Augustan poets. Collins's "Ode to Evening" (1747) became very popular and influenced John Keats in particular, who shared Collins's interest in melancholy and nighttime, as well as the form of the ode. Collins addresses Eve, goddess of the evening, in the formal, anthropomorphic terms of the classical odes ("now the bright-haired Sun/ Sits in yon western Tent"), but the poet's longing for the melancholic effects of darkness on the "weak-eyed bat" and on the ancient pile of ruins looks ahead to the Romantic movement in poems like Keats's "Ode on Melancholy" (1819). Unlike other eighteenth-century night poems, often referred to as the "graveyard school" (including the Irish poet Thomas Parnell's "Night-Piece on Death" [1721], and Edward Young's "Night Thoughts" [1742]), Collins's ode speaks not directly of death, but rather appreciates the coming of night in all seasons because, out of doors, "Fancy, Friendship, Science, rose-lip'd Health" flourish best under the "gradual dusky Veil" of night.

Samuel Taylor Coleridge rejects the notion of pathetic fallacy—giving human emotion to the natural world, and particularly finding melancholy in night sounds—in his "conversational poem" "The Nightingale" (1798). His conversation is with William and Dorothy Wordsworth as they walk together one still, April evening and hear the nightingale's song. He refers to Milton's "Il Penseroso" (c. 1631), in which the speaker calls the bird "most musical, most melancholy." In a footnote, Coleridge allows this identification because it is the dramatization of the speaker's own melancholy, but he still warns against the human impulse to ascribe emotion to nature. "In nature there is nothing melancholy," he argues, but some sad man filled the world with his own sadness, and poets have taken up the nightingale's burden of man's sorrow. Far better, says Coleridge, for the poet to love nature for itself, "surrendering his whole spirit, of his song/And of his fame forgetful!" Realizing that people will continue to find the nightingale's song melancholy, Coleridge still urges his friends to recognize that Nature's "sweet voices" are "always full of love/And joyance," and the nightingale is "merry." He describes the bird as being awakened into song by the moon's appearance from behind a cloud, just as the eolian harp (in Coleridge's poem of that name) was awakened by the wind. The poem closes with Coleridge's recollection of the moon's good effect on his young son. Once when the baby awoke out of a nightmare, he took him outside where the sight of the moon instantly calmed and brightened him. Coleridge wants his son to grow up associating nighttime with joy, not melancholy.

The Romantic poet Percy Bysshe Shelley speaks of night as his creative time in "To Night" (1820). Addressing the Spirit of Night, Shelley makes him a mysterious, even dangerous, figure, suggesting the mixture of joy and fear with which many writers of the time associated their relationship with their imagination. It brought freedom and vision, but sometimes it took them to terrifying depths as well. The Spirit of Night has spent the day in a mysterious eastern cave weaving dreams "of joy and fear,/Which make thee terrible and dear." In stanza two, the poet tells the Night to woo the Day into sleep by kissing her into oblivion and blinding her with his hair. Stanza three marks the poet's impatience as the slow day passes; he awaits Night as he would a lover. In stanza four, he is wooed by Night's brother, Death, and his child, Sleep, the two usual associates of Night, but in the final stanza he rejects them, knowing that they will come in their own time. But now he needs "beloved Night."

Emily Brontë's relationship with the night is similarly described as a courtship in "The Night-Wind" (1840). The poet is sitting by an open window in a summer midnight when the wind lifts her hair and talks to her of death. She tells the wind that its "wooing voice is kind," but she wishes to keep her human soul separate from the natural world. Blow through the flowers and trees, she tells it, but "leave my human feelings/In their own course to flow." The poem suggests a fear of losing herself in an imaginative identification with the night wind. It woos her persistently, kissing her warmly and threatening to win her " 'gainst thy will." The Romantic poets' attachment to melancholy is strong in the temptation offered by the wind when he reminds her that they have always been friends. The last stanza notes that a time will come when death separates her from the natural world and she will be immune to the wind's caress, lying "beneath the church-yard stone."

COUNTRY HOUSE POEMS

Poems that pay tribute to the stately homes of the British Isles (and their owners) usually concentrate on the beauty of their extensive grounds. They were most popular in the seventeenth and eighteenth centuries, when formal gardens were greatly admired. Implicit in the idea of the cultivated garden was the notion that man could improve upon nature. A landowner would dam streams to make them flow in chosen directions; topiary, or shaping hedges and trees into particular shapes, was popular; and classical form—careful arrangement of flower beds and statuary— was preferred to natural growth. The gardens were designed to be pleasing to the eye from the house, the center of the estate, and to the lord and lady, center of civilized life in the country. Best known of these poems is Ben Jonson's "To Penshurst," the Kent home of Sir Philip Sidney's family (open today to the public), written in 1616. Jonson begins his description by telling Penshurst that it is superior to the highly ornate houses built for show by tasteless owners wishing to show off to their visitors. Jonson's portrait of Penshurst's beauties—its walks, copse, ponds, and orchards— is a tribute to the generous hospitality of the Sidneys, for the purpose of the grounds is to provide ample food for their table. The grounds feed the sheep and cattle; the copse provides pheasant and partridge, who are "willing to be killed" for the table; the fish "run into thy net"; and eels leap into the fisherman's hand. Even children can easily reach the peaches and apricots that hang from the trees in the orchard. The house and grounds are thus an extension of their generous owner, existing to provide food and nourishment for all and sundry and doing so willingly. This notion of the landowner as steward and the land as valued for its bounty is typical of the seventeenth and eighteenth centuries, when wild nature was somewhat feared, but cultivated nature—improved by the hand of man—was mankind's rightful inheritance, according to the Bible. Jonson goes further, however, in suggesting that Penshurst is almost a return to the Golden Age. The emphasis in the poem is on the readiness of the land and the animals to yield themselves up for food—abundance is everywhere, without seeming effort on the part of the fisherman or the hunter.

With ownership of the land came a heavy responsibility, however, and Jonson praises the Sidneys' generosity to all comers, not just fellow landed gentry. The house itself was not built at the expense of the builders: "No man's ruin, no man's groan" went into its construction. All the neighbors wish them well and bring their own small contributions— peasant food like capons and apples—to the table, where they are all welcome to share the food that the lord himself eats (unlike many big houses, where the lower classes and the servants would have received a very different diet). By addressing the estate in the poem, Jonson identifies Penshurst with its owner and attributes the moral qualities of benevolence and generosity to both. Owner and land work together in harmony for the good of a feudal society dependent upon the lord and his lady's good stewardship (the lady is praised for her excellent housewifery). The children are being trained to live similarly religious, virtuous lives, accepting their responsibility as landowners. The poem ends with a nice distinction between the ornate but useless houses of the wealthy, and the plainer but useful and harmonious Penshurst:

> Those proud, ambitious heaps, and nothing else,
> May say, their lords have built, but thy lord dwells.

King James I is mentioned as visiting Penshurst, a reference to his proclamation telling the gentry to live in their country homes, not in London, because the social structure of England depended upon the good stewardship of the landed gentry and their support of their communities. This notion is evident also in the novels of Jane Austen.

Contemporary with "To Penshurst" was Aemilia Lanyer's tribute to her patron Margaret Clifford, countess of Cumberland, entitled "The Description of Cooke-ham" (1611). The estate belonged to the countess's brother, but the poem describes the natural elements of the estate preparing for her arrival and mourning her departure. The emphasis here is not on the countess's benevolence (although it is mentioned in passing) but on her virtue and grace, which the natural world admired and aimed to please. The poem is heavily marked by what John Ruskin was to label "pathetic fallacy," the attributing of emotion to nonhuman elements of nature to show their sympathy with the people in the scene. Thus "each arbor, bank, each seat, each stately tree,/Thought themselves honored in supporting thee." When the countess departs, the trees weep and shed their leaves in an attempt to win her pity. The purpose of the poem is not to elucidate the harmony between estate and lady, as in "To Penshurst," but to flatter Lanyer's patron with the notion of the estate's adoration of her.

Other country house poems include Thomas Carew's "To Saxham" and "To my friend G.N. from *Wrest*" (1640), both influenced by "To Penshurst" in their evocation of a hospitable, feudal society where the land happily contributes to the feeding of the poor. Carew, however, also emphasizes the country estate as an innocent retreat, safe from the dangers of court intrigue and plotting leading up to the regicide of Charles I in 1649 (Carew died in 1640). His hospitality is less egalitarian than Jonson's also, as the guests do not enjoy equal entertainment. Robert Herrick, another Cavalier poet, praises the lord for his equal generosity to all in "A Panegerick to Sir Lewis Pemberton" (1648). The idealized, pastoral world of the shepherd has been replaced by the real world of benevolent, socially responsible gentry who are able to uphold the old courtly ideals of gentlemanly conduct. Andrew Marvell's long poem "Upon Appleton House" (1651) is a tribute to Lord Fairfax, a retired general on the parliamentary side of the civil war, and his daughter Mary, for whom Marvell served as tutor from 1651 to 1653. A Puritan, Marvell succeeded his friend John Milton as Oliver Cromwell's Latin Secretary in 1657. The poem, while celebrating the beauties of Nun Appleton and his pleasant years there, is also an allegory about the Reformation and the Civil War. Marvell's attitude to nature is very different from that of the other country house poets. At Nun Appleton he also wrote "The Garden" and four "Mower" (1681) poems that emphasize man as the master of nature, controlling it and not always kindly (as is suggested by "mowing" with its connotation of Death wielding his scythe). "The Mower's Song" (1681) compares the cruelty of the mower's lover to his cruelty to the grass. He expects nature to sympathize with his suffering, and he intends to mow down the grass just as Juliana will mow him down. "The Mower Against Gardens" (1681) accuses man after the Fall of using his new vice to interfere with nature and, through science, alter the natural colors and scents of the flowers and meddle with natural propagation. So busy are we in creating artificial gardens that the "sweet fields do lie forgot."

TOPOGRAPHICAL POETRY

Similar to the country house poems, topographical poems were mostly written in the eighteenth century. Samuel Johnson defined topographical poetry as "local poetry, of which the fundamental object is some particular landscape . . . with the addition of . . . historical retrospection or incidental meditation." Many topographical poems describe the view from a high point, and although they often include a country house and grounds, they concentrate on the landscape rather than the relationship between the owners and the estate. Sir John Denham's "Cooper's Hill" (1642) became the model. Other examples are Alexander Pope's "Windsor Forest" (1713), Sir Samuel Garth's "Claremont" (1715), John Dyer's "Grongar Hill" (1726), discussed in the Active and Contemplative Lives section, and Richard Jago's "Edge-hill" (1767).

VILLAGE LIFE

When Alexander Pope defined Pastoral poetry in 1704, he noted that it must present only the happy side of a shepherd's life and conceal the miserable side—the winter nights spent digging sheep out of snowdrifts, the poor diet, the loneliness, and the poverty that was the real lot of most British shepherds. Pope recognized that the Pastoral was a formal literary convention, intended to show off the poet's technical skill and provide an escape from life's worries. While the country house poems tended to glorify the life of the gentry, Oliver Goldsmith's much-loved poem "The Deserted Village" (1770) painted an idyllic picture of a way of life that had disappeared with the growing wealth of landowners and farmers. "Sweet Auburn! loveliest village of the plain" was created partly from Goldsmith's memories of his childhood in Lissoy, Ireland, and partly from a longing for a simpler, less materialistic way of life. The "one only master" who has taken over the common land previously farmed by many, each growing just what his family needed, has ruined the land with his greed and neglect: "Ill fares the land, to hastening ills a prey,/Where wealth accumulates, and men decay." Goldsmith charges the new landowners (as did Jonathan Swift in Ireland) with destroying the old ways to live in opulence and luxury. The "bold peasantry," deprived of their land, have been forced into the towns or to emigration. As he walks round the deserted village, lamenting the loss of its cottages, its neglected woods, and overgrown gardens, he acknowledges that his dream had always been to retire to his childhood home. Now he has to rely on his memory in order to describe the village of his youth for the reader, and paint vivid portraits of its once-colorful inhabitants in the manner of Chaucer's Prologue to his *Canterbury Tales* (c. 1387). The village preacher, "passing rich with forty pounds a year," was the antithesis of the greedy modern farmer in his open-hearted charity to all in need, deserving or not. The schoolmaster, dreaded by truant schoolboys who wisely pretended to laugh at his jokes, was the admiration of the village for his extensive knowledge. The simple village louts would gaze in amazement when he argued with the parson: "And still they gazed, and still the wonder grew,/That one small head could carry all he knew."

Goldsmith contrasts the simple, humble, and pleasant life of the old village with the horrors to which the villagers were forced to flee. The city means luxury and vice for the wealthy, prostitution and misery for the poor. Emigration takes them to a foreign land, populated by a motley variety of wild beasts in a harsh climate, so different from the temperate weather, lush countryside, and friendly birds and animals of the village. The "various terrors" of the foreign shore include blazing suns, poisonous fields, scorpions, rattlesnakes, tigers, savage men, and tornadoes. The villagers take all their virtues with them—"Contented toil, and hospitable care,/And kind connubial tenderness . . . and piety . . . and steady loyalty, and faithful love."

Goldsmith's poem was immensely popular when it was first published. Thomas Gray, whose "Elegy written in a Country Churchyard" (1751) is a similar portrait of village life, praised it, and the German philosopher and writer Johann Wolfgang von Goethe was so impressed that he immediately translated it into German. Edmund Burke also admired it. Thomas Macaulay pointed to philosophical problems within the poem, however, noting that the village of the past sounded like an English village, but the deserted village must have been an Irish village because it was the Irish who were driven to emigration. But no Irish village was ever remotely like the idyllic Auburn of the poem. Goldsmith's biographer, John Forster, agreed that Goldsmith oversimplified his argument in making trade and larger farms the destroyer of all virtue and happiness. In the character sketches in particular, however, "The Deserted Village" has remained a favorite evocation of a simpler time, when humble virtues were valued more than possessions and luxury.

George Crabbe took exception to Goldsmith's idealizing, and in "The Village" (1783) he offered what he considered a more realistic portrait of village life. Crabbe takes issue with the whole notion of Pastoral poetry— the idealizing of a shepherd's life as described by Pope and pursued as a poetic exercise by English poets studying classical modes. While Pope maintained that the Pastoral "consists in exposing the best side only of a shepherd's life, and in concealing its miseries," Crabbe set out not "these real ills to hide/In tinsel trappings of poetic pride." He considered it an insult to the poor to depict them as idyllically happy when the truth was so different, at least for English shepherds. Crabbe knew rural poverty in his own life, so he was sympathetic to the seamier side of country life. In his landscape, "thistles stretch their prickly arms afar,/ And to the ragged infant threaten war." He overturns Goldsmith's portrait of a "bold peasantry" cheerfully playing games on the village green, and rather than seeing nature as a benevolent bestower of food and plenty, Crabbe depicts the land as impoverished, giving with a "niggard hand." Unlike the supportive community of Goldsmith's village, Crabbe's rural society ignores its old people, who end their days in the workhouse, its miseries described in chilling and realistic detail. Although Crabbe's village was never as popular as Goldsmith's, it had many admirers including Sir Walter Scott, and it brought to poetry a concern for social conditions that was taken up by the city poets of the nineteenth century.

THE ROMANTIC MOVEMENT

The Romantic movement in British poetry is generally accepted to have begun with the French Revolution of 1789. By 1830 it had run its course, with the deaths of the major poets of the movement (John Keats in 1821, Percy Bysshe Shelley in 1822, Lord Byron in 1824, and Samuel Taylor Coleridge in 1834). William Wordsworth lived until 1850, but his best poetry was written around the turn of the century. The poets associated with romanticism shared certain similarities that arose as a reaction against eighteenth-century classicism and rationalism, and that corresponded with the rise of the democratic movement inspired by the French and American revolutions.

The literature of the eighteenth century, especially during the Augustan Age in the first half of the century, was characterized by its urbanity, wittiness, and polished style. Most of the writers of the time were city dwellers, advocates of civilized life and interested in man as a species rather than as individual personality. Alexander Pope's "An Essay on Man" (1733) (actually a long poem) was typical of the eighteenth-century emphasis on rational discourse. Eccentricity—individual differences— was somewhat feared. Nature, too, was preferable when tamed by human hand. Scottish scenery, with its high mountains and wild rivers, was all very well in theory, but most writers of the time preferred the tame, structured landscape of the country park. Later in the century, a reaction against the formalism of the Augustans arose in a renewed interest in the sublime, based on an ancient Greek work, *On the Sublime*, which had been translated into French in 1674. By the sublime Edmund Burke and other English writers meant nature on a grand scale—the huge waterfalls, soaring peaks, and rushing cataracts of untamed nature. To Burke, the sublime suggested terror and danger and was associated with solitude, darkness, and vastness. Writers on the sublime had a new appreciation for such wildness, and accompanying nature's impressive power and wonder was a renewed interest in human grandeur, specifically the emotions and passions, and especially the imagination. The wildness and variety of nature came to symbolize the creative mind for writers who valued perception and inspiration more than reason. An appreciation of the sublime was also an appreciation of nature as the creation of God. The mighty waterfall or the mountain storm embodied God's omnipotence and might. The new interest in grand scenery, as well as being a reaction against the neat, formal classicism of eighteenth-century gardens, was also inspired by an increase in travel to more remote and wild areas. The European Alps became a favorite destination for young British travelers on the "Grand Tour," and many of them ventured into wild regions unknown in the more moderate scenery of the British Isles. European descriptions entered British poetry in poems such as Percy Bysshe Shelley's "Mont Blanc" (1816), in which Shelley recreates the vast, serene majesty of the mountain while trying to understand whether the power he feels comes from God. Mont Blanc cannot answer, and Shelley finds the power in the human mind rather than in a creator. The mountain is governed by "the secret strength of things/ Which governs thought."

Coinciding with this new respect for wildness and eccentricity in nature and in individual emotion was a movement toward democracy— an interest in ordinary people, their lives and speech—inspired by the revolutions. Rather than man as a species, the Romantics valued the individual; rather than Pope's "An Essay on Man," William Wordsworth wrote poems about specific, individualized country people such as "Michael" (1800), about a real shepherd, not the idealized shepherd of the classical Pastoral mode. Wordsworth and Samuel Taylor Coleridge set out some of the requirements for this new style of poetry in a preface to the 1802 edition of their *Lyrical Ballads*. The Romantic poets were revolutionary in many ways, championing political and personal freedom as well as experimentation in literary form. Shelley's cry to the west wind— that it blow through him and inspire him—became symbolic of the new attitudes the Romantic poets brought to literature.

When Robert Burns, an Ayrshire plowman, published his first volume of poems in 1786, he seemed to epitomize this pre-Romantic reaction against the well-educated, classical, urban literature of most of the eighteenth century. Here was a country man who personified the Golden Age figure of the pastoral shepherd/poet, uneducated and naturally endowed with the poetic gift. Another anti-classical movement of the eighteenth century, primitivism, idealized such a figure in contrast to the civilized, cultured man of letters. Burns was far from being a Pastoral ideal, of course, and he was also quite well educated, but coming at the beginning of the Romantic period he has become symbolic of the movement, especially as he also championed democracy ("A Man's a Man for A' That"[1795]) and wrote about common people in their own language. As a plowman he was instinctively and genuinely in touch with the natural world, and his poems spoke powerfully of the beautiful hills and streams of southwest Scotland. One of Burns's best-loved nature poems is "To a Mouse," composed, according to his brother, while he was still holding the plow that turned up the creature's nest in a field in November 1785. Burns feels guilty for his clumsy, human destruction of the mother mouse's home—"I'm truly sorry Man's dominion/Has broken Nature's social union"—and he queries that dominion, pondering the relationship between man and the beasts of the field. He invests the mouse with more native grace and sensitivity than he has himself, noting that her "ill opinion" of him (obvious in her small terror) is justified. She is the finer creature when he calls himself "thy poor, earth-born companion,/An' fellow mortal!" When he ponders her ruined home, the loss of all her hard work and planning, and the realization that she will have to start over again to be protected against the harsh winter weather (it was then November), he realizes how alike men and mice are: "The best laid plans o' Mice and Men/Gang aft agley [go often awry],/An' lea'e us nought but grief an' pain/For promis'd joy!" Finally, he envies the mouse for living only in the present, whereas he can grieve over past mistakes and look to the future with apprehension.

Often compared to Burns was the English village poet John Clare, whose first volume of poems, *Poems Descriptive of Rural Life and Scenery*

(1820), was recommended by the publisher because it was written by a "genuine" young peasant. Clare admired the Romantic poets with whom he was a contemporary, but he criticized Keats for describing nature from his imagination, not from his senses. Clare's poetry was inspired by his acute observation of his rural world in Northamptonshire, and although his early popularity waned, his nature poems are still enjoyed for their sensitivity to the English landscape. His "Mouse's Nest" (c. 1835) describes a scene similar to Burns's but without Burns's reflections on the mouse's terror and the complex relationship between man and nature.

The first poets to theorize about the new attitudes to poetry that came to be known as the Romantic movement were William Wordsworth and Samuel Taylor Coleridge, whose joint publication, *Lyrical Ballads*, was published in 1798. One of Coleridge's earliest poems, written in 1795, was "The Eolian Harp," which describes a quiet evening as the poet and his new wife, Sara, sit together outside their cottage at Clevedon, near Bristol. The only sound is a mild breeze drifting through the strings of an eolian harp that has been placed in a window of the cottage, a popular musical "wind chime" of the time. Many of the Romantic poets liked the metaphor of the eolian harp because it beautifully symbolized for them the union of nature (the wind) and man (the musical instrument), and the perfect but natural sound that could be created by that union. The sound of the harp connects Coleridge to the world of nature—"the one life within us and abroad"—and he speculates on the wind blowing through the harp as a symbol of the energy of life itself:

> And what if all of animated nature
> Be but organic harps diversely framed,
> That tremble into thought, as o'er them sweeps
> Plastic and vast, one intellectual breeze,
> At once the Soul of each, and God of All?

In the last stanza, however, Coleridge, inspired by Sara's Christianity, rejects this pantheistic view and separates God the creator from nature, his creation. His musings about "one intellectual breeze" are merely human pride, the "shapings of an unregenerate mind."

Coleridge's little son, Hartley, is at the heart of one of Coleridge's most beautiful poems, "Frost at Midnight" (1798). The poet and the sleeping baby are sitting companionably together in the still house, while the frost silently forms on the window pane and an owl hoots in the darkness outside. Time seems suspended, the only moving thing a piece of soot ("film") fluttering on the grate. Coleridge identifies his own quiet spirit with the film, and then chides himself for always needing to find in his surroundings the "echo or mirror" of his own mood (just as in "The

Nightingale" [1798] he criticized our temptation to call the bird melancholy). In the next stanza, watching the fire reminds him of his school days in London, when, a homesick child, he would gaze into the flames and dream of his birthplace in Devonshire. He remembers how the next day he would continue to dream in class, watching the door expectantly for the arrival of the absent friend from home that, according to local lore, seeing the film on the grate was supposed to portend. The third stanza shifts to the sleeping baby. In the father's deep love for his little son, he envisages a different childhood for him because he will be raised in the countryside, where God's "eternal language" can be seen and heard in the mountains, lakes, and shores. Not for Hartley the lonely, isolated life of the London schoolboy, closed off from family and nature with only the "sky and stars" to comfort him. The final stanza returns the poem to the opening image of the frost on the window pane. All seasons shall be "sweet" to his son—summer and winter,

> Or, if the secret ministry of frost
> Shall hang them up in silent icicles,
> Quietly shining to the quiet Moon.

Coleridge reinforces the stillness and calm of the opening. While his mind has wandered from the past of his own childhood into the future of his child, the baby has slept on, and the frost has silently woven a pattern that holds and reflects the moonlight as the harp and the nightingale have held and transformed the forces of wind and light. Coleridge sees mankind as similarly engaging with God through nature, both receiving and then giving: "Great Universal Teacher! He shall mould/Thy spirit, and by giving make it ask."

The poet's relationship to the natural world was central to William Wordsworth's life and work, and nearly all of his poems incorporate this theme in some way. His "Ode: Intimations of Immortality from Recollections of Early Childhood" (1802–1804; discussed in the Immortality section) lays out the development of his relationship with the natural world, from his innate, joyous sense of union with nature when he was a small child, to his role as "Nature's Priest" as a youth, and finally to a more distanced sense of companionship with nature rather than a mystical connection. Another starting point to studying Wordsworth's view of nature is his long poem "The Prelude," written between 1798 and 1805, but revised over several years and finally published after Wordsworth's death in 1850. Subtitled "Growth of a Poet's Mind," the poem traces Wordsworth's close relationship with the natural world from his infancy in the Lake District, to his travels in the French Alps, and his return to the Lakes, finding in nature a constant source of spiritual renewal and consolation when personal and social troubles threaten to overwhelm him. In nature he also found the inspiration for his poetic creativity, as his imagination entered into a union with the beauty of his surroundings. When this bond began to weaken as he grew older, his gifts as a poet also decreased.

As well as in his "Ode: Intimations of Immortality," Wordsworth's understanding of his relationship with nature can be found in "Lines Composed a few miles above Tintern Abbey" (1798). The poem describes Wordsworth's return to this lovely part of south Wales after an absence of five years; he wrote the poem in his head during a four-day walking tour with his sister, Dorothy. In the first part of the poem Wordsworth is looking again on the "steep and lofty cliffs," the river valley, and the small farms, and he remembers how powerfully in the five intervening years that scene has inspired him through his imagination when he has been far away, " 'mid the din/Of towns and cities." The scene's first effect on him is a moral one. Nature for Wordsworth was a moral force that had the power to make people more compassionate. Morality came not from education or religion (the civilizing influences valued by the eighteenth-century rationalists and by evangelical Christianity) but from innate impulses strengthened by nature's beauty. The eighteenth-century French philosopher Jean-Jacques Rousseau had similarly argued that children were best educated in natural surroundings, away from the corrupting influences of "civilized" life and institutions. In the poem, Wordsworth speaks of the influence of a beautiful landscape on "that best portion of a good man's life,/His little, nameless, unremembered, acts/Of kindness and of love."

The second impulse of the remembered scene—the "beauteous forms" as he calls the Wye valley and its surroundings—is more personal. He describes a meditative state, inspired by the landscape, that takes him into a kind of suspension: "we are laid asleep/In body, and become a living soul." In this moment of quiet harmony and deep joy, "We see into the life of things." Such solace and peace have often come to him through an act of the imagination, when he is far away in the hum of the city. That he will be able to recreate the scene in later years comforts him because he realizes that even now he is very different in his response to nature than he was even five years before. What will he be like in the future? He recalls the stages of his life and his changing relationship with his natural surroundings, as he does in the "Ode: Intimations of Immortality." As a young boy he was like a small animal, wholly at one with the natural world in which he ran and played. Later, his love for the wild cataracts and mountains (like the poets of the sublime) was almost overwhelming. His passion for them was frightening in its intensity, and pure emotion. Nature then "was all in all." Now, he no longer feels with the ardor of youth, but he is recompensed with a deeper and more intellectual understanding of the oneness of man and nature. He hears "the still, sad music of humanity" in the landscape. The "mind of man" is "deeply interfused" with the world of nature:

A motion and a spirit, that impels
All thinking things, all objects of all thought,
And rolls through all things.

The union of the poet's senses with what his senses perceive—of the poet himself and nature—becomes "the anchor of my purest thoughts, the nurse,/The guide, the guardian of my heart, and soul/Of all my moral being." The poem concludes with an address to Dorothy, Wordsworth's sister, with whom he lived for most of his life (even while he was married), and who shared his love of nature. Their love for each other is bound up in their response to nature, who "never did betray/The heart that loved her."

A well-known short lyric that makes the same philosophic point about natural scenes recollected later, in the imagination, is "I wandered lonely as a cloud" (1804). Known as Wordsworth's daffodil poem, it is intensely English in its description of "a crowd,/A host of golden daffodils." The scene unites land, sky, and water in its evocation of the spring scene, which later "flash[es] upon that inward eye/Which is the bliss of solitude." In the *Preface to the Lyrical Ballads*, in which Wordsworth and Coleridge set out their new view of poetry, Wordsworth described poetry as "the spontaneous overflow of powerful feelings," specifically "emotion recollected in tranquillity." Better than the scene itself, then, for creative purposes, is the scene when recalled in the imagination of the meditative poet.

Wordsworth described nature as his nurse, guide, guardian, all in all. In the companion poems "Expostulation and Reply" and "The Tables Turned" (1798) he debates the role of nature as teacher. In the first poem, William is chided by Matthew for wasting his time contemplating nature. He should be reading books and learning from the experience of others. William replies that "we can feed this mind of ours/In a wise passiveness." Our ears, eyes, and bodies cannot help but learn from nature. In "The Tables Turned," William chides his friend for wasting his time reading books. "Let Nature be your Teacher," he urges:

One impulse from a vernal wood
May teach you more of man,
Of moral evil and of good,
Than all the sages can.

The Romantic favoring of emotion over reason, spontaneity over deliberation, impulse over careful analysis, is evident in William's famous declaration, "We murder to dissect."

One of Wordsworth's best-known early sonnets, "The world is too much with us" (1802), regrets that modern life is taking us away from an appreciation of the natural world. Better to be a pagan with a belief in the divinity of nature than a modern man with no beliefs at all. By 1833, however, Wordsworth had tempered his criticism of the industrial world. In his late sonnet "Steamboats, Viaducts, and Railways" he argues that these products of the Industrial Revolution are not wholly antagonistic to nature; in fact, "Nature does embrace/Her lawful offspring in Man's art. . . ." Man's accomplishments are essential to progress and an integral part of the created, natural world.

Percy Bysshe Shelley, like the other Romantic poets, was happiest in the world of nature, either in England or on the Continent (France and Italy), where he lived for the last few years of his short life. Shelley and John Keats are considered the second wave of romanticism, the first phase of Wordsworth and Coleridge having been brought to an end by the government of William Pitt, which feared radical ideas and brought in some more repressive measures. The pro-radical movement was revived in 1808–1809 with agitation for peaceful parliamentary reform. Shelley was the most revolutionary of these Romantics, a passionate reformer whose own enormous energy and emotional sensitivity drove his personal and literary lives. He wrote some of the most beautiful of British poems about nature, transforming his acute sympathy with his surroundings into unforgettable lyric poetry. His "To a Skylark" (1820) and "Ode to the West Wind" (1819) are discussed in the Art, Imagination, and Inspiration section, because although they powerfully describe the natural landscape, their purpose is to recreate the power of nature to inspire the poet's revolutionary thoughts through the wind and the bird's song. In "The Cloud" (1820) Shelley's intense sympathy with the natural world is evident. Spoken by the cloud itself, the poem personifies the cloud as a godlike, life-giving power that sweeps over the earth bringing rain, wind, and shade, but also hail, snow, and thunder. All of nature is personified in the manner of the ancient Greek myths, and the whole universe is characterized by a violent but creative female energy that is immortal:

> I am the daughter of Earth and Water,
>   And the nursling of the Sky;
> I pass through the pores of the ocean and shores;
>   I change, but I cannot die.

John Keats was also a second-phase Romantic poet, and like Shelley, nature for Keats was a way into a Platonic ideal and immortal world. Most of Keats's poems that are concerned with the relationship between the poet and nature ("Ode to a Nightingale" [1819] most importantly) are discussed in the Art, Imagination, and Inspiration section of this survey. His "To Autumn" discussed above in this section is characteristic of Keats and his emotional attachment to the English landscape.

POST-ROMANTICISM

The Romantic movement in British poetry had arisen at a particular time in history, in response to the democratic movement fostered by the French and American revolutions, and as a reaction against the rationalism of the eighteenth century. But its legacy continued in a new respect for natural beauty rather than cultivated gardens, and a moral rather than theological concern with the relationship between man and the natural world. The Wordsworthian belief that nature is our best teacher and moral guide and the poet's main source of inspiration has continued to influence our thinking, particularly in the twentieth century, when industrialism and technology have increasingly distanced most of us from the natural world. Unfortunately, however, romanticism lent itself to excess, and in the hands of inferior poets the Romantic poets' introspective obsession with their own emotions and spiritual growth became sentimental and trivial. As a reaction against declining romanticism, some of the Imagist poets of the early twentieth century, such as T. S. Eliot, condemned poets who wrote about the English countryside, considering it a limited, provincial topic. But there have been several fine twentieth-century British poets who, because they came from rural backgrounds, have powerfully described the landscape and lamented the passing of the old rural ways.

Thomas Hardy wrote many poems about rural life in his native Dorset, poems marked by a keen observation of the particulars of scenery. Hardy rejected the Romantic idealizing of the natural world as a teacher or universal mother, and his poems reflect both a love for the beauty of nature and also an appreciation for its neutrality in human affairs. Hardy was more inclined to see nature as, in Tennyson's words, "red in tooth and claw" (the cruelty and ruthlessness of animals seeking food), rather than as a benevolent and comforting presence. In "In a Wood" (1887) he addresses the trees, telling them that he came to the wood seeking a respite from "man's unrest." But in the wood he finds even the trees at war with each other, elbowing each other for room, turning cankered, pricking and stinging, even choking each other as the ivy does the elm. The final stanza rejects the comfort of trees in favor of man's world instead, where at least affection and "life-loyalties" can be found among the rivalries. The last four lines of each stanza exactly fit the rhythm of the second verse of the British national anthem, "God Save the Queen."

Hardy's loss of religious faith placed him in a hostile universe, the only resource being human decency and mutual support. His own place in the world he describes best in "Afterwards" (1917). In each of the five stanzas, someone who knew Hardy will ponder a particular detail of nature—the delicacy of spring leaves, a hawk in flight, a hedgehog shuffling over a lawn, a starry sky, the sound of the wind cutting a church bell's ring—and remember that Hardy "used to notice such things." He is immortalized not in a union with some universal mother but in the memories of friends. The natural world is full of beauty and mystery, but for Hardy there is no sentimental connection with it. The friends will remember that he tried to protect animals like the little hedgehog from harm (as so many of us do, removing them from the path of speeding cars on country roads), but his attempts were largely futile.

"Snow in the Suburbs" (1925) is a delightful description of nature in the city. The first stanza describes snow falling silently on road and fence, no wind to disturb the gentle movement of the flakes as they swirl together in a "fleecy fall." The second stanza moves from the snow to a sparrow, whose arrival on a branch triggers a small avalanche of snow that almost swallows him whole. Flying on, the bird sets off a rush of other minor slides. In the final stanza of only four lines, the bird's enemy, the speaker's black cat, enters the scene. But although a predator, he is worthy of sympathy also, finding himself, like the bird, in a hostile, white world. Thin, hungry, and looking for refuge, he makes his appeal to the watcher, who opens the door for him. Again, it is the human world that is required to be charitable and kind.

One of Hardy's most famous poems is "The Darkling Thrush," written on December 31, 1900, to mark the beginning of a new century. The poem opens with the poet leaning on a gate looking into a wood, the image marking the transition from one century to the next. It is midwinter and the departing century, as evidenced by Hardy's surroundings, has been bleak indeed. It is the end of the day, the end of the year, the end of the century—the end, seemingly, of man's dreams and strivings. No one is about in this barren landscape, and the bare branches of the shrubs look "like strings of broken lyres" against the winter sky, a reminder that the Romantic poets' idealizing of nature is no longer possible for Hardy. The death of the year and the century is made manifest in the second stanza, when the dead fields seemed to be the nineteenth-century's corpse. All within and without the poet is desiccated and sere. Suddenly, though, the desolation is broken by birdsong. The source of this joyful sound is not a beautiful young skylark, however, but "an aged thrush, frail, gaunt, and small," seemingly as shrunken and spiritless as the land and the poet. As the poet looks around at the joyless landscape, emblematic of his own despair at the state of mankind at the end of the nineteenth century, he can only wonder at the bird's innocence and presume that the bird has some kind of hope which the poet cannot share. The poem bears witness to Hardy's sense that nature is separate from and indifferent to man. For Hardy there is no identification with the bird as there had been for Shelley and Keats, no release from earthly sorrows and despair.

Of the poets writing about nature in the first two decades of the twentieth century, the best is Edward Thomas, whose work was not well known until quite recently. Thomas wrote widely about the countryside in reviews and books before, with the encouragement of Robert Frost, turning to poetry. He wrote nearly 150 poems between 1914 and his death, at the age of thirty-nine, in 1917. Thomas had voluntarily joined the Royal Artillery, and he was killed by a shell while on duty in France.

Thomas's many poems about the countryside all reflect his strong belief that in nature we are in touch with the generations of people who have walked over the same land and admired the same vistas. We share a nature that responds to the land in a certain way. This sense of continuity through the generations is particularly strong in Europe (compared, say, to the huge tracts of open land in North America), where the land has been cultivated for centuries. "Adlestrop" (1915) is a short poem that subtly captures this sense of history that can be contained just in the place names of rural England. The poet recalls how one hot June day, his train pulled unexpectedly into Adlestrop station. The simple details of the poem—"The steam hissed. Someone cleared his throat./ No one left and no one came/On the bare platform."—create a sense of time suspended in this almost deserted village, cut off from the new current of life as so many of the old villages were. From the deserted platform he moves to the wild flowers—willow-herb and meadowsweet, as aromatic as their names—that characterize the English countryside. The picture then moves to an even more generalized vision of the sky and a blackbird singing, giving rise to the poem's climax:

> a blackbird sang
> Close by, and round him, mistier,
> Farther and farther, all the birds
> Of Oxfordshire and Gloucestershire.

Thomas is conjuring here with the old place names of England, in which are contained the essence of the English countryside. The name Adlestrop, captured in a moment on a hot June afternoon, is as quintessentially England as is the blackbird, the embodiment of all English birds.

In "The Manor Farm" (1914) Thomas writes eloquently of the importance of the human presence in the rural landscape. It is February, and winter is slowly turning toward spring in the strengthening rays of the sun that are beginning to melt the "rock-like mud" of the road. But the poet claims not to "value that thin gliding beam" until he comes upon the signs of civilization, the church, the yew tree (planted long ago in most English churchyards), and the manor farm. The countryside seems to be self-contained on that February day, the only sound that of three cart-horses swishing away a solitary fly with their tails. But the poem ends with an evocation of the human history whose roots lie deep in the English countryside. The sun has awakened "a season of bliss unchangeable" that has lain "safe under tile and thatch for ages since/This England, Old already, was called Merry." Thomas often hearkens back to England's more settled past, when time moved more slowly, life was governed by the seasons, and custom bound people together in harmony with their landscape. Like Oliver Goldsmith's "Deserted Village" over a century before, Thomas's poems regret the passing of the old ways but they also find in landscape a way of connecting with the centuries of people who have walked the same paths, climbed the same hills, and gazed out over the same sea that surrounds "England's green and pleasant land."

∞◊∞

"The Human Seasons," John Keats
    WiR; EnRP
"The Flower," George Herbert
    NAEL-1; OBEV
"Cuckoo Song," anonymous
    ImPo; NAEL-1; OBEV; SB; TFi; TrGrPo-1
"Spring, the sweet spring," Thomas Nashe
    ImPo; OBEV; TFi; TrGrPo-1
"The Soote Season," Henry Howard, earl of Surrey
    NAEL-1; OBEV
"Lines Written in Early Spring," William Wordsworth
    NAEL-2; OAEL-2
"The Shepeardes Calender," Sir Edmund Spenser
    NAEL-1; OAEL-1
"The Seasons" (extracts), James Thomson
    NAEL-1; OAEL-1
"To Spring," William Blake
    NAEL-2
"To Summer," William Blake
    WiR

"To Autumn," William Blake
    NAEL-2; WiR

"To Winter," William Blake
    WiR

"To Autumn," John Keats
    ImPo; NAEL-2; OAEL-2; OBEV; TFi; TrGrPo-2

"On the Grasshopper and the Cricket" ("The poetry of earth is never dead"), John Keats
    ImPo; OAEL-2; TrGrPo-2

"A Nocturnal Reverie," Anne Finch
    ECP; NAEL-1; OBEV; SB

"Ode to Evening," William Collins
    BL; ECP; ImPo; NAEL-1; OAEL-1; OBEV; TFi; TrGrPo-1

"The Nightingale," Samuel Taylor Coleridge
    EnRP

"To Night," Percy Bysshe Shelley
    NAEL-2; OAEL-2; TFi; TrGrPo-2

"The Night-Wind," Emily Brontë
    NAEL-2

"To Penshurst," Ben Jonson
    NAEL-1; OAEL-1; OBEV; TFi

"The Description of Cooke-ham," Aemilia Lanyer
    NAEL-1

"To Saxham," Thomas Carew
    NoP

"A Panegerick to Sir Lewis Pemberton," Robert Herrick
    CaPo

"Upon Appleton House," Andrew Marvell
    NAEL-1; OAEL-1

"The Mower's Song," Andrew Marvell
    NAEL-1

"The Mower Against Gardens," Andrew Marvell
    NAEL-1; OAEL-1

"The Deserted Village," Oliver Goldsmith
    BL; ECP; ImPo; NAEL-1; OAEL-1; TFi; TrGrPo-1

"The Village," George Crabbe
    BL; ECP; NAEL-1; OAEL-1; TrGrPo-1

"Mont Blanc," Percy Bysshe Shelley
    NAEL-2; OAEL-2

"To a Mouse," Robert Burns
    BL; ECP; ImPo; NAEL-2; OAEL-2; OBEV; TFi; TrGrPo-1

"Mouse's Nest," John Clare
    NAEL-2

"The Eolian Harp," Samuel Taylor Coleridge
    NAEL-2; OAEL-2

"Frost at Midnight," Samuel Taylor Coleridge
    NAEL-2; OAEL-2; TFi

"The Prelude" (excerpts), William Wordsworth
    NAEL-2; OAEL-2

"Lines Composed a few miles above Tintern Abbey," William Wordsworth
    ImPo; NAEL-2; OAEL-2; OBEV; TFi; TrGrPo-2

"I wandered lonely as a cloud," William Wordsworth
    ImPo; NAEL-2; OAEL-2; OBEV; TFi; TrGrPo-2

"Expostulation and Reply," William Wordsworth
    NAEL-2; OAEL-2

"The Tables Turned," William Wordsworth
    NAEL-2; OAEL-2

"The world is too much with us," William Wordsworth
    ImPo; NAEL-2; OAEL-2; TFi; TrGrPo-2

"Steamboats, Viaducts, and Railways," William Wordsworth
    NAEL-2

"The Cloud," Percy Bysshe Shelley
    NAEL-2

"In a Wood," Thomas Hardy
    BAVP

"Afterwards," Thomas Hardy
    BAVP; OBEV; SB; TFi; TrGrPo-2

"Snow in the Suburbs," Thomas Hardy
    BAVP; OAEL-2

"The Darkling Thrush," Thomas Hardy
    BAVP; NAEL-2; OAEL-2; OBEV; TFi; TrGrPo-2
"Adlestrop," Edward Thomas
    NAEL-2
"The Manor Farm," Edward Thomas
    not anthologized; available in editions of Thomas's poetry

Old Age

⚌

Old age seems to be a subject that concerns male poets rather than female ones, perhaps because old men have always appeared to have more value to society than old women, and therefore they are more willing to expose their feelings about aging. The theme occurs in poems about "Time and Change" also, but the poems discussed here are those that focus on old age specifically, rather than the more general idea of time passing.

The Elizabethan poet George Peele praises old age in *Polyhymnia* (1590), his tribute to Queen Elizabeth I's retiring servant, Sir Henry Lee (1531–1611). The famous closing song, "His golden locks time hath to silver turned," reminds us of what the old knight has lost: his hair is grey; his helmet, once glistening, is now a hive for bees; his home is a cottage, not the court. But then he reminds us of the more important and lasting virtues that the old knight still retains; although "beauty, strength, youth are flowers but fading seen;/Duty, faith, love, are roots, and ever green." The old knight serves on his knees now, rather than on his horse; he prays for his queen instead of fighting for her.

Many of Shakespeare's sonnets are concerned with the passing of time and therefore aging, but the one most centrally about growing old is Sonnet 73, "That time of year thou mayst in me behold" (1609). The time of year is autumn, and the metaphors for the poet's sense that he is growing old are all chosen as representing transitional times. In the first quatrain he is autumn, when "yellow leaves or none or few do hang." Summer, his youth, is over, but the winter of old age is not yet upon him. In the second quatrain the speaker is twilight, again a transitional time between daylight (youth) and night. This metaphor deepens the poet's sense of aging as he recalls that the night so soon to descend is "death's second self that seals up all in rest." The third quatrain introduces a third transitional metaphor: a dying fire that paradoxically is put out by the source of its earlier heat, as the logs become ash that smothers the dying embers. The image suggests that the speaker's exuberant youth has led to this sense of growing old. As often happens in Shakespeare's sonnets, however, the drift of the poem shifts in the closing couplet. The speaker returns to the listener who "mayst . . . behold" the speaker's advancing age. But now he tells the listener that their love is all the stronger because they know they are soon to be parted by death.

One of the most inventive poems about old age is the Renaissance poet George Gascoigne's "The Lullaby of a Lover" or "Gascoigne's Lullaby" (1573). The poet seeks to put to sleep the many "wanton babes" that trouble his old age. The first is his "youthful years," whose interests are put to sleep in the following stanzas. His "gazing eyes" must no longer be enticed by beautiful women for "every glass may now suffice/ To show the furrows in my face." Next, he puts to sleep his will, which now must be ruled by reason. If his will sleeps, his body will rest also. That thought leads to the last request, that his sexual desire be stilled also. The final stanza stresses the difference between the woman's soothing lullaby to her baby, and the poet's bittersweet lullaby to his youth and vigor: "I can no more delays devise, /But welcome pain, let pleasure pass."

Thomas Hardy takes up Gascoigne's lament that the mirror brings him only regret in his poem "I Look into My Glass" (1898). Hardy might be comforted by Gascoigne's lullaby when he pleads that his heart could be as wasted as his skin, for then he would not be so conscious of the hearts that no longer love him. Alas, he says, time both steals and retains, leaving him an old man's body but a young man's desires.

A more philosophic acceptance of the old man's sense of loss is expressed in John Masefield's "On Growing Old" (1919), a poem composed of two Shakespearean sonnets. The speaker, sitting by the fire with a book and his old dog, addresses Beauty, the spirit of the created world whose beauties he can recreate through memory, just as he can find the fire's beauty in its embers. In the second stanza he compares his lot to that of younger people in the prime of life. While they enjoy the abundance and riches of the world, he asks Beauty for only wisdom and passion; with them, even his old age will continue to hold promise. The speaker's optimism is undercut, however, by the failure of imagination at the end of the poem. The earlier images of aging—his own state reflected in the fire, the yellow leaves of the book, the "withered wire" that "moves a thin ghost of music in the spinet"—are more convincing than the old man's explained desire for passion.

The Irish poet William Butler Yeats hated growing old, and as he found his youthful energy and good health waning, old age became a central theme in his poetry. In 1922 he seemed to be at the peak of his career. He had returned to Ireland from England, received two honorary degrees from Irish universities, became a senator in the new Free State, and in 1924 received the Nobel Prize. But at the same time civil war was buffeting Ireland and Yeats felt too old to be politically active. In 1926 Yeats was confronted by the significance of old age when he visited a Montessori school and wrote about the contrast between himself and the young pupils in "Among School Children." In the schoolroom, watching the children reminds him of his old friend (unnamed in the poem) Maud Gonne, and how she had once told him about an incident in her school days that had suddenly brought tragedy to the sensitive child. Remembering the traumas of his own youth, Yeats had sympathized and felt at one with her. He looks around the schoolroom, wondering if any of the children have also suffered childish hurts, and he seems to see his old friend before him, first as a child and then as an old woman, as he too is old. In stanza five he wonders if women would go through the pains of childbirth if they could see their babies as the old people they will become. Even the great philosophers, Plato, Aristotle, and Pythagoras, turned into frightening old scarecrows. In stanza seven he finds permanence only in images: the holy images worshiped by nuns (a nun is teaching the class), and the image of the perfect child, worshiped by mothers. These images "break hearts" because they remind us that "man's enterprise" is fleeting and mortal, but we create them because we seek some kind of permanence. The final stanza seems to return to the opening description of the children in the schoolroom, learning their modern lessons. The children stare at him in some amazement. How can he bridge the gap between youth and age? Work, especially "modern," dull, and repetitive school work, must not destroy the soul of the child, he argues. Labor enriches us only when the body does not suffer for the soul, when beauty is not the result of despair, and when wisdom is not dependent upon long hours of tedious study. Just as he had felt a sympathetic unity with Maud Gonne, so he now sees an ideal union in a chestnut tree that is at once young and old and in a woman who is a part of the dance she performs. The schoolchildren perhaps share in this union, before a "harsh reproof" such as the one that shattered Maud Gonne begins to age and bruise them into scarecrows.

In "Sailing to Byzantium" (1926), written when Yeats was sixty-one, he rejects Ireland as "no country for old men" because its inhabitants are caught up in the physical and sexual; the poet seeks instead a land where "unageing intellect" is valued. The second stanza opens with the famous image of the old man as a scarecrow. Yeats finds the place where the old can find a soul in Byzantium (now Istanbul), the ancient seat of Plato's Academy and the capital of Eastern Christianity. There he can reject the mortal body, so honored by the youth in Ireland, and find instead immortality in the holy city. He asks the sages of the old city to free his soul from his body, and transport him to an eternal world of art. Recalling Keats's evocation of such an immortal world in his "Ode to a Nightingale" (1819), the poem closes with Yeats's identification with the nightingale of legend that sang for the emperor in Hans Christian Andersen's story. He rejects his human, mortal body and takes instead an artificial, artistic body of a bird created by Greek goldsmiths. In this new, mechanical body he will continue to be a poet, singing in Byzantium. This identification recalls James Joyce's connection between "the artist as a young man," Stephen Dedalus, and Dedalus the inventor (artificer) of Greek mythology. For both writers, writing is associated with artifice, a deliberate, willful creation rather than the unrestrained, thoughtless sensuality of nature that Yeats associates with the young. And yet the poem ends with the poet, immortalized as a nightingale, singing of the mortal, temporal world.

T. S. Eliot's "Gerontion" (1920) is narrated by the "little old man" of the title, but the poem is concerned with the approaching spiritual death of the western world rather than the individual death of the speaker. A difficult poem with—like all of Eliot's verse—many allusions to other works, "Gerontion" uses its narrator, a dried-up, spiritually thirsty old man, to exemplify and expose the corruption and emptiness at the heart of twentieth-century life. His house is rotten and his head is empty. The old man has no sense of the past and no belief because the modern world demands proof of God's existence. Eliot echoes Matthew 12, in which Christ tells the doubters, "an evil and adulterous generation seeketh after a sign." Eliot recalls the coming of Christ "the tiger" into the world, but the poem laments the modern world's failure to follow him. Spiritually dry and near death, like the old narrator, Western society awaits renewal, when "the tiger springs in the new year."

Eliot's "The Love Song of J. Alfred Prufrock" (1911) is a poem with many themes, but its most lasting impression is of the sense of being old, so often brought on by regret, disappointment, or loss. Prufrock narrates the poem to a listener but the "you" to whom he speaks is the reader, or, more likely, Prufrock himself as he vacillates in his mind, desperately attempting to get up the courage to approach a woman. The poem contrasts Prufrock's humble, even sordid life in the poorer part of town (the images suggest a "poor relation," or a gentleman who has fallen on bad times) and the civilized, comfortable life of the women with whom he wishes to associate. The poem traces Prufrock's indecisiveness as he imagines the meeting and tries to get up the courage to go through with it. He has time, he hopes, to prepare himself for the encounter, to put on a suitable front that will impress these formidable ladies. But when he imagines himself reaching the door and then changing his mind, his vision of his descent down the staircase reminds him that he is approaching middle age when the women see his departing head from above and note his thinning hair.

Prufrock realizes that his life has been unfulfilled and futile, hovering on the edge of the upper-class society of which he so desperately wishes to be a part. That he has "measured out [his] life with coffee spoons" neatly sums up the triviality of his life and contrasts strongly with his fervent desire to be a hero (or at least be thought a hero). But two metaphors remind him of his fear and lack of self-confidence: the women's eyes pin him to the wall like a butterfly captured by a collector. Recalling the sexual attraction of the women, he sees himself as a lowly and frightened crab skittering off sideways from their touch. Finally he imagines his proposition to the women as they lounge together on the floor after tea. But he knows he will never have the nerve to approach her, and so he begins to retreat from the encounter in his mind. He rationalizes backing out—the woman would have tricked him, playing games and pretending that he has misunderstood her. But having backed out, he is left only with the realization of his failure. He is not the hero after all— rather than Hamlet, he is only Polonius, or maybe even the Fool. And so his fear that he is too old to attract a woman is realized, and suddenly he *is* old, with nothing to look forward to except the conventional activities of old age. He will roll up his trousers and paddle in the sea; he will comb his hair in an attempt to hide his bald spot. Joining the ranks of the elderly British who retire to the seaside, he will seek mermaids instead of flesh-and-blood women, but even the mermaids will evade him. At the end of the poem, he wakes to the reality of his lost hopes and empty dreams and finds himself drowning. "I grow old . . . I grow old" laments the balding Prufrock, articulating for generations of readers the bitter knowledge that life has passed one by.

ᴇᴏᴅᴅᴏ

"His golden locks time hath to silver turned," George Peele
    TrGrPo-1

Sonnet 73, "That time of year thou mayst in me behold," William Shakespeare
    ImPo; NAEL-1; OAEL-1; OBEV; TFi; TrGrPo-1

"The Lullaby of a Lover" ("Gascoigne's Lullaby"), George Gascoigne
    TrGrPo-1

"I Look into My Glass," Thomas Hardy
    NAEL-2

"On Growing Old," John Masefield

ImPo

"Among School Children," William Butler Yeats
ImPo; NAEL-2; TFi; TrGrPo-2

"Sailing to Byzantium," William Butler Yeats
ImPo; NAEL-2; OAEL-2; OBEV; TFi

"Gerontion," T. S. Eliot
ImPo; NAEL-2; OAEL-2; TFi

"The Love Song of J. Alfred Prufrock," T. S. Eliot
NAEL-2; OAEL-2; OBEV; TFi; TrGrPo-2

Patriotism

❦

Poems about war and political events are often also patriotic, but the poems discussed in this section are those whose central theme is love of one's country and, often, excessive love that sees one's native land as inherently superior to all others. England has a reputation for such patriotism due to its central role in world affairs since the Renaissance. The turbulent history of Ireland has also raised up heroes and nationalistic fervor, however, and Ireland's many poets, novelists, and playwrights have for centuries chafed against English rule.

William Butler Yeats's "Easter 1916" concerns a week-long rebellion of Irish nationalists against the British government, which had long been delaying the promise of independence for Ireland and was now too busy with World War I to consider it. Fifteen of the leading rebels were executed, bringing their cause renewed support. Yeats supported Irish nationalism because he saw Britain as exemplifying modern materialism and greed, and he thought an independent Ireland would be better able to maintain its ties with an ancient, more heroic culture, associated with the songs and legends of the western coast. Like many Irishmen, he had revered earlier Irish heroes like Charles Parnell, Wolfe Tone, and John O'Leary (about whom he wrote in "September 1913"), and these new heroes had become martyrs in the Irish cause. The poem suggests an ambivalence in Yeats's view of their sacrifice. Was it worth it, and were they just ordinary people whose deaths made them noble?

The poem's first stanza describes the ordinary, drab life of the speaker and his fellow office workers. But after the rebellion, all is overturned, and a "terrible beauty is born." The second stanza describes some of the rebels—Countess Markiewicz, Padraic Pearse, Thomas MacDonagh, Major John MacBride—as belonging to the laughably innocent former times, when they all wore "motley" like jesters and were just playacting until fate cast them in the role of hero. The third stanza describes the single-mindedness of the nationalists as a stone in the stream that diverts the course of history and is the only thing in nature not to change. But the stone, formed by enchantment from the rebels' hearts, will disturb the current of life. The implication of stonyheartedness is taken up in the final stanza, when the poet suggests that a delayed sacrifice can turn a heart to stone. And for what purpose? Perhaps it is the province of God, not man, to effect real change so that lives are not lost. Finally, he queries the need for a rebellion at all. Perhaps the British government will actually honor their promise. But as patriots, the rebels have become immortalized in the nation's heart. Whatever their shortcomings and mundane faults before the rebellion, from now on they are transformed.

The most famous British patriotic poem, still sung today as an alternative national anthem, is James Thomson's "Ode: Rule, Britannia," written in 1740 to music by Thomas Arne, for a masque honoring the prince of Wales. It remained popular for the next 200 years, but its jingoistic sentiments—Britain as the God-chosen "dread and envy" of all other nations—appalled many Britons including Charles Dickens, whose novels frequently satirized the type of nationalistic Englishman who believed implicitly in the song's sentiments. Its chorus, proudly announcing that "Britons never will be slaves," was altered in the musical version to the easily ridiculed "never never never shall be slaves." It became the marching song for British imperialism in the nineteenth century, when the idea that "all thine shall be the subject main,/And every shore it circles thine" was irresistible.

Hugely popular in its time was Rudyard Kipling's hymn "Recessional," written to honor the sixtieth anniversary of Queen Victoria in 1897 (the Diamond Jubilee). Kipling tempers the patriotism of "Rule Britannia" by reminding the British that while they may boast of their conquests around the world (and the Queen's jubilee had inspired much self-congratulation), they must never forget to be humble before God, under whose hand the British maintain their empire. When the smoke of battle has melted away into boasts and bragging they would do well to bring to God a contrite heart. Each of the first four stanzas ends with a variation of the refrain that includes the now-famous Remembrance Day words, "Lest we forget!"

Patriotism is usually associated with male writers, connected as it often is with war and aggression. The nineteenth-century poet Felicia Dorothea Hemans is the best-known patriotic woman writer with verses such as "The Homes of England" (1827). Like "Ode: Rule, Britannia," this celebration of England's greatness has also been the source of many comic parodies, especially of the opening lines, which declare "The stately Homes of England,/How beautiful they stand!" The first three stanzas describe the stately homes and their contented residents, peaceful and blessed amid the beauties of the English landscape. The fourth stanza finds the same quiet enjoyment in the homes of the poor, the cottage homes of England. The final stanza brings the two worlds together in an injunction that patriotic countrymen may arise in both classes "to guard each hallow'd wall!" Children must be raised in a grateful spirit of love for God and country.

Robert Browning's "Home-Thoughts from Abroad" (1845) opens with the well-known lines, "Oh, to be in England/Now that April's there." Like most travelers, Browning wearies for the countryside of his native land, and the poem captures many of the scents and sounds of an English spring, so much more verdant and fragrant than drier Italy, whose "gaudy melon-flower" cannot compete, for Browning, with England's bright buttercups. The coming of spring reminds Browning of the well-known harbingers of that season—the new growth on the trees, the sound of birdsong, and the burgeoning of flowers in the hedgerows.

Most patriotic of the poems written during World War I was Rupert Brooke's "The Soldier" (1914). While many war poets wrote of their experiences at the front and speak of the general horror, not distinguishing between friend and foe in the universal grief over young lives lost, Brooke wrote "The Soldier" and four other sonnets about war while he was still in training. This less personal connection with the topic of the poem may partly explain its detached, abstract tone and language, which have made it one of the quintessential English poems. When Brooke, a handsome, athletic, and intellectual graduate of Rugby and Cambridge, died five months later of blood poisoning on his way to the Dardanelles just before his twenty-eighth birthday, he became England's epitome of the soldier he had immortalized in verse. In the sonnet, the soldier asks of his countrymen, "If I should die, think only this of me:/That there's some corner of a foreign field/That is forever England." The identification of the Englishman with his native soil—raised and nurtured, like that soil, by English sun, English air, English rivers—continues as the dominant idea in the poem. His dust is a "richer dust" than that of the foreign land in which he is buried. In the sestet, the soldier is freed from "all evil" as in death he becomes a "pulse in the Eternal mind." But even in heaven he is still an Englishman, returning in the innocence of death to the innocence of his English childhood, a world of laughter and friends, gentleness and peace, "under an English heaven."

Brooke's patriotism, revered at the time of his death in 1915, became the subject of attack as World War I progressed into the horrors of the Somme. Later war poets like Siegfried Sassoon and Wilfrid Owen, who experienced life and death in the trenches, had no time for Brooke's idealistic portrait of a soldier's death (although Owen shared Brooke's naive optimism at the beginning of the war). Extreme patriotism lends itself to the kind of ridicule and parody that has dogged the patriotic poems of Thomson, Hemans, and Brooke. Browning's longing for England, however, expresses a genuine love for the sights and scents of one's homeland that all exiles can understand. Such nostalgia is central to the Scottish temperament and appears in such well-known verses as Robert Burns's "My Heart's in the Highlands" (1790):

> Farewell to the Highlands, farewell to the North,
> The birthplace of valour, the country of worth;
> Wherever I wander, wherever I rove,
> The hills of the Highlands for ever I love.

⚬⚬⚬⚬⚬

"Easter 1916," William Butler Yeats
  NAEL-2; OAEL-2; TFi
"Ode: Rule Britannia," James Thomson
  NAEL-1
"Recessional," Rudyard Kipling
  BAVP; NAEL-2; TFi; TrGrPo-2
"The Homes of England," Felicia Dorothea Hemans
  NAEL-2
"Home-Thoughts from Abroad," Robert Browning
  ImPo; NAEL-2; TFi; TrGrPo-2
"The Soldier," Rupert Brooke
  NAEL-2; TFi; TrGrPo-2
"My Heart's in the Highlands," Robert Burns
  ImPo

Politics and Human Rights

ᕙᏍᏀᏍᕚ

Percy Bysshe Shelley spoke for many poets when he called them "the unacknowledged legislators of the world." For Shelley, poets had a particular power of imaginative vision to understand the times in which they lived and also to be prophets of what lay ahead. It was a poet's responsibility to use his poetic gifts for political means for the betterment of society. It is frequently argued in response that literature cannot be political without sacrificing art to ideology. But good poets write good poetry, regardless of the subject matter, and many fine poems have been written about specific political events. Others take up the theme of human rights and the democratic movement more generally and have become lasting expressions of liberty and justice. Burns's "A Man's a Man for A' That" (1795) is such a poem. Some of the most famous British poems, such as Spenser's *The Faerie Queen* (1590, 1596) and John Milton's *Paradise Lost* (1667), lend themselves to allegorical political readings, while others are overtly about political events.

Many poems were written in praise of Oliver Cromwell, the leader of the army that beheaded King Charles I in 1649 and brought in parliamentary rule in place of the monarchy. Cromwell became Lord Protector and head of the new Commonwealth in 1653. It was a troubled time, when families were often pitted against each other and religion (the Parliamentary party were Protestants, the royal family of Stuarts, Catholic) was a large part of the conflict. The complexity of the Civil War and its aftermath was best expressed by Andrew Marvell in his poem "An Horation Ode Upon Cromwell's Return from Ireland" (1650). Marvell admired Cromwell and supported the movement toward democracy, but he also questioned the violence of the regicide and painted a heroic portrait of Charles's patient acceptance of his fate:

He nothing common did or mean
Upon that memorable scene,
    But with his keener eye
    The ax's edge did try.

Cromwell's defeat of the Irish in 1650 was important to the revolutionaries because they interpreted it as a sign of God's support of the regicide. The poet acknowledges Cromwell's providential right to govern but also fears his energy and power. He compares him to Zeus, making his "fiery way" to the top of the rebel army as the representative of "angry heaven's flame." Marvell refers to Cromwell's trickery—he "wove a net"—that ensured the death of Charles I, but in comparing the regicide to the assassination of Julius Caesar he reminds us that no violent action can be without consequences. The fate of England now stems from a "bleeding head." Marvell's sense that Cromwell's ends were not without ruthless means is evident in his ironic reference to the Irish, who had just been violently overthrown, as being the best able to attest to his goodness and fitness for "highest trust." The conclusion of the poem, however, suggests that so far Cromwell has been humble in acting for parliament and the people rather than for his own glory. He will continue to conquer for the prosperity of the republic, though, and Marvell warns the Scots to "shrink underneath the plaid" because they will be Cromwell's next conquest. Again, Marvell is equivocal as he ends the poem by citing Machiavelli's observation that when violent means are used to gain power, violence will be required to maintain it.

John Milton (1608–1674) devoted his life to public causes and his writing—both poetry and prose—to the service of his countrymen. He addressed all the central issues of his turbulent times—religion, the Civil War, free speech, even divorce (he argued in favor of it at a time when such views were generally unacceptable)—in pamphlets and poems. He was forty-one in 1649 when King Charles I was beheaded, and he became the Latin Secretary for the parliament that succeeded the monarchy and then for Oliver Cromwell when he became the Lord Protector in 1653. Milton wrote in praise of Cromwell in his sonnet "To the Lord General Cromwell, May 1652," urging him not to give up the fight for "peace and truth" even though he had been victorious over the Scots (as Marvell had predicted). "Peace hath her victories/No less renowned than war," and the threat now, in Milton's view, is the movement toward a paid clergy and government control of spiritual matters. As in "Lycidas" (1637), in which he describes corrupt clergy as wolves sneaking into the sheepfold, such clergy are "hireling wolves whose gospel is their maw"—for they are motivated by greed.

Milton's sonnet "On the Late Massacre in Piedmont" (1655) is one of his most famous. Here he takes up the cause of a small group of Protestants in northern Italy and southern France who were brutally massacred by the armies of the Catholic duke of Savoy. The poem, an appeal to God to right the wrong done to his innocent followers, reenacts in sound the violent attack on this mountain people, as the lines flow from one to the next like the women and children who were tumbled down the mountainside:

> Forget not: in thy book record their groans
>   Who were thy sheep and in their ancient fold
> Slain by the bloody Piedmontese that rolled
>   Mother with infant down the rocks. Their moans
> The vales redoubled to the hills, and they
>   To heaven.

One of the most famous and sustained of political poems is John Dryden's "Absalom and Achitophel," written in 1681 as a defense of King Charles II, who had been restored to the throne in 1660. His brother James, a Catholic, was next in succession, but the House of Commons proposed an Exclusion Bill that would bar all Catholics from the throne. The supporters of this movement were led by the earl of Shaftesbury, who urged Charles II's illegitimate son, the duke of Monmouth, to take over the throne. Dryden wrote the poem at the request of King Charles, to restore faith in his leadership and unmask the rebels as dangerous anarchists. To add weight to his poem, Dryden wrote it as a political allegory based on the biblical story of King David and his son Absalom, who at the urging of Achitophel rebels against his father's authority and attempts to take the throne. When he is killed, David regrets his death, crying out the famous lament, "O Absalom, my son, my son!"

Dryden published the poem after Charles II had dissolved parliament, thus putting an end to the Exclusion Bill, and after the earl of Shaftesbury had been arrested for treason. The threat of rebellion was thus less acute, but Dryden still saw the need to restore a sense of law and order after a dangerously troubled period that reminded him of the unrest following the regicide of King Charles I in 1649. He had to be diplomatic in the poem: not too critical of the duke of Monmouth, who was still his father's favorite; and not too critical of Charles II's well-known infidelities. Using an allegorical style, where the characters are all disguised as biblical figures, helped to give dignity and seriousness to his attack and also gave Charles the attributes of kingship accorded to King David. The parallels between the two stories had already been noted by Dryden's contemporaries: both sons were spoiled favorites of their fathers, and both were encouraged to rebel by self-serving flatterers, Achitophel, and the earl of Shaftesbury. Dryden was able to find biblical counterparts for all of his characters except for James, Charles's brother and the next in succession to the throne.

The poem is written in heroic couplets and much of the tone is serious, but Dryden departs from the epic form in the opening, where he excuses Charles's many adulteries by referring to David's promiscuity as sanctioned by the Bible because it occurred "in pious times . . . Before polygamy was made a sin" by the priesthood. The story behind the duke of Monmouth's (Absalom's) rebellion is based, however, on his illegitimacy. One of the crucial scenes in the poem is Achitophel's temptation of Absalom, in which the wily rebel overcomes Absalom's loyalty to his father by playing on Absalom's resentment at being excluded from the succession because of his illegitimacy. Achitophel flatters the handsome young man, urging his father's increasing weakness and the son's popularity with the people. Because his illegitimacy rankles with him, Absalom is easily won over.

The most memorable parts of the poem are the brilliant sketches of the rebels. Achitophel's temptation of Absalom recalls the devil's smooth-tongued tempting of Eve in the Garden of Eden (as described by Milton in *Paradise Lost*, written in 1667). Just as the devil disguised himself as a snake, Achitophel "sheds his venom" in his silky words. Achitophel, representing the earl of Shaftesbury, is a treacherous figure, motivated by hatred of the king and burning personal ambition. Dryden acknowledges Shaftesbury's honesty and fairness as a judge, and regrets that he was not content to limit his powers to that important role. His character, unfortunately, was too unstable, his love of danger and excitement too great to remain in quiet waters: "when the waves went high/He sought the storms. . . ." Dryden depicts him as a restless, unhappy man whose cleverness was akin to madness. Small in stature, Shaftesbury had a burning impatience that made him reckless, and therefore dangerous to the peace of the state. His body was too small to contain his "fiery soul, which, working out its way,/Fretted the pygmy body to decay,/And o'er-informed the tenement of clay."

Shaftesbury's fellow rebels include a cast of self-serving confidence tricksters such as George Villiers, the duke of Buckingham and a rival playwright of Dryden's. Appearing as Zimri in the poem, Villiers is satirized as a man of extremes and excess, continually shifting his interests and his loyalties: "in the course of one revolving moon,/Was chymist, fiddler, statesman, and buffoon." He switched his allegiance from the monarchy to the rebels, but was not clever enough to lead. Like the other rebels, Villiers was dangerous because of his lack of moderation, an extremist who was "Stiff in opinions, always in the wrong;/Was everything by starts, and nothing long." Slingsby Bethel, a sheriff of London who packed the juries with Whigs and therefore acquitted the king's enemies, including Shaftesbury, appears in the poem as Shimei. Dryden identifies him as a religious hypocrite, and he cleverly turns biblical language into an attack on Slingsby Bethel's perverted and extreme piety. How can a zealous lover of God hate his king, asks Dryden, when the king is God's representative on earth. But Shimei turned his apparent godliness to the rebel cause. He "never broke the Sabbath, but for gain," and "loved his wicked neighbor as himself." Shimei has amassed wealth but makes a merit of parsimony and asceticism. His servants are half-starved, his guests unfed, his cooks idle: "Cool was his kitchen, though his brains were hot." Dryden goes so far as to compare Shimei ironically with Christ, drawing an analogy between the disciples and Shimei's fellow rebels:

> When two or three were gathered to declaim
> Against the monarch of Jerusalem,
> Shimei was always in the midst of them.

Titus Oates, disguised as Corah in the poem, was the instigator of the Popish Plot that in 1678 stirred up a violent and unjustified fear that Catholics were plotting to assassinate King Charles II, set fire to London, and reestablish the Catholic Church. Oates, a well-known swindler, presented the king with false documents alleging the plot. Despite his reputation, rumors spread about the threatened persecution of Protestants, playing into the hands of the rebels, who wanted to prevent the passing of the succession to Charles's Catholic brother, James. In the poem, Dryden ironically castigates Corah by comparing him to the false witnesses who condemned Stephen, the first Christian martyr. If anyone testified against Corah, he just said that they were part of the plot.

Absalom (the duke of Monmouth) falls prey to Achitophel's goading that he is excluded from the succession by the most unfair of reasons, his illegitimacy. Flattered by Achitophel's reminder that the people love him and he has all the qualities of kingship, Absalom sets out across the country to sound out the people and gauge his support. But Dryden interrupts the narrative with a statement of his own belief in the necessity for a royal succession that cannot be altered by the people. The king, he argues, cannot be at the mercy of a foolish and fickle populace. Mob rule can take over and anarchy is the result. Dryden then contrasts the portraits of the rebels with an account of the king's friends—not self-serving and immoderate, but generous and reasonable men. The poem concludes with David's speech to the nation, based on an address that Charles II gave at Oxford. Continuing Dryden's call for a succession untouched by the fickle will of the people, David draws attention to the lawlessness of the rebels and the dangers of populist rule. He points to the hypocrisy of the rebels in pretending that they are acting for the public good, and he reminds his audience that he has been patient and merciful with his enemies. The rebels, he says, will ultimately destroy themselves because their motives are false and their methods unlawful. Dryden concludes by reasserting Charles II's divine right. His speech is validated by God, and a "new time" ensues in which law and justice prevail.

The Romantic poets took up many political causes, inspired by the wave of democratic fervor in Europe following the Declaration of Independence of the United States in 1776 and the French Revolution of 1789. Finally the rights of the common man rather than church and aristocracy were being championed, and the poets at the beginning of the nineteenth century took up the cause of ordinary—especially rural—people. Robert Burns, the "plowman" poet from Ayrshire, Scotland, was not at the center of political life, but he was well read, and once he became famous and feted by the upper classes of Edinburgh (who patronized him as a "rustic" poet), he was in a position to comment on the injustices of the class system. His poem "A Man's a Man for A' That" (1795) is a well loved defense of the ordinary man. Honesty, worth, independence of mind, and good sense belong in as large measure to the poor as to the privileged. The lord "wha struts, and stares, and a' that,/Though hundreds worship at his word,/He's but a coof [dolt] for a' that." Burns concludes his comic attack (comic, but deeply felt) with a warning that the triumph of "sense and worth" is coming, and "Man to Man the world o'er,/Shall brothers be for a' that." Burns died a year later.

Percy Bysshe Shelley came from a much more privileged background than Burns. An aristocrat, he attended Oxford University (until expelled for writing a pamphlet on atheism), but he shared Burns's flouting of conventional morality (both ignored traditional views of fidelity) and his democratic defense of the ordinary man, if from a much more intellectual perspective. Shelley was four years old when Burns died, so he lived to see a resurgence of reactionary policies and restrictive measures in the wake of the French Revolution. A depression added to the grievances of the working classes. In 1819 his "Song to the Men of England" was a war cry like Burns's on behalf of the rural working man, but it decries the aristocracy not for being foolish, arrogant dolts but for being parasites on the hardworking farmers and weavers who keep the wealthy well fed and clothed. The "Song" became a rallying cry for the labor movement in its succinct, scathing attack on privilege:

> Wherefore feed and clothe and save
> From the cradle to the grave
> Those ungrateful drones who would
> Drain your sweat—nay, drink your blood?

In the same year, Shelley's sonnet "England in 1819" was a scorching attack on British institutions following the Peterloo Massacre of August

16, 1819, in which many peaceful protestors were brutally put down by cavalry in St. Peter's field, near Manchester. The sonnet begins at the apex of British institutions with King George III, "an old, mad, blind, despised and dying King." Next follow the princes, hangers-on at the trough of privilege, whom Shelley scathingly describes as clinging "leechlike to their fainting country . . . Till they drop, blind in blood, without a blow." In the middle of the poem are the victims of this corrupt ruling class, "A people starved and stabbed in the untilled field." The soldiers wield a "two-edged sword" because they are destroying what they should be defending. In the closing lines of the poem he moves to institutions and laws rather than the people that control them. The church, he says, is just empty ritual, acting at odds with Christ's injunction to love each other. The government has imposed restrictions on the freedom of religion of those outside the Anglican church, whose rightful grievances will result in another revolution (a "glorious Phantom," like the Glorious Revolution of 1660) that will, ghostlike, emerge from the grave to "illumine our tempestuous day."

In 1819 Shelley also wrote "To Sidmouth and Castlereagh" in response to the government's restrictive measures following the Battle of Waterloo, when fear of a British revolution was widespread. Viscount Castlereagh was foreign secretary and Viscount Sidmouth was home secretary when unrest escalated into the Peterloo Massacre. Shelley addresses them as a series of cruel, vicious birds and fish, dangerous and predatory: "two empty ravens" who smell "fresh human carrion"; "two gibbering night-birds"; "a shark and dogfish" waiting for a dinner of African slaves, thrown over the sides of the slave ships; finally in the last stanza, a new beast in every line—vultures, scorpions, wolves, crows, "vipers tangled into one." Shelley makes no other comment; his metaphors are only too damning.

William Wordsworth wrote a more general condemnation of the injustices of British institutions in his sonnet "London, 1802." He had just returned from France, with whom Britain was at war, and he was struck by the indifference and apathy of the British people. He addresses John Milton in the sonnet because Milton's own sonnets had called for individual freedom, tempered by a strong sense of personal responsibility and duty. England, Wordsworth writes, is "a fen/Of stagnant waters." He uses metonymy—"altar" for the church, "sword" for the army, "pen" for the literati, "fireside" for the common people, and "hall and bower" for the privileged classes—to implicate all the English in a general malaise. "We are selfish men," he writes, needing Milton's "cheerful godliness" that was ready to perform the "lowliest duties" of life.

In the twentieth century, the world wars have provoked the largest and most impassioned poetic responses to political events. These poems are discussed in the War section. One poem that is more generally about human suffering, however, is Edward Thomas's "The Owl," written in 1914, before he enlisted. Thomas describes stopping for food and lodging at an inn one autumn night. Tired, cold, and hungry, he appreciates the refuge, when the melancholy cry of an owl reminds him that others— "soldiers and poor"—are still out in that cold night, "quite barred out" from the comfort that he is now enjoying. The haunting sound of the owl is a fine contrast to the songs of skylarks and other songbirds that bring joy to the heart of the listener in many poems. As the poet sits in the warmth of the inn, the cry of the owl speaks for the voiceless who are not rejoicing. While modern readers may no longer look to poets for a criticism of society and its ills, as earlier centuries did, many poets still take seriously their responsibility to speak out for those who lack the poet's eloquent voice.

❧⚮☙

"An Horatian Ode Upon Cromwell's Return from Ireland," Andrew Marvell
> BL; NAEL-1; OAEL-1; OBEV; TFi

"To the Lord General Cromwell, May 1652," John Milton
> BL; NAEL-1; TrGrPo-1

"On the Late Massacre in Piedmont," John Milton
> BL; NAEL-1; OBEV; TFi

"Absalom and Achitophel," John Dryden
> NAEL-1

"A Man's a Man for A' That," Robert Burns
> ImPo; NAEL-2; OAEL-2; TFi; TrGrPo-1

"Song to the Men of England," Percy Bysshe Shelley
> TrGrPo-2

"England in 1819," Percy Bysshe Shelley
> NAEL-2; OAEL-2; OBEV; TFi; TrGrPo-2

"To Sidmouth and Castlereagh," Percy Bysshe Shelley
> NAEL-2

"London, 1802," William Wordsworth
> NAEL-2; TrGrPo-2

"The Owl," Edward Thomas
> NAEL-2; OAEL-2; TFi

Pride and Vanity

❦

Pride has always been considered the most serious of human failings. For the ancient Greek dramatists, pride, or *hubris*, was the flaw that defeated all the tragic heroes because in their heroic desire to do good (bolstered by the admiration of their people) they overstepped human bounds and began to think themselves gods. Often the tragic fall came about because the hero in his pride thought he could avoid his destiny. Oedipus was such a blinded man. Told by the oracle that he would grow up to murder his father and marry his mother, he fled his home and traveled to Thebes, not knowing that the parents from whom he was running had adopted him. Oedipus's predicament evokes pity and fear in us, as Aristotle said all good tragedies must, because he cannot be faulted for trying to evade such a cruel fate. His error was in taking his destiny into his own hands, challenging the gods and thinking he could outwit them.

In the Judeo-Christian tradition, pride is the most serious of the seven deadly sins because all others stem from it. Here, too, pride is setting oneself against God, and the consequences of such pride are the subject of many stories in English. The legend of Dr. Faust (as told in Christopher Marlowe's play *Doctor Faustus* [c. 1588]), for example, is the story of a man who sells his soul to the devil in exchange for superhuman powers. In Milton's *Paradise Lost* (1667), pride is the devil's sin that results in his expulsion from heaven. Pride is the tragic flaw of many of Shakespeare's heroes, and as in *Oedipus Rex* (c. 430 B.C.) it is often associated with blindness (Oedipus blinds himself at the end, when at last he sees the truth) because pride is a mental blindness to one's place in creation.

Vanity is less serious than pride. The preacher in Ecclesiastes warns us that the earthly life is all vanity: our petty desires, worries, and conceits are nothing in the grand scheme of things. "One generation passeth away, and another generation cometh; but the earth abideth forever." "The vanity of human wishes," as Samuel Johnson was to title a long poem on this subject in 1749, has been the source of much gentle humor and comic satire. William Drummond of Hawthornden neatly captured the frailty of our ambitions and high reputation in "This life, which seems so fair" (1656). Drummond's simile compares our short and puffed-up lives to the soap bubbles that children enjoy blowing about. The bubble seems to hover firmly in the sunlit air, but just when it is at its most magnificent and admired, it suddenly "turns to nought" because it was nought to begin with.

Geoffrey Chaucer poked fun at the vanity of many of his pilgrims in *The Canterbury Tales* (c. 1387), especially where Christian humility was expected. The Prioress, for example, prides herself on her French accent and sings hymns through her nose with more concern for the impression she is making than the meaning of the words. His portrait is kindly, though, and he clearly likes his prioress, with her overly genteel table manners and misplaced affection for dogs rather than parishioners. His Wife of Bath is larger than life and a bundle of vanities, especially in church, where she insists on her superior position in the village hierarchy. If she is not first in line to put her money in the plate, she is so miffed that she gives nothing at all. In her red hat and soft leather shoes she likes to make an impression as she sweeps down the aisle. But again, Chaucer speaks with kindness about this most recognizable churchgoer.

Robert Burns's "To a Louse" (1785) pokes fun at another Wife of Bath, the well-dressed matron who attends church to be seen and believes a pious life is a moral life. Sitting behind a well-dressed lady, Burns sees a louse on her bonnet and speculates about the difference between the lowly, despised insect and the fine lady who is unaware of its presence and would be horrified if she knew. Her ignorance of the discrepancy between her vanity and the ugly little insect (always associated with the lower classes and lack of hygiene) becomes a way of recognizing that self-righteous pride in ourselves is foolish: "O wad some Pow'r the giftie gie us/To see oursels as others see us!"

One of the masters of the character sketch in British poetry, as acute an observer of human nature as Chaucer, was the Victorian poet Robert Browning, and many of his dramatic monologues reveal a personality caught up in pride and vanity. The most famous, "My Last Duchess" (1842), is a study of pride in a husband and is discussed in the Marriage section of this book. His earlier poem "Porphyria's Lover" (1834) is similarly about power in a relationship and can also be seen as a study of wounded pride. Browning first published it with another poem under the title "Madhouse Cells," drawing attention to the deranged state of mind of the speaker. The monologue takes place inside that mind, and tells the story of Porphyria's arrival at the speaker's lonely and humble hut. Porphyria is wet and cold from the storm, but she brings warmth and life into the cold room by her presence and by making "the cheerless grate/Blaze up." At first, she is the dominant figure in their relationship, and he seems to be passive to the point of inertia. She calls him, and "when no voice replied,/She put my arm about her waist. . . ." We learn that she comes from a higher class and a family that considers him beneath them. She has been at a party, but left it to join her lonely lover. She loves him, but she is "too weak" to break the bonds of "pride, and vainer ties" that connect her to her upper-class world. Listening to her, the speaker realizes that she worships him, and in that triumphant moment he "found/A thing to do": wishing to keep her in his power forever, he strangles her. The remainder of the poem reveals the speaker's determined (and insane) justification of his action, based on wounded pride as a poor man patronized by a wealthier woman. She felt no pain, he assures himself. When he opens her eyes, they still laugh "without a stain." When he releases the long tresses with which he had strangled her, the blood returns to her cheek and she seems to blush when he kisses her. Just as the Duke in "My Last Duchess" desires to own his Duchess, and actually turns her into a picture after having her killed, the speaker here has turned Porphyria into a possession. She becomes just "the smiling rosy little head," reduced to a thing—"it had its utmost will" (she had told him that her fondest wish was to be his forever). The poem ends with the macabre picture of the speaker and Porphyria seated together, her head propped on his shoulder. As he speaks the poem, we learn that they have sat thus all night, "and yet God has not said a word!" In the madman's gloating pride, he considers himself above reproach. There are many echoes of Keats's "The Eve of St. Agnes" (1819) in the poem, but Browning was more interested than was Keats in the psychology of the individual mind and how to convey that mind in poetry.

In "Sordello" (1840) an early work about a poet, Browning outlines what was to become his method in writing the monologues for which he became famous. Each human being has a special point of view and separate spiritual life. An evil man cannot live with the knowledge of his evil acts, so he creates, "through a maze of lies,/His own conceit of truth." Thus the Duke and Porphyria's lover rationalize the murders of the women they have failed to dominate or control in life. Browning's purpose in his monologues is to "impart the gift of seeing" to his audience, laying bare the "incidents in the development of a soul." Browning's strength is in delineating those souls and their individual dramas. The "Soliloquy of the Spanish Cloister"(1839) is another study of pride and vanity, this time by a monk in a Spanish monastery who is muttering his annoyance with a fellow monk, Brother Lawrence, while tending the hated brother's monastery garden. The poem is a soliloquy rather than a dramatic monologue because the monk is talking out loud to himself rather than to a listener whose presence is evident in the dramatic monologue even though his responses are not heard. The success of the soliloquy, however, is that, as in the dramatic monologue, the main effect is an ironic discrepancy between the monk's view of himself and our view of him. In this poem, humor rather than horror (as in "Porphyria's Lover") is the result. The monk takes out his anger at Brother Lawrence by attacking the brother's flowers with mischievous glee ("He-he! There his lily snaps!"). Our speaker prides himself on his Christianity while condemning Brother Lawrence for his frailties, even wishing him dead, so strongly does he hate him. He makes fun of Brother Lawrence's fastidiousness in the dining room, but then criticizes him for draining his drink in one gulp. Our speaker prides himself on drinking his in three sips, to illustrate the Trinity, and placing his utensils in a cross, unconsciously revealing the shallowness of his piety. He accuses Brother Lawrence of having a mistress—brown Dolores—but the fervor with which he describes her suggests his own lascivious thoughts. In the last three stanzas he craftily thinks up ways of sending Brother Lawrence to hell. He will trick him into uttering a heresy on his deathbed, which will "send him flying/Off to hell, a Manichee." Or he will slip a page of a licentious French novel into Brother Lawrence's sieve as he is gathering greengages, so that he cannot fail to read it and be damned immediately. Our speaker fails to notice that the book is his, and he is clearly very familiar with its contents. Finally he plans to sell his soul to Satan, Faust-like, but extricate himself in the nick of time while condemning Brother Lawrence. At the end of the poem the reader is in no doubt who is the humble Christian in the poem, and who the vain and jealous sinner, burning up with hatred for his fellow monk.

A more complex portrait of un-Christian pride and vanity is Browning's dramatic monologue "The Bishop Orders His Tomb at Saint Praxed's Church" (1844). The setting, in sixteenth-century Rome, is the deathbed of the Bishop, from which he is giving his final commands to his "nephews" gathered around his bed. The poem opens with the central irony: the Bishop quotes from Ecclesiastes, "Vanity, saith the preacher, vanity!" As a bishop on his deathbed, his thoughts should indeed be with his eternal life, recognizing the triviality of earthly desires. But the Bishop's monologue reveals a man wholly caught up in vanity, both in life and after death, for he has called his "nephews" together to ensure that his tomb will be the grandest in the church, and his resting place the most advantageous. So bound up in the vanities of the world is he that he conceives of himself when entombed as though he will still have his senses. Even in death he will be trying to outwit his long-time rival, the former bishop Old Gandolf, whose resting place will not be nearly so well placed in the old church.

The brilliance of the poem lies in Browning's skill at showing through the monologue the old Bishop's waning faculties. Like all the speakers in the dramatic monologues, he is anxious to maintain his view of himself, both to himself and to others (his "own conceit of truth" in Browning's words). But because he is old and near death, his guard keeps dropping and in his confused ramblings his real life and personality are revealed. Almost at once he lets slip that the boys around the bed are his sons, not his nephews. The Bishop has had a long-term relationship with a woman whose beauty allowed him to feel a superiority to Old Gandolf. Remembering that she is gone recalls him to his reason for calling the boys here: he is dying and has plans to make. The irony of the churchman wholly dedicated to the world of the flesh and possessions is inherent in the choice of church—Saint Praxed's, named for Saint Praxedes, a charitable woman who gave away all she had to the poor— and in the juxtaposition of the Bishop's praise for the church's peace, immediately followed by the truth: "I fought/With tooth and nail to save my niche, you know." The Bishop describes his tomb in highly sensuous terms, gloating over its "peach-blossom marble . . . rosy and flawless." Old Gandolf has only "paltry onion-stone," and in the confusion of the Bishop's mind he could be thinking of the peachy stone of his tomb or the peachy complexion of his mistress, whom Old Gandolf also coveted. The Bishop lets down his guard again in revealing to the boys that he stole and hid a valuable stone—lapis lazuli—when his church burned down. Now they are to dig it up for his tomb.

Like many another proud man, the Bishop hopes to avoid his mortality by creating a monument to himself. So real is this elaborate tomb that he imagines himself lying in it with all his senses, able to see and hear the mass, feel the candle flame, and taste the incense smoke. He is so afraid of relinquishing the material wealth that has made him happy and given him status that he cannot face eternal life except in terms of earthly possessions. From time to time the realization of death confronts him but his mind glides away into the stone of the tomb again, a fine metaphor for the Bishop's materialistic life:

> Swift as a weaver's shuttle fleet our years:
> Man goeth to the grave, and where is he?
> Did I say basalt for my slab, sons?

In ordering his tomb he requests a jumble of Christian and pagan imagery—The Savior at his Sermon on the Mount beside Pan and nymphs—the juxtaposition again illuminating the discrepancy between the life the Bishop should have lived, and the life he did live.

Thinking that the boys are whispering, he accuses them of spending the Bishop's money on themselves and scrimping on the tomb. Realizing that they have power over him now, however, he promises them material goods, "and mistresses with great smooth marbly limbs," the Bishop's mind again connecting his lifelong passion for women with his new passion for the stone of his tomb. But as the poem draws to its conclusion, the stone metaphor becomes all too apparent as an emblem of the Bishop's heart. He has never loved his sons—again he accuses them of treachery and threatens to cut them off with nothing—and he never really loved their mother. He sees their eyes "glitter like [their] mother's for [his] soul," suggesting that he has always shut himself away behind his love of ornament and show and his intense desire to eclipse Old Gandolf. As the sons draw away from the bedside he realizes that his life has been an empty one of vain wishes and proud boasts. He accuses them of ingratitude, the last rationalization of a mind that refuses to accept the truth. His parting lines find him still obsessed with besting his old rival:

> And leave me in my church, the church for peace,
> That I may watch at leisure if he leers—
> Old Gandolf, at me, from his onion-stone,
> As still he envied me, so fair she was!

One of the most famous examples of human pride is the story of Daedalus and his son Icarus. Daedalus, a skillful Athenian craftsman, had been imprisoned with Icarus in a labyrinth on the island of Crete. He made wings for them from wax and feathers and together they flew out of the maze, but the young Icarus was proud of his ability to fly and soared higher and higher, until he was too close to the sun. Its heat melted the wax on the wings and Icarus plunged into the sea and drowned (this part of the Mediterranean near Crete is still called the Icarian Sea). Icarus's story is often recounted when writers and artists want to illustrate the old proverb "Pride goeth before a fall." It also illustrates another dimension to human pride, however, because Icarus's desire to fly high is also a noble aspiration. When does human endeavor—the desire to know more and extend the boundaries of human achievement—become a prideful attempt to be godlike? The sixteenth-century Flemish artist Pieter Brueghel painted Icarus's descent, the boy's leg all that remains in view as he disappears into the sea. Meanwhile life goes on around him—a farmer plows his field, a ship sails by—completely unaffected by one boy's tragedy.

W. H. Auden wrote "Musée des Beaux Arts" (1938) in response to Brueghel's painting. For Auden, the event is about the suffering involved in failure, a subject that the old painters knew well, he tells us. Individual human suffering—of monumental import to the sufferer—happens in the midst of ordinary events and makes no difference at all. In the second part of the poem, Auden finely paraphrases the painting in long sweeping lines that imitate the leisurely activities happening around the fall of young Icarus. The first stanza suggests that even Christ's birth and suffering affect only the old; children "did not specially want it to happen." The reference to Christ, buried in the middle of the poem, reminds us that he lived and died in humility, free from human vanity and aspiration.

Thomas Hardy's poem "The Convergence of the Twain" (1912) sets human pride in the form of the *Titanic* against the greater forces of nature—the iceberg that sank this triumph of human engineering. He depicts the once mighty ship lying, the victim of "human vanity," among the fish who ponder man's folly. Worms crawl unconcerned, over the mirrors that for a short time flattered the vain, pampered passengers. Man's pride has been humbled by the "Immanent Will" that fashioned the iceberg as carefully as the builders fashioned the magnificent ship, and no one saw their fated collision:

> Alien they seemed to be:
> No mortal eye could see
> The intimate welding of their later history.

The "human vanity" of the *Titanic* or the preacher's warning in Ecclesiastes is a more comprehensive pride in human accomplishments than is often meant when we refer to someone as "vain." Many poets have satirized the more trivial concern with personal beauty that vanity often suggests, the apotheosis being Alexander Pope's incomparable "The Rape of the Lock," written as a mild rebuke to a frivolous young belle, Arabella Fermor, in 1712 (the poem we now read is a later, revised version of 1717). When a feud had erupted between two families because a young man, Lord Petre, had treacherously cut off a lock of Arabella's hair, a mutual friend asked Pope (a friend of both families) to write about the "rape" and diffuse the bad temper that had resulted. Pope turned the event into a mock epic, writing of it as though it were of monumental importance in order to show how very trivial it was. In doing so he also satirized the whole social world of the English upper classes and their leisurely, shallow, and self-serving lives.

The satire on vanity plays out through the elaborate battle of the sexes that Pope describes as though it were an epic battle of heroic proportions. The poem opens with the heroine, Belinda, preparing for a day of tea drinking and cards with her friends. In epic poems, the human combatants are aided by supernatural forces, which in this epic are spirits taken from Rosicrucian philosophy. According to this belief, when a woman dies her spirit becomes sprites from one of the four elements. Sylphs live in air and come from agreeable women; they both encourage a woman to be flirtatious and protect her honor. Nymphs live in water and come from changeable women; salamanders live in fire and come from hot-tempered women; and gnomes live underground and come from ill-tempered or prudish women. These sprites take part in the action, helping or hindering the human actors in the drama. At the beginning of the poem, Belinda is still asleep and her chief sylph, Ariel, has whispered to her the epic dream warning of "some dread event." Like the epic hero, however, Belinda forgets Ariel's words as soon as her eyes open. Her preparation for battle is described in heroic terms and draws comic attention to the confusion of values in the high society of Pope's day. Her dressing table is her altar, at which she "begins the sacred rites of Pride" with her "inferior priestess," her maid. Among the accoutrements of battle—her cosmetics and perfumes—can be found her Bible, of no more importance to her than her powders and puffs. Aided by her sylphs (her army), she arms herself for the battle like an epic hero putting on his armor, but central to the hero's preparations would be some sort of genuine prayer for divine aid.

Canto two opens with Belinda's sunlike arrival on the Thames, where the villainous Baron sees her beautiful hair and determines to steal a lock. He, too, has prepared for battle by worshiping at the altar of love, which he has built from French romances and the trophies of his former conquests: garters, gloves, and old love letters. One of the most delightful passages in the poem occurs at line fifty-five of Canto two, in which the army of sylphs is described in language that beautifully evokes the airy, ephemeral color and lightness of the sylphs. In a parody of Satan in John Milton's *Paradise Lost* (1667; on which Pope relies most heavily for his epic elements), Ariel musters his troops and gives them instructions on guarding Belinda in the upcoming battle. Pope's satire on the perversion of moral values among the upper classes (the valuing of "vanities" like beauty, flirtations, parties, and clothes) is often expressed through the rhetorical device of *zeugma*, where a moral quality is linked to a trivial one as though they were of equal importance. In his warning about the coming battle, Ariel tells his army that Belinda might "stain her honor, or her new brocade,/Forget her prayers, or miss a masquerade,/Or lose her heart, or necklace, at a ball. . . ."

Canto three enacts the battle by placing Belinda and the Baron as adversaries at a game of Ombre, the cards representing the warriors and the table the field of battle. The description of the card game is brilliantly suggestive of the battle of the sexes, a complicated game with rules that are easily broken. Belinda wins, and exultingly goes to tea (the epic banquet after the battle), but the Baron is already plotting his revenge. Provided with a small pair of scissors by Clarissa, he snips off a lock of

Belinda's hair. The sylphs are powerless to prevent it because they have discovered that Belinda is secretly in love, and therefore cannot be helped any further by the sprites of flirtation and fickleness.

Canto four contains the epic journey to the underworld, in which Ariel is replaced by Umbriel, a gnome, who travels to the Cave of Spleen (the equivalent of Milton's hell) to obtain the female weapons of "sighs, sobs, and passions, and the war of tongues . . . fainting fears,/Soft sorrows, melting griefs, and flowing tears." The loss of the lock is equated in this society with the loss of Belinda's honor, and Thalestris encourages Belinda in her rage, asking her if for this she put up with "torturing irons" to curl her hair and all the other afflictions suffered by young women in the name of vanity. Belinda pretends to regret that she ever went to Hampton Court that day. Why didn't she stay home saying her prayers and keeping her "charms concealed from mortal eye,/Like roses that in deserts bloom and die." This argument, in reverse, is a favorite one of the *carpe diem* poets who know that their Belindas would rather lose a lock of hair any day than bloom unseen in the desert.

Canto five opens with some sensible advice from Clarissa. She wonders why beauty is so highly prized and reminds Belinda, "How vain are all these glories, all our pains,/Unless good sense preserve what beauty gains. . . ." Hair turns gray and good looks quickly fade, so it is important to remain good humored: "Charms strike the sight, but merit wins the soul." No one ever listens to good advice, however, and the battle of the sexes merely resumes with added gusto in a delightful parody of an epic struggle. Belinda throws snuff at the Baron, making him sneeze, before drawing her epic dagger (a hairpin) for a final thrust. Belinda demands the return of her lock, but it is nowhere to be found. The poem ends with the consolation that it has been spirited into the skies to become a new constellation; when "all those tresses shall be laid in dust" her lock will make Belinda immortal.

This brief summary of the poem does little justice to Pope's wit and inventiveness, but as a poem about vanity and pride, "The Rape of the Lock" is the quintessential expression of a society driven by those most human of weaknesses. Pope's tone is never cynical or even critical of his foolish young friend. When in Canto two he declares, "If to her share some female errors fall,/Look on her face, and you'll forget 'em all," he is admitting to the pleasure that both sexes derive from their youthful flirtations. Only occasionally does the poem remind us of the implications for society of the upper classes' vanity and self-absorption. At lunchtime, Pope notes, "the hungry judges soon the sentence sign,/And wretches hang that jurymen may dine. . . ." The complacency of the upper classes was to be severely shaken by the French Revolution less than eighty years later, and by the wave of democratic revolt in the next century, when the satirical deflating of the vanities of the wealthy would become the province of novelists rather than poets.

❧❧❧

"This life, which seems so fair," William Drummond of Hawthornden
    SB; TrGrPo
"The General Prologue," *The Canterbury Tales*, Geoffrey Chaucer
    NAEL-1; OAEL-1
"To a Louse," Robert Burns
    ECP, NAEL-2
"Porphyria's Lover," Robert Browning
    BAVP; NAEL-2; TrGrPo-2
"Soliloquy of the Spanish Cloister," Robert Browning
    BAVP; NAEL-2; OAEL-2; OBEV; TrGrPo-2
"The Bishop Orders His Tomb at Saint Praxed's Church," Robert Browning
    BAVP; NAEL-2; OAEL-2; TFi
"Musée des Beaux Artes," W. H. Auden
    NAEL-2; ImPo; TFi
"The Convergence of the Twain," Thomas Hardy
    NAEL-2; OAEL-2; OBEV; TFi
"The Rape of the Lock," Alexander Pope
    ImPo; NAEL-1; OAEL-1; TrGrPo-1

Rebellion and Conformity

❧

Rebellion and conformity is a theme usually associated with youth, especially the transitional years between childhood and adulthood when children typically challenge the restrictions of adult life, perhaps in the knowledge that soon the pressures of earning a living and taking on adult responsibilities will be inevitable. It is also a theme more commonly associated with the novel, which lends itself to following the progress of a child to adulthood in the *Bildungsroman*. Poets have approached it with a variety of attitudes, however, and have not restricted the discussion to young people.

George Crabbe (1754–1832) is not well known now, except for his long poem "The Village" (c. 1815), but one of his lyrics, "The Whistling Boy" (c. 1815), neatly confronts the question of rebellion in youth. The first stanza tells the story of the whistling boy, a young plowman who yearns to break free from his dull life and become a soldier, but "he knows not how/To leave the land he loves so well." In the second stanza, a village girl who loves him decides not to follow her dream of a different, more exciting life in London. The third stanza compares the speaker's fear of rebellion to that of the boy and the maid. Vacillating between resolve to go and reluctance to leave familiar scenes, which "to minds disturbed . . . appear/In melancholy charms arrayed," the speaker fails to make up his mind, a dilemma that was probably Crabbe's own. As a boy he worked as a day laborer in the country while studying to be a doctor. Eventually someone paid for him to go to London, where he went into the ministry rather than the medical profession.

Alfred, Lord Tennyson's "Locksley Hall" also drew on the poet's own experience. Written in 1837–1838, the poem was influenced by Tennyson's bitter discovery that the young woman with whom he had fallen in love, the wealthy Rosa Baring, was a shallow flirt. The speaker of this dramatic monologue is a disgruntled young man who in the opening lines tells his friends to go on without him, sounding the horn for him when they are ready. Tennyson said of the poem that it "represents young life, its good side, its deficiencies, and its yearnings." The speaker is full of self-pity and righteous indignation. Caught between a love and respect for the past (symbolized by Locksley Hall) and a fierce desire to break away from it and flout convention, he is alternately contemptuous and sadly yearning. The poem is written in rhyming trochaic couplets that provide a sense of forward motion, but the speaker, like Crabbe's, is also fearful of the unknown future. He speaks of clinging to the present "for the promise that it closed," the intention being "enclosed" or possible, but the implication suggesting something more limiting.

The young man's immediate complaints form the basis for his vacillation between rebellion and conformity. He describes his girlfriend's rejection of him, charges her with bowing to her family's wishes, and accuses her of folly in choosing a man with "a range of lower feelings and a narrower heart than mine!" Then he looks into her future: her unworthy husband will drag her down in his coarseness, holding her "something better than his dog, a little dearer than his horse." In his bitter disappointment he rails against the social conventions that have taken her from him, and reminds her that some day she will look back on her rejection of him with regret. Finally, a baby will replace him in her affections, though, and will even reconcile her to her brutish husband.

Having dealt with his lost love, who took the path of conformity to her family and society, the speaker ponders his own future, foreseeing a break with dull routine: "I must mix myself with action, lest I wither by despair." Like Ulysses in Tennyson's poem of that name, this speaker desperately wants to live life to the fullest, but Victorian society does not offer anything to those without wealth ("Every door is barred with gold, and opens but to golden keys"). Even war is not heroic now, when paid service "helps the hurt that Honor feels." In the most famous passage in the poem, the speaker laments the passing of his more hopeful youth. Amy's rejection has made him feel old (like T. S. Eliot's "J. Alfred Prufrock"), and he remembers his youthful visions:

> For I dipped into the future, far as human eye could see,
> Saw the Vision of the world, and all the wonder that would be;
> Saw the heavens fill with commerce, argosies of magic sails,
> Pilots of the purple twilight, dropping down with costly bales;
> Heard the heavens fill with shouting, and there rained a ghastly dew
> From the nations' airy navies grappling in the central blue;
> Far along the world-wide whisper of the south wind rushing warm,
> With the standards of the peoples plunging through the thunderstorm;

Till the war drum throbbed no longer, and the battle flags were furled
In the Parliament of man, the Federation of the world.

Tennyson's predictions are very accurate here, in his vision of airplanes, the role of the air force in war, parachutes, and finally a United Nations. The young man's rebellious thoughts are quelled, however, by the disappointment of his lost love. Rather than the airy visions of his youth, now he sees the progress of science and human evolution as slow moving. Again, the speaker sounds like Ulysses when he remarks, "Knowledge comes, but wisdom lingers, and I linger on the shore,/And the individual withers, and the world is more and more." Hearing his friends' bugle call, he again rejects his background as "a trampled orphan" and tries to rouse himself to break away from his bitter resentment and disappointment. He envisions a retreat from civilized Victorian society and its improvements—a "march of mind" that has produced the steamship, the railway, and "the thoughts that shake mankind." No, he will escape to an island paradise where "some savage woman . . . shall rear my dusky race." He sees his children running wild in the forest, "not with blinded eyesight poring over miserable books." But as soon as he conjures up this rebellious vision, he realizes that it would be a step backward, a rejection of the progress of mankind in knowledge and culture. In a fine line that epitomizes the favorite Victorian linking of the railway with human progress, he urges, "Forward, forward let us range,/Let the great world spin forever down the ringing grooves of change." At the end of the poem he realizes that disappointment has not disabled him completely. In an echo of Milton's "Lycidas," in which the mourning shepherd sets out at the end for "fresh woods and pastures new," the speaker leaves Locksley Hall behind as "the mighty wind arises, roaring seaward, and I go." An odd mixture of youthful rant, lyrical evocation of times past, and prophetic glimpse of the century to follow, "Locksley Hall" remains a quintessentially Victorian poem, best known now, perhaps, for its often-quoted line, "In the spring a young man's fancy lightly turns to thoughts of love."

Thomas Hardy's "The Ruined Maid" (1866) is a clever defense of sexual nonconformity. The poem takes the form of a dialogue between a village girl and an old friend from the village whom she encounters on a city street. Amelia now lives in town, and the village girl is surprised to find her sporting fine clothes and flashy jewelry. The poem upsets the conventional notion that a promiscuous woman is "ruined." Hardy was taking issue with the self-righteous moralists who enjoyed the notion that sexual promiscuity in women led to disease, poverty, and misery. Even if she were "ruined" by an unscrupulous man (as so many servant girls were, by the young gentlemen of the house), the conventional view of Victorian England was that she deserved her miserable fate because she had transgressed an important moral law. To the village girl's increasing surprise that Amelia has actually prospered and acquired manners and even an upper-class, educated accent, 'Melia replies pertly that her success is all due to being "ruined." We are not told whether 'Melia is a high-class prostitute or a kept woman, but the poem clearly favors her position through the shift in the village girl's attitude from condescension to outright jealousy. At the same time, Hardy makes clear his real target of attack: the miserable living conditions of the village girl, whose only hope for a better life is the street. The hardness of her life, once shared by 'Melia, is strongly contrasted with 'Melia's new luxury. Her work-roughened hands and bruised face have been transformed into ladylike gloves and fine complexion. "Ruined" is the state of the conventional village girl, not the rebel, and the poem powerfully takes issue with a society that condemns its working-class women to such hardship while offering no way of bettering themselves other than promiscuity. Conventional morality condemned sexual freedom when it should have been condemning the grinding poverty that led to prostitution.

Society's condemnation of the rebel is partly the subject of Seamus Heaney's "Punishment" (1975). Heaney had been strongly affected by a Danish archaeologist's descriptions of bodies found preserved in peat bogs. Many of the people described in P. V. Glob's book *The Bog People* are believed to be sacrificial victims put to death as bridegrooms for the Mother Goddess of the earth. "Punishment," however, is about a young girl from the first century A.D. whose body was discovered in Germany in 1951. She had been blindfolded and her head shaved, and she was so light that a stone had been used to submerge her in the bog as punishment for adultery. Heaney calls her his "poor scapegoat" and admits that he too would have cast "stones of silence" in not preventing her death. He is referring here to the biblical story of the stoning of the woman taken in adultery. Christ tells the stone-throwers that only those without sin can cast a stone. Heaney suggests that in standing silently by in the face of injustice we are equally guilty of letting it happen. The poem then moves to contemporary Ireland, where Heaney sees a parallel between the bog girl and her "betraying sisters" who were condemned—tarred, shaved, and tied to railings—by the IRA for associating with British soldiers. He sees their punishment for rebellion against the accepted ideology as the finding of a scapegoat, and he implicates himself in the ease with which we all cast stones at societal scapegoats. He said nothing when the Irish women were humiliated. Although he would feel "civilized outrage" he still understood his collusion with the perpetrators as "tribal, intimate revenge." In apologizing to the young bog girl for being a voyeur of her mutilated but preserved body, he also does so to the Irish women in whose punishment he silently acquiesced. The poem is a powerful reminder that scapegoating those who seem to rebel against the supposed norms of society has been a fact of human life for centuries, and is still going on because we all passively allow it to happen. "Punishment" in the end refers to the poet as well as to the young victims.

The most sustained satire on the conformity imposed by governments and bureaucracies is W. H. Auden's "The Unknown Citizen" (1939). Narrated by the bland voice of a nameless civil servant, the poem describes the blameless life of a "citizen," identified only by his number on a tombstone erected by the state. In all things, this ideal citizen conformed to government requirements and societal expectations of behavior. All the different departments of government—the Bureau of Statistics, the social workers, the research and marketing offices, the Public Opinion group—have examined his behavior and found it faultless. Auden is satirizing the utilitarian and statistical approach to human affairs, which has no time for individuality but judges the citizen according to his usefulness for the greater good. Utilitarianism as preached by Jeremy Bentham at the end of the eighteenth century considered the greatest happiness of the greatest number as the measure of right and wrong. This citizen passes the test because he always "served the Greater Community." A man of moderation, he was a model of the bureaucratic statistics. The civil servant dismisses as absurd any suggestion that the citizen was unhappy; if he had been, the government would have been the first to know. As well as satirizing conformity, Auden is also attacking government interference in private matters, and the modern obsession with counting, evaluating, and reporting on human affairs in order to establish "normal" behavior and "trends." A similar description of a bland, conformist life is Matthew Prior's "An Epitaph" (1718), discussed in this survey in the Marriage section.

❧

"The Whistling Boy," George Crabbe
    TrGrPo-1
"Locksley Hall," Alfred, Lord Tennyson
    BAVP; ImPo; NAEL-2; OAEL-2
"The Ruined Maid," Thomas Hardy
    NAEL-2; TFi
"Punishment," Seamus Heaney
    NAEL-2
"The Unknown Citizen," W. H. Auden
    NAEL-2

Regret, Consolation, and Melancholy

❦

Many poems in this survey express regret or offer consolation because most human relations are touched at some time by feelings of regret for deeds done or not done, words said or not said. Consolation, if it happens at all, comes in different forms; sometimes the poet is left only with deep feelings of loss or disappointment, or with a consolation that fails to offer real solace. Closely related to regret is melancholy, a state of mind that has always been associated with the acutely sensitive poetic temperament that prefers solitude and is inclined to introspection and sadness.

One of the oldest poems written in England (in Old English, and therefore now mainly read in translation) is "The Wanderer" (c. 975). In this elegiac poem, the wanderer's philosophic speculation on life is set in a brief framework. The wanderer is an elderly warrior, far from home, whose companions and lord are dead. His meditation urges endurance, moderation, and patience under suffering. He offers advice on what it is to be wise, and how life's pains and losses lead to a humble, holy heart. The poem is famous for its use of the "ubi sunt" ("where are they?") convention of the medieval Latin poem.

Many of Shakespeare's sonnets express regret, but the most sustained sonnet on this theme is Sonnet 30, "When to the sessions of sweet silent thought" (1709). In the first stanza the speaker tells us that when he remembers the past he laments how many of the things he had hoped for did not happen. Recalling these "old woes" reminds him of the time he has wasted, perhaps with the suggestion that he is wasting time now in recalling them. In the second quatrain he specifies what some of these losses are, which now bring a tear to his eye: valued friends now dead; old love affairs; "many a vanished sight." At this point in the poem the reader can sense a gentle self-mockery in the speaker's tone: that he sighs, wails, drowns an eye, and moans suggests that he is only too aware of the danger of submerging himself in useless regret and self-pity. The third quatrain strengthens the central metaphor of a counting house or a court of law—a formal calling to account, in remembrance, for what has been lost. The "sessions" of silent thought suggest the sitting of a court; he "summon[s] up" past memories, as a witness is called to testify. In the third quatrain he mourns again over old grievances, and "tell[s] o'er/The sad account" of those losses, which he pays for again, as though he had not already lamented them previously. Describing losses and regrets as a monetary transaction suggests that the speaker is all too aware that when in this frame of mind we too easily pile misery on misery, deliberately creating a sense of regret. As always in Shakespeare, the closing couplet shifts the poem into another vein. The consolation for his losses is the friend to whom he has been moaning: "But if the while I think on thee, dear friend,/All losses are restored, and sorrows end."

Regret was a favorite theme of the Romantic poets, who enjoyed analyzing their emotions, especially melancholy. After the emphasis on sanity, common sense, and rational thought of the eighteenth century, the pre-Romantics at the end of the 1700s turned instead to the darker corners of the mind, evident in their interest in the Gothic and its attributes: haunted castles, mysterious inmates, guttering candles, high winds swirling the clouds past a huge moon, and owls hooting in the night. Poems of regret and melancholy often incorporated such symbols of a distressed or even diseased mind.

Samuel Taylor Coleridge's "Dejection: An Ode" (1802) began as a verse letter to Sara Hutchinson, his friend William Wordsworth's future sister-in-law, with whom Coleridge (who was unhappily married) had fallen in love. He later shortened it considerably and removed any references to Sara, changing them to "Lady." As well as the disappointment of his marriage, Coleridge was also suffering a sense that his intuitive sympathy with the natural world was abating. He had just read Wordsworth's "Ode: Intimations of Immortality" (1802–1804), in which Wordsworth regretted the loss of an instinctual sympathy with the nature that he had known as a boy. For Coleridge, this loss seemed also to mean the loss of his powers as a poet.

The poem begins with a quotation from the "Ballad of Sir Patrick Spens," in which the seaman warns that the position of the moon foretells a deadly storm. In the first stanza, Coleridge sees the same warning and predicts that the "tranquil" night will soon give way to "rain and squally blast." At one time he would have been invigorated by the thought of such a storm coming—the sounds would have "raised" and inspired his soul. He asks for such an inspiration now, to "startle this dull pain." In a state of lethargy, he is no longer at one with the natural world and able to respond to it. Stanza two elaborates on this sense of dull separation from a scene that should engage and inspire him. He gazes "with how blank an eye!" at the darkening sky and realizes that he is unmoved by it. He feels empty, "a grief without a pang, void, dark, and drear," a grief that he cannot express. He is "heartless," and can only see, not feel, the beauty of the night sky.

A short stanza three attributes his failure to respond not to the scene in front of him but to his own inner "genial spirits," his creative impulses, which have become deadened. In stanza four he recognizes that the creative connection between himself and nature has to come from him. The poet's soul allows him to see the world in a different, higher light, and without that soul he is just like "the poor loveless ever-anxious crowd" for whom the natural world is "inanimate" and "cold." The loss of that soul is the reason for his intense regret and desolation. In stanza five he defines the "strong music in the soul" as "Joy that ne'er was given,/Save to the pure." Again, he distinguishes the pure in heart, who experience the world in a light that is "undreamt of by the sensual and proud." The Lady (Sara) has this purity of heart that he no longer finds in himself. Stanza six tries to explain how he came to lose his "shaping spirit of Imagination," the joy that allowed him to turn misfortunes into "dreams of happiness." He had hope because he drew strength from the natural world. Now afflictions prevent him from realizing that joy; each misery "suspends what nature gave me at my birth" and he has grown into the habit of dejection.

Stanza seven returns to the growing storm outside, taking him away from the "viper thoughts" that beset him. The picture of the storm is tortured and mad, a perversion of the creative wind that he had spoken of in the first stanza. It is spring, but a wild and destructive spring, and a wind that speaks of war, "groans of trampled men, with smarting wounds." Suddenly the madness abates, however, and the wind tells the story of Lucy Gray from Wordsworth's poem of that name, a child who sets out alone with a lantern to light her mother home, but disappears in the storm. The concluding stanza prays that the Lady will awaken after the storm to the joyful connection with the world that he used to feel: "To her may all things live, from pole to pole,/Their life the eddying of her living soul!"

Coleridge's lament that he sees, but no longer feels, the beauties of nature, is echoed in William Wordsworth's "Resolution and Independence" (1802), a poem that Coleridge thought was entirely characteristic of Wordsworth. Based on a real encounter, the poem begins with the poet, a "Traveller," setting out onto the moors on a glorious morning following a storm. The natural world is at one, united by the love of the sun that shines alike on grass, raindrops, and hare, and at first the poet shares in that joy. But suddenly and unexplicably the joy "can no further go" and he is plunged from the height of happiness into an equally deep dejection that has no cause or association, just a "dim sadness—and blind thoughts." The Traveller, trying to account for this change of mood, realizes that he had unrealistically thought of himself as a "happy Child of the earth," as free from care as the hare and the bird he sees flying above him. He has lived as though life could be perpetual summer, that "all needful things" (Christ's phrase to Martha for love) would come "unsought/To genial faith." Thinking about other poets, he realizes that their lives have not been sunny at all, despite their gifts. In stanza six he recalls Coleridge's deep unhappiness, and in seven he remembers Thomas Chatterton, who committed suicide, and Robert Burns, who died young, both victims of their poetic gifts that took them out of the common sphere of activity. "By our own spirits are we deified:/We Poets in our youth begin in gladness;/But thereof come in the end despondency and madness."

At this point Wordsworth's thoughts are suddenly arrested, whether by "peculiar grace" or "a leading from above" he doesn't know. He sees a man "before me unawares," a phrase that recalls Coleridge's ancient mariner, who blesses the sea snakes "unawares" and in that act of grace begins his spiritual redemption. The old man is a leech gatherer, and Wordsworth describes him as though he were almost primordial, a creature of the pool from which he seems suddenly to have arisen. He is ancient, "not all alive nor dead," someone who has lived long enough to have regained the innate wisdom of the very young. His body is bent into almost a complete circle, his "feet and head/Coming together in life's pilgrimage." He is weighed down by the pains of living, and is supported now by a staff, which he uses to stir the water, searching for leeches. Wordsworth falls back on the conventional remark to a stranger: isn't it a nice day! But the old man replies with quiet dignity "above the reach/Of ordinary men" in lofty, well-chosen words like a poet or a religious man who knows what is due to man and God. The old man's story is a simple one: he travels the countryside gathering leeches for a living, resting wherever God provides a place. His calm resignation and sense of duty (resolution and independence) mesmerize Wordsworth and draw him out of his desolate state. Seeming to hear the old man in a dream, he regards him as heaven-sent "to give me human strength, by apt admonishment." Wordsworth is shamed by the old man's quiet resilience under suffering, and he seeks his help in overcoming his previous misery, "the fear that kills." The old man merely repeats the story of his quest for leeches, growing more difficult every year—"Yet still I persevere." Wordsworth seems to be only half-listening to the man's tale; he is "troubled" by the old man's presence in this remote place, and as the old man tells his story yet again, Wordsworth is able to recreate him in his imagination and see him as a part of the natural world. He knows that if dejection overtakes him again, he need only remember the "decrepit Man" who had "so firm a mind." The poet's self-pity is shamed by the simple dignity of the independent, solitary leech gatherer.

John Keats's "Ode on Melancholy" (1819) also takes up the subject of the sudden plunge from joy into despair, when "the melancholy fit shall fall/Sudden from heaven like a weeping cloud." In the first stanza, Keats warns the reader seeking a melancholy state not to toy with the ancient places, plants, and animals associated with melancholy and death: Lethe, the river of forgetfulness; the poisonous wolf's bane and nightshade; yew berries, beetles, and death-moths; the owl, bird of night. Do not let these be "a partner in your sorrow's mysteries" because they will numb the senses into unconsciousness and "drown the wakeful anguish of the soul." The poet suggests that melancholy is a state of mind that must be embraced fully so that the mysteries can be plumbed. In the second stanza he describes the mood of melancholy as falling "sudden from heaven" as a spring rain descends on the countryside. The image of spring rain continues as he advises the seeker after melancholy to "glut [his] sorrow" on the beauties of the natural world—a morning rose, a rainbow, spring peonies. That Keats is ironically considering the self-pity involved in states of melancholia is suggested, however, when he recommends that if one's mistress raves in anger, take her hand "and feed deep, deep upon her peerless eyes."

Stanza three opens with the reminder that "she dwells with Beauty—Beauty that must die," referring to the mistress and also to Melancholy herself. She also dwells with Joy, who is always ready suddenly to depart, as Wordsworth found in "Resolution and Independence." Even pleasure turns to "poison" in the moment of ecstasy. Melancholy, he suggests, lives "In the very temple of Delight." True melancholy, in other words, belongs not to the nighttime Gothic world of owls, nightshade, and wolf's bane, but to moments in our lives when we are feeling most joyful and least melancholic. Only those who truly feel joy can also enjoy (as the poet "feeds" upon his mistress's eyes) melancholy. Melancholy, personified as a lover, will consider such a suffering soul her trophy, because she has truly possessed him. Melancholy is born from the dreadful realization of the transience of beauty, joy, and pleasure.

This sense of the fragility of human happiness is strong in the poetry of Percy Bysshe Shelley, a contemporary of Keats and, like many of the Romantic poets, a rebel and reformer who felt passionately about freedom and democracy but whose short lyrics also contain some of poetry's finest expressions of pure emotion. Shelley drowned off the coast of Italy in 1822, just a month before his thirtieth birthday, so he did not live to write about regret and loss from the perspective of old age. But his emotional life was turbulent, and many of his poems—especially those he wrote near the end of his short life—were tinged with a melancholy sense of lost opportunities and vain hopes. An earlier poem, "Stanzas Written in Dejection—December 1818, near Naples," was, like Coleridge's "Dejection: An Ode" (1802), an expression of personal grief and pain. Shelley had married Harriet Westbrook when they were both still teenagers, and he had been expelled from Oxford for writing a pamphlet, "The Necessity of Atheism." After the birth of a son he deserted Harriet for Mary Wollstonecraft Godwin, with whom he eloped to Switzerland in 1814. He invited Harriet to join them but she declined, and not long after she drowned herself. He lost custody of their two children, married Mary and moved to Italy, where their baby daughter died. Suffering ill health and loss of faith in his poetic ability, he wrote five stanzas, comparing his lonely, miserable state with the beautiful scene before him. Again there is some self-pity in the poet's gloomy reflections on his lot as he examines his lethargy and dull, aching sense of futility: "I could lie down like a tired child/And weep away the life of care/Which I have borne and yet must bear/Till Death like Sleep might steal on me." In the final stanza he imagines friends grieving over his dead body, just as he will lament the passing of the lovely day. This thought reminds him of his self-indulgent complaint, because his broken heart "insults" the day with its "untimely moan." If he were to die, men might regret his passing even though they do not love him. The passing of the lovely day, however, will remain in the mind.

Two brief lyrics written near the end of his short life are well-known expressions of the theme of regret and loss. "O World, O Life, O Time" (1824), like Tennyson's "Break, break, break" (1834), depends on monosyllables to convey the poet's sense of stonyhearted despair as he contemplates the loss of his youth and the "glory" of those days. Joy has fled, and the seasons "Move my faint heart with grief, but with delight/No more, O never more!" The eight-line poem "A Dirge" (1821) draws on the natural world to convey a lament for "the world's wrong!" Rough wind, wild wind, sad storm, bare woods, deep caves, and dreary man— John Ruskin would find Shelley's dependence on pathetic fallacy (the attributing of human emotion to insensate things) forced, as the winds moan, the cloud knells, the "sad" storm rains tears, and the sea wails. More effective is "When the lamp is shattered" (1822), discussed in the Love section of this commentary.

Alfred, Lord Tennyson is also associated with poems of regret and loss, his whole life and poetic career having been overshadowed by the death of his friend Arthur Hallam when they were young men. "Tears, Idle Tears" (1847) is perhaps the quintessential British poem about regret, because it captures the intangible, unexplained emotion that is often associated with a general feeling of uneasiness and restlessness, a feeling that cannot be attached to any specific cause. Rather, it is often, as in Tennyson's poem, inspired by a landscape. The inspiration for the poem was Tintern Abbey on an autumn day (scene of Wordsworth's famous poem about lost youth, and also near Hallam's grave at Clevedon). Tennyson explained that the sorrow expressed in the poem had no specific cause; "it was rather the yearning that young people occasionally experience for that which seems to have passed away from them for ever." The tears that arise unbidden to the poet's eyes are "idle" because they have no immediate purpose; they are not inspired by a particular event but rather arise in the heart "from the depth of some divine despair." At such times humankind seems to share in a universal sadness inspired by the fading of summer into autumn (many children's books evoke this feeling, such as *Charlotte's Web* [1952] and *The Wind in the Willows* [1908]).

For Tennyson, the autumn fields around the ancient abbey remind him "of the days that are no more." Tennyson's images of this reminder are sharp, however; he does not fall into vague memories, despite the intangible nature of his sense of loss. In stanza two, the days are as "fresh" as "the first beam glittering on a sail/That brings our friends up from the underworld." "Fresh" and "glittering" establish the pang of remembrance of the dead as acute and fully realized, not just a faint ache. The image of the ship's arrival turns into an image of the ship's retreating— sinking "with all we love below the verge" in the red glow of sunset— because the return of the dead to the mind can only be fleeting. Thus the days are "so sad, so fresh."

In the third stanza, the image is of a dying man, the memories now "sad and strange" as the soul slips away with the coming of dawn. Just as memories of the dead have brought tears to the poet's eyes in a "strange" conjunction of past and present, so the dying man recognizes the strangeness of leaving the world just as day is dawning. His "dying ears" hear the sounds of awakening birds, and his "dying eyes" watch the room lightening for the last time as "the casement slowly grows a glimmering square." The dying man hovers between the "underworld" and this world, a transitional state (like autumn) that is the poet's state as well as he stands in the present while acutely conscious of "the days that are no more."

The last stanza gives physical expression to the mental loss. The dead friend is remembered physically through the body: "Dear as remembered kisses after death." Such kisses are as much missed as those imagined by "hopeless fancy" when one's love is unrequited. Such fanciful wished kisses, existing only in the mind of the dreamer, are like the ache of desire in the poet, as he remembers the days that are no more. Those days, which have been "fresh," "sad," and "strange," are at the end of the poem "deep as love" and "wild with all regret" because the poet has been absorbed into his recollection of a lost past. He is deep in the "divine despair" from which the recollections came, and his sense of pain is not just a dull ache but a wildness, a disorientation that overtakes the person lost in remembrance. The final line sums up this losing of one's bearings (the state of being "surprised by joy" as Wordsworth expresses it in the sonnet of that name): "O Death in Life, the days that are no more!"

Recollecting days and friends that are gone brings a sharpness of pain that is palpable. The movement of the poem takes the reader from a vague sense of recollection—"idle" tears gathering in the eyes while "thinking on the days that are no more"—to a recognition that those thoughts can overwhelm the present, bringing the lost past before the mind and the senses as distinctly as the autumn fields themselves. Tennyson offers no conventional consolation. The immediacy of grief and the tendency of memories to flood into the consciousness as though those lost times were still present are part of the human condition.

❦

"The Wanderer," anonymous

> NAEL-1; OAEL-1

Sonnet 30, "When to the sessions of sweet silent thought," William Shakespeare

> ImPo; NAEL-1; OAEL-1; TFi; TrGrPo-1

"Dejection: An Ode," Samuel Taylor Coleridge

> NAEL-2; OAEL-2; TFi

"Resolution and Independence," William Wordsworth

> NAEL-2; OAEL-2; SB; TFi

"Ode on Melancholy," John Keats

> ImPo; NAEL-2; OAEL-2; OBEV; TFi; TrGrPo-2

"Stanzas Written in Dejection—December 1818, near Naples," Percy Bysshe Shelley

> NAEL-2

"O World, O Life, O Time," Percy Bysshe Shelley

> NAEL-2; TrGrPo-2

"A Dirge," Percy Bysshe Shelley

> NAEL-2; TrGrPo-2

"Tears, Idle Tears," Alfred, Lord Tennyson

> ImPo; NAEL-2; OAEL-2; OBEV; TFi; TrGrPo-2

Religion

❧✦☙

Spiritual questions have been explored in poetry from earliest times. What is our place in the universe? Is there a greater power at work in our lives? Where did the world come from? Most religious poetry in English belongs to the seventeenth century, in the genius of John Donne, John Milton, George Herbert, and Henry Vaughan, but faith and doubt were explored again in the nineteenth century when the Romantic poets (especially Blake, Wordsworth, and Coleridge) brought a new sense of spirituality to the rationalism of the eighteenth century. Later, the Victorian poets lived in an age when faith was under attack from the findings of scientists such as the geologist Charles Lyell and the biologist Charles Darwin, whose discoveries cast doubt on the literal truth of the Bible. Tennyson's "In Memoriam A.H.H." (1850) is the most sustained examination of Victorian doubt, but other Victorian poets like Christina Rossetti held firm in their faith. In the twentieth century, also, some poets have taken up the subject of general attitudes to religion while others have expressed an individual faith. In all ages, poetry has been the basis of hymns and songs of worship and praise. A few of the most famous of these are included here. Poems that touch on religious themes will also be found in the Immortality and Death sections of this volume.

The seventeenth century was a time of appalling religious unrest. Following the conversion of England to Protestantism by Henry VIII in the middle of the sixteenth century, Catholics lived under severe restrictions for most of the 1600s. John Donne (1573–1631), who figures largely also in the Love section of this volume, came from a well-known Catholic family that had suffered severe persecution. An exceptionally clever man, Donne attended Oxford University but was not allowed to receive a degree. He converted to the Church of England (Anglicanism), and after taking part in the campaign against Catholic Spain, he worked as private secretary to Sir Thomas Egerton, Lord Keeper of the Great Seal, until his secret marriage to Egerton's niece, Anne More, caused his dismissal. (Sir Thomas later forgave Donne and gave him and his now large family an allowance.) By now well known as a talented writer of poetry and anti-Catholic pamphlets, Donne was urged by King James I to take holy orders in the Church of England. In 1615 he did so, and in 1621 he became the dean of St. Paul's.

Donne's religious poetry is as startling and unconventional as his love poetry, and just as the love poetry uses religious metaphors, his relationship with God is often described in highly physical, even erotic terms. His nineteen Holy Sonnets include the famous "Death be not proud" (1633), which is discussed in this volume in the Death section, and number 14, "Batter my Heart" (1633). In this sonnet, Donne addresses God directly, urging him in a series of striking metaphors to take his soul by force because Donne's faith is too weak. Overturning the vision of Christ as the gentle shepherd, Donne pleads, "Batter my heart, three-personed God; for you/As yet but knock, breathe, shine, and seek to mend." Donne loved paradox, and in the first of several in the sonnet he asks God to throw him down so that he may stand up; only through God's strength can he be strong. A powerful alliteration—"bend/Your force to break, blow, burn, and make me new"—ends the first quatrain. The second quatrain contains a striking extended simile in which Donne compares himself to a town that has been usurped by the devil. He wants to let God take the town over, but his Reason ("your viceroy in me,"—Reason was seen as the human attribute that allowed us to comprehend God) is too weak to resist the devil's temptations. The sestet introduces an even more startling metaphor when Donne tells God that he is "betrothed" to God's enemy. Pleading with God to divorce him from the devil, he concludes the poem with two disturbing paradoxes: unless God "enthralls" him he will never be free; unless God "ravishes" him, he will never be chaste. The sonnet powerfully expresses Donne's sense of his own weak will that cannot be brought to God by gentle means, or by his own efforts.

Donne wrote several hymns including the famous "A Hymn to God the Father" (1633), in which he asks God for forgiveness of his sins through a series of pleas. In the first two stanzas, Donne asks for forgiveness through four questions that begin "Wilt Thou forgive?" But in the third stanza, questioning paradoxically gives way to certainty when Donne speaks of the sin of fear that there is no afterlife, that "when I have spun/My last thread, I shall perish on the shore." Donne does not have to ask for God's forgiveness for this sin because the answer has already been provided in Christ's death: "at my death Thy Son/Shall shine as he shines now, and heretofore."

George Herbert was influenced by his older friend John Donne to write religious verse and, at the age of thirty-six, to become a minister of the Anglican church. A gentle, saintly man, Herbert was also blessed with a sharp wit and inventive imagination that lent surprise and passion to his deeply felt poetry. But unlike Donne, Herbert did not look to secular metaphors to express his beliefs; rather, he turned to the Bible and even to the building of the church itself for his inspiration. "The Altar" (1633), for example, is one of Herbert's "emblem" poems, where the subject of the poem is found in the form as well. Shaped like an altar, the poem begins with two lines of iambic pentameter followed by two lines of iambic tetrameter, forming the top. Eight lines of iambic dimeter form the column supporting the top, and the pedestal is the top lines reversed. The poem speaks of the poet's heart as an altar, created by God and formed to give praise. "Easter Wings" (1633), shaped in the form of two sets of angels' wings, makes powerful use of this unusual form. In each of the two stanzas, the first five lines gradually decrease in length from the first line's ten syllables to the fifth line's two syllables. The second half of the stanza reverses this decrease, moving out from two syllables to a final ten. This pattern exemplifies the meaning of the lines, which takes the reader from the abundance of God's creation to the Fall and man's becoming "most poor." The second half of the stanza, beginning "With thee," finds the poet rising like a lark and expanding back into fullness through God's grace. In the second stanza the movement occurs within the poet's own life as through sin he became "Most thin." Again "With thee" begins the rising action as the poet again finds wings through God's strength, provided by Christ's death.

"The Pulley" (1633) reverses the Greek myth of Pandora, who opened a magic box that released evils into the world but left hope behind in the box. In the poem, God pours blessings on the world—strength, beauty, wisdom, honor, pleasure—but he keeps rest behind. Herbert puns on the word "rest" and its two meanings of repose and what remains. God says, "Yet let him keep the rest,/But keep them with repining restlessness" so that man will always turn back to God and will not be satisfied by material gifts. The pulley is thus a metaphor for God's creating man and drawing him back to him.

In "The Collar" (1633), Herbert takes on Donne's tone of remonstrance with God, beginning with the poet's cry, "I struck the board and cried, no more!" The title suggests a restriction or even a sense of slavery, and in the poem Herbert rails against being tied by conventional piety and Christian practice. He complains that he has accomplished nothing, that his efforts have all been wasted and unproductive. But at the end of the poem, he takes up Donne's paradox that only God can grant true freedom: "But as I raved and grew more fierce and wild/At every word,/Methoughts I heard one calling, *Child!*"/And I replied, "*My Lord.*"

John Milton is considered by many the finest poet to have written in

English. A formidable scholar from a young age, Milton decided on a career as a poet when he was at Cambridge. In the Civil War that tore England apart in the middle of the seventeenth century, Milton, a Puritan, was at the center of Cromwell's Commonwealth that beheaded Charles I and established a republic until the monarchy was restored in 1660. During these years as Latin Secretary to the republican government, Milton published a large number of pamphlets on topics ranging from divorce and freedom of the press to politics and the reformation of the church. His masterpiece, of course, is *Paradise Lost* (1667), an epic poem whose intention was to try and understand the origin and nature of sin, death, and suffering by recounting Adam and Eve's fall from the Garden of Eden and Satan's raising of a rebellion in hell to overthrow God and regain heaven. By now Milton was blind, a condition which many of his contemporaries blamed on his liberal views about divorce and his support of the regicide of Charles I. His blindness raised many questions for Milton also, and in order to answer them he wrote one of his finest poems about his relationship with God.

"When I consider how my light is spent" (1652?) (or "On His Blindness") is a Petrarchan sonnet. Its divisions of thought are not divided into three quatrains and a couplet, as in Shakespeare's sonnets, but into an octave (eight lines), which often poses a question, and a sestet (six lines), which provides the answer. Milton's question concerns his ability to use his God-given writing talent, now that he is blind. Does God expect him to produce as much work as he did before? The octave pursues this question through its allusion to the parable of the talents (Matthew 25:14–30). In this parable Christ tells of the master who gives pieces of money (talents) to his servants and asks them to use them wisely. The servants who invested the money and returned more to the master were praised, but the servant who buried his (being afraid of losing it) was cast into darkness. The parable is usually interpreted as meaning that we must put our gifts (talents) to use for the glory of God; to hide or ignore them is a sin. But Milton turns the parable around by playing on the dual meaning of talent (both money and his gift for writing). He regrets that his light (eyesight) is "spent" (gone, or used as money is), and the "one talent which is death to hide" is now "useless." He wishes to present his "true account" to God, as a clerk would in a counting house. But Milton prepares for the answer to his question—"Doth God exact day-labor, light denied?"—when he refers to serving his "Maker." The difference between Maker and Master (which is the word the reader expects) becomes clear in the sestet, when Patience, the personification of accepting God's will, replies to the question Milton has "fondly" (foolishly) asked. God is Milton's Maker, not his Master, and he therefore does not require any "return" on his gift. It is freely given. As Patience explains: "God doth not need/Either man's work or his own gifts. Who best/Bear his mild yoke, they serve him best." A line break in the sentence "His state/Is kingly" draws attention to the concluding lines, in which Patience describes the Kingdom of Heaven, in which the lower angels are depicted as busily running errands ("thousands at his bidding speed,/And post o'er land and ocean without rest"). The greater virtue is reserved for those placed at the right hand of God: "They also serve who only stand and wait." Milton argues here for justification through faith alone, not through good works, and the poem actually enacts the concept of grace. Just as the answer comes to Milton unbidden, so God's grace is freely given and cannot be earned.

The eighteenth-century poet William Cowper is not well known today, but a few of his poems have remained with us, as well as several that were set to music as the Olney hymns, written with John Newton, the author of "Amazing Grace." Best known of Cowper's hymns is "Light Shining Out of Darkness," or "God moves in a mysterious way/His wonders to perform" (1772), in which in a series of images he reminds us that the darkest hours mean the coming of light: "The bud may have a bitter taste,/But sweet will be the flower." Trust in God's plan, he says, for it will always bring blessings. Cowper was a deeply troubled man whose peaceful life was shattered by periodic lapses into insanity that caused him to believe himself damned for sinning against the Holy Ghost. His most moving account of this fear is found in "The Castaway" (1799), a poem that Virginia Woolf used to great effect in her novel *To the Lighthouse* (1927). The poem is a narrative describing the fate of a man washed overboard in an Atlantic storm. (Cowper had read the story in George, Lord Anson's memoir, *Voyage* [1748], and Anson's grief at the loss of his man is mentioned in the poem.) Cowper, terrified that God has rejected him, identifies himself strongly with the man in the opening stanza when he calls him "such a destined wretch as I," but this identification fades in the graphic description of the man's plight. The narrative moves relentlessly through eleven six-line stanzas, the ending foretold from the beginning, but nonetheless dreaded. In each stanza the first four lines rhyme abab, with iambic tetrameter alternating with iambic trimeter. The concluding two lines form a rhyming couplet of iambic tetrameter lines, which strikes a knell of impending tragedy as each couplet reminds us of the man's fate, despite the efforts of his shipmates to save him. They throw over lifelines—casks, coops, floated cord—but in his despairing state he thinks they will not risk their own lives to save him. Ironically, this despair keeps him fighting. He "waged with death a lasting strife,/Supported by despair of life." The connection between the drowning man and the poet is chillingly made in the closing stanza. God did not intervene; help did not come; he drowns, deserted by his shipmates. The final three lines bring the poem back to Cowper and his desperate sense of his separation from God, which gives the whole poem a startling resonance:

> We perished, each alone;
> But I beneath a rougher sea,
> And whelmed in deeper gulfs than he.

There are few more memorable descriptions of despair in British poetry.

The Romantic poets at the beginning of the nineteenth century brought an unorthodox approach to Christianity that in Blake and Wordsworth was mystical and prophetic rather than theological (adhering to accepted church teachings), although Blake's poetry is steeped in biblical references. Blake was unorthodox and rebellious in his beliefs, and he formulated a complicated mythology of spiritual life that is sometimes contradictory and often puzzling. Because Blake's religious views require an understanding of this mythology, this survey is not going to embark on a discussion of his religious poems, other than the ones from his "Songs of Innocence and of Experience," which are discussed in that section of this survey.

Very different from Blake was Robert Burns, his Scottish contemporary, who wrote "Holy Willie's Prayer" (1789) as a comic attack on self-righteous, hypocritical Calvinists whose adherence to the doctrine of the "elect" allowed them to believe themselves chosen by God, while others are damned. While Calvin did not intend this doctrine to free believers from the responsibility to lead godly lives, many people found it a convenient crutch. The doctrine of the elect came to Scotland through John Knox, and Burns satirizes the attitudes of many of his fellow Ayrshire villagers in "Holy Willie," whose story was based on a real person, as Burns explains in a preface to the poem. Willie is the pharisee in the biblical story of the pharisee and the publican who went up to the temple to pray. The rich pharisee thanks God for making him a good man, not like the miserable little publican. The publican quietly prays, "Oh God, be merciful to me, a sinner." Holy Willie takes great pride in his elect state. He brags of his sexual misdemeanors, suggesting that God leads him into sin so that he won't be proud. At the same time he condemns others for their faults and even calls on God to punish them severely. Burns's rendering of Holy Willie's voice adds to the effect of the monologue, which depends on the reader's forming a very different picture of Willie than he thinks he is creating. A similar technique became a favorite of the Victorian poet Robert Browning.

Samuel Taylor Coleridge's most famous and sustained poem is "The Rime of the Ancient Mariner" (1797), a story within a story that has much in common with the old ballads. Too long for detailed discussion here, the poem can be read on many levels, but much of its rich symbolism suggests a religious interpretation. The poem opens with a fairy-tale device: the ancient mariner—who we learn later is doomed to tell his story over and over again—fixes upon a visitor at a wedding with his "glittering eye" and sits him down to listen to the tale. The mariner's story can be seen in the tradition of the journey to the underworld (in classical literature), the dark night of the soul, or the journey through the valley of the shadow of death. Sailing with his crew through the ice and snow of the South Pole, the mariner sees an albatross looming out of the mist: "As if it had been a Christian soul,/We hailed it in God's name." The journey to the underworld is initiated by the committing of a crime or sin, in this case the mariner's inexplicable killing of the innocent bird, whom the sailors had seen as a good omen because it had brought the wind and led them out of the snow and ice, back toward the north. In Part 2, the dire consequences of the mariner's crime become horribly evident when the ship is becalmed under a blistering sun, "as idle as a painted ship/Upon a painted ocean." The setting is indeed hellish—symbolic of spiritual death, the mariners are parched ("Water, water, every where,/Nor any drop to drink") and the sea is alive with "slimy things." The mariners hang the albatross around the mariner's neck as a sign of his sin and to mark him out as the cause of their peril: the guilty one. The albatross appears to symbolize Christ at this point, as it replaces the cross on the mariner's neck.

In Part 3 the mariners, burning to death under the constant sun, suddenly spot a sail in the distance, but it turns out to be a skeleton ship with a terrifying crew: a woman—Life-in-death—and her companion, Death. These two nightmare figures are engaged in a game of dice for the souls of the mariners, and the woman wins the ancient mariner, who watches horrified as his crewmates die one by one. Left alone in the valley of the shadow of death with "a thousand thousand slimy things," the ancient mariner suffers agonies of guilt and misery. Unable to pray, or die (his heart is "as dry as dust"), he feels cursed by the men whose death he has caused. But the chance for redemption comes when, at the lowest point in his journey, he sees some beautiful water snakes:

> O happy living things! No tongue
> Their beauty might declare:
> A spring of love gushed from my heart,
> And I blessed them unaware.

With this selfless connection with the living world, the mariner's spiritual torpor ("Death-in-life") is lifted and the albatross falls from his neck, allowing him to return from the underworld. He sleeps, waking to rain and the renewal of the spirit. The wind rises, and the mariners mysteriously become animated by "a blessed troop of angelic spirits," as Coleridge explains in his side notes to the poem. "They raised their limbs like lifeless tools—We were a ghastly crew," and the ship sails on. Spirits tell the mariner that although he has confessed his guilt, he must continue to do penance, which comes in the form of his dead shipmates' curse for bringing their fates upon them. They "fixed on me their stony eyes,/That in the Moon did glitter." Finally, the curse is lifted, the mariner reaches home, and the men are transformed into angels as the mariner is welcomed by the Pilot and the Hermit, who will wash away the mariner's guilt for killing the albatross. When the mariner's ship suddenly sinks, the Pilot rescues him, and the mariner begs the Hermit to hear his confession and grant him absolution. The mariner is Everyman, the ordinary man who commits a crime without knowing why (which suggests his sinful nature), and who has to continue to seek absolution through confession. That is why he has told his tale to the wedding guest.

Coleridge thought that he had made the moral too obvious, when in the closing stanzas the mariner tells the wedding guest:

> He prayeth best, who loveth best
> All things both great and small;
> For the dear God who loveth us,
> He made and loveth all.

Coleridge is right in thinking that the power of the poem is not so much in its moral as in its eerie depiction of the mariner's journey through ice and snow and blistering sun on an airless ocean. The archetypal, dreamlike images in the poem have captured the imaginations of many readers.

Many of Alfred, Lord Tennyson's poems are concerned with faith, from his six-line "Flower in the Crannied Wall" (1869) ("... if I could understand/What you are, root and all, and all in all,/I should know what God and man is") to his long account of his personal struggle with religious doubt in "In Memoriam A.H.H." (1850). When his close friend Arthur Hallam died suddenly at the age of twenty-two, Tennyson's faith—particularly his faith in an afterlife—was severely tried. Because Tennyson's concern was essentially with the question of immortality, this poem is discussed at length in that section of this survey. It is also included in the Christmas section and Death of the Young Section.

Most of the poetry written by Christina Rossetti (1830–1894) was religious. Like many Christians, she renounced her earthly life and looked forward to an afterlife with God; thus many of her poems are about her death and are discussed in that section of this survey. Rossetti never married but lived a quiet and devout life. She, too, had her moments of despair, however, expressed in such poems as "A Better Resurrection" (1857) in which she describes her life as "like a faded leaf ... a frozen thing . . . a broken bowl." Seeing "no everlasting hills" when she lifts her eyes, she prays to Jesus to bring her spiritual strength and renewal, and in the writing of the poem that strength comes. Through a series of similes in the second stanza, Rossetti remembers that the leaf is renewed in the spring. But the final stanza calls on renewal through Christ rather than through natural processes. The "broken bowl" of her life will not only be made whole but will become the communion cup from which Christ will drink. Rossetti also wrote the popular but rather mournful Christmas carol "In the Bleak Midwinter" (1872).

Perhaps the most famous of Victorian religious poets was Gerard Manley Hopkins (1844–1889). Hopkins attended Oxford University, where, under the influence of the earlier Oxford Movement and John Henry Newman (who had converted to Roman Catholicism in 1845), he also converted to Catholicism and became a Jesuit priest. Because his poetry was not published until 1918, many years after his death (he had left his manuscripts with his friend and fellow poet, Robert Bridges), and because his poetry is characterized by unusual, experimental rhythm, he is often thought of as a modern poet. But his religious poetry also has its roots in the Romantic movement of the nineteenth century in its emphasis on the natural world as an expression of the divine. His sonnet "God's Grandeur" (1877) reminds us that in an industrial age we are often blind to God's eternal presence in the world. Hopkins's metaphors are often startling and fresh, many times employing the language of electricity. The world is "charged" with "the grandeur of God" that will "flame out, like shining from shook foil." (In a letter, Hopkins explained that this image referred to the flashes of light produced when a sheet of gold foil was shaken.) God's grandeur "gathers to a greatness, like the ooze of oil/Crushed." These images link the divine with the material world as a reminder that God is in all things even though the toil of everyday work seems to separate us from him. Hopkins uses repetition in the line "Generations have trod, have trod, have trod" to emphasize his sense of man's alienation from the divine; "all is seared with trade; bleared, smeared with toil." He speaks of "man's smudge" as the product of seeking gain; the foot, now shod, no longer feels the earth beneath it. The second stanza returns to God's grandeur. Noting that "Nature is never spent," Hopkins (like Milton in "On His Blindness") plays upon "spent" to contrast the narrow, mercantile world of trade and profit with the abundant, eternal world of God's gifts. The poem closes with a fine image of the Holy Ghost as a bird (favorite metaphor in the biblical psalms), who bends over the world "with warm breast and with ah! bright wings."

"The Windhover," a sonnet dedicated to Christ, most fully exemplifies the energy that inspires both Hopkins's rhythms and his religious devotion. The poem has to be read in its entirety for the effect of Hopkins's "sprung rhythm" to be appreciated, but the poem finds in the hovering kestrel (or windhover as it is known, for its ability to hang on the wind) an expression of Christ himself. Hopkins draws on the language of falconry, in which a bird is released to the air from the wrist of his master. As the bird swoops "in his ecstasy," Hopkins marvels at his "mastery" of the wind, and the poem becomes a devotion to "the fire that breaks from thee then." In the closing three lines (while a sonnet in form, Hopkins separates the poem into an octave and two tercets), two images refer to the transforming power of Christ's sacrifice when a seemingly ordinary event is charged with beauty. A plow, moved by the "sheer plod" of the farmer, yet shines among the furrows, and the "blue-bleak embers" are transformed to "gash gold-vermilion."

Hopkins fell into a deep depression after his appointment as professor of classics at University College, Dublin. Away from his familiar surroundings and overworked in a demanding but tedious occupation— being in charge of examinations for Ireland—Hopkins felt separated from God and wrote several so-called "Terrible sonnets" that powerfully evoke his despair and sense of worthlessness. "That Nature Is a Heraclitean Fire and of the Comfort of the Resurrection" (1888), however, is a startling poem that moves from the ever-changing nature of the created world to the certainty of the resurrection. From a "Jack, joke, poor potsherd, patch, matchwood," Hopkins becomes "all at once what Christ is . . . immortal diamond."

The poem that for many encapsulates the Victorians' sense of faith disappearing from the world is Matthew Arnold's "Dover Beach" (1851). Arnold is addressing his new wife as they gaze out of a window overlooking the English Channel at dusk. The poem achieves a fine melancholy through the use of enjambment, similar to Tennyson's in "Ulysses" (1833), in lines such as the opening ones:

> The tide is full, the moon lies fair
> Upon the straits;—on the French coast the light
> Gleams and is gone;

Sounds then take over this melancholy as the poet listens to "the grating roar/Of pebbles which the waves draw back, and fling,/At their return, up the high strand," bringing "the eternal note of sadness in." The sound of the waves on the shore reminds him of the long ages of human suffering; the ancient Greeks heard it then, as he hears it now, the "turbid ebb and flow/Of human misery." The fourth stanza eloquently relates the ebbing of the tide to the withdrawal of faith from the world. The Sea of Faith once encircled the world, but now

> I only hear
> Its melancholy, long, withdrawing roar,

Retreating, to the breath
Of the night-wind, down the vast edges drear
And naked shingles of the world.

In the concluding stanza, Arnold finds that only in human love can they find solace from the death of the spirit. He and his wife are

. . . here as on a darkling plain
Swept with confused alarms of struggle and flight,
Where ignorant armies clash by night.

The plain recalls Tennyson's "ringing plains of windy Troy" in "Ulysses," but it is also a reference to the Greek historian Thucydides' account of the battle of Epipolae, during which the Athenians, invading Sicily in the dark, attacked many of their own men by mistake. The wider reference, however, is to life without faith, to the anarchy that many Victorians saw as the inevitable result of industrialism and the withdrawal of faith from the world.

Arnold's friend Arthur Hugh Clough is remembered now mainly for his short poem "Say not the struggle nought availeth" (1848). Written three years before "Dover Beach," it takes up the same imagery of the ocean but finds hope in it, not loss. Through three metaphors, the poem reminds us that when life seems most hopeless it is often just a failure to see the greater picture. The smoke of the battlefield may conceal from the weary, despairing soldier that his comrades are actually winning. The "tired waves, vainly breaking" on the shore may seem, like Arnold's sea of faith, not to be gaining any ground, but far away, where the rivers and creeks are formed, "came, silent, flooding in, the main." Finally, he looks not just to the sunrise for hope, but to the sunset. While the rising sun may climb slowly, when one faces westward, "look, the land is bright."

Thomas Hardy, best known as a novelist, returned to poetry for the last thirty years of his life. Many of his poems (and his novels) confront his sense that he would like to believe in God, but he finds that at the end of the nineteenth century he cannot. In "A Cathedral Facade at Midnight" (1897) (the fine detail in the poem is influenced by Hardy's training as an architect), Hardy finds no human solace in the old building. He describes the moonlight as it drifts across the walls of the cathedral, illuminating the carved figures of saints, prophets, and kings and queens, put there when man still believed that the earth was the center of the universe. The figures seem to sigh with regret that the ancient religion that created them has disappeared completely under the relentless march of Reason.

In the absence of religious belief, a providential view of why events happen to us is replaced by the belief that life is random, and we are often victims of chance. In his early poem "Hap" (1866), Hardy suggests that he would have found it easier to bear suffering if he could attribute it to a vengeful god who took pleasure in causing pain to mortals. Then at least his misery would have had some purpose and meaning. When everything is just "Crass Casualty," why could he not have been awarded more happiness and less grief?

Equally a victim of chance, but with greater strength to survive what Hamlet called "the slings and arrows of outrageous fortune," was W. E. Henley, a contemporary of Hardy's. Henley suffered much ill health and wrote "Invictus" (1875) while he was in the hospital. It has remained a favorite war cry on behalf of the human spirit that will not bow to the "bludgeonings of chance." In his suffering through a night that is "black as the pit from pole to pole," Henley looks to a future that holds out no hope. In a world without faith, only the strength of his own soul can keep him soldiering on: "I am the master of my fate;/I am the captain of my soul." Henley's poem is a lasting testament to the Victorian belief in self-reliance and determination, often at odds with his society's equally strong sense of anxiety and regret, as found in Arnold's "Dover Beach" and the poems of Hardy.

One of the most poignant expressions of twentieth-century loss of faith is Philip Larkin's "Church Going" (1954). The title suggests a congregation of worshipers faithfully and regularly attending church each Sunday. But instead, there is just one visitor to the church—the speaker—and there is no service in progress. The emptiness of the church, symbolizing the passing of religious belief in England, is chillingly foreshadowed in the opening lines. The church is empty, devoid of anything "going on"—a service or a wedding or a funeral—and he lets the heavy door "thud shut." And yet something makes it different from a museum or a stately home that is no longer used, for the speaker, already hatless, takes off his cycle-clips "in awkward reverence." What is that difference? The speaker leaves the church after a short time, thinking that it wasn't worth the visit. But he did stop, and he often does stop in churches. Why? What will become of them, he ponders, when faith is completely dead and the churches no longer have a purpose to fulfill. Will they become objects of superstition or historical oddities? Finally he examines his own attraction to the church. For him, it represents a solidity of human activity, a calm center in the midst of "suburb scrub" where the crucial events of human life—the sacraments of "marriage, and birth, and death"—are properly acknowledged. Even if what was once thought divine providence is now only a natural human compulsion to seriousness, it is still a human yearning that finds fulfillment in the church building itself, its ancient form (the cross on the ground) and familiar furnishings of pew, wood, and stone. Here one can grow wise.

❦

Holy Sonnet 14 ("Batter my Heart"), John Donne
ImPo; OAEL-1; NAEL-1; TFi

"A Hymn to God the Father," John Donne
NAEL-1; OAEL-1; OBEV; TFi; TrGrPo-1

"The Altar," George Herbert
NAEL-1; OAEL-1; TrGrPo-1

"Easter Wings," George Herbert
NAEL-1; OAEL-1; TFi

"The Pulley," George Herbert
ImPo; NAEL-1; OAEL-1; TFi; TrGrPo-1

"The Collar," George Herbert
ImPo; NAEL-1; OAEL-1; SB; TFi; TrGrPo-1

"On His Blindness" ("When I consider how my light is spent"), John Milton
BL; ImPo; NAEL-1; OAEL-1; OBEV; TFi; TrGrPo-1

"God moves in a mysterious way," William Cowper
ImPo; OBEV; TFi; TrGrPo-1

"The Castaway," William Cowper
ECP; NAEL-1; OAEL-1; OBEV

"Holy Willie's Prayer," Robert Burns
ECP; NAEL-2; OAEL-1; TFi

"The Rime of the Ancient Mariner," Samuel Taylor Coleridge
ImPo; NAEL-2; OAEL-2; OBEV; SB; TFi; TrGrPo-2

"Flower in the Crannied Wall," Alfred, Lord Tennyson
BAVP; ImPo; NAEL-2; TFi; TrGrPo-2

"A Better Resurrection," Christina Rossetti
BAVP

"God's Grandeur," Gerard Manley Hopkins
BAVP; ImPo; NAEL-2; OAEL-2; OBEV; TFi; TrGrPo-2

"The Windhover," Gerard Manley Hopkins
BAVP; NAEL-2; OAEL-2; OBEV; TFi

"That Nature Is a Heraclitean Fire and of the Comfort of the Resurrection," Gerard Manley Hopkins

NAEL-2; OAEL-2

"Dover Beach," Matthew Arnold

 ImPo; NAEL-2; OAEL-2; OBEV; SB; TFi; TrGrPo-2

"Say not the struggle nought availeth," Arthur Hugh Clough

 BAVP; ImPo; NAEL-2; OAEL-2; OBEV; TFi; TrGrPo-2

"A Cathedral Facade at Midnight," Thomas Hardy

 not anthologized; available in editions of Hardy's poetry

"Hap," Thomas Hardy

 BAVP; ImPo; NAEL-2; OAEL-2

"Invictus," W. E. Henley

 ImPo; NAEL-2; TrGrPo-2

"Church Going," Philip Larkin

 ImPo; NAEL-2; OAEL-2; TFi

Sleep

Another universal theme, sleep (or the lack of it), affects everyone. The poet who cannot get to sleep writes a poem about it. Suffering poets yearn for it, and yet it often eludes those most in need of it: the troubled and careworn. Sleep is usually personified in poetry as the poet addresses it as a god, pleading for it to bring its gifts of revitalizing repose. Sleep is usually seen as the balm that brings about renewal, and the best-known passage in English describing sleep's restorative powers is Macbeth's tortured speech in Shakespeare's famous play. Having murdered Duncan, Macbeth realizes that his conscience will give him no peace:

> Methought I heard a voice cry "Sleep no more!
> Macbeth does murder sleep," the innocent sleep,
> Sleep that knits up the raveled sleave of care,
> The death of each day's life, sore labor's bath,
> Balm of hurt minds, great nature's second course,
> Chief nourisher in life's feast. (*Macbeth*, 2.2.39–44, 1606)

Because sleep doesn't come just when we wish it, it is sometimes personified as a fickle lover, and poets often wonder why it visits other people and not them. In its more universal sense (even the worst insomniac sleeps eventually), however, it is associated with death, because the sleeping person most closely resembles the dead. In Greek mythology, the personification of Sleep, Somnus, was Death's brother. He lived in a deep valley, out of the sun and engulfed in shadowy twilight. No sounds disturb his slumber except the flowing of the river Lethe, which brings forgetfulness, another blessing of sleep for a troubled mind. Morpheus, son of Somnus, was the god of dreams, from whose name we derive morphine, a sleeping drug made from poppies (thus poppies too are part of the imagery surrounding sleep).

Samuel Daniel's "Care-charmer Sleep, son of the sable Night" from his sonnet cycle "Delia" (1592) takes up these mythological allusions in addressing Sleep as Death's brother. Daniel asks for release from his daytime cares, which paradoxically are the blackness of his life, while sleep brings light. Daniel rejects dreams also, because they will only raise false hopes that will be shattered on waking, adding more grief to the sorrow of the "shipwreck" of his "ill-adventured youth."

One of the finest poems about sleep is Sir Philip Sidney's "Come sleep! O Sleep the certain knot of peace" from his sonnet cycle *Astrophil and Stella* (1582). A popular convention of love poetry is to describe the sleepless lover, tossing on his lonely bed in an agony of unrequited or spurned love. Sidney's poem adopts the convention by appealing to Sleep as a god and offering him gifts in return for Sleep's great gift of a good night's rest. In the opening quatrain he offers several definitions of sleep: the "certain knot" (reliable source) of peace; the restorer of wit; the easer of sorrow; "the poor man's wealth, the prisoner's release,/The indifferent judge between the high and low." Most of these definitions take up the common identification of sleep with death, for poems about death frequently see it also as the great leveler. In the second quatrain Astrophil addresses Sleep as his shield or protector against the arrows of despair, and as the peacemaker who will end the "civil wars" of a vexed mind that disturb his rest. If Sleep will bring him peace, the poet will repay him, and in the third quatrain he offers to Sleep the aids to a good night's rest that the poet can provide: smooth pillows, comfortable bed, a quiet, dark bedroom, sweet-smelling herbs, and "a weary head." If Sleep still does not come, despite these inducements, he will find the source of the poet's insomnia: Stella's image dancing in his head, the cause of his miserable civil wars.

Many poets have written love poems about the sight of their lover sleeping. The Elizabethan love poet Thomas Campion hopes that his sleeping lover will wake in a friendlier mood in "Sleep, Angry Beauty" (1617). Comparing her to a sleeping lion, he is enjoying seeing "those lips shut up, that never kindly spoke." In sleep, her beauty seems harmless: clearly this is a lover whose disdain, even bad temper, he fears. In the second stanza the poet suggests that the woman is now feeling guilty about her treatment of him. He notices that in sleep she is weeping because "dreams often more than waking passions move." In the final couplet, Campion addresses the god of sleep, asking him to plead his cause with the woman when she is in the softer mood inspired by sleep so that she may wake in a better frame of mind.

Campion's contemporary Thomas Dekker is the author of "Golden slumbers kiss your eyes" (1603), a song made popular by the Beatles 400 years later and one of many famous lullabies written to lull infants to sleep. Typically, sleep is depicted as a mother or other protector, shielding the child from the harmful realities of life to come. Punning on the word "care," Dekker tells the child that sleep protects it from the cares of life, while at the same time the child deserves that protection and has to be cared for: "Care is heavy, therefore sleep you;/You are care, and care must keep you."

Francis Quarles (1592–1644) takes up the traditional child's prayer, asking for God's protection through the night, in "A Good Night" (1635), one of his "emblem" poems that were once very popular. The emblem poems took a passage from the Bible as their inspiration, and "A Good Night" recalls Psalm 121, which describes God as the unslumbering protector and preserver. In the first four lines Quarles reminds his sleeper that he is in God's ever-watchful care. The next four lines assert that our consciences are untroubled in sleep; compared with that peace of mind, "the music and the mirth of kings/Are all but very discords."

The prolific late-eighteenth-century poet Charlotte Smith helped to reestablish the sonnet form in British poetry. One of her "Elegiac Sonnets" is "To Sleep" (1784), an address to Morpheus that takes up the popular request for sleep's universal healing powers, available to king and peasant alike. The sonnet is Shakespearean in form, and in the first quatrain Smith calls on Sleep to bring her release from her "aching head" by shedding poppies (the source of morphine, a sleeping drug) on her "sad temples." From her own distress, Smith moves in the second quatrain to Sleep's partiality in coming more easily to some than to others. Calling upon the troubled King Henry IV's speech in Shakespeare's *Henry IV, Part Two* (c. 1597), in which he accuses Sleep of bringing repose to the ship's boy and not to him ("Uneasy lies the head that wears a crown"), Smith reiterates Henry's accusation that Sleep is "partial" and rewards the poor more than the rich. In the third quatrain, the village girl is also blessed with sweet slumber. In the final couplet, Smith returns to her own sleepless state, begging for the "opiate aid" that will bring her release from anxiety and tears. Her unhappiness is emphasized by the extra two syllables in the last line, forming an alexandrine (iambic hexameter) and drawing out her sense of despair:

> But still thy opiate aid does thou deny
> To calm the anxious breast; to close the streaming eye.

Sleep was a favorite topic of the Romantic poets, who admired Smith and for whom sleep was of interest because of its relationship to dreams, the source of unconscious and often surprising revelations and visions not accessible during waking hours. Sleep is thus not so much restorative as creative, allowing the mind to enter a different realm, a mysterious other world like the afterworld reached in death. In William Wordsworth's sonnet "To Sleep" (1807), this world is welcome, if elusive. Wordsworth begins with a conventional address, a soothing quatrain on the thoughts that the poet had hoped would bring sleep: "A flock of sheep that leisurely pass by,/One after one; the sound of rain, and bees/ Murmuring; the fall of rivers, winds and seas,/Smooth fields, white sheets of water, and pure sky." None of these restful visions has worked: the word "Sleepless!" marks the giving up of sleep-inducing thoughts and the recognition that night is nearly over and the birds will soon herald the coming of day, after a third night without sleep. That day will be cheerless without the "blessed barrier" of sleep that brings "fresh thoughts and joyous health" to the mind.

Samuel Taylor Coleridge's "The Pains of Sleep" (1802) is not one of his best poems, and he referred to it as "dogrels." Taking a very different approach, Coleridge here dreads sleep because it brings him not welcome dreams but appalling nightmares. He wrote to his friend Southey that fear of these "Horrors" kept him sitting up night after night. Rather than taking opiates to induce sleep, he had given them up, the withdrawal of which may have been the cause of the nightmares. In the first stanza Coleridge recalls how he usually goes to bed with a "sense of supplication" rather than a formal prayer because he senses that "eternal strength and wisdom" surround him and protect him through divine love. He falls asleep "in humble trust." How different, then, is his shouted prayer of the previous night that opens the second stanza. Tortured by a "fiendish crowd of shapes and thoughts," he is beset by a sense of guilt—of "intolerable wrong"—for he knows not what crimes. Is he the sinner or the victim? He doesn't know, for all is chaos and confusion of "life-stifling fear, soul-stifling shame." The third stanza enacts Coleridge's exhaustion after two nights of such torment, when sleep "seemed to me/Distemper's worst calamity." When his own screams wake him on the third night, he finds relief in tears and in the recognition that his nightmares are undeserved because he does not harbor evil thoughts and desires. "Natures deepliest stained with sin" will understandably have horrifying dreams, but why do they pursue him, who seeks only to love and be loved.

Sleep is often used as a euphemism for death, especially in Christian terms. The dead sleep dreamlessly in their beds under the earth, until they wake on the Day of Judgment, roused by the trumpet's call. Christina Rossetti's "Sleeping at Last" (1896) is characteristic of this metaphor. One of the most powerful evocations of sleep's affinity to death is John Keats's "Sonnet to Sleep" (1819). Addressing sleep, Keats acknowledges its power to comfort and protect from the worries of the day, but he does so in language that powerfully suggests death instead. This affinity is characteristic of Keats, who wrote most of his poetry in the two years following his brother's death, when he knew that his own early death was imminent. He calls sleep the "soft embalmer," suggesting that in sleep we are indeed dead. As sleep closes our eyes, we find ourselves in darkness, "enshaded in forgetfulness divine." So earnestly does Keats seek such forgetfulness that he implores sleep to overtake him even as he is writing this "hymn," waiting only for the closing amen. In seeking sleep and the darkness of oblivion he will shut out the light of the passed day that will otherwise "shine upon my pillow, breeding many woes." Keats then differentiates between the darkness of sleep and the darkness of the bedroom. Conscience is awakened in the dark of the room; it "hoards its strength" for that quiet time, when, like a blind mole, it burrows into his waking thoughts. To prevent the mole of guilt and regret from entering his thoughts, he calls on sleep to overtake him in a closing image that eerily conveys death rather than just sleep:

> Turn the key deftly in the oiled wards,
> And seal the hushed casket of my soul.

Elsewhere, Keats writes of sleep as creative and life affirming rather than as deadening oblivion. In "Sleep and Poetry" (1816), sleep is described in terms of its superiority to many different impressions: more gentle than a summer breeze; more soothing than bees; more serene than Cordelia's countenance; more "full of visions than a high romance." Only poetry offers the soul more—high praise indeed for sleep.

Alfred, Lord Tennyson's "Sweet and Low," from "The Princess" (1849), is a lullaby that perfectly creates the rhythm of a cradle rocking back and forth. Like Keats's life, Tennyson's was overshadowed by death, and that connection is evident even in this gentle lullaby for a child. He implores the "wind of the western sea" to blow over "the rolling waters" and "come from the dying moon" to "blow him again to me." These images remind the reader of Tennyson's favorite metaphor for death: the soul heading westward with the tide. In stanza two, the "Father" who will come soon is thus more likely the child's heavenly father, especially as "sleep and rest, sleep and rest" recall the notion of death as a "rest" (as Hamlet puns in his closing line, "The rest is silence"). The father comes with "silver sails all out of the west/Under the silver moon," suggesting the nursery rhyme notion of the father returning from months at sea, but also implying a divine rather than a human visit, although both meanings are held in balance.

Another lyric from "The Princess" is the lovely "Now Sleeps the Crimson Petal," discussed in this survey in the Love section. Few poems have created a better sense of sleepy languor than this one, in which the speaker and his surroundings (a palace) are gradually overtaken by unconsciousness as the mind slides away into dream.

Tennyson's narrative poem "The Lotos-Eaters" (1842) takes up the Romantic idea of a yearning for escape from the griefs of life, just as Keats yearns to enter the bird's world in "Ode to a Nightingale" (1819). Many of Tennyson's poems express such a desire, and in "The Lotos-Eaters" he uses an episode from Homer's *The Odyssey* as the basis for the emotion. While returning from the Trojan War, Odysseus and his crew, exhausted and disconsolate about ever reaching home, arrive at a land where, in Tennyson's words, "it seemed always afternoon." The place seems enchanted, swooning in the still, languorous air. Around the boat gather the natives, the "mild-eyed melancholy Lotos-eaters." When Odysseus's men eat the lotos fruit, they immediately lose all desire to continue their journey. Lethargy overtakes them, and their senses become deadened. Voices seem far away, and the waves seem "to mourn and rave/On alien shores." Sitting on the shore, they think of their homeland as a dream, and the return voyage as a weariness not to be endured any longer. The mariners sing a "Choric Song" in which they gladly embrace oblivion and freedom from the pain of daily life in a dream world luxuriously described. Tennyson may be referring here to the dream state brought on by opium, a common drug of the time for easing pain and worry and inducing sleep. The landscape includes opium's source, the poppy, which "from a craggy ledge . . . hangs in sleep." The mariners grumble about their lot in life. Why should they alone of nature's creatures have to toil and fret?

As in many "sleep" poems, the sleep induced by the lotos flower is akin to death as the mariners cry, "Give us long rest or death, dark death, or dreamful ease." The mariners do not seek oblivion so much as melancholy, however. They want to give themselves over to remembrance, a living in the past that takes them away from their present work:

> To lend our hearts and spirits wholly
> To the influence of mild-minded melancholy;
> To muse and brood and live again in memory,
> With those old faces of our infancy
> Heaped over with a mound of grass,
> Two handfuls of white dust, shut in an urn of brass!

The lotos flower will take them into their remembrances of the dead, the land involuntarily recreated in "Tears, Idle Tears" (1847). Finally, they reject the troubled world of the living, for "slumber is more sweet than toil . . . O, rest ye, brother mariners, we will not wander more."

Siegfried Sassoon (1886–1967) is best known as a war poet. The speaker of "Falling Asleep" (1919) is an officer who has returned to England, and the experience he describes is probably based on Sassoon's own return to England, wounded, in 1917 and again in 1918. Lying in bed, he drifts off to sleep in a confused but contented blur of sounds around him (doors shutting and feet padding in the quiet house, its occupants retiring for the night) and outside the window (whispering trees, hounds in the park, herons, and owls). As consciousness slips away his mind returns to the battle scene he has left. He blots out the horror of that scene by fixing on pleasant thoughts from the day—music, a song about a soldier, a bright white room (suggesting he is in a hospital)—that brings "radiance," calm, and peace to his dream of soldiers marching with sunlight on their faces. Finally, as he drifts off to sleep, the recovered sanity of being in England engulfs him, and the world of war is "fading past [him] into peace." For the shell-shocked soldier, sleep is indeed the lovelorn Astrophil's "certain knot of peace . . . the balm of woe."

☙❧

"Care-charmer Sleep, son of the sable Night," Samuel Daniel
ImPo; OBEV; TFi; TrGrPo-1
Sonnet 39, *Astrophil and Stella* ("Come sleep! O Sleep the certain knot of peace"), Sir Philip Sidney
NAEL-1; OBEV; TFi; TrGrPo-1
"Sleep, Angry Beauty," Thomas Campion
TrGrPo-1
"Cradle Song" ("Golden slumbers kiss your eyes"), Thomas Dekker
OBEV; TrGrPo-1
"A Good Night," Francis Quarles
TrGrPo-1
"To Sleep," Charlotte Smith
NAEL-2
"To Sleep," William Wordsworth
TrGrPo-2
"The Pains of Sleep," Samuel Taylor Coleridge
NAEL-2
"Sonnet to Sleep," John Keats
NAEL-2
"Sleep and Poetry" (excerpts), John Keats
NAEL-2; OAEL-2
"Sweet and Low," from "The Princess," Alfred, Lord Tennyson

NAEL-2; TrGrPo-2

"The Lotos-Eaters," Alfred, Lord Tennyson

BAVP; NAEL-2; OAEL-2

"Falling Asleep," Siegfried Sassoon

MoBrPo; OxBTC

Time and Change

꩜

The passing of time is another immortal human theme, as important to the ancients as it is to us. We tend to think of the industrial world as being the first to experience time as fast moving, and certainly modern technology has sped up many events, such as letter writing, travel, and the construction of buildings. But the Romans coined the phrase *tempus fugit*, or time flies, and Job in the Bible says movingly, "My days are swifter than a weaver's shuttle . . . oh remember that my life is wind" (Job 7:6–7). The fear of time as fleeting often leads to the personification of Time as the great devourer, as Ovid noted in his phrase *tempus edax rerum*, or time, consumer of things. Ovid's *Metamorphoses*, Book 15, has been an important influence on British poets writing about time and change. Ovid uses natural metaphors to describe the swift passing of human time, and the ever-changing nature of human and universal affairs. Time, he says, is like a river in constant flux, or like waves relentlessly flowing toward the shore. He compares the four stages of human life—childhood, maturity, middle age, old age—to the four seasons. Metamorphoses mean transformations, and while most of Ovid's long poem retells the myths in which a human is transformed into something else—Io into a cow, Daphne into a laurel tree, Narcissus into a flower— Book 15 also emphasizes that beneath the ever-present changing of the elements, the natural world, and human life itself there exists a permanence; everything changes into something else and therefore does not die.

The shortness of human life is often understood in terms of the natural world, where the brevity of life for plants and animals is all too obvious. The seventeenth-century poet Robert Herrick is famous for his *carpe diem* poem "Gather ye rosebuds while ye may" (1648) in which he reminds young women that, like roses, they will soon age and wither. He simi-

251

larly compares human life to that of a flower in "To Daffodils" (1648), in which he laments that "we weep to see/You haste away so soon." Herrick upsets the conventional alternating of iambic tetrameter lines with iambic trimeters to draw attention to the plight of mortal man. Just as the flower withers before noon, so man also finds his life over too soon:

> We die,
> As your hours do, and dry
> Away
> Like to the Summer's rain.

A. E. Housman's "Loveliest of Trees" (1896) similarly compares the brevity of human life to the startlingly beautiful but short-lived spring blossoms of the cherry tree. Remembering that human life spans a mere seventy years, and twenty are already past, the poet sets out to enjoy the spring blossoms while he can. But the last line reminds us forcibly of life's brevity: the cherry trees of spring are hanging not with the white of Eastertide, but with the "snow" of winter.

Many of Shakespeare's sonnets take up the subject of time, especially the notion of the poem itself conferring immortality on the short-lived human subject of the sonnet. Sonnet 60 (1609) opens with the compelling simile, taken from Ovid's *Metamorphoses*. "Like as the waves make towards the pebbled shore,/So do our minutes hasten to their end." The relentlessness of time (and an incoming tide) is emphasized in the next two lines, which describe the minutes (and the waves) as overtaking the one coming before in the same unvaried direction. The second quatrain considers the action of time on human life. In childhood, time seems to move slowly; the baby "crawls to maturity." But when he reaches it, time starts to take away the gift of life that it had bestowed. The third quatrain explains this shift to time the destroyer: taking up the favorite image of Father Time holding a scythe to mow us down, the quatrain finds Time plowing furrows in the beautiful youth's brow, and devouring that which it had created. The closing couplet does not offer immortality to the subject of the sonnet as convincingly as do some of Shakespeare's other sonnets; the poem only seeks to stand fast against the ravages of time ("his cruel hand") by praising the worth of the loved one.

In Sonnet 15 "When I consider everything that grows" (1609), Shakespeare again contrasts Time's gift in creating youth with Time's cruelty in destroying that same youth. His central metaphor compares human life to plant life: all created things are perfect for just a moment, and men, like plants, grow and flourish, only to find that growth suddenly checked and diminished. In the third quatrain, the poet addresses the young man (the subject of many of Shakespeare's sonnets) directly, telling him that while the brevity of his youthfulness makes him all the more attractive, "wasteful time" is still waiting to turn youth's day into man's night. The poem returns to the plant metaphor in the closing couplet, where the poet declares war on Time. While Time destroys the young man, the poet will "engraft [him] new," or recreate him through the poem, as a plant is propagated by grafting a young branch onto an old stock.

Ovid's awareness that change is at work in all created things is echoed in Percy Bysshe Shelley's poem "Mutability" (1814). Like Ovid and others, Shelley compares human mutability with natural change, seeing us in the first stanza as clouds that for a short time block out the moon, only to be engulfed by the darkness of night. In stanza two, he compares human life to a "forgotten lyre," an old wind harp whose "dissonant strings" responded erratically to the wind blowing through them, and whose sound could never be repeated. This idea is pursued in the third stanza, in which Shelley finds such random moodiness in people also. Sleep comes but is poisoned by bad dreams; day comes, but "one wandering thought" spoils it; our moods lead us from one extreme to another. Summing up in the fourth stanza, Shelley finds only mutability a certainty because our joys and sorrows wax and wane: "Man's yesterday may ne'er be like his morrow."

Many poems discussed in other sections of this volume are concerned with time and change, but from the perspective of innocence becoming experience, love, immortality, *carpe diem*, even death. (See, for example, Tennyson's fine poem of regret, "Tears, Idle Tears" [1847], which he said was about "the sense of the abiding in the transient.") A particularly beautiful poem that touches upon many other themes but is essentially about time is William Butler Yeats's "The Wild Swans at Coole," written in 1916 when Yeats was once again visiting his friend Lady Gregory's home at Coole Park in Ireland. As in Shakespeare's Sonnet 73 "That time of year thou mayst in me behold" (1609), in which the poet compares his advancing age to autumn and to dusk, Yeats (at the age of fifty-one) describes fifty-nine swans on a lake in an October twilight. He recalls that he has been counting the swans at this time of year for nineteen years, and as he watches them mount into the sky he is led to compare their seemingly unchanging beauty with his own changed circumstances. Nineteen years ago, he "trod with a lighter tread." But love's youthful promise has not been fulfilled, and now he is a disappointed man. (His beloved Maud Gonne had once again refused his offer of marriage.) The swans, in contrast, live in a freer world of water and air, attached always to their partner, their hearts still young. They could be the very same swans that he counted nineteen years before, because the world of change does not seem to touch them in the natural, ever-renewing beauty of Coole Park. They circle back to the lake as he watches, reinforcing this sense that for all living forms except humankind, the individual representative embodies the whole.

E. B. White comes to the same realization in his essay "Once More to the Lake" (1941), when he sees a dragonfly and it seems to be the same dragonfly that he saw on the lake many years earlier, when he was a boy. White, too, is both troubled and comforted by the contrast between man's mutability and nature's permanence. At the end of the poem Yeats foresees his death, a culmination of his acute sense of life passing, when he will awaken to another world, leaving the birds for the delight of other eyes.

Where is permanence to be found during times of cataclysm and devastating change, such as in wartime? The answer for many poets lay in nature—as in Yeats's swans—or in art, as in Keats's Grecian urn or Shakespeare's sonnets. Thomas Hardy finds some kind of permanence in three images in his "In Time of 'The Breaking of Nations' " (1915), written during World War I but inspired by an insight realized in Cornwall during the Franco-Prussian War in 1870. The first image of an old farmer and his horse, nodding over their plowing, suggests the permanence of the peasant worker, attached to the land in an ancient ritual that is handed down from generation to generation and thus seems timeless. The second image is of "thin smoke without flame" drifting upward from piles of grass. The third is a young couple whose growing love is an old story that also transcends time and place, and ensures the continuation of the human race, despite the carnage of war.

Seamus Heaney also turns to the agricultural worker as the link with an older, more permanent time. "The Forge" (1969) tells of a visit to a blacksmith's forge. The narrator seems to stand on the threshold of the building, appropriately poised between the old, unchanging world of the smithy and the new, hectic, modern world outside. Outside, rusting metal from the forge suggests that the work is no longer needed or valued. So what is hidden in the dark inside the forge? The inhabitant is unseen at first, his presence evident only in the noise of hammering, the shower of sparks, and the hiss of hot horseshoe hitting cold water. The anvil—sign of his craft—is hidden somewhere in the gloom. Darkness still pervades the poem, but now the blacksmith emerges as a kind of priest, the anvil his "altar" where he creates not just form but also music. He does not go beyond the door, leaning there on the threshold, the link between past and present as he observes the steady flow of traffic where horses used to clatter. The blacksmith's days are numbered, but the narrator recognizes the value of his ancient work as the blacksmith goes back inside "to beat real iron out, to work the bellows."

While Ovid and succeeding generations of poets have written about change in nature and in man's life, it is perhaps only the industrial world of the past two centuries that has been acutely aware of the pace of change in society and our man-made surroundings. Many twentieth-century poets, like Heaney, write of the passing of the old ways and the old craftsmen, disappearing under the tide of industrial and technological innovation. For city poets, the passing of time is equally poignant as the gaslights and steam trains give way to electricity and the bustle of late-twentieth-century life. Sir John Betjeman, poet laureate from 1972 until his death in 1984, wrote many poems about English life and places, and in "Monody on the Death of Aldersgate Street Station" (1966) he laments the "desecration" of London, choosing that word to identify the passing of the old trains with the passing of Christianity from English life. As he conjures up the ringing of the many church bells on a London Sunday morning, he remembers how that sound would in turn bring to mind the London of the distant past, when the Thames and the Fleet rivers flowed silently out to green meadows. His church, now demolished, the old walls broken and overgrown, no longer rings to the sound of the prayer book readings or the rich ticking of the old clock. As the last train puffs away in the final stanza, the snow falls deadeningly, and the poet, "the lost generation" who loved the steam train and gas light, rejects the improvements of the modern, soulless city.

A more abstract depiction of the theme of time is offered in Philip Larkin's "Days" (1953) and "Nothing to Be Said" (1961). "Days" is a short poem that asks what days are for, replying that they are for living in. We waken into them over and over again, and they bring us happiness. Sometimes we seek an escape from them, to live somewhere else, but that involves the doctor (who deals with death) and the priest (who offers a spiritual life). Larkin's picture of these alternatives is comic: the long-coated experts "running over the fields." "Nothing to Be Said" returns to the central theme of poems about time and change: time moves us inexorably toward death. The first stanza unites all people the world over in their common recognition that living means growing closer to death. Stanza two finds that the many ways of living are just "ways of slow dying." This recognition "means nothing" to some people; others respond that there is "nothing to be said." And yet poets will continue to find something to say about this universally troubling theme.

⊙⌒⋏⌒⊙

"To Daffodils," Robert Herrick
    BL; TFi; TrGrPo-1
"Loveliest of Trees," A. E. Housman
    ImPo; NAEL-2; OAEL-2; TFi; TrGrPo-2

Sonnet 60, "Like as the waves make towards the pebbled shore," William Shakespeare

    ImPo; NAEL-1; OBEV; TFi

Sonnet 15, "When I consider everything that grows," William Shakespeare

    NAEL-1; TrGrPo-1

"Mutability," Percy Bysshe Shelley

    NAEL-1; OAEL-1

"The Wild Swans at Coole," William Butler Yeats

    NAEL-2; TFi

"In Time of 'The Breaking of Nations,' " Thomas Hardy

    NAEL-2; OAEL-2; TFi

"The Forge," Seamus Heaney

    NAEL-2

"Monody on the Death of Aldersgate Street Station," Sir John Betjeman
not anthologized; available in editions of Betjeman's poetry

"Days," Philip Larkin

    OBEV

"Nothing to Be Said," Philip Larkin

    OxBTC

War

∾∾∾

Few topics in poetry elicit such strong and contradictory responses in both poets and readers as does war. Typical of the extremes of opinion are two poems about the Battle of Ypres in World War I, the war that has given rise to most of the poems on this vexed subject. Three years after Ypres, in 1917, A. E. Housman published "Epitaph on an Army of Mercenaries" in *The Times* to commemorate the bravery of the paid soldiers and thank them for holding up a world that God had abandoned. He was scathingly answered by the Scottish poet Hugh MacDiarmid in "Another Epitaph on an Army of Mercenaries"; MacDiarmid called Housman's poem "a God-damned lie." According to MacDiarmid's short epitaph, the mercenaries knew nothing of saving the world; they were "professional murderers." MacDiarmid even sees the mercenaries as damaging to civilized life; "in spite of all their kind" human dignity and worth struggle to survive. In every battle, every war, there have been some who see the necessity for combat and defend the soldiers, while others see only hypocrisy, arrogant leadership, and sentimental jingoism. Poems that are concerned specifically with the question of duty are discussed in the Duty section of this survey. Other famous war poems that are essentially patriotic propaganda rather than about war as an event will be found in the Patriotism section. Rupert Brooke's "The Soldier" (1914), for example, is such a poem and was highly influential at the beginning of World War I.

A soldier's duty to his king and country in time of war was often described as a marriage because the loyalty of the soldier to his king and country had to be absolute, and had to take precedence over all other loyalties. This metaphor is central to the Cavalier poet Richard Lovelace's famous lyric "To Lucasta, Going to the Wars." Lovelace was a soldier who fought on the side of the king in the civil wars that tore England

and Scotland apart in the seventeenth century. He wrote his "Lucasta" poems while imprisoned for ten months in 1648. The speaker is addressing his mistress, explaining with regret that from her "chaste breast and quiet mind/To war and arms I fly." The pun in the word "arms," suggesting both the lover's human arms and the soldier's military arms, indicates the metaphor of warfare as a love affair that Lovelace plays upon in the poem. The second stanza makes the identification even more absolute when he tells Lucasta that he chases a "new mistress" in the field of combat, and he will "embrace" not Lucasta but "a sword, a horse, a shield." The third stanza assures her that she will learn to appreciate his "inconstancy" because his heartfelt sense of honor and duty strengthens his love for her. The honor of the soldier makes possible the strong heart of the lover; a man without a sense of honor to king and country would be an ignoble husband. Lovelace's soldier steers clear of any emotional language that might remind Lucasta of the realities of the battlefield. Rather than concrete nouns he uses abstracts, and the formal stanzas—four lines of alternating tetrameters and trimeters rhyming abab—are reassuringly civilized and controlled, and therefore calming.

An ironic or cynical view of war, very different from Lovelace's, became a central thread of war poetry, especially in the poems written during World War I, when most of the British poems about war were written. A famous eighteenth-century poem also takes an ironic stance. Robert Southey's "The Battle of Blenheim" (1798) was written as a criticism of the glorifying of that battle in England. At an engagement of the War of Spanish Succession in August 1704, near the village of Blenheim, Bavaria (now West Germany), the English and Austrian forces under the duke of Marlborough defeated the French and Bavarians. Despite the loss of 4,500 English and Austrian soldiers, and a huge number of wounded, the Battle of Blenheim was always hailed as a great victory, and the duke of Marlborough became one of the most commanding figures in Europe. Southey's poem is set one summer evening in a cottage garden in Germany, some years after the battle. A child playing in the garden finds a skull, which his grandfather tells him would have been "some poor fellow" who "fell in the great victory." The poem then employs the favorite ironic device of looking at adult affairs through the eyes of a child. The boy and his sister want to know what they were fighting for, but the old man does not know; all he knows is that it was "a famous victory" that saw his father's house burned to the ground and many of the country people killed. The children, of course, declare it a wicked thing, and ask what good came of it. Again the old man does not know. Historians credit Marlborough's victories over the French with importantly containing the increasing aggression of France in Europe, and they would accuse Southey of naïvete in reducing a complex political issue to the level of a simple peasant grandfather and two children.

But one of the central problems of war is the conflict between political leaders, who are usually far from the battlefield, and the civilians who find themselves the victims of a war that seems to have no bearing on their lives.

British war poetry is now almost exclusively thought of as poetry written before and during World War I (also known as the Great War), often by soldier-poets like Richard Lovelace, but from the perspective of the battlefield, not the boudoir. There were two waves of World War I poetry, the first generally idealistic and hopeful, and intensely nationalistic (as in Rupert Brooke's sonnets "The Dead" and "The Soldier," written soon after the beginning of the war in 1914); the second war was much more cynical and bleak, following the disastrous losses in the Battle of the Somme of 1916. But not all of the early poetry was idealistic. Thomas Hardy was seventy-four in 1914, and his perspective was thus very different from that of the eighteen year olds who were enlisting for the good of their country. Hardy was an established and committed poet who naturally turned his attention to what was to become one of the most savage losses of human life in history. In "Channel Firing," written in April of 1914, just four months before the outbreak of war, Hardy's speakers are skeletons in a churchyard near the English Channel. Awakened by the sound of gunnery practice over the channel (the expression, "loud enough to awaken the dead" is a popular one in England), they sit bolt upright in their coffins, thinking that Judgment Day has come. Criticism of the impending war is voiced by God, who tells the skeletons that it is not God's work but man's. The skeletons then discuss man's sorry state that seems to be moving into greater insanity rather than toward the civilization that the Victorians had envisaged as human progress. The parson regrets that he wasted so much time on fruitless preaching; he would have been better to sit in the pub. The poem closes by looking behind the graveyard both in place (to England) and in time (to the past) rather than to the sea and Europe, and to the world war in preparation. The sound of the guns can be heard at Stourton Tower, Camelot, and Stonehenge, ancient places that represent England's legendary past, part history and part myth, the past of King Alfred, King Arthur, and the prehistoric worshipers at Stonehenge. Like the gunners in the channel, Alfred (ninth century) and Arthur (fifth century) were associated with defending the south of the island against invaders, the Danes and Saxons respectively. Stonehenge is the oldest evidence of people living in southwest England, 2,000 years before Christ. Hardy thus reminds us of the deep and troubled roots of English history and perhaps hints at the arrogance of those who see our own times as all-important. That Stonehenge is "starlit" suggests the neutrality of the universe in the face of human events.

Thomas Hardy's "In Time of 'The Breaking of Nations,' " written in

1915 (and discussed in this survey under "Time and Change") pictures a man and his old horse "harrowing clods" and a pair of lovers; both remind us of the continuation of human life while war across the channel seems to threaten that certainty. These images of farming and love recur with the same import in Edward Thomas's "As the Team's Head Brass," written in May 1916, two months before the Battle of the Somme and eight months before Thomas was sent to the Western Front at the age of thirty-nine. The title, which is the first half of the opening line of the poem, refers to the harness on the lead horse of a team that is plowing the field while the poet watches from a fallen elm tree. As well as the farmer and the poet, this rural scene also includes two lovers, who at the beginning of the poem disappear into the wood, to emerge at the end. Their lovemaking thus provides a silent backdrop against which to understand the conversation that takes place in snatches between the poet and the farmer, who passes with his team every ten minutes as he plows a square of wild mustard. The farmer tells him that the elm tree fell in a blizzard, and it will be cleared away after the war. The two then, in snatches of conversation, discuss the war. The farmer asks if the poet has "been out"? The effects of the war on this quiet corner of England—on the land as well as the people—become the topic of their desultory conversation. The tree would have been cleared away by now had the farmer's mate not been killed on his second day in France. The poet would not have been sitting on the tree; everything would have changed. The farmer suggests it would have been a better world, but then recalls that there may be a larger plan at work that is actually bringing about good. The poem ends with a sense of the continuity of life despite the destruction of war and blizzards. The lovers, symbolic of fertility and the propagation of life, reappear. Although it is "for the last time" (and sadly it probably was Thomas's last view of spring plowing—he was sent to France the following January and was killed just three months later), he continues to watch the earth breaking and falling under the plow. The ending seems to evoke not just the destruction of war (the men stumbling and falling in the clay fields of France) but also the persistence of nature, and man, to endure, just as the woodpecker earlier in the poem must have endured the loss of his elm tree home.

Thomas Hardy and Edward Thomas were already established poets when they wrote about the war. But several young men have become inextricably linked with World War I because they wrote about it and died in it, sometimes just days before the Armistice, before their talent could properly flower. Their view of the war is colored by their experiences on the battlefield, a reality sharply at odds with the idealism with which so many of them set out, fired by innocent patriotic zeal. In their youthful promise cut tragically short, they represented a whole generation of young men who died in World War I, and their poems gave voice to the thousands who died with them. Others survived the war, and their depictions of what they experienced in the trenches remain the works for which they are now remembered. Ivor Gurney, for example, was a musician, not a poet, when he was sent to France and lived through some of the darkest days of the war. Poisoned with gas, he was sent home in 1917, but his experiences left him unbalanced and he suffered from mental illness until his death in 1937. Like Hardy and Thomas, Gurney contrasts the experience of war with rural, settled England. In "To His Love," published in 1919, the speaker is a friend of a dead soldier addressing the soldier's lover and speaking for their shared grief. He recalls their times together on the Severn River, whose calm, blue beauty Gurney often contrasted with the Somme in France, where the most horrifying of the battles took place. The speaker can only hope that memories of the dead man's idyllic past in England will cover over the recent memories of his bloody death in France. Cover him in the violets of the Severn, he tells her, because purple violets represent the nobility with which he died.

After 1915 not many poets could write about the nobility of dying in the war. Gurney's "The Silent One" (1954) is a much more graphic and biting comment on the crucial class distinctions of the war. The middle classes became officers on signing up; the working classes were the private soldiers, subject to harsher living and fighting conditions and abuse from the unscrupulous among the officers. Gurney was a private, and "The Silent One" poignantly describes an incident that occurred to a fellow private. This man climbs the barbed wire separating the front from attack and is immediately shot. The speaker, however, is not so heroic. Seeing no hole in the fence, he chooses instead to lie low and fight with the others, his only chance. Suddenly an upper-class officer's voice suggests to Gurney, in the roundabout, characteristically polite manner of his class, that perhaps he could crawl through that hole in the fence. Just as politely, Gurney rejects the offer. The exchange, maintaining a level of civility and manners totally at odds with the request (there was no hole, and following the order would mean death "on the wires," like the silent one), draws attention to the gulf that existed between the officers and the men. The nobility of the private is evident in the final few lines of the poem, when he thinks of music, and, while swearing, is yet "Polite to God." The closing line reminds us that although he has rejected the officer's polite order, he cannot refuse indefinitely. Twice he retreats, and twice he returns to the wire.

Siegfried Sassoon belonged to the officer class, but in his poetry and later in his anti-war work he demonstrated a genuine sympathy for the "Tommies," or common soldiers. Sassoon came from a privileged background, attended Cambridge, lived comfortably in the country, and had begun to publish poetry when he joined up in 1914 at the age of twenty-eight. An idealist, Sassoon was hit hard by the realities of war, and his poetry of the Front was an attempt to wake up his countrymen back in England to the truth hidden by official statements and ignored by complacent nationalism. Many of his poems are bitterly ironic attacks on churchmen ("They"), the top brass ("The General"), and even the women of England ("Glory of Women"). The first poem to come out of his horrifying experiences in the war was "The Rear-Guard," written in a hospital in England after he was wounded while serving on the Hindenburg Line in April 1917. The poem graphically describes a British officer groping his way along a dank tunnel in search of headquarters. When he encounters a body, he assumes the man is sleeping and tries to kick him awake to help him find the exit; in the glow of his flashlight, of course, he sees a corpse in whose eyes he can still read the agony of the death that came ten days earlier. Alone, the soldier stumbles on until, seeing light filtering down, he climbs out of the tunnel, "Unloading hell behind him step by step." The poem is full of detail indicating that the tunnel has been home to the German soldiers serving there. The human form is at first just another obstacle to stumble over, and the speaker is impatient with it, his excuse being his lack of sleep. Such humanizing details link the German and the British soldiers trapped in a hellish atmosphere of death and decay.

It was perhaps providential that Siegfried Sassoon was to cross paths with the other major voice of World War I, Wilfred Owen. Sassoon (who survived the war) was sent home shell-shocked to Craiglockhart, a psychiatric hospital in Scotland, where he met Owen and encouraged his writing as well as his growing pacifism. Owen, who returned to the Front in 1918 and was killed just a week before the end of the war, wrote the poem that has come to exemplify the experience of the young men who went off to World War I full of nationalistic pride and a sense of duty and service to their country. "Dulce et Decorum Est" (1917–1918) takes its title from the Roman poet Horace: "It is sweet and fitting" ("pro patria mori—to die for one's country"). The poem takes us to the heart of trench warfare, to the mud, the sickness, the poison gas, the stench of death. Owen turns upside down Richard Lovelace's smooth, mellifluous address to Lucasta. Instead of noble generalizations ("faith," "honor"), Owen plunges us into the sickening center of the war with concrete, highly emotive words. Reading it, we hear the soldiers "coughing like hags," smell the greenish poison gas swirling around them, a deadly vapor, and see the unfortunate man, too late in getting on his gas mask, "guttering, choking, drowning." Everything about the poem is disturbing, from its graphic, even lurid, vocabulary, to its jerky, uneven rhythms: "Gas! GAS! Quick boys!" But Owen's purpose was exactly that: to shake his countrymen and -women out of their complacency and apathy and to bring before their eyes and hearts the true horror of the war across the channel.

Lovelace's soldier wanted to reassure Lucasta that going to war was as tame an endeavor as falling in love. He had to divorce the realities of war from the idealistic notion of "honor," and it was easy to do so when he was sitting beside her in the comfort of England. Owen is addressing his countrymen from the trenches, and his final statements are full of bitterness and rancor. If those back home could see what he has seen, they would not tell children "the old Lie" that Horace first declared. Owen was referring to the many young men (some even lied about their age, so keen were they to join up) who were encouraged to join the war effort by appeals to their nationalism and sense of duty and honor. When those who encouraged them then failed to support them, and through bungled and inept planning brought about the unnecessary deaths of almost an entire generation of men, Owen can be forgiven for rejecting out of hand the notion of death in war being "sweet and fitting," so horrifying were the realities of those deaths.

In 1917 and 1918, Wilfred Owen wrote a series of poems about the war that established him as a poet of great promise. His "Anthem for Doomed Youth" was written in response to a preface to a volume of poems published in 1916 (*Poems of Today*) that spoke glibly of a young poet who had "gone singing to lay down his life for his country's cause" to the sound of "the passing-bells of Death." Owen's "anthem" contains not the sweet and patriotic sounds described in the preface but "only the monstrous anger of the guns./Only the stuttering rifles' rapid rattle." Instead of the peaceful choirs of English churches, they hear only "the shrill, demented choirs of wailing shells," a reference to a line in Keats's "To Autumn" (1819) that contrasts Keats's peaceful rural scene with the mechanical horror of warfare. In "Futility," Owen again draws attention to the perversion of the natural world in warfare. "Move him gently into the sun," urges the first line, because the sun has always awakened the sleeping boy before. Now, in death, he is impervious to the awakening rays, rays that bring to life dead seeds and "the clays of a cold star." What is the point of earth's creation if it ends in premature death for so many? Owen seems to be answering Keats's declaration, "The poetry of earth is never dead." The war has upset the natural order, when young limbs, "full-nerved, still warm," cannot be stirred.

Isaac Rosenberg was a poor Jewish boy from London who was embarking on a career as an artist and poet when he enlisted at the age of twenty-five, hoping to provide an income for his mother. Unlike Sassoon and Owen, who were middle class and officers, Rosenberg was a regular soldier and suffered even more acute deprivations and suffering than they did. He was killed in April 1918, but his war poems have ensured his reputation as a poet whose considerable talents were abruptly cut short. In "Break of Day in the Trenches" (1916), Rosenberg uses the same device as John Donne in "The Flea" (1633) to overcome barriers—in

Donne's poem the speaker tells his mistress that the flea has bitten both of them so in its body their blood is already united; her opposition to sex is thus already answered, with no harm done. Rosenberg's lowly creature is a rat who, as Rosenberg tells it, will be shot if the authorities find out that it has touched his hand and will now cross No Man's Land to touch a German hand. Free from the political and nationalistic ambitions that have put the Englishman and the German at war, the lowly rat, he says, has a better chance of survival than the two athletic, fine-limbed men. The rat's failure to distinguish between the men and the two camps nicely points to the stupidity of the conflict—the "whims of murder" that will likely see both men die before the end. They are the miserable creatures, cornered and vulnerable, not the rat. To the rat the conflict is inexplicable; the bombs tear apart "still heavens." The poem is framed by another natural emblem (and one that has become the symbol for World War I), the poppy. The soldier puts one behind his ear at the beginning of the poem; at the end he has saved it from destruction temporarily, but both poppy and man are doomed to die—the poppy's roots are mingled with the corpses, their blood running red in the flowers that "are ever dropping."

Rosenberg's "Returning, We Hear the Larks" (1917) reminds us of the very different use to which poetry was put during World War I by the soldier-poets. So many poems have spoken rapturously of birds—nightingales and larks especially—and their glorious songs, free from the bonds of earth and mortality. Here Rosenberg takes up this ancient poetic emblem to portray the fine line the living soldiers tread each day, surrounded by death on all sides. Returning from a night exercise, exhausted and fearful, they hear with "strange joy" the sound of birdsong "showering on our upturned list'ning faces." But the larks' song does not herald freedom and inspiration for the war-poet; however joyful the sound, he knows that death could just as easily drop on them from the night sky. Two fine images close the poem and elaborate the close connection between joy and death: a blind man dreams on the shore, not knowing that danger lurks in the tides beside him, and a sleeping girl dreams, unaware of a serpent lurking. How incongruous is a world in which the sound of larks ascending can in seconds be replaced by the sound of bombs screaming through the night sky.

The poetry of World War II has never been as well known as that from the first, because the images of trench warfare created by the poets of the so-called Great War seemed to capture for all time the experience of war. The senselessness of World War I and the devastating errors committed by those in authority made the slaughter of the young soldiers all the more memorable and appalling. But some powerful war poetry emerged from World War II also, from poets such as Edith Sitwell (1887–1964), whose "Still Falls the Rain" (1942) was written in response to the terrifying German air attack on London in 1940, during the Battle of Britain. Like Rosenberg's "Returning, We Hear the Larks," "Still Falls the Rain" contrasts the deadly, man-made bombs falling from the sky with the life-giving, natural falling of rain or birdsong. But Sitwell's poem moves the image into a recreation of Christ's death, symbol of man's inhumanity to man and the coming of the darkness that has reached its deepest gloom in World War II. The poem ends with the hope of Christ's redemption for the sins of mankind.

Although the justification for Britain's entry into World War II was more obvious than for World War I (Germany had occupied much of the Continent and had begun its attack on Britain), the question of class and the ill-preparedness of many of the upper-class officers remained a question to be addressed by the poets. Keith Douglas knew about war—his father had won the Military Cross in World War I, but he deserted his family when Douglas was only eight. He began writing poetry at an early age, and after attending Oxford University enlisted in the army and was sent to North Africa, where he fought in the Desert Campaign against Rommel. He survived injury, but was killed in the Normandy invasion of 1944. Douglas's poems are much less cynical in their tone than those of Sassoon or Owen, even when he is addressing the folly of the officers and the senselessness of many aspects of a war that was supposed to be re-creating the heroes of old. Many war poems deal with the way the war changed the old ways, and Douglas finds the stiff-upper-lipped training of the English upper classes not only inadequate but ludicrously incongruous to the circumstances of modern warfare. The famous old expression that the Battle of Waterloo was won on the playing fields of Eton summed up the long-held belief that the principles of gamesmanship and good manners taught in the schools of young gentlemen were all that were needed to defeat the barbarous enemy. Douglas's poems find that attitude still disastrously embraced by the officers of World War II. "Gallantry" (1943) describes the deaths of three young men, each one of whom goes politely to his grave. They are "doomed" just as Owen's young men are the "doomed race," doomed perhaps by the Colonel, who casually tells a joke over the microphone while the men follow orders that will kill them. The "perfectly mannered flesh" of one of them is doomed because he "open[ed] the door" for a bomb, just as he had been taught to do in school. The surviving Colonel deems them brave, but even the bombs themselves find the war amusing, and the earth politely receives them.

In "Aristocrats" (1943), Douglas compares the cavalrymen of the North African campaign to the knights of old, whose nobility was unchallenged, their purpose unassailable. One of the men comments, "It's most unfair," as he crawls across the sand, his leg amputated by a German tank. The poet's response is sad amazement at the soldier's clinging to past ideals of chivalry. They are becoming unicorns, he says, fools and heroes, to be laughed at and admired. They see the cavalry charge as a steeplechase, the desert their school playing fields. Douglas takes World War II soldiers out of their specific time and place to comment more generally on the nature of war and heroism and the demands made on the modern soldier to maintain an outmoded chivalric ideal.

eণ৬ে

"Epitaph on an Army of Mercenaries," A. E. Housman
     NAEL-2; OBEV
"Another Epitaph on an Army of Mercenaries," Hugh MacDiarmid
     NAEL-2
"To Lucasta, Going to the Wars," Richard Lovelace
     BL; ImPo; NAEL-1; OAEL-1; OBEV; TFi; TrGrPo-2
"The Battle of Blenheim," Robert Southey
     SB; TFi; TrGrPo-2
"Channel Firing," Thomas Hardy
     ImPo; NAEL-2; OAEL-2; OBEV; TFi
"In Time of 'The Breaking of Nations,' " Thomas Hardy
     NAEL-2; OAEL-2; TFi
"As the Team's Head Brass," Edward Thomas
     NAEL-2
"To His Love," Ivor Gurney
     NAEL-2
"The Silent One," Ivor Gurney
     NAEL-2; SB
"The Rear-Guard," Siegfried Sassoon
     NAEL-2
"Dulce et Decorum Est," Wilfred Owen
     NAEL-2; OAEL-2; OBEV; TFi
"Anthem for Doomed Youth," Wilfred Owen
     ImPo; OAEL-2; OBEV; TFi
"Futility," Wilfred Owen
     MoBrPo; NAEL-2
"Break of Day in the Trenches," Isaac Rosenberg

NAEL-2; OAEL-2; OBEV; SB; TFi

"Returning, We Hear the Larks," Isaac Rosenberg

    NAEL-2; OAEL-2

"Still Falls the Rain," Edith Sitwell

    NAEL-2; TFi

"Gallantry," Keith Douglas

    NAEL-2

"Aristocrats," Keith Douglas

    NAEL-2

Biographical Sketches

❧

MATTHEW ARNOLD (1822–1888) was educated at Rugby School, whose headmaster was his famous father, Thomas (immortalized in Thomas Hughes's novel *Tom Brown's Schooldays*). Arnold attended Oxford, where he was a close friend of Arthur Hugh Clough. He married in 1851 and became an inspector of schools, a post he held for thirty-five years. He was also a professor of poetry at Oxford. Arnold wrote a few fine poems, but he is now better known as a social and literary critic. His *Culture and Anarchy* stressed the importance of the liberal arts in a cultured society.

W(YSTAN) H(UGH) AUDEN (1907–1973) began to write poetry at Oxford University. His first collection was published with great success by T. S. Eliot at Faber and Faber in 1930. He collaborated with the playwright Christopher Isherwood and the composer Benjamin Britten, who set some of his poems to music. After a brief visit to Spain during the 1937 Civil War, where he intended to fight on the side of the Republicans, Auden moved to the United States and became an American citizen in 1946. He returned to England in 1956 to become a professor of poetry at Oxford University. As well as a large body of poetry, Auden was also a literary critic in works such as *The Dyer's Hand* (1962).

ANNA LETITIA BARBAULD (1743–1825) was well educated by her father, a college teacher, and the scientist Dr. Joseph Priestley. Her first volume of poems was published in 1773 and sold very well. After her marriage, she ran a boys' school with her husband and wrote school books for children. After her husband's death, she became a leading radical and an important editor, critic, and writer in London.

JOHN BARBOUR (c. 1320–1395) was a Scottish churchman and auditor of the exchequer. The authorship of much of his poetry is disputed except for his epic history of the Scottish hero Robert the Bruce, *The Bruce* (1376).

SIR JOHN BETJEMAN (1906–1984) was a Londoner. He attended Oxford at the same time as W. H. Auden but did not receive a degree. Betjeman became a professional writer in 1931, and in 1972 his popularity as a witty commentator on English life led to his appointment as poet laureate.

WILLIAM BLAKE (1757–1827) apprenticed as an engraver, and throughout his life his art was an integral part of his poetry. He married Catherine Boucher in 1782, and the following year his *Poetical Sketches* was published. In 1789 *Songs of Innocence* was published with his own engravings, followed by *Songs of Experience* in 1794. A free thinker, Blake conceived his own complicated mystical vision which he explored in such works as *The Book of Thel* and *The Marriage of Heaven and Hell*. Misunderstood in the nineteenth century, Blake is now valued as a prophetic voice who urged an apocalyptic rebirth of spirituality in the early days of the Industrial Revolution. This concern (best known in his poem *Jerusalem*), was shared by the Romantic poets, who were his immediate successors.

ANNE BRADSTREET (c. 1612–1672) was born in England but emigrated to America in 1630 with her husband. Her poems were published in 1650 in London, but she is recognized as the first American woman poet.

ROBERT BRIDGES (1844–1930) attended Oxford University and then became a doctor. His first volume of poetry appeared in 1873. Six volumes had been published by 1905 and he was appointed poet laureate in 1913. He was an adviser to Oxford University Press and one of the founders of the Society for Pure English. Among his many contributions to English literature was his editing and publishing of the poetry of his friend Gerard Manley Hopkins.

EMILY BRONTË (1818–1848) lived with her novelist sisters Charlotte and Anne at Haworth Parsonage, Yorkshire. She attended Cowan Bridge School (the hardships of which are graphically recorded in Charlotte Brontë's *Jane Eyre*), but other than brief sojourns away,

Emily lived entirely in the parsonage. She and her sisters and brother Branwell created imaginary heroic worlds for which Emily wrote many dramatic poems. Charlotte, Emily, and Anne published their poetry under the pseudonyms Currer, Ellis, and Acton Bell in 1846. Emily's only novel, *Wuthering Heights*, was published in 1847. In 1848 she succumbed to the tuberculosis that had already taken the lives of three of her sisters. Emily's strong religious faith and heightened imagination are evident in her poetry.

RUPERT BROOKE (1887–1915) was educated at Rugby School, where his father taught. A handsome man, he excelled at Cambridge and began to write poetry, publishing in the famous *Georgian Poetry* series. He joined the Royal Navy in 1914 and took part in the defense of Antwerp. On his return he wrote five "War Sonnets" that immediately came to represent British patriotism: the Dean of St. Paul's Cathedral read "The Soldier" during a sermon in 1915. He died of blood poisoning a few months later while en route to Gallipoli and was buried in Greece. Brooke came to epitomize the fine young men whose promising futures were tragically cut short by the Great War.

ELIZABETH BARRETT BROWNING (1806–1861) was the eldest of eleven children of Edward Barrett, a dictatorial father who did not want his children to marry. Elizabeth's extensive literary and classical education was largely self-directed, and by the time she was thirty she was a respected poet, despite her confinement to her room due to poor health. Her courtship and secret elopement with Robert Browning in 1846 have been the subject of several plays and films. The couple moved to Italy and had one son. Her love poems to Robert, *Sonnets from the Portuguese*, are now her best-loved works, but she also wrote about social injustices such as slavery (her father had been a plantation owner) and child labor. In her verse novel *Aurora Leigh* she attacked Victorian restrictions on women, especially on women writers.

ROBERT BROWNING (1812–1889), the son of a London bank clerk, benefitted from his father's extensive library and interest in art and literature. When John Stuart Mill called his first long poem "Pauline" "morbid self-consciousness," Browning tried playwriting and then found his forte in the dramatic monologue, a form that removed the poet's own voice from the poem. He married Elizabeth Barrett Browning in 1846, lived in Italy with her until her death in 1861, and then returned to London.

ROBERT BURNS (1759–1796) was the son of a poor farmer in Ayrshire, Scotland. He was well educated at local schools, where he started writing poetry. Burns continued to farm in Ayrshire, the setting of many of his poems. His first published collection, *Poems, chiefly in the Scottish Dialect*, (1786) was unexpectedly successful and he was hailed in Edinburgh as an uneducated "ploughman poet" with innate genius. Burns's fondness for the "lassies" inspired many of his famous love poems, but he is also still valued for his championing of human rights and democracy. Burns's birthday, January 25, is celebrated at Burns' Night dinners all around the world, at which his "To a Haggis" is recited over that uniquely Scottish meat dish. And the new year is traditionally greeted by the singing of Burns's "Auld Lang Syne."

GEORGE GORDON, LORD BYRON (1788–1824) was raised in Scotland but inherited Newstead Abbey and a title in 1798. Although he had a club foot, he was a handsome and flamboyant man when he attended Cambridge and acquired a reputation as a libertine and a wastrel. A member of the House of Lords, he traveled abroad frequently and had a series of love affairs that damaged his reputation at home. He moved to Italy permanently in 1816. His literary reputation was established in 1812 with *Childe Harold's Pilgrimage*. Byron died of fever while fighting for Greek independence. His large body of poetry, including *Don Juan*, has been highly influential in Europe as well as in England.

THOMAS CAMPION (1567–1620) was educated at Cambridge, trained as a lawyer, but became a physician in 1605. He was famous in his own day as a singer and songwriter, and he wrote several masques for Kind James I's court. Campion dropped out of favor until the end of the nineteenth century, but he is now regarded as one of the finest Elizabethan poets.

THOMAS CAREW (1595–1640) was one of the "Cavalier poets," a member of King Charles I's court and a supporter of the Royalist cause. After graduating from Oxford, Carew served abroad as a diplomat for several years. He wrote masques for the court and enjoyed a life of ease, dying before the regicide of his patron the king.

CHARLES CAUSLEY (1917–   ) was born and still lives in Cornwall. The local traditions of folk songs influenced Causley's poetry, some of which was inspired by his experiences in the Royal Navy from 1940 to 1946. A school teacher, Causley has also written extensively for children.

THOMAS CHATTERTON (1752–1770) began to write poetry as a school boy in Bristol. He is best known for his "Rowley" poems, which he pretended were the work of a fifteenth-century poet. He moved to London in 1770 and committed suicide soon after, ending a tragic short life that captured the imaginations of the Romantic poets a few years later.

GEOFFREY CHAUCER (c. 1343–1400) is the preeminent writer of the Middle Ages. The son of a vintner in London, he served in the army and then held many positions with the court, traveling as a diplomat to France, Genoa, and Florence. Back in England, he was a controller of customs for the port of London, a justice of the peace, a member of parliament for Kent, and the clerk of the king's works, an important position overseeing the royal residences and parks. His poetry, strongly influenced by European writers and philosophers, often took the form of the dream vision, but he is best loved for the memorable sketches of English people of all classes and professions found in *The Canterbury Tales*.

JOHN CLARE (1793–1864) was a Northamptonshire laborer. When he was sixteen, his unrequited love for a wealthier girl brought on the mental illness that plagued Clare for most of his life. His first collection of poems, *Poems Descriptive of Rural Life and Scenery*, was well received in London and he was feted as a "peasant poet," but the fame was short-lived and his life was dogged by ill health and poverty. He wrote some of his best poems in Northampton County Asylum, and he is now recognized for his evocations of country life.

ARTHUR HUGH CLOUGH (1819–1861) was a contemporary of Matthew Arnold at Rugby School and Oxford University. He went on to a variety of posts in education and government, and lectured in the United States. The religious doubt and general anxiety evident in his poems are characteristic of the Victorian age in which he lived.

SAMUEL TAYLOR COLERIDGE (1772–1834) was born in Ottery St. Mary, Devon, the son of the vicar. He was a classmate of the writers Charles Lamb and Leigh Hunt at school in London and went on to Cambridge University. Although brilliant, he dropped out and enlisted briefly in the army, from which he was rescued by his brothers. An idealistic scheme to start a commune in America with his friend and fellow poet Robert Southey led to his unfortunate marriage to Sara Fricker, sister of Southey's fiancée. Coleridge and Sara moved to Clevedon on the west coast of England and then to Nether Stowey, Somerset, where he and William Wordsworth formed a close partnership as poets. They established new attitudes to poetry (later to be known as Romanticism) in their *Lyrical Ballads* (1798). Most of Coleridge's best poetry was written at this time. After traveling in Germany, both poets moved to the Lake District, where Coleridge fell in love with Sara Hutchinson, Wordsworth's future sister-in-law. Now addicted to opium, Coleridge traveled abroad alone before separating from his wife. In later life he lived with a surgeon in London and wrote his famous work of literary criticism, *Biographia Literaria*.

WILLIAM COLLINS (1721–1759) was educated at Oxford and in London befriended Samuel Johnson and James Thomson. His twelve odes appeared to little acclaim in 1746, but they have since been influential in the writings of succeeding poets, particularly the Romantics. He lived unhappily and in isolation near Oxford, suffering from depression.

RICHARD CORBET (1582–1635) was a gardener's son, educated at Oxford University. He was chaplain to King James I, bishop of Oxford, and bishop of Norwich, but he also enjoyed Ben Jonson's company at the Mermaid Tavern and wrote cheerful, light verse.

ABRAHAM COWLEY (1618–1667) was the son of a London stationer. He was well educated at school, where he began to write poetry, and at Cambridge University. A Royalist, Cowley served as secretary to one of the Stuarts when they fled to France. Returning to England, he was imprisoned as a spy for a short time. With the Restoration, Cowley returned to favor, studied medicine at Oxford, and ended his life quietly in the country. His poetry included Pindaric odes, whose form was taken up by later Restoration writers such as Dryden.

WILLIAM COWPER (1731–1800), the son of a clergyman in Hertfordshire, suffered from melancholia and depression from an early age, having been bullied at school. He became a lawyer, but when he was offered a controversial clerkship in the House of Lords he attempted suicide. Cowper suffered under the belief that he was damned, and although he enjoyed some happier times living quietly with religious friends in the country, he had periodic bouts of insanity. As well as his poetry, Cowper wrote several famous hymns.

GEORGE CRABBE (1754–1832) was a poor country boy training to be a doctor when a move to London brought him to the attention of Edmund Burke, who helped to publish his work and encouraged him to become a clergyman. He returned to his native Aldborough and then obtained a post with the Duke of Rutland in Dorsetshire. His poem "The Village," written in response to Goldsmith's more idealistic portrait in "The Deserted Village," was admired by many writers including Sir Walter Scott, Jane Austen, and Thomas Hardy.

SAMUEL DANIEL (1562–1619) attended Oxford University and became a tutor. As a court poet he wrote masques and plays for King James I. The Romantic poets admired him but he is now remembered only for his sonnet sequence *Delia*.

W(ILLIAM) H(ENRY) DAVIES (1871–1940) was born to Welsh country people. He had little formal education and spent several years living by his wits in North America. His experiences were recounted in *The Autobiography of a Super-Tramp* (1908), including his losing a leg in a train accident while gold-seeking in the Klondike. George Bernard Shaw promoted his writing, and he produced eighteen volumes of poetry, to some acclaim from other writers of the time. His writing was simple and optimistic, his subject matter usually the natural world.

THOMAS DEKKER (1570?–1632) was a Londoner who lived in cheerful poverty, enduring several spells in prison for debt. A playwright, he collaborated with many of his contemporaries including Ben Jonson, Michael Drayton, and Thomas Middleton. Like Defoe and Dickens in later centuries, Dekker painted realistic portraits of London life, especially the sufferings of poor people and animals.

EDWARD DE VERE, 17TH EARL OF OXFORD (1550–1604), attended Cambridge University. His favor at court was affected by his quarrelsome nature; he had a famous row with Sir Philip Sidney on a tennis court, and reputedly threatened to kill him. In 1920 an argument was made for his authorship of Shakespeare's plays and poems, and an active group of "Oxfordians" is still trying to earn universal recognition for him.

JOHN DONNE (1572–1631) was related to Sir Thomas More on his mother's side. He attended Oxford (and possibly Cambridge) University but as a Catholic was unable to earn a degree. After traveling abroad, Donne studied law and converted to the Church of England, his family having experienced considerable persecution as Catholics. He accompanied the earl of Essex in his campaigns against Spain and then became secretary to Sir Thomas Egerton, Lord Keeper of the Great Seal. His advancement in politics (he was elected an MP in 1601) was curtailed when he antagonized Egerton by secretly marrying Lady Egerton's niece. Dismissed from service, Donne spent the next few years struggling to provide for a large family by writing. New patrons rescued him and he entered the church in 1615, holding several important positions. In 1621 he became Dean of St. Paul's and began a career as a formidable preacher. Donne wrote both devotional poetry and erotic love poetry with unique vitality and striking, often disturbing images. Disapproved of by the eighteenth century, Donne was rediscovered by T. S. Eliot in the twentieth and is considered the greatest of the "metaphysical poets."

KEITH DOUGLAS (1920–1944) was the son of a World War I hero. He was educated at Oxford University where he was tutored by the war poet Edmund Blunden. He published poetry in the 1930s, but he is remembered for the vivid poems that were inspired by his experiences fighting against Rommel's Africa Corps in Egypt. He was killed on June 6, 1944 in Normandy.

MICHAEL DRAYTON (1563–1631) was a prolific writer at the time of Shakespeare. Little is known about his life, but he wrote sonnets, odes, plays, and patriotic and historical verses. His best-known work is the sonnet sequence *Idea*, thought to have been composed for Sir Henry Goodere's daughter Anne.

WILLIAM DRUMMOND OF HAWTHORNDEN (1585–1649) was named for his estate near Edinburgh, Scotland. Educated as a lawyer, Drummond traveled extensively and discovered the work of many continental poets before settling down to a reclusive literary life at his estate, enriched by his vast library. Ben Jonson visited him in 1618. Some of Drummond's poetry was inspired by the death of his fiancée on the eve of their wedding. A Royalist at the time of the Civil Wars, Drummond died not long after the regicide of King Charles I.

JOHN DRYDEN (1631–1700) came from a Puritan family that supported Cromwell's Protectorate, but he changed his allegiance to Charles II on the Restoration of the monarchy in 1660 and was appointed poet laureate in 1668. When James II was crowned, Dryden became a Catholic and lost his laureateship with the deposing of James in 1688. Dryden supported himself by his prolific writing of plays and poems, and he also wrote important literary criticism, including *An Essay of Dramatic Poesy* (1668).

SIR EDWARD DYER (1543–1607) attended Oxford University and then became a member of Queen Elizabeth's court. A close friend of Sir Philip Sidney, he wrote an elegy on Sidney's death, one of the few poems by Dyer that have survived.

JOHN DYER (1699–1757) was a Welsh clergyman whose poetry was set in the hill country of his home. His long epic poem "The Fleece" was about the wool trade in the earliest days of industrialism.

T(HOMAS) S(TEARNS) ELIOT (1888–1965) was born in St. Louis, Missouri, and studied at Harvard, the Sorbonne, Paris, and Oxford University. He remained in England, becoming a British subject and Anglican in 1927. His first volume of poems, *Prufrock and other Observations*, appeared in 1917. Employed by Lloyd's bank, Eliot also joined the staff of the literary magazine *The Egoist* and then founded *The Criterion*, which opened with Eliot's *The Waste Land* and ran until 1939. Eliot was one of the most influential writers of his time, partly through his position as director of the publishing firm Faber and Faber, and partly through his considerable output of essays of literary criticism as well as poetry and plays.

ANNE FINCH, COUNTESS OF WINCHILSEA (1661–1720) was the daughter of Sir William Kingsmill and became a maid of honor to the Duchess of York. She married Colonel Heneage Finch, who became fourth Earl of Winchilsea. She was a friend of the major writers of the day including Pope, Swift, and John Gay. Her first collection of poems appeared in 1713.

GEORGE GASCOIGNE (1539–1578) attended Cambridge University and became a lawyer in London. He was involved in various scandals and lawsuits which led to his being disinherited by his father and banned from taking a seat in parliament. He served as a soldier in the Netherlands for two years and returned to a better position in Queen Elizabeth I's court. He is recognized now as having been an early innovator of many literary forms in English, including the novel and blank verse satire.

OLIVER GOLDSMITH (c. 1730–1774), the son of an Irish clergyman, attended Trinity College, Dublin. He failed in his attempts to follow careers in the church and medicine and became a reviewer and magazine writer instead, starting his own publication, *The Bee*, in 1759. He was befriended by Samuel Johnson and achieved success with his poems *The Traveller* and *The Deserted Village*, his novel *The Vicar of Wakefield*, and his play *She Stoops to Conquer*.

THOMAS GRAY (1716–1771) came from a humble London family but was educated at Eton (where he became friends with Horace Walpole) and Cambridge University. After touring the continent, Gray settled in Cambridge, where he published his famous "Elegy Written in a Country Churchyard" with the help of Walpole. He lived a retiring life, refusing the offer of the poet laureateship but accepting a professorship at Cambridge. Gray was a precursor of the Romantic poets in his interest in the countryside, the picturesque, and old Norse and Welsh poetry.

ROBERT GREENE (1558–1592) attended Cambridge University but went on to a profligate career in London, living with lowlifes until his death, reputedly from an overindulgence in pickled herrings and wine but more probably from the plague. His prose romances looked forward to the novel, and his plays (in which his best-known poetry appeared) achieved some success, especially *Orlando Furioso.*

IVOR GURNEY (1890–1937) attended the Royal College of Music on a scholarship and became a composer of songs. Wounded while serving on the Western Front, he was hospitalized in Rouen, France. His first volume of poems about the war, *Severn and the Somme,* was published in 1917, followed by *War's Embers* in 1919. He went on to fight at Paschendale but the effects of poison gas troubled him for the rest of his life, which he would pass almost entirely in mental hospitals. He continued to write poetry and compose music for the poetry of A. E. Housman and Edward Thomas.

THOMAS HARDY (1840–1928) lived most of his life in Dorset, England, the setting of his "Wessex" novels. The son of a stonemason, he became an architect on leaving school and began writing poetry and novels. The success of his fourth novel, *Far from the Madding Crowd,* in 1874 allowed him to pursue writing full time, and he published twelve more novels over the next twenty years. When his 1895 novel, *Jude the Obscure,* was harshly criticized, he returned to his first love, poetry. Some of Hardy's best poems were inspired by his unhappy marriage to Emma Gifford, who died in 1912. Hardy's early loss of religious faith, leading to a strong fatalism, is also a central theme in his poetry and fiction.

SEAMUS HEANEY (1939–) comes from a farming family in Northern Ireland. He attended Queen's University, Belfast, where he became a lecturer in poetry. He and his family moved to Eire in 1972. Heaney has been an invited professor of poetry at the University of California, Berkeley, at Harvard University, and at Oxford University. His first collection of poems, *Death of a Naturalist*, appeared in 1966 and he has published collections regularly ever since. In 1995 Heaney was awarded the Nobel Prize for Literature.

FELICIA DOROTHEA HEMANS (1793–1835) was deserted by first her father (when she was fourteen) and then her husband (after six years of marriage and five children). Her lyrics often take up the subject of women's responsibilities in the domestic sphere, but other narrative poems tell unusual stories of warlike, avenging women warriors. She published fourteen volumes of poetry, the first when she was only fifteen, and was immensely popular in her time, particularly in the United States.

WILLIAM ERNEST HENLEY (1849–1903) had a childhood ailment that in 1873 resulted in his spending a year in the Edinburgh Infirmary. His "Hospital Sketches," poems written at that time, were published in the *Cornhill Magazine* in 1875. He met Robert Louis Stevenson in Edinburgh and together they wrote several plays; he was also the model for Long John Silver in Stevenson's *Treasure Island*. Henley was an influential magazine editor in London, publishing and encouraging many famous writers.

GEORGE HERBERT (1593–1633), the son of a noble family, had a distinguished career as a student at Cambridge University, where he began writing the devotional poetry that would occupy his life. He was influenced by his mother's friend John Donne to become a poet and a clergyman, obtaining several positions in central England. Herbert loved church music and church architecture (an interest which is central to his poetry), and he helped to restore a ruined country church. The power of Herbert's religious poetry was recognized by Coleridge at the beginning of the nineteenth century, and he is now highly regarded for his intellectual, profound mysticism.

ROBERT HERRICK (1591–1674) came from a family of goldsmiths in London and attended Cambridge University, where he trained for the Anglican church. In London he was one of Ben Jonson's "sons," young poets who were influenced and encouraged by the older, established poet. Herrick moved to a church position in Devon, where he at first found country life boring. In a well-known story he threw his sermon at his indifferent congregation, but he also came to celebrate country life and customs in his poetry. A Royalist, Herrick is also known as one of the "Cavalier poets," famous for their graceful, witty lyrics, often about love.

THOMAS HOOD (1799–1845) was the son of a London bookseller. He played an important role in nineteenth-century publishing as the editor of many periodicals including his own *Hood's Magazine*, and he was a friend of many of the writers of the day, including Charles Lamb and Charles Dickens. Hood's poetry was mostly gently satiric or comic, but "The Song of the Shirt" and "The Dream of Eugene Aram" (about a murder) were also popular.

GERARD MANLEY HOPKINS (1844–1889) began writing poetry seriously at Oxford University, where he excelled. When he became a Roman Catholic in 1866 he burned most of his poetry. As a priest he reconciled his profession and his art by writing devotional poetry to the glory of God as evidenced in the beauty of the natural world. A Jesuit lecturer, he spent his last five years unhappily as an administrator and professor at University College, Dublin. Here he wrote the so-called "Terrible Sonnets" that depict a deep depression. Most of Hopkins's work was published posthumously by his Oxford friend and fellow poet Robert Bridges. Hopkins died of typhoid in Ireland.

A(LFRED) E(DWARD) HOUSMAN (1859–1936) was born in Shropshire, the setting for many of his poems. He attended Oxford University, but despite a brilliant mind he failed his examinations and became a government clerk for ten years. After extensive private study of the classics, he became a professor of Latin at University College, London in 1892; in 1911 he was appointed a professor at Cambridge University. *A Shropshire Lad*, Housman's most famous collection of poetry, appeared in 1896 and became very popular.

HENRY HOWARD, EARL OF SURREY (1517?–1547) was descended from royalty and grew up in the court, where he took part in several campaigns in Europe. With Wyatt, he helped to establish the sonnet form in England and may have invented the English rhyme scheme (rather than the Italian form used by Petrarch). He also experimented with blank verse. Howard's hot temper led to many escapades, and he was executed for an alleged attempt to succeed King Henry VIII.

ELIZABETH JENNINGS (1926–) comes from a Catholic family and was educated at Oxford University. Her first collection of poems was published in 1953. While her early work was sometimes associated with that of the Movement poets (see Larkin, for example), her later work takes up personal rather than societal themes.

BEN JONSON (1572–1637) was the posthumous son of a clergyman. Jonson attended Westminster School and then worked for his stepfather, a bricklayer. He served in the army in Flanders and on returning to London became an actor, dramatist, and manager. His first play, *Every Man in His Humour*, included Shakespeare in the cast, and the two writers became close friends, meeting at the Mermaid Tavern with other members of "the tribe of Ben." He wrote many masques for King James I, who granted him a pension in 1616. He received an honorary degree from Oxford and became a lecturer at Gresham College in London.

JOHN KEATS (1795–1821) was orphaned young. Apprenticed to be a surgeon in north London, he began writing poetry at an early age and gave up his medical career to devote himself to it. Leigh Hunt published his first poems in *The Examiner* and introduced him to Shelley, Wordsworth, and Coleridge. A collection appeared in 1817, to highly critical reviews that attacked him as an uneducated Londoner. In 1818 Keats's brother Tom died of tuberculosis, an illness that took Keats's life in 1821. Keats fell in love with Fanny Brawne in 1819, the year in which he wrote most of his famous odes and other poems that established him as central to the Romantic movement. In 1820 he went to Italy for his health but survived for only three months.

RUDYARD KIPLING (1865–1936) was born in Bombay, India, but educated in England. He worked in India as a journalist while publishing the poetry that would make his name when he returned to England in 1889. In 1892 he married an American, with whom he lived in Vermont for four years. After traveling in South Africa, he settled in England. Kipling was awarded the Nobel Prize for literature in 1907. His wide range of writing, much of it about colonialism and British India, includes his collected poems (*Departmental Ditties*, 1886), short stories (*Plain Tales From The Hills*, 1888), novels (*Kim* is considered his masterpiece), and works for children including *Just-So Stories* and *The Jungle Book*.

LETITIA ELIZABETH LANDON (1802–1838) used the pseudonym L.E.L. A Londoner, she earned a good living from her five volumes of poetry and four novels. Her relationships with gentlemen friends in the literary world attracted some gossip. She was engaged briefly to Charles Dickens's biographer John Forster but married George Maclean, a colonial governor in west Africa. She died there of poisoning, under suspicious circumstances.

AEMILIA LANYER (1569–1645) was the daughter of Italian-Jewish court musicians. She lived in court circles and in 1611 published a volume of poems that contain religious and feminist themes.

PHILIP LARKIN (1922–1985) attended Oxford University and then worked for many years as a librarian at Hull University. The first of his four volumes of poetry was published in 1944. Larkin was associated for some years with the Movement, a group of English writers who commented unsentimentally on contemporary life. Influenced at first by W. B. Yeats, Larkin soon rejected the modernist movement of T. S. Eliot and Ezra Pound for the native English tradition that led to Thomas Hardy. He edited *The Oxford Book of Twentieth-Century English Verse* in 1973.

D(AVID) H(ERBERT) LAWRENCE (1885–1930) was raised in Nottinghamshire, the sickly child of a miner and a schoolteacher, who encouraged him to become better educated than his father. He earned a teacher's certificate and taught for two years, but ill health following the death of his mother forced him to turn to writing instead. His first novel, *Sons and Lovers*, recounts his early years and his love for her. Lawrence married Frieda von Richthofen and together they lived a restless and impoverished life in Europe, Mexico, and New Mexico. Lawrence was criticized—even charged criminally—for obscenity and immorality, but he is now highly regarded as a novelist, short-story writer, and poet.

RICHARD LOVELACE (1618–1657) A courtier and Cavalier poet, he came from a wealthy Kent family. As a Royalist he was imprisoned several times, lost his fortune and spent the last ten years of his life destitute. The poems he wrote in prison, for Lucasta, are believed to have been written for Lucy Sacheverell, who married someone else believing that Lovelace had died.

HUGH MACDIARMID (1892–1978) was the penname of the Scottish poet Christopher Murray Grieve. MacDiarmid was a nationalist; he founded the National Party of Scotland and hoped for a cultural Renaissance, reviving the medieval Scottish poets (William Dunbar and Robert Henryson) whom he found superior to Robert Burns and his weaker followers. A Communist, MacDiarmid wrote political poetry and is best known for *A Drunk Man Looks at the Thistle*. His interest in and experiments with language and dialect are similar to James Joyce's, and he is now regarded as the successor to Burns as Scotland's preeminent poet.

CHRISTOPHER MARLOWE (1564–1593), the son of a shoemaker, graduated from Cambridge University with B.A. and M.A. degrees. The details of his unorthodox career in London are sketchy, but he was charged with various offences and was killed in a tavern brawl in 1593. Marlowe's genius is evident in his plays (especially *Doctor Faustus*, *The Jew of Malta*, and *Tamburlaine*), and he had considerable influence on his contemporaries, including Shakespeare.

ANDREW MARVELL (1621–1678) was the son of a clergyman. He attended Cambridge University, lived abroad, and then settled in London. He wrote some of his most famous "garden" poems while employed as a tutor at Nun Appleton, Yorkshire, and went on to a position as tutor for a relative of Oliver Cromwell. He succeeded Milton as Latin secretary to Cromwell's Council of State and continued to be involved in the chaotic politics of the Restoration. Marvell's reputation as a "metaphysical poet" was revived by T. S. Eliot in the twentieth century.

JOHN MASEFIELD (1878–1967) joined the merchant navy at the age of thirteen. At seventeen he jumped ship and stayed in America for some years, working various jobs, reading, and writing poetry. On returning to England, he worked for the *Manchester Guardian* and pursued a literary career, publishing fifty volumes of poetry, over twenty novels, several plays, and a variety of other works. "Cargoes" appeared in *Ballads and Poems* (1910). He was appointed poet laureate in 1930 and received the Order of Merit in 1935.

ALICE MEYNELL (1847–1922) lived an active literary life as editor, poet, and journalist, publishing essays in the major newspapers and journals of the day. She became a Roman Catholic in 1868 and many of her poems are religious or domestic. She was also concerned with women's rights.

JOHN MILTON (1608–1674) is considered by many to be the equal of Shakespeare as the greatest of English poets. His father, a London scrivener and musician, recognized his son's genius in childhood and raised him to become a poet. During his seven years at Cambridge University he began to write seriously in Latin and English while training for the ministry. Returning home to Horton, Buckinghamshire, he continued his education and writing, then traveled abroad for two years. Milton settled in London and became active in politics, writing pamphlets in defense of human liberties such as divorce and freedom of the press. Milton's first two wives died in childbirth. During the Commonwealth, Milton, a Puritan, held the post of Latin Secretary to the Council of State. At the restoration of the monarchy in 1660 he lost his privileges and was arrested and fined. Now blind and in straightened circumstances, Milton began his epic poem *Paradise Lost*, dictating it to his daughters. He married for a third time in 1663. Milton has been a major influence on later poets, many of whom wrote tributes to him.

LADY MARY WORTLEY MONTAGU (1689–1762), the daughter of an aristocratic family, was educated at home. She married in 1712 and traveled with her husband, an ambassador. On returning to London she became a lively part of the Augustan literary scene, enjoying poetic sparring with Alexander Pope. After 1739 the Montagus lived abroad, and her letters became a large part of her literary legacy.

THOMAS NASHE (1567–1601) was educated at Cambridge University on a bursary and then earned his living in London writing satirical pamphlets, poetry, and prose. He is best known now for *The Unfortunate Traveller* (1594), a precursor to the realistic novel. His poetry also depicted the London of his time.

WILFRED OWEN (1893–1918), the son of a railway-worker in Shropshire, taught in France before joining the army to fight in World War I. He met the poet Siegfried Sassoon, who encouraged his writing of poetry when they were both invalided to a hospital in Edinburgh. Owen returned to the front and was awarded a Military Cross for bravery. One month later he was killed in action, one week before the armistice. Owen's small body of poetry was not recognized until some years later, but he is now regarded as one of the most powerful antiwar voices in English.

GEORGE PEELE (1556–1596) was the son of the Clerk of Christ's Hospital. He was educated at Oxford University and then became a writer in London, producing plays, pageants, and a variety of poetry.

KATHERINE PHILIPS (1631–1664) called herself "The Matchless Orinda" in her poems written for her friends that extolled the virtues of women's friendships. She married at seventeen an M.P. and Presbyterian magistrate, who was much older than she. A Royalist, Philips wrote political poems in support of the monarchy as well as a variety of other verse. She died of smallpox.

ALEXANDER POPE (1688–1744) was known as the "wasp of Twickenham" because of his bitingly sarcastic tongue, his crippled body, and his home on the Thames near London. As a Roman Catholic he was unable to live in central London or attend university. Pope was a child prodigy, writing brilliant verse from an early age. He was a central figure in the active literary coterie of the Augustan age and is still considered the master of the satire in heroic couplets. Pope held intellectual sparring matches in verse with many of his contemporaries.

MATTHEW PRIOR (1664–1721) was the son of a joiner who attended Cambridge University under the patronage of Lord Dorset. He worked as secretary to the English ambassador in the Netherlands, and then as a secret agent in Paris. The Treaty of Utrecht in 1713 was known as "Matt's Peace" because of Prior's role in the negotiations. Prior's fortunes rose and fell, but he was supported by aristocratic friends who valued his varied poetry and prose.

FRANCIS QUARLES (1592–1644) was a courtier, educated at Cambridge University. He lived abroad as a member of Princess Elizabeth's retinue, was secretary to the Primate of Ireland, and returned to London as city chronologer. His many poems include biblical paraphrases that he called "Emblems."

SIR WALTER RALEGH (1552–1618) probably did not cover a puddle with his cloak to save Queen Elizabeth's shoes, but he was still a dashing figure, an elegant courtier, statesman, explorer, and poet. He colonized parts of North America for Queen Elizabeth I with his half-brother Sir Humphrey Gilbert; he fought in Ireland and in Spain with the earl of Essex; and he searched for gold in Guiana (now Venezuela). Having fallen out of favor with the queen when he married one of her maids of honor, his attachment to the court ended completely with the succession of James I, who imprisoned him for suspected treason. Ralegh was released from the Tower (where he had languished for thirteen years with his wife and family) to conduct another expedition to Guiana, but it ended disastrously and Ralegh was executed. He wrote a *History of the World* while in prison.

MARY ROBINSON (1758–1800) was a beautiful actress (a favorite of David Garrick, manager of Drury Lane Theatre), who began to write poems while imprisoned with her spendthrift husband in debtor's prison. She was befriended by the Duchess of Devonshire, to whom she dedicated her first volume in 1775. She continued to write throughout her checkered career. Her sonnet sequence *Sappho and Phaon* (1796) led to her being known as "the English Sappho." She enjoyed the company of some of the radical thinkers of the day, in-

cluding Coleridge and Mary Wollstonecraft, and at that time wrote
satires in the manner of Swift and Pope for the *Morning Post*.

ISAAC ROSENBERG (1890–1918) came from a Russian family. He grew
up in east London where he wrote poetry and painted. He attended
the Slade School of Art and was supported in his writing by Ezra
Pound. He was killed in World War I and is now best known for
his realistic war poetry.

CHRISTINA ROSSETTI (1830–1894) belonged to an artistic and literary
family of Italian refugees in London. Her brothers Dante Gabriel and
William Michael were part of the artistic group the Pre-Raphaelite
Brotherhood, to whose magazine, *The Germ*, Christina contributed
poems. Her ill health confined her to home, looking after their ailing
father while pursuing her calling as a poet. She was a devout high
Anglican and turned down two offers of marriage on religious
grounds.

SIEGFRIED SASSOON (1886–1967) attended Cambridge University and
was encouraged in a poetic career by his mother. He enlisted to fight
in World War I, but he was a pacifist and spoke against the war
when he was invalided to a hospital in Edinburgh, where he met
Wilfred Owen. Sassoon survived the war, and although he published novels, diaries, autobiographies, and devotional poetry with
some success, he is best known now as a poet of World War I.

WILLIAM SHAKESPEARE (1564–1616) was born and raised in Stratford-
upon-Avon, the son of a local shopkeeper who was also a bailiff and
justice of the peace. At the age of eighteen Shakespeare married Anne
Hathaway, eight years his senior. Little is known about Shakespeare's
life, but by 1694 he was active in a theater company in London known
as the Lord Chamberlain's Men. Their theater was the Globe, and
they became the King's Men when James I succeeded to the throne
in 1603. Anne and their children remained in Stratford, to which
Shakespeare returned before his death. Controversy still surrounds
the attribution and dating of Shakespeare's plays because they were
not published officially until after his death. The sonnets were first
published in 1609.

PERCY BYSSHE SHELLEY (1792–1822) was the son of a Member of Parliament for Sussex. A radical from childhood, he attended Oxford
University but was expelled in 1811 for promoting atheism. He
eloped with a sixteen-year-old, Harriet Westbrook, and they had
two children before Shelley left her for Mary Godwin, with whom

he lived abroad. Unconventional in his domestic life and revolutionary in his politics, Shelley befriended Byron in Italy and continued to write poems and essays, including his famous *Defence of Poetry*. With Byron and Keats, Shelley belonged to the "second wave" of Romantic poets, and he was critical of the increasing conservatism of Wordsworth and Coleridge. He drowned in a boating accident, a volume of Keats's poems in his pocket.

JAMES SHIRLEY (1596–1666) was educated at Oxford and Cambridge and became a clergyman and school teacher. He wrote many plays for the London and Dublin theaters until the theaters were closed by the Puritans during the Interregnum. Shirley and his wife died in the Great Fire of London.

SIR PHILIP SIDNEY (1554–1586) was born at Penshurst Place, Kent (immortalized by Ben Jonson). After attending both Oxford and Cambridge, he traveled abroad and then became a courtier, embodying the qualities now associated with a "Renaissance man": poet, literary patron, scholar, courtier, and soldier. His sonnet sequence *Astrophil and Stella* (which inspired many later sonnets) was written for Lord Essex's daughter Penelope Deveraux, but he married Frances Walsingham. His 1579 essay, *A Defence of Poetry*, is one of the earliest works of English literary criticism. Sidney died heroically in the Netherlands, defending the Dutch against the Spanish. Legend has it that, mortally wounded, he passed a water bottle over to another soldier with the words "Thy necessity is greater than mine."

DAME EDITH SITWELL (1887–1964) came from an aristocratic Yorkshire family. Like her brothers Osbert and Sacheverell, she supported the Modernist movement in literature and art, and Edith edited the literary magazine *Wheels* for five years. Her poetry, as eccentric and radical as she was, was most successful during World War II.

CHARLOTTE SMITH (1749–1806) grew up in Sussex. She was married at the age of fifteen to a West Indies merchant who proved a disastrous, insolvent husband. With a large family to support, Charlotte moved to Brighton, Sussex, and earned a living from writing. Her *Elegiac Sonnets*, published in 1784, were popular, but she was better known as a novelist.

STEVIE (FLORENCE MARGARET) SMITH (1902–1971) lived in London with her aunt. She wrote three novels and eight volumes of poetry, which she illustrated and also read aloud at public readings.

ROBERT SOUTHEY (1774–1843) was a rebel in his youth, like many of the Romantic poets. He was expelled from Westminster School for writing against flogging, and went on to Oxford University, where he met Samuel Taylor Coleridge. His 1793 epic poem *Joan of Arc* saw the French Revolution as overthrowing tyranny and introducing a new Eden. With Coleridge he planned to establish an ideal commune in America, but it never materialized. Southey lived in the Lake District, near Wordsworth and Coleridge, and devoted his life to writing. Like other young rebels, Southey became conservative later, accepting the poet laureateship in 1813 and writing for the Tory *Quarterly Review*, a change of heart that Byron and others ridiculed.

ROBERT SOUTHWELL (1561–1595) was educated in Italy and became a Roman Catholic priest. He returned to his native England in 1586, where the reign of Protestant Queen Elizabeth outlawed the practicing of Catholicism. In 1592, while celebrating Mass, he was captured, and after three years of torture and imprisonment (during which he wrote most of his devotional poetry), he was executed. Southwell was declared a saint in the Roman Catholic Church in 1970.

EDMUND SPENSER (1552–1599) was the son of a London clothmaker. He attended Cambridge University and then obtained an appointment with the Earl of Leicester, through whom he met Sir Philip Sidney, Leicester's nephew. He moved to Ireland in 1580 as secretary to the Lord Deputy, and although he always wished to obtain an appointment in England, he never did. Spenser's most famous work is *The Faerie Queen*, an allegory about Elizabethan England, but he also wrote the sonnet sequence *Amoretti* for his second wife, Elizabeth Boyle, whom he married in 1594. After Irish rebels destroyed his home, he returned to London where he died in poverty.

ROBERT LOUIS STEVENSON (1850–1894) was the only and sickly child of a lighthouse engineer in Edinburgh. Because of his health, he studied law rather than engineering, but he pursued a literary career and lived abroad in search of a climate more beneficial to his weak chest. He married an American, Fanny Osbourne, in 1880. He published a variety of works including several plays in collaboration with W. E. Henley. Stevenson is best known for his writings for children including the novels *Treasure Island* and *Kidnapped* and his *Child's Garden of Verses*. His last few years were spent in the South Seas, and he died in Samoa.

SIR JOHN SUCKLING (1609–1642) attended Cambridge University, leaving when he inherited a vast fortune. After touring the continent, he became a feted member of the court and one of the "Cavalier poets," a gallant and witty writer of lyrics and plays. As a Royalist he was eventually forced to flee to France, where he died.

JONATHAN SWIFT (1667–1745) grew up in Ireland though of English descent. He attended Trinity College, Dublin, and became secretary to Sir William Temple in Moor Park, England. On taking orders he returned to Ireland, where eventually he became dean of St. Patrick's Cathedral. Active in politics through his many associations with first the Whig and then the Tory governments in London, Swift is best known for his pamphlets and satires such as *Gulliver's Travels*. He was also a central figure in the London literary scene. Some of his poetry was inspired by his affection for "Stella" (Esther Johnson), whom he met at Moor Park.

ALFRED, LORD TENNYSON (1809–1892) was raised in the large and chaotic family of a country parson in Somersby, Lincolnshire, and educated at Cambridge, where he became close friends with another young poet, Arthur Henry Hallam. Hallam died suddenly in 1833, inspiring many of Tennyson's best poetry including "In Memoriam A.H.H.," written over seventeen years. Tennyson married Emily Sellwood after a long courtship, and he endured many years of financial strain until his reputation as the age's favorite poet secured his income. He was appointed poet laureate in 1850. Tennyson's interest in the Arthurian legends is evident in such poems as "Idylls of the King" and "The Lady of Shalott."

DYLAN THOMAS (1914–1953) grew up in Swansea, Wales, the son of a schoolteacher. A poet from youth, Thomas became a journalist and filmmaker in London. He was well known as a broadcaster in England and the United States, where he conducted several lecture tours. He is best known for his fondness for alcohol and his radio play *Under Milk Wood*. His essay "A Child's Christmas in Wales" is a delightful evocation of his childhood.

(PHILIP) EDWARD THOMAS (1878–1917) attended Oxford University, married young, and lived in Kent. He was making a living as a writer when Robert Frost encouraged him to take up poetry. Because Thomas enlisted in the army and was killed in action in World War I, he is often associated with the war poets, but he is also one of the finest poets of the English countryside.

JAMES THOMSON (1700–1748) was a Scot, educated at Edinburgh University. His most influential poem, "The Seasons," was written in London between 1726 and 1730. Thomson traveled abroad as a tutor and enjoyed success with the London writers of the time.

CHIDIOCK TICHBORNE (1558?–1586) was a staunch Catholic who was involved in a plot to assassinate Queen Elizabeth I. The other conspirators escaped, but Tichborne was captured and pled guilty. He is immortalized in the poem he wrote on the eve of his execution.

THOMAS TRAHERNE (1637–1674) was the son of a shoemaker who attended Oxford University as a commoner and became a clergyman. He lived a devout, quiet life. Traherne's poems were not published in his lifetime; many of them were discovered in manuscripts on a London bookstall in 1896 and are now highly valued. Traherne's belief in childhood innocence and spiritual awareness is akin to Wordsworth's.

HENRY VAUGHAN (1621–1695) came from an old Welsh family, whose linguistic roots can be heard in his poetry. He studied at Oxford University and the Inns of Court in London (training for the law) but returned to Wales at the beginning of the Civil War. Vaughan's first volume of devotional poetry, *Silex Scintillans*, suggested his religious conversion and was also critical of the Puritan regime. Vaughan practiced medicine and continued to write religious verse in a mystical vein. He greatly admired the poetry of George Herbert.

EDMUND WALLER (1606–1687) was educated at Eton and Cambridge. As a member of parliament he changed sides frequently, serving on the side of the king or against him as fortune dictated through the Civil War years. As a poet he was greatly admired by John Dryden, and he was one of the earliest poets to use the heroic couplet form that would dominate English poetry in the eighteenth century.

OSCAR WILDE (1854–1900) was born in Ireland but remained in England after attending Oxford University. A flamboyant leader of an artistic Aesthetic Movement, he published his first collection of poems in 1881, but he is best known for his plays (including *The Importance of Being Earnest*) and fairy tales. Wilde was married with children, but in 1895 he was imprisoned for practicing homosexuality. On his release, bankrupt, in 1897 he went to France, where he died.

WILLIAM WORDSWORTH (1770–1850) grew up in the Lake District that would become his later home and was always his poetic inspiration. The significance of his childhood to his growth as a poet is the subject of many of Wordsworth's poems, including *The Prelude*. He attended Cambridge University without enthusiasm and then traveled extensively on the continent. In France he fell in love with Annette Vallon, who bore him a daughter, Carolyn. As for many others, Wordsworth's early enthusiasm for the French Revolution was tempered with time and his radical views became conservative. Wordsworth settled with his sister Dorothy in Somerset to be near his new friend, Samuel Taylor Coleridge. The two poets published the *Lyrical Ballads* in 1798. The following year the Wordsworths moved to Dove Cottage in the Lake District, and in 1802 Wordsworth married Mary Hutchinson. Although Wordsworth's best poetry was written in his early years, his reputation as a poet grew steadily. He lived a comfortable life, despite emotional upheavals including a falling out with Coleridge (which was never completely healed) and the deaths of two of his children. He was appointed poet laureate in 1843. Wordsworth's dedication to nature, childhood, the imagination, and the common man had a lasting influence. John Stuart Mill credited Wordsworth with restoring his faith in human affection after Mill's father's rigid Utilitarianism had caused a mental breakdown.

SIR HENRY WOTTON (1568–1639) became a friend of John Donne at Oxford University. He followed his family into diplomacy, serving as secretary and spy for the earl of Essex. While an ambassador in Europe, he wrote the now well-known definition of his calling: "An ambassador is an honest man, set to lie abroad for the good of his country." Wotton's small body of poetry is well regarded. Izaak Walton published his biography in 1670.

LADY MARY WROTH (1587–1651?), the niece of Sir Philip Sidney, grew up in Penshurst, the estate immortalized by Ben Jonson, whose patron she became. Jonson wrote several poems in her honor and admired her as a poet. She married at seventeen, was widowed young, and carried on a long-term love affair with her married cousin, the earl of Pembroke. Wroth is now recognized as an important early voice in women's poetry, offering a female perspective on love and politics in her romance *Urania* and her sonnet sequence *Pamphilia to Amphilanthus*.

SIR THOMAS WYATT (c. 1503–1542) attended Cambridge University at the age of thirteen and later traveled widely on the continent as a diplomat for Henry VIII. In Italy he discovered the love sonnets of Petrarch (1304–1374), which he translated and introduced to England. A courtier, Wyatt was involved with Anne Boleyn before her marriage to Henry VIII, and he was twice imprisoned in the Tower of London.

WILLIAM BUTLER YEATS (1865–1939) was the son and nephew of Irish artists. He studied art in Dublin for three years before turning to writing and editing. He became active in Irish nationalism, promoting Irish culture through helping to establish the Gaelic League and the Irish National Theatre, for which he wrote plays. He also served as a senator of the Irish Free State from 1922 to 1928. Yeats became an important poet, moving from nationalistic themes to a complicated symbolism that he developed through his poetry, based on the automatic writing of his wife, whom he married in 1917 after years of rejection by Maud Gonne, a fervent nationalist who repeatedly rejected his offers of marriage. In 1923 Yeats received the Nobel Prize for literature.

Further Reading

Arp, Thomas. *Perrine's Sound and Sense. An Introduction to Poetry.* 8th ed. Fort Worth: Harcourt Brace, 1992.

Brooks, Cleanth, and Robert Penn Warren. *Understanding Poetry.* 4th ed. New York: Holt, Rinehart, Winston, 1976.

Furniss, Tom, and Michael Bath. *Reading Poetry. An Introduction.* Englewood Cliffs, N.J.: Prentice Hall, 1996.

Fussell, Paul. *Poetic Metre and Poetic Form.* New York: Random House, 1979.

Hamilton, Ian, ed. *The Oxford Companion to Twentieth-Century Poetry.* Oxford: Oxford University Press, 1994.

Hirsch, Edward. *How to Read a Poem and Fall in Love with Poetry.* New York: Harcourt Brace, 1999.

Hollander, John. *Rhyme's Reason: A Guide to English Verse.* New Haven: Yale University Press, 1981.

Leavis, F. R. *Revaluation: Tradition and Development in English Poetry.* Westport, Conn.: Greenwood, 1975.

Preminger, Alex, and T.V.F. Brogan, eds. *The New Princeton Encyclopedia of Poetry and Poetics.* Princeton: Princeton University Press, 1993.

Ricks, Christopher. *The Force of Poetry.* Oxford: Oxford University Press, 1984.

Schmidt, Michael. *Lives of the Poets.* London: Phoenix, 1999.

Smith, Barbara Herrnstein. *Poetic Closure: A Study of How Poems End.* Chicago: University of Chicago Press, 1968.

Steele, Michael. *All the Fun's in How You Say a Thing.* Athens: Ohio University Press, 1999.

Williams, Miller. *Patterns of Poetry: An Encyclopedia of Forms.* Baton Rouge: Louisiana State University Press, 1986.

Index

About the Author

RUTH GLANCY is Associate Professor of English at Concordia University College of Alberta, Canada, where she teaches courses in British literature and poetry. She is the author of several books on Dickens including *The Student Companion to Charles Dickens* (Greenwood, 1999). She has also edited his Christmas writings.